Hibernate in Action

Hibernate in Action

CHRISTIAN BAUER
GAVIN KING

MANNING

Greenwich
(74° w. long.)

For online information and ordering of this and other Manning books, please visit
www.manning.com. The publisher offers discounts on this book when ordered in
quantity. For more information, please contact:

Special Sales Department
Manning Publications Co.
209 Bruce Park Avenue   Fax: (203) 661-9018
Greenwich, CT 06830   email: manning@manning.com

  Manning Publications Co.   Copyeditor: Tiffany Taylor
209 Bruce Park Avenue   Typesetter: Dottie Marsico
Greenwich, CT 06830   Cover designer: Leslie Haimes

ISBN 1932394-15-X

Second, corrected, printing October 2004
Printed in the United States of America
3 4 5 6 7 8 9 10 – VHG – 07 06 05

contents

1 *Understanding object/relational persistence*   *1*

foreword

Relational databases are indisputably at the core of the modern enterprise.

While modern programming languages, including Java™, provide an intuitive, object-oriented view of application-level business entities, the enterprise data underlying these entities is heavily relational in nature. Further, the main strength of the relational model—over earlier navigational models as well as over later OODB models—is that by design it is intrinsically agnostic to the programmatic manipulation and application-level view of the data that it serves up.

Many attempts have been made to bridge relational and object-oriented technologies, or to replace one with the other, but the gap between the two is one of the hard facts of enterprise computing today. It is this challenge—to provide a bridge between relational data and Java™ objects—that Hibernate takes on through its object/relational mapping (ORM) approach. Hibernate meets this challenge in a very pragmatic, direct, and realistic way.

As Christian Bauer and Gavin King demonstrate in this book, the effective use of ORM technology in all but the simplest of enterprise environments requires understanding and configuring how the mediation between relational data and objects is performed. This demands that the developer be aware and knowledgeable both of the application and its data requirements, and of the SQL query language, relational storage structures, and the potential for optimization that relational technology offers.

Not only does Hibernate provide a full-function solution that meets these requirements head on, it is also a flexible and configurable architecture. Hibernate's developers designed it with modularity, pluggability, extensibility, and user customization in mind. As a result, in the few years since its initial release,

Hibernate has rapidly become one of the leading ORM technologies for enterprise developers—and deservedly so.

This book provides a comprehensive overview of Hibernate. It covers how to use its type mapping capabilities and facilities for modeling associations and inheritance; how to retrieve objects efficiently using the Hibernate query language; how to configure Hibernate for use in both managed and unmanaged environments; and how to use its tools. In addition, throughout the book the authors provide insight into the underlying issues of ORM and into the design choices behind Hibernate. These insights give the reader a deep understanding of the effective use of ORM as an enterprise technology.

Hibernate in Action is the definitive guide to using Hibernate and to object/relational mapping in enterprise computing today.

LINDA DEMICHIEL
Lead Architect, Enterprise JavaBeans
Sun Microsystems

preface

Just because it is possible to push twigs along the ground with one's nose does not necessarily mean that that is the best way to collect firewood.

—Anthony Berglas

Today, many software developers work with Enterprise Information Systems (EIS). This kind of application creates, manages, and stores structured information and shares this information between many users in multiple physical locations.

The storage of EIS data involves massive usage of SQL-based database management systems. Every company we've met during our careers uses at least one SQL database; most are completely dependent on relational database technology at the core of their business.

In the past five years, broad adoption of the Java programming language has brought about the ascendancy of the object-oriented paradigm for software development. Developers are now sold on the benefits of object orientation. However, the vast majority of businesses are also tied to long-term investments in expensive relational database systems. Not only are particular vendor products entrenched, but existing legacy data must be made available to (and via) the shiny new object-oriented web applications.

However, the tabular representation of data in a relational system is fundamentally different than the networks of objects used in object-oriented Java applications. This difference has led to the so-called *object/relational paradigm* mismatch. Traditionally, the importance and cost of this mismatch have been underestimated, and tools for solving the mismatch have been insufficient. Meanwhile, Java developers blame relational technology for the mismatch; data professionals blame object technology.

Object/relational mapping (ORM) is the name given to automated solutions to the mismatch problem. For developers weary of tedious data access code, the good news is that ORM has come of age. Applications built with ORM middleware can be expected to be cheaper, more performant, less vendor-specific, and more able to cope with changes to the internal object or underlying SQL schema. The astonishing thing is that these benefits are now available to Java developers for free.

Gavin King began developing Hibernate in late 2001 when he found that the popular persistence solution at the time—CMP Entity Beans—didn't scale to nontrivial applications with complex data models. Hibernate began life as an independent, noncommercial open source project.

The Hibernate team (including the authors) has learned ORM the hard way—that is, by listening to user requests and implementing what was needed to satisfy those requests. The result, Hibernate, is a practical solution, emphasizing developer productivity and technical leadership. Hibernate has been used by tens of thousands of users and in many thousands of production applications.

When the demands on their time became overwhelming, the Hibernate team concluded that the future success of the project (and Gavin's continued sanity) demanded professional developers dedicated full-time to Hibernate. Hibernate joined jboss.org in late 2003 and now has a commercial aspect; you can purchase commercial support and training from JBoss Inc. But commercial training shouldn't be the only way to learn about Hibernate.

It's obvious that many, perhaps even most, Java projects benefit from the use of an ORM solution like Hibernate—although this wasn't obvious a couple of years ago! As ORM technology becomes increasingly mainstream, product documentation such as Hibernate's free user manual is no longer sufficient. We realized that the Hibernate community and new Hibernate users needed a full-length book, not only to learn about developing software with Hibernate, but also to understand and appreciate the object/relational mismatch and the motivations behind Hibernate's design.

The book you're holding was an enormous effort that occupied most of our spare time for more than a year. It was also the source of many heated disputes and learning experiences. We hope this book is an excellent guide to Hibernate (or, "the Hibernate bible," as one of our reviewers put it) and also the first comprehensive documentation of the object/relational mismatch and ORM in general. We hope you find it helpful and enjoy working with Hibernate.

acknowledgments

Writing (in fact, creating) a book wouldn't be possible without help. We'd first like to thank the Hibernate community for keeping us on our toes; without your requests for the book, we probably would have given up early on.

A book is only as good as its reviewers, and we had the best. J. B. Rainsberger, Matt Scarpino, Ara Abrahamian, Mark Eagle, Glen Smith, Patrick Peak, Max Rydahl Andersen, Peter Eisentraut, Matt Raible, and Michael A. Koziarski. Thanks for your endless hours of reading our half-finished and raw manuscript. We'd like to thank Emmanuel Bernard for his technical review and Nick Heudecker for his help with the first chapters.

Our team at Manning was invaluable. Clay Andres got this project started, Jackie Carter stayed with us in good and bad times and taught us how to write. Marjan Bace provided the necessary confidence that kept us going. Tiffany Taylor and Liz Welch found all the many mistakes we made in grammar and style. Mary Piergies organized the production of this book. Many thanks for your hard work. Any others at Manning whom we've forgotten: You made it possible.

about this book

We introduce the object/relational paradigm mismatch in this book and give you a high-level overview of current solutions for this time-consuming problem. You'll learn how to use Hibernate as a persistence layer with a richly typed domain object model in a single, continuing example application. This persistence layer implementation covers all entity association, class inheritance, and special type mapping strategies.

We teach you how to tune the Hibernate object query and transaction system for the best performance in highly concurrent multiuser applications. The flexible Hibernate dual-layer caching system is also an important topic in this book. We discuss Hibernate integration in different scenarios and also show you typical architectural problems in two- and three-tiered Java database applications. If you have to work with an existing SQL database, you'll also be interested in Hibernate's legacy database integration features and the Hibernate development toolset.

Roadmap

Chapter 1 defines object persistence. We discuss why a relational database with a SQL interface is the system for persistent data in today's applications, and why hand-coded Java persistence layers with JDBC and SQL code are time-consuming and error-prone. After looking at alternative solutions for this problem, we introduce object/relational mapping and talk about the advantages and downsides of this approach.

Chapter 2 gives an architectural overview of Hibernate and shows you the most important application-programming interfaces. We demonstrate Hibernate configuration in managed (and non-managed) J2EE and J2SE environments after looking at a simple "Hello World" application.

Chapter 3 introduces the example application and all kinds of entity and relationship mappings to a database schema, including uni- and bidirectional associations, class inheritance, and composition. You'll learn how to write Hibernate mapping files and how to design persistent classes.

Chapter 4 teaches you the Hibernate interfaces for read and save operations; we also show you how transitive persistence (persistence by reachability) works in Hibernate. This chapter is focused on loading and storing objects in the most efficient way.

Chapter 5 discusses concurrent data access, with database and long-running application transactions. We introduce the concepts of locking and versioning of data. We also cover caching in general and the Hibernate caching system, which are closely related to concurrent data access.

Chapter 6 completes your understanding of Hibernate mapping techniques with more advanced mapping concepts, such as custom user types, collections of values, and mappings for one-to-one and many-to-many associations. We briefly discuss Hibernate's fully polymorphic behavior as well.

Chapter 7 introduces the Hibernate Query Language (HQL) and other object-retrieval methods such as the query by criteria (QBC) API, which is a typesafe way to express an object query. We show you how to translate complex search dialogs in your application to a query by example (QBE) query. You'll get the full power of Hibernate queries by combining these three features; we also show you how to use direct SQL calls for the special cases and how to best optimize query performance.

Chapter 8 describes some basic practices of Hibernate application architecture. This includes handling the SessionFactory, the popular ThreadLocal Session pattern, and encapsulation of the persistence layer functionality in data access objects (DAO) and J2EE commands. We show you how to design long-running application transactions and how to use the innovative detached object support in Hibernate. We also talk about audit logging and legacy database schemas.

Chapter 9 introduces several different development scenarios and tools that may be used in each case. We show you the common technical pitfalls with each approach and discuss the Hibernate toolset (hbm2ddl, hbm2java) and the integration with popular open source tools such as XDoclet and Middlegen.

Who should read this book?

Readers of this book should have basic knowledge of object-oriented software development and should have used this knowledge in practice. To understand the application examples, you should be familiar with the Java programming language and the Unified Modeling Language.

Our primary target audience consists of Java developers who work with SQL-based database systems. We'll show you how to substantially increase your productivity by leveraging ORM.

If you're a database developer, the book could be part of your introduction to object-oriented software development.

If you're a database administrator, you'll be interested in how ORM affects performance and how you can tune the performance of the SQL database management system and persistence layer to achieve performance targets. Since data access is the bottleneck in most Java applications, this book pays close attention to performance issues. Many DBAs are understandably nervous about entrusting performance to tool-generated SQL code; we seek to allay those fears and also to highlight cases where applications should *not* use tool-managed data access. You may be relieved to discover that we don't claim that ORM is the best solution to every problem.

Code conventions and downloads

This book provides copious examples, which include all the Hibernate application artifacts: Java code, Hibernate configuration files, and XML mapping metadata files. Source code in listings or in text is in a fixed-width font `like this` to separate it from ordinary text. Additionally, Java method names, component parameters, object properties, and XML elements and attributes in text are also presented using fixed-width font.

Java, HTML, and XML can all be verbose. In many cases, the original source code (available online) has been reformatted; we've added line breaks and reworked indentation to accommodate the available page space in the book. In rare cases, even this was not enough, and listings include line-continuation markers. Additionally, comments in the source code have been removed from the listings.

Code annotations accompany many of the source code listings, highlighting important concepts. In some cases, numbered bullets link to explanations that follow the listing.

Hibernate is an open source project released under the Lesser GNU Public License. Directions for downloading Hibernate, in source or binary form, are available from the Hibernate web site: www.hibernate.org/.

The source code for all CaveatEmptor examples in this book is available from http://caveatemptor.hibernate.org/. The CaveatEmptor example application code is available on this web site in different flavors: for example, for servlet and for EJB deployment, with or without a presentation layer. However, only the standalone persistence layer source package is the recommended companion to this book.

An upcoming book from Manning, *WebWorks in Action* by Patrick Lightbody et al., is a good companion to this book. Both book use the CaveatEmptor example application and you will learn how to write a presentation layer using WebWork with a Hibernate persistence layer. The example source code for both books will be available on the CaveatEmptor web site.

About the authors

Christian Bauer is a member of the Hibernate developer team and is also responsible for the Hibernate web site and documentation. Christian is interested in relational database systems and sound data management in Java applications. He works as a developer and consultant for JBoss Inc. and lives in Frankfurt, Germany.

Gavin King is the founder of the Hibernate project and lead developer. He is an enthusiastic proponent of agile development and open source software. Gavin is helping integrate ORM technology into the J2EE standard as a member of the EJB 3 Expert Group. He is a developer and consultant for JBoss Inc., based in Melbourne, Australia.

about Hibernate3 and EJB 3

The world doesn't stop turning when you finish writing a book, and getting the book into production takes more time than you could believe. Therefore, some of the information in any technical book becomes quickly outdated, especially when new standards and product versions are already on the horizon.

Hibernate3, an evolutionary new version of Hibernate, was in the early stages of planning and design while this book was being written. By the time the book hits the shelves, there may be an alpha release available. However, the information in this book is valid for Hibernate3; in fact, we consider it to be an essential reference even for the new version. We discuss fundamental concepts that will be found in Hibernate3 and in most ORM solutions. Furthermore, Hibernate3 will be mostly backward compatible with Hibernate 2.1. New features will be added, of course, but you won't have problems picking them up after reading this book.

Inspired by the success of Hibernate, the EJB 3 Expert Group used several key concepts and APIs from Hibernate in its redesign of entity beans. At the time of writing, only an early draft of the new EJB specification was available; hence we don't discuss it in this book. However, after reading *Hibernate in Action*, you'll know all the fundamentals that will let you quickly understand entity beans in EJB 3.

For more up-to-date information, see the Hibernate road map: www.hibernate.org/About/RoadMap.

author online

Purchase of *Hibernate in Action* includes free access to a private web forum where you can make comments about the book, ask technical questions, and receive help from the author and from other users. To access the forum and subscribe to it, point your web browser to www.manning.com/bauer. This page provides information on how to get on the forum once you are registered, what kind of help is available, and the rules of conduct on the forum. It also provides links to the source code for the examples in the book, errata, and other downloads.

Manning's commitment to our readers is to provide a venue where a meaningful dialog between individual readers and between readers and the authors can take place. It is not a commitment to any specific amount of participation on the part of the authors, whose contribution to the AO remains voluntary (and unpaid). We suggest you try asking the authors some challenging questions lest their interest stray!

about the title and cover

By combining introductions, overviews, and how-to examples, Manning's *In Action* books are designed to help learning and remembering. According to research in cognitive science, the things people remember are things they discover during self-motivated exploration.

Although no one at Manning is a cognitive scientist, we are convinced that for learning to become permanent it must pass through stages of exploration, play, and, interestingly, re-telling of what is being learned. People understand and remember new things, which is to say they master them, only after actively exploring them. Humans learn *in action*. An essential part of an In Action guide is that it is example-driven. It encourages the reader to try things out, to play with new code, and explore new ideas.

There is another, more mundane, reason for the title of this book: our readers are busy. They use books to do a job or solve a problem. They need books that allow them to jump in and jump out easily and learn just what they want, just when they want it. They need books that aid them *in action*. The books in this series are designed for such readers.

About the cover illustration

The figure on the cover of *Hibernate in Action* is a peasant woman from a village in Switzerland, "Paysanne de Schwatzenbourg en Suisse." The illustration is taken from a French travel book, *Encyclopedie des Voyages* by J. G. St. Saveur, published in 1796. Travel for pleasure was a relatively new phenomenon at the time and travel guides such as this one were popular, introducing both the tourist as well as the armchair traveler, to the inhabitants of other regions of France and abroad.

The diversity of the drawings in the *Encyclopedie des Voyages* speaks vividly of the uniqueness and individuality of the world's towns and provinces just 200 years ago. This was a time when the dress codes of two regions separated by a few dozen miles identified people uniquely as belonging to one or the other. The travel guide brings to life a sense of isolation and distance of that period and of every other historic period except our own hyperkinetic present.

Dress codes have changed since then and the diversity by region, so rich at the time, has faded away. It is now often hard to tell the inhabitant of one continent from another. Perhaps, trying to view it optimistically, we have traded a cultural and visual diversity for a more varied personal life. Or a more varied and interesting intellectual and technical life.

We at Manning celebrate the inventiveness, the initiative, and the fun of the computer business with book covers based on the rich diversity of regional life two centuries ago brought back to life by the pictures from this travel book.

Understanding
object/relational persistence

This chapter covers

- Object persistence with SQL databases
- The object/relational paradigm mismatch
- Persistence layers in object-oriented applications
- Object/relational mapping basics

The approach to managing persistent data has been a key design decision in every software project we've worked on. Given that persistent data isn't a new or unusual requirement for Java applications, you'd expect to be able to make a simple choice among similar, well-established persistence solutions. Think of web application frameworks (Jakarta Struts versus WebWork), GUI component frameworks (Swing versus SWT), or template engines (JSP versus Velocity). Each of the competing solutions has advantages and disadvantages, but they at least share the same scope and overall approach. Unfortunately, this isn't yet the case with persistence technologies, where we see some wildly differing solutions to the same problem.

For several years, persistence has been a hot topic of debate in the Java community. Many developers don't even agree on the scope of the problem. Is "persistence" a problem that is already solved by relational technology and extensions such as stored procedures, or is it a more pervasive problem that must be addressed by special Java component models such as EJB entity beans? Should we hand-code even the most primitive CRUD (create, read, update, delete) operations in SQL and JDBC, or should this work be automated? How do we achieve portability if every database management system has its own SQL dialect? Should we abandon SQL completely and adopt a new database technology, such as object database systems? Debate continues, but recently a solution called *object/relational mapping* (ORM) has met with increasing acceptance. Hibernate is an open source ORM implementation.

Hibernate is an ambitious project that aims to be a complete solution to the problem of managing persistent data in Java. It mediates the application's interaction with a relational database, leaving the developer free to concentrate on the business problem at hand. Hibernate is an non-intrusive solution. By this we mean you aren't required to follow many Hibernate-specific rules and design patterns when writing your business logic and persistent classes; thus, Hibernate integrates smoothly with most new and existing applications and doesn't require disruptive changes to the rest of the application.

This book is about Hibernate. We'll cover basic and advanced features and describe some recommended ways to develop new applications using Hibernate. Often, these recommendations won't be specific to Hibernate—sometimes they will be our ideas about the *best* ways to do things when working with persistent data, explained in the context of Hibernate. Before we can get started with Hibernate, however, you need to understand the core problems of object persistence and object/relational mapping. This chapter explains why tools like Hibernate are needed.

First, we define persistent data management in the context of object-oriented applications and discuss the relationship of SQL, JDBC, and Java, the underlying technologies and standards that Hibernate is built on. We then discuss the so-called *object/relational paradigm mismatch* and the generic problems we encounter in object-oriented software development with relational databases. As this list of problems grows, it becomes apparent that we need tools and patterns to minimize the time we have to spend on the persistence-related code of our applications. After we look at alternative tools and persistence mechanisms, you'll see that ORM is the best available solution for many scenarios. Our discussion of the advantages and drawbacks of ORM gives you the full background to make the best decision when picking a persistence solution for your own project.

The best way to learn isn't necessarily linear. We understand that you probably want to try Hibernate right away. If this is how you'd like to proceed, skip to chapter 2, section 2.1, "Getting started," where we jump in and start coding a (small) Hibernate application. You'll be able to understand chapter 2 without reading this chapter, but we also recommend that you return here at some point as you circle through the book. That way, you'll be prepared and have all the background concepts you need for the rest of the material.

1.1 What is persistence?

Almost all applications require persistent data. Persistence is one of the fundamental concepts in application development. If an information system didn't preserve data entered by users when the host machine was powered off, the system would be of little practical use. When we talk about persistence in Java, we're normally talking about storing data in a *relational database* using SQL. We start by taking a brief look at the technology and how we use it with Java. Armed with that information, we then continue our discussion of persistence and how it's implemented in object-oriented applications.

1.1.1 Relational databases

You, like most other developers, have probably worked with a relational database. In fact, most of us use a relational database every day. Relational technology is a known quantity. This alone is sufficient reason for many organizations to choose it. But to say only this is to pay less respect than is due. Relational databases are so entrenched not by accident but because they're an incredibly flexible and robust approach to data management.

A relational database management system isn't specific to Java, and a relational database isn't specific to a particular application. Relational technology provides a way of sharing data among different applications or among different technologies that form part of the same application (the transactional engine and the reporting engine, for example). Relational technology is a common denominator of many disparate systems and technology platforms. Hence, the relational data model is often the common enterprise-wide representation of business entities.

Relational database management systems have SQL-based application programming interfaces; hence we call today's relational database products *SQL database management systems* or, when we're talking about particular systems, *SQL databases.*

1.1.2 *Understanding SQL*

To use Hibernate effectively, a solid understanding of the relational model and SQL is a prerequisite. You'll need to use your knowledge of SQL to tune the performance of your Hibernate application. Hibernate will automate many repetitive coding tasks, but your knowledge of persistence technology must extend beyond Hibernate itself if you want take advantage of the full power of modern SQL databases. Remember that the underlying goal is robust, efficient management of persistent data.

Let's review some of the SQL terms used in this book. You use SQL as a *data definition language* (DDL) to create a database schema with CREATE and ALTER statements. After creating tables (and indexes, sequences, and so on), you use SQL as a *data manipulation language* (DML). With DML, you execute SQL operations that manipulate and retrieve data. The manipulation operations include *insertion,* *update,* and *deletion.* You retrieve data by executing queries with *restriction, projection,* and *join* operations (including the *Cartesian product*). For efficient reporting, you use SQL to *group, order,* and *aggregate* data in arbitrary ways. You can even nest SQL statements inside each other; this technique is called *subselecting.* You have probably used SQL for many years and are familiar with the basic operations and statements written in this language. Still, we know from our own experience that SQL is sometimes hard to remember and that some terms vary in usage. To understand this book, we have to use the same terms and concepts; so, we advise you to read appendix A if any of the terms we've mentioned are new or unclear.

SQL knowledge is mandatory for sound Java database application development. If you need more material, get a copy of the excellent book *SQL Tuning* by Dan Tow [Tow 2003]. Also read *An Introduction to Database Systems* [Date 2004] for the theory, concepts, and ideals of (relational) database systems. Although the relational database is one part of ORM, the other part, of course, consists of the objects in your Java application that need to be persisted to the database using SQL.

1.1.3 Using SQL in Java

When you work with an SQL database in a Java application, the Java code issues SQL statements to the database via the *Java DataBase Connectivity* (JDBC) API. The SQL itself might have been written by hand and embedded in the Java code, or it might have been generated on the fly by Java code. You use the JDBC API to bind arguments to query parameters, initiate execution of the query, scroll through the query result table, retrieve values from the result set, and so on. These are low-level data access tasks; as application developers, we're more interested in the business problem that requires this data access. It isn't clear that we should be concerning ourselves with such tedious, mechanical details.

What we'd really like to be able to do is write code that saves and retrieves complex objects—the instances of our classes—to and from the database, relieving us of this low-level drudgery.

Since the data access tasks are often so tedious, we have to ask: Are the relational data model and (especially) SQL the right choices for persistence in object-oriented applications? We answer this question immediately: Yes! There are many reasons why SQL databases dominate the computing industry. Relational database management systems are the only proven data management technology and are almost always a *requirement* in any Java project.

However, for the last 15 years, developers have spoken of a *paradigm mismatch*. This mismatch explains why so much effort is expended on persistence-related concerns in every enterprise project. The paradigms referred to are object modeling and relational modeling, or perhaps object-oriented programming and SQL. Let's begin our exploration of the mismatch problem by asking what *persistence* means in the context of object-oriented application development. First we'll widen the simplistic definition of persistence stated at the beginning of this section to a broader, more mature understanding of what is involved in maintaining and using persistent data.

1.1.4 Persistence in object-oriented applications

In an object-oriented application, persistence allows an object to outlive the process that created it. The state of the object may be stored to disk and an object with the same state re-created at some point in the future.

This application isn't limited to single objects—entire graphs of interconnected objects may be made persistent and later re-created in a new process. Most objects aren't persistent; a *transient* object has a limited lifetime that is bounded by the life of the process that instantiated it. Almost all Java applications contain a mix of persistent and transient objects; hence we need a subsystem that manages our persistent data.

Modern relational databases provide a structured representation of persistent data, enabling sorting, searching, and aggregation of data. Database management systems are responsible for managing concurrency and data integrity; they're responsible for sharing data between multiple users and multiple applications. A database management system also provides data-level security. When we discuss persistence in this book, we're thinking of all these things:

- Storage, organization, and retrieval of structured data
- Concurrency and data integrity
- Data sharing

In particular, we're thinking of these problems in the context of an object-oriented application that uses a *domain model*.

An application with a domain model doesn't work directly with the tabular representation of the business entities; the application has its own, object-oriented model of the business entities. If the database has ITEM and BID tables, the Java application defines Item and Bid classes.

Then, instead of directly working with the rows and columns of an SQL result set, the business logic interacts with this object-oriented domain model and its runtime realization as a graph of interconnected objects. The business logic is never executed in the database (as an SQL stored procedure), it's implemented in Java. This allows business logic to make use of sophisticated object-oriented concepts such as inheritance and polymorphism. For example, we could use well-known design patterns such as *Strategy, Mediator,* and *Composite* [GOF 1995], all of which depend on polymorphic method calls. Now a caveat: Not all Java applications are designed this way, nor should they be. Simple applications might be much better off without a domain model. SQL and the JDBC API are perfectly serviceable for dealing with pure tabular data, and the new JDBC *RowSet* (Sun JCP, JSR 114) makes CRUD operations even easier. Working with a tabular representation of persistent data is straightforward and well understood.

However, in the case of applications with nontrivial business logic, the domain model helps to improve code reuse and maintainability significantly. We focus on applications with a domain model in this book, since Hibernate and ORM in general are most relevant to this kind of application.

If we consider SQL and relational databases again, we finally observe the mismatch between the two paradigms.

SQL operations such as projection and join always result in a tabular representation of the resulting data. This is quite different than the graph of interconnected objects used to execute the business logic in a Java application! These are fundamentally different models, not just different ways of visualizing the same model.

With this realization, we can begin to see the problems—some well understood and some less well understood—that must be solved by an application that combines both data representations: an object-oriented domain model and a persistent relational model. Let's take a closer look.

1.2 The paradigm mismatch

Figure 1.1 A simple UML class diagram of the user and billing details entities

The paradigm mismatch can be broken down into several parts, which we'll examine one at a time. Let's start our exploration with a simple example that is problem free. Then, as we build on it, you'll begin to see the mismatch appear.

Suppose you have to design and implement an online e-commerce application. In this application, you'd need a class to represent information about a user of the system, and another class to represent information about the user's billing details, as shown in figure 1.1.

Looking at this diagram, you see that a `User` has many `BillingDetails`. You can navigate the relationship between the classes in both directions. To begin with, the classes representing these entities might be extremely simple:

```
public class User {
    private String userName;
    private String name;
    private String address;
    private Set billingDetails;

    // accessor methods (get/set pairs), business methods, etc.
    ...
}
public class BillingDetails {
    private String accountNumber;
    private String accountName;
    private String accountType;
    private User user;
```

```
        //methods, get/set pairs...
        ...
    }
```

Note that we're only interested in the state of the entities with regard to persistence, so we've omitted the implementation of property accessors and business methods (such as `getUserName()` or `billAuction()`). It's quite easy to come up with a good SQL schema design for this case:

```
create table USER (
    USERNAME VARCHAR(15) NOT NULL PRIMARY KEY,
    NAME VARCHAR(50) NOT NULL,
    ADDRESS VARCHAR(100)
)

create table BILLING_DETAILS (
    ACCOUNT_NUMBER VARCHAR(10) NOT NULL PRIMARY Key,
    ACCOUNT_NAME VARCHAR(50) NOT NULL,
    ACCOUNT_TYPE VARCHAR(2) NOT NULL,
    USERNAME VARCHAR(15) FOREIGN KEY REFERENCES USER
)
```

The relationship between the two entities is represented as the foreign key, USERNAME, in BILLING_DETAILS. For this simple object model, the object/relational mismatch is barely in evidence; it's straightforward to write JDBC code to insert, update, and delete information about user and billing details.

Now, let's see what happens when we consider something a little more realistic. The paradigm mismatch will be visible when we add more entities and entity relationships to our application.

The most glaringly obvious problem with our current implementation is that we've modeled an address as a simple `String` value. In most systems, it's necessary to store street, city, state, country, and ZIP code information separately. Of course, we could add these properties directly to the User class, but since it's highly likely that other classes in the system will also carry address information, it makes more sense to create a separate `Address` class. The updated object model is shown in figure 1.2.

Should we also add an ADDRESS table? Not necessarily. It's common to keep address information in the USER table, in individual columns. This design is likely to perform better, since we don't require a table join to retrieve the user and address in a single query. The nicest solution might even be to create a user-defined

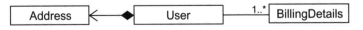

Figure 1.2   The **User** has an **Address**.

SQL data type to represent addresses and to use a single column of that new type in the USER table instead of several new columns.

Basically, we have the choice of adding either several columns or a single column (of a new SQL data type). This is clearly a problem of *granularity*.

1.2.1 *The problem of granularity*

Granularity refers to the relative size of the objects you're working with. When we're talking about Java objects and database tables, the granularity problem means persisting objects that can have various kinds of granularity to tables and columns that are inherently limited in granularity.

Let's return to our example. Adding a new data type to store Address Java objects in a single column to our database catalog sounds like the best approach. After all, a new Address type (class) in Java and a new ADDRESS SQL data type should guarantee interoperability. However, you'll find various problems if you check the support for user-defined column types (UDT) in today's SQL database management systems.

UDT support is one of a number of so-called *object-relational extensions* to traditional SQL. Unfortunately, UDT support is a somewhat obscure feature of most SQL database management systems and certainly isn't portable between different systems. The SQL standard supports user-defined data types, but very poorly. For this reason and (whatever) other reasons, use of UDTs isn't common practice in the industry at this time—and it's unlikely that you'll encounter a legacy schema that makes extensive use of UDTs. We therefore can't store objects of our new Address class in a single new column of an equivalent user-defined SQL data type. Our solution for this problem has several columns, of vendor-defined SQL types (such as boolean, numeric, and string data types). Considering the granularity of our tables again, the USER table is usually defined as follows:

```
create table USER (
    USERNAME VARCHAR(15) NOT NULL PRIMARY KEY,
    NAME VARCHAR(50) NOT NULL,
    ADDRESS_STREET VARCHAR(50),
    ADDRESS_CITY VARCHAR(15),
    ADDRESS_STATE VARCHAR(15),
    ADDRESS_ZIPCODE VARCHAR(5),
    ADDRESS_COUNTRY VARCHAR(15)
)
```

This leads to the following observation: Classes in our domain object model come in a range of different levels of granularity—from coarse-grained entity classes like

User, to finer grained classes like Address, right down to simple String-valued properties such as zipcode.

In contrast, just two levels of granularity are visible at the level of the database: tables such as USER, along with scalar columns such as ADDRESS_ZIPCODE. This obviously isn't as flexible as our Java type system. Many simple persistence mechanisms fail to recognize this mismatch and so end up forcing the less flexible representation upon the object model. We've seen countless User classes with properties named zipcode!

It turns out that the granularity problem isn't especially difficult to solve. Indeed, we probably wouldn't even list it, were it not for the fact that it's visible in so many existing systems. We describe the solution to this problem in chapter 3, section 3.5, "Fine-grained object models."

A much more difficult and interesting problem arises when we consider domain object models that use *inheritance*, a feature of object-oriented design we might use to bill the users of our e-commerce application in new and interesting ways.

1.2.2 *The problem of subtypes*

In Java, we implement inheritance using super- and subclasses. To illustrate why this can present a mismatch problem, let's continue to build our example. Let's add to our e-commerce application so that we now can accept not only bank account billing, but also credit and debit cards. We therefore have several methods to bill a user account. The most natural way to reflect this change in our object model is to use inheritance for the BillingDetails class.

We might have an abstract BillingDetails superclass along with several concrete subclasses: CreditCard, DirectDebit, Cheque, and so on. Each of these subclasses will define slightly different data (and completely different functionality that acts upon that data). The UML class diagram in figure 1.3 illustrates this object model.

We notice immediately that SQL provides no direct support for inheritance. We can't declare that a CREDIT_CARD_DETAILS table is a subtype of BILLING_DETAILS by writing, say, CREATE TABLE CREDIT_CARD_DETAILS EXTENDS BILLING_DETAILS (...).

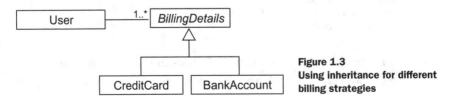

Figure 1.3
Using inheritance for different billing strategies

In chapter 3, section 3.6, "Mapping class inheritance," we discuss how object/relational mapping solutions such as Hibernate solve the problem of persisting a class hierarchy to a database table or tables. This problem is now quite well understood in the community, and most solutions support approximately the same functionality. But we aren't quite finished with inheritance—as soon as we introduce inheritance into the object model, we have the possibility of *polymorphism*.

The User class has an association to the BillingDetails superclass. This is a *polymorphic association*. At runtime, a User object might be associated with an instance of any of the subclasses of BillingDetails. Similarly, we'd like to be able to write queries that refer to the BillingDetails class and have the query return instances of its subclasses. This feature is called *polymorphic queries*.

Since SQL databases don't provide a notion of inheritance, it's hardly surprising that they also lack an obvious way to represent a polymorphic association. A standard foreign key constraint refers to exactly one table; it isn't straightforward to define a foreign key that refers to multiple tables. We might explain this by saying that Java (and other object-oriented languages) is less strictly typed than SQL. Fortunately, two of the inheritance mapping solutions we show in chapter 3 are designed to accommodate the representation of polymorphic associations and efficient execution of polymorphic queries.

So, the mismatch of subtypes is one in which the inheritance structure in your Java model must be persisted in an SQL database that doesn't offer an inheritance strategy. The next aspect of the mismatch problem is the issue of object *identity*. You probably noticed that we defined USERNAME as the primary key of our USER table. Was that a good choice? Not really, as you'll see next.

1.2.3 *The problem of identity*

Although the problem of *object identity* might not be obvious at first, we'll encounter it often in our growing and expanding example e-commerce system. This problem can be seen when we consider two objects (for example, two Users) and check if they're identical. There are three ways to tackle this problem, two in the Java world and one in our SQL database. As expected, they work together only with some help.

Java objects define two different notions of *sameness*:

- Object identity (roughly equivalent to memory location, checked with a==b)
- Equality as determined by the implementation of the equals() method (also called *equality by value*)

On the other hand, the identity of a database row is expressed as the primary key value. As you'll see in section 3.4, "Understanding object identity," neither equals() nor == is naturally equivalent to the primary key value. It's common for several (nonidentical) objects to simultaneously represent the same row of the database. Furthermore, some subtle difficulties are involved in implementing equals() correctly for a persistent class.

Let's discuss another problem related to database identity with an example. In our table definition for USER, we've used USERNAME as a primary key. Unfortunately, this decision makes it difficult to change a username: We'd need to update not only the USERNAME column in USER, but also the foreign key column in BILLING_DETAILS. So, later in the book, we'll recommend that you use *surrogate keys* wherever possible. A surrogate key is a primary key column with no meaning to the user. For example, we might change our table definitions to look like this:

```
create table USER (
    USER_ID BIGINT NOT NULL PRIMARY KEY,
    USERNAME VARCHAR(15) NOT NULL UNIQUE,
    NAME VARCHAR(50) NOT NULL,
    ...
)

create table BILLING_DETAILS (
    BILLING_DETAILS_ID BIGINT NOT NULL PRIMARY KEY,
    ACCOUNT_NUMBER VARCHAR(10) NOT NULL UNIQUE,
    ACCOUNT_NAME VARCHAR(50) NOT NULL,
    ACCOUNT_TYPE VARCHAR(2) NOT NULL,
    USER_ID BIGINT FOREIGN KEY REFERENCES USER
)
```

The USER_ID and BILLING_DETAILS_ID columns contain system-generated values. These columns were introduced purely for the benefit of the relational data model. How (if at all) should they be represented in the object model? We'll discuss this question in section 3.4 and find a solution with object/relational mapping.

In the context of persistence, identity is closely related to how the system handles caching and transactions. Different persistence solutions have chosen various strategies, and this has been an area of confusion. We cover all these interesting topics—and show how they're related—in chapter 5.

The skeleton e-commerce application we've designed and implemented has served our purpose well. We've identified the mismatch problems with mapping granularity, subtypes, and object identity. We're almost ready to move on to other parts of the application. But first, we need to discuss the important concept of *associations*—that is, how the relationships between our classes are mapped and handled. Is the foreign key in the database all we need?

1.2.4 *Problems relating to associations*

In our object model, associations represent the relationships between entities. You remember that the `User`, `Address`, and `BillingDetails` classes are all associated. Unlike `Address`, `BillingDetails` stands on its own. `BillingDetails` objects are stored in their own table. Association mapping and the management of entity associations are central concepts of any object persistence solution.

Object-oriented languages represent associations using *object references* and collections of object references. In the relational world, an association is represented as a *foreign key* column, with copies of key values in several tables. There are subtle differences between the two representations.

Object references are inherently directional; the association is from one object to the other. If an association between objects should be navigable in both directions, you must define the association *twice*, once in each of the associated classes. You've already seen this in our object model classes:

```
public class User {
    private Set billingDetails;
    ...
}

public class BillingDetails {
    private User user;
    ...
}
```

On the other hand, foreign key associations aren't by nature directional. In fact, *navigation* has no meaning for a relational data model, because you can create arbitrary data associations with *table joins* and *projection*.

Actually, it isn't possible to determine the multiplicity of a unidirectional association by looking only at the Java classes. Java associations may have *many-to-many* multiplicity. For example, our object model might have looked like this:

```
public class User {
    private Set billingDetails;
    ...
}

public class BillingDetails {
    private Set users;
    ...
}
```

Table associations on the other hand, are always *one-to-many* or *one-to-one*. You can see the multiplicity immediately by looking at the foreign key definition. The following is a one-to-many association (or, if read in that direction, a many-to-one):

```
USER_ID BIGINT FOREIGN KEY REFERENCES USER
```

These are one-to-one associations:

```
USER_ID BIGINT UNIQUE FOREIGN KEY REFERENCES USER
BILLING_DETAILS_ID BIGINT PRIMARY KEY FOREIGN KEY REFERENCES USER
```

If you wish to represent a many-to-many association in a relational database, you must introduce a new table, called a *link table*. This table doesn't appear anywhere in the object model. For our example, if we consider the relationship between a user and the user's billing information to be many-to-many, the link table is defined as follows:

```
CREATE TABLE USER_BILLING_DETAILS (
    USER_ID BIGINT FOREIGN KEY REFERENCES USER,
    BILLING_DETAILS_ID BIGINT FOREIGN KEY REFERENCES BILLING_DETAILS
    PRIMARY KEY (USER_ID, BILLING_DETAILS_ID)
)
```

We'll discuss association mappings in great detail in chapters 3 and 6.

So far, the issues we've considered are mainly structural. We can see them by considering a purely static view of the system. Perhaps the most difficult problem in object persistence is a dynamic. It concerns associations, and we've already hinted at it when we drew a distinction between *object graph navigation* and *table joins* in section 1.1.4, "Persistence in object-oriented applications." Let's explore this significant mismatch problem in more depth.

1.2.5 *The problem of object graph navigation*

There is a fundamental difference in the way you access objects in Java and in a relational database. In Java, when you access the billing information of a user, you call aUser.getBillingDetails().getAccountNumber(). This is the most natural way to access object-oriented data and is often described as *walking the object graph*. You navigate from one object to another, following associations between instances. Unfortunately, this isn't an efficient way to retrieve data from an SQL database.

The single most important thing to do to improve performance of data access code is to *minimize the number of requests to the database.* The most obvious way to do this is to minimize the number of SQL queries. (Other ways include using stored procedures or the JDBC batch API.)

Therefore, efficient access to relational data using SQL usually requires the use of joins between the tables of interest. The number of tables included in the join determines the depth of the object graph you can navigate. For example, if we need to retrieve a User and aren't interested in the user's BillingDetails, we use this simple query:

```
select * from USER u where u.USER_ID = 123
```

On the other hand, if we need to retrieve the same User and then subsequently visit each of the associated BillingDetails instances, we use a different query:

```
select *
from USER u
left outer join BILLING_DETAILS bd on bd.USER_ID = u.USER_ID
where u.USER_ID = 123
```

As you can see, we need to know what portion of the object graph we plan to access when we retrieve the initial User, *before* we start navigating the object graph!

On the other hand, any object persistence solution provides functionality for fetching the data of associated objects only when the object is first accessed. However, this piecemeal style of data access is fundamentally inefficient in the context of a relational database, because it requires execution of one select statement for each node of the object graph. This is the dreaded *n+1 selects problem.*

This mismatch in the way we access objects in Java and in a relational database is perhaps the single most common source of performance problems in Java applications. Yet, although we've been blessed with innumerable books and magazine articles advising us to use StringBuffer for string concatenation, it seems impossible to find any advice about strategies for avoiding the n+1 selects problem. Fortunately, Hibernate provides sophisticated features for efficiently fetching graphs of objects from the database, transparently to the application accessing the graph. We discuss these features in chapters 4 and 7.

We now have a quite elaborate list of object/relational mismatch problems, and it will be costly to find solutions, as you might know from experience. This cost is often underestimated, and we think this is a major reason for many failed software projects.

1.2.6 *The cost of the mismatch*

The overall solution for the list of mismatch problems can require a significant outlay of time and effort. In our experience, the main purpose of up to 30 percent of the Java application code written is to handle the tedious SQL/JDBC and the manual bridging of the object/relational paradigm mismatch. Despite all this effort, the end result still doesn't feel quite right. We've seen projects nearly sink due to the complexity and inflexibility of their database abstraction layers.

One of the major costs is in the area of modeling. The relational and object models must both encompass the same business entities. But an object-oriented purist will model these entities in a very different way than an experienced relational data modeler. The usual solution to this problem is to bend and twist the object model until it matches the underlying relational technology.

This can be done successfully, but only at the cost of losing some of the advantages of object orientation. Keep in mind that relational modeling is underpinned by relational theory. Object orientation has no such rigorous mathematical definition or body of theoretical work. So, we can't look to mathematics to explain how we should bridge the gap between the two paradigms—there is no elegant transformation waiting to be discovered. (Doing away with Java and SQL and starting from scratch isn't considered elegant.)

The domain modeling mismatch problem isn't the only source of the inflexibility and lost productivity that lead to higher costs. A further cause is the JDBC API itself. JDBC and SQL provide a *statement-* (that is, command-) oriented approach to moving data to and from an SQL database. A structural relationship must be specified at least three times (Insert, Update, Select), adding to the time required for design and implementation. The unique dialect for every SQL database doesn't improve the situation.

Recently, it has been fashionable to regard architectural or pattern-based models as a partial solution to the mismatch problem. Hence, we have the entity bean component model, the data access object (DAO) pattern, and other practices to implement data access. These approaches leave most or all of the problems listed earlier to the application developer. To round out your understanding of object persistence, we need to discuss *application architecture* and the role of a *persistence layer* in typical application design.

1.3 *Persistence layers and alternatives*

In a medium- or large-sized application, it usually makes sense to organize classes by concern. Persistence is one concern. Other concerns are presentation, workflow, and business logic. There are also the so-called *"cross-cutting"* concerns, which may be implemented generically—by framework code, for example. Typical cross-cutting concerns include logging, authorization, and transaction demarcation.

A typical object-oriented architecture comprises layers that represent the concerns. It's normal, and certainly best practice, to group all classes and components responsible for persistence into a separate *persistence layer* in a *layered system architecture.*

In this section, we first look at the layers of this type of architecture and why we use them. After that, we focus on the layer we're most interested in—the persistence layer—and some of the ways it can be implemented.

1.3.1 *Layered architecture*

A *layered architecture* defines interfaces between code that implements the various concerns, allowing a change to the way one concern is implemented without significant disruption to code in the other layers. Layering also determines the kinds of interlayer dependencies that occur. The rules are as follows:

- Layers communicate top to bottom. A layer is dependent only on the layer directly below it.
- Each layer is unaware of any other layers except for the layer just below it.

Different applications group concerns differently, so they define different layers. A typical, proven, high-level application architecture uses three layers, one each for presentation, business logic, and persistence, as shown in figure 1.4.

Let's take a closer look at the layers and elements in the diagram:

- *Presentation layer*—The user interface logic is topmost. Code responsible for the presentation and control of page and screen navigation forms the presentation layer.
- *Business layer*—The exact form of the next layer varies widely between applications. It's generally agreed, however, that this business layer is responsible for implementing any business rules or system requirements that would be understood by users as part of the problem domain. In some systems, this layer has its own internal representation of the business domain entities. In others, it reuses the model defined by the persistence layer. We revisit this issue in chapter 3.

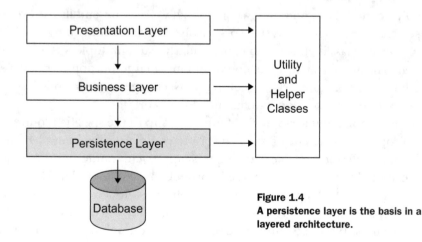

Figure 1.4
A persistence layer is the basis in a layered architecture.

- *Persistence layer*—The persistence layer is a group of classes and components responsible for data storage to, and retrieval from, one or more data stores. This layer necessarily includes a model of the business domain entities (even if it's only a metadata model).

- *Database*—The database exists outside the Java application. It's the actual, persistent representation of the system state. If an SQL database is used, the database includes the relational schema and possibly stored procedures.

- *Helper/utility classes*—Every application has a set of infrastructural helper or utility classes that are used in every layer of the application (for example, `Exception` classes for error handling). These infrastructural elements don't form a layer, since they don't obey the rules for interlayer dependency in a layered architecture.

Let's now take a brief look at the various ways the persistence layer can be implemented by Java applications. Don't worry—we'll get to ORM and Hibernate soon. There is much to be learned by looking at other approaches.

1.3.2 *Hand-coding a persistence layer with SQL/JDBC*

The most common approach to Java persistence is for application programmers to work directly with SQL and JDBC. After all, developers are familiar with relational database management systems, understand SQL, and know how to work with tables and foreign keys. Moreover, they can always use the well-known and widely used DAO design pattern to hide complex JDBC code and nonportable SQL from the business logic.

The DAO pattern is a good one—so good that we recommend its use even with ORM (see chapter 8). However, the work involved in manually coding persistence for each domain class is considerable, particularly when multiple SQL dialects are supported. This work usually ends up consuming a large portion of the development effort. Furthermore, when requirements change, a hand-coded solution always requires more attention and maintenance effort.

So why not implement a simple ORM framework to fit the specific requirements of your project? The result of such an effort could even be reused in future projects. Many developers have taken this approach; numerous homegrown object/relational persistence layers are in production systems today. However, we don't recommend this approach. Excellent solutions already exist, not only the (mostly expensive) tools sold by commercial vendors but also open source projects with free licenses. We're certain you'll be able to find a solution that meets your requirements, both business and technical. It's likely that such a solution will do a great deal more, and do it better, than a solution you could build in a limited time.

Development of a reasonably full-featured ORM may take many developers months. For example, Hibernate is 43,000 lines of code (some of which is much more difficult than typical application code), along with 12,000 lines of unit test code. This might be more than your application. A great many details can easily be overlooked—as both the authors know from experience! Even if an existing tool doesn't fully implement two or three of your more exotic requirements, it's still probably not worth creating your own. Any ORM will handle the tedious common cases—the ones that really kill productivity. It's okay that you might need to hand-code certain special cases; few applications are composed primarily of special cases.

Don't fall for the "Not Invented Here" syndrome and start your own object/relational mapping effort just to avoid the learning curve associated with third-party software. Even if you decide that all this ORM stuff is crazy, and you want to work as close to the SQL database as possible, other persistence frameworks exist that don't implement full ORM. For example, the iBATIS database layer is an open source persistence layer that handles some of the more tedious JDBC code while letting developers handcraft the SQL.

1.3.3 *Using serialization*

Java has a built-in persistence mechanism: *Serialization* provides the ability to write a graph of objects (the state of the application) to a byte-stream, which may then be persisted to a file or database. Serialization is also used by Java's Remote Method Invocation (RMI) to achieve pass-by value semantics for complex objects. Another usage of serialization is to replicate application state across nodes in a cluster of machines.

Why not use serialization for the persistence layer? Unfortunately, a serialized graph of interconnected objects can only be accessed as a whole; it's impossible to retrieve any data from the stream without deserializing the entire stream. Thus, the resulting byte-stream must be considered unsuitable for arbitrary search or aggregation. It isn't even possible to access or update a single object or subgraph independently. Loading and overwriting an entire object graph in each transaction is no option for systems designed to support high concurrency.

Clearly, given current technology, serialization is inadequate as a persistence mechanism for high concurrency web and enterprise applications. It has a particular niche as a suitable persistence mechanism for desktop applications.

1.3.4 Considering EJB entity beans

In recent years, Enterprise JavaBeans (EJBs) have been a recommended way of persisting data. If you've been working in the field of Java enterprise applications, you've probably worked with EJBs and entity beans in particular. If you haven't, don't worry—entity beans are rapidly declining in popularity. (Many of the developer concerns will be addressed in the new EJB 3.0 specification, however.)

Entity beans (in the current EJB 2.1 specification) are interesting because, in contrast to the other solutions mentioned here, they were created entirely by committee. The other solutions (the DAO pattern, serialization, and ORM) were distilled from many years of experience; they represent approaches that have stood the test of time. Unsurprisingly, perhaps, EJB 2.1 entity beans have been a disaster in practice. Design flaws in the EJB specification prevent *bean-managed persistence* (BMP) entity beans from performing efficiently. A marginally more acceptable solution is *container-managed persistence* (CMP), at least since some glaring deficiencies of the EJB 1.1 specification were rectified.

Nevertheless, CMP doesn't represent a solution to the object/relational mismatch. Here are six reasons why:

- CMP beans are defined in one-to-one correspondence to the tables of the relational model. Thus, they're too *coarse grained*; they may not take full advantage of Java's rich typing. In a sense, CMP forces your domain model into first normal form.

- On the other hand, CMP beans are also too *fine grained* to realize the stated goal of EJB: the definition of reusable software components. A reusable component should be a *very* coarse-grained object, with an external interface that is stable in the face of small changes to the database schema. (Yes, we really did just claim that CMP entity beans are both too fine grained and too coarse grained!)

- Although EJBs may take advantage of implementation inheritance, entity beans don't support polymorphic associations and queries, one of the defining features of "true" ORM.

- Entity beans, despite the stated goal of the EJB specification, aren't portable in practice. Capabilities of CMP engines vary widely between vendors, and the mapping metadata is highly vendor-specific. Some projects have chosen Hibernate for the simple reason that Hibernate applications are much more portable between application servers.

- Entity beans aren't serializable. We find that we must define additional *data transfer objects* (DTOs, also called *value objects*) when we need to transport data to a remote client tier. The use of fine-grained method calls from the client to a remote entity bean instance is not scalable; DTOs provide a way of batching remote data access. The DTO pattern results in the growth of parallel class hierarchies, where each entity of the domain model is represented as both an entity bean and a DTO.

- EJB is an *intrusive* model; it mandates an unnatural Java style and makes reuse of code outside a specific container extremely difficult. This is a huge barrier to unit *test driven development* (TDD). It even causes problems in applications that require batch processing or other offline functions.

We won't spend more time discussing the pros and cons of EJB 2.1 entity beans. After looking at their persistence capabilities, we've come to the conclusion that they aren't suitable for a full object mapping. We'll see what the new EJB 3.0 specification can improve. Let's turn to another object persistence solution that deserves some attention.

1.3.5 *Object-oriented database systems*

Since we work with objects in Java, it would be ideal if there were a way to store those objects in a database without having to bend and twist the object model at all. In the mid-1990s, new object-oriented database systems gained attention.

An object-oriented database management system (OODBMS) is more like an extension to the application environment than an external data store. An OODBMS usually features a multitiered implementation, with the backend data store, object cache, and client application coupled tightly together and interacting via a proprietary network protocol.

Object-oriented database development begins with the top-down definition of host language bindings that add persistence capabilities to the programming language. Hence, object databases offer seamless integration into the object-oriented application environment. This is different from the model used by today's relational databases, where interaction with the database occurs via an intermediate language (SQL).

Analogously to ANSI SQL, the standard query interface for relational databases, there is a standard for object database products. The Object Data Management Group (ODMG) specification defines an API, a query language, a metadata language, and host language bindings for C++, SmallTalk, and Java. Most object-oriented database systems provide some level of support for the ODMG standard, but to the best of our knowledge, there is no complete implementation. Furthermore, a number of years after its release, and even in version 3.0, the specification feels immature and lacks a number of useful features, especially in a Java-based environment. The ODMG is also no longer active. More recently, the Java Data Objects (JDO) specification (published in April 2002) opened up new possibilities. JDO was driven by members of the object-oriented database community and is now being adopted by object-oriented database products as the primary API, often in addition to the existing ODMG support. It remains to be seen if this new effort will see object-oriented databases penetrate beyond CAD/CAM (computer-aided design/modeling), scientific computing, and other niche markets.

We won't bother looking too closely into why object-oriented database technology hasn't been more popular—we'll simply observe that object databases haven't been widely adopted and that it doesn't appear likely that they will be in the near future. We're confident that the overwhelming majority of developers will have far more opportunity to work with relational technology, given the current political realities (predefined deployment environments).

1.3.6 *Other options*

Of course, there are other kinds of persistence layers. XML persistence is a variation on the serialization theme; this approach addresses some of the limitations of byte-stream serialization by allowing tools to access the data structure easily (but is itself subject to an object/hierarchical impedance mismatch). Furthermore, there is no additional benefit from the XML, because it's just another text file format. You can use stored procedures (even write them in Java using SQLJ) and move the problem into the database tier. We're sure there are plenty of other examples, but none of them are likely to become popular in the immediate future.

Political constraints (long-term investments in SQL databases) and the requirement for access to valuable legacy data call for a different approach. ORM may be the most practical solution to our problems.

1.4 *Object/relational mapping*

Now that we've looked at the alternative techniques for object persistence, it's time to introduce the solution we feel is the best, and the one we use with Hibernate: ORM. Despite its long history (the first research papers were published in the late 1980s), the terms for ORM used by developers vary. Some call it *object relational mapping*, others prefer the simple *object mapping*. We exclusively use the term *object/relational mapping* and its acronym, ORM. The slash stresses the mismatch problem that occurs when the two worlds collide.

In this section, we first look at what ORM is. Then we enumerate the problems that a good ORM solution needs to solve. Finally, we discuss the general benefits that ORM provides and why we recommend this solution.

1.4.1 What is ORM?

In a nutshell, object/relational mapping is the automated (and transparent) persistence of objects in a Java application to the tables in a relational database, using metadata that describes the mapping between the objects and the database. ORM, in essence, works by (reversibly) transforming data from one representation to another.

This implies certain performance penalties. However, if ORM is implemented as middleware, there are many opportunities for optimization that wouldn't exist for a hand-coded persistence layer. A further overhead (at development time) is the provision and management of metadata that governs the transformation. But again, the cost is less than equivalent costs involved in maintaining a hand-coded solution. And even ODMG-compliant object databases require significant class-level metadata.

> **FAQ**   *Isn't ORM a Visio plugin?*   The acronym ORM can also mean *object role modeling*, and this term was invented before object/relational mapping became relevant. It describes a method for information analysis, used in database modeling, and is primarily supported by Microsoft Visio, a graphical modeling tool. Database specialists use it as a replacement or as an addition to the more popular *entity-relationship modeling*. However, if you talk to Java developers about ORM, it's usually in the context of object/relational mapping.

An ORM solution consists of the following four pieces:

- An API for performing basic CRUD operations on objects of persistent classes
- A language or API for specifying queries that refer to classes and properties of classes
- A facility for specifying mapping metadata
- A technique for the ORM implementation to interact with transactional objects to perform dirty checking, lazy association fetching, and other optimization functions

We're using the term ORM to include any persistence layer where SQL is autogenerated from a metadata-based description. We aren't including persistence layers where the object/relational mapping problem is solved manually by developers hand-coding SQL and using JDBC. With ORM, the application interacts with the ORM APIs and the domain model classes and is abstracted from the underlying SQL/JDBC. Depending on the features or the particular implementation, the ORM runtime may also take on responsibility for issues such as optimistic locking and caching, relieving the application of these concerns entirely.

Let's look at the various ways ORM can be implemented. Mark Fussel [Fussel 1997], a researcher in the field of ORM, defined the following four levels of ORM quality.

Pure relational

The whole application, including the user interface, is designed around the relational model and SQL-based relational operations. This approach, despite its deficiencies for large systems, can be an excellent solution for simple applications where a low level of code reuse is tolerable. Direct SQL can be fine-tuned in every aspect, but the drawbacks, such as lack of portability and maintainability, are significant, especially in the long run. Applications in this category often make heavy use of stored procedures, shifting some of the work out of the business layer and into the database.

Light object mapping

Entities are represented as classes that are mapped manually to the relational tables. Hand-coded SQL/JDBC is hidden from the business logic using well-known design patterns. This approach is extremely widespread and is successful for applications with a small number of entities, or applications with generic, metadata-driven data models. Stored procedures might have a place in this kind of application.

Medium object mapping

The application is designed around an object model. SQL is generated at build time using a code generation tool, or at runtime by framework code. Associations between objects are supported by the persistence mechanism, and queries may be specified using an object-oriented expression language. Objects are cached by the persistence layer. A great many ORM products and homegrown persistence layers support at least this level of functionality. It's well suited to medium-sized applications with some complex transactions, particularly when portability between different database products is important. These applications usually don't use stored procedures.

Full object mapping

Full object mapping supports sophisticated object modeling: composition, inheritance, polymorphism, and "persistence by reachability." The persistence layer implements transparent persistence; persistent classes do *not* inherit any special base class or have to implement a special interface. Efficient fetching strategies (lazy and eager fetching) and caching strategies are implemented transparently to the application. This level of functionality can hardly be achieved by a homegrown persistence layer—it's equivalent to months or years of development time. A number of commercial and open source Java ORM tools have achieved this level of quality. This level meets the definition of ORM we're using in this book. Let's look at the problems we expect to be solved by a tool that achieves full object mapping.

1.4.2 Generic ORM problems

The following list of issues, which we'll call the *O/R mapping problems,* are the fundamental problems solved by a full object/relational mapping tool in a Java environment. Particular ORM tools may provide extra functionality (for example, aggressive caching), but this is a reasonably exhaustive list of the conceptual issues that are specific to object/relational mapping:

1 *What do persistent classes look like?* Are they fine-grained JavaBeans? Or are they instances of some (coarser granularity) component model like EJB? How *transparent* is the persistence tool? Do we have to adopt a programming model and conventions for classes of the business domain?

2 *How is mapping metadata defined?* Since the object/relational transformation is governed entirely by metadata, the format and definition of this metadata is a centrally important issue. Should an ORM tool provide a GUI to manipulate the metadata graphically? Or are there better approaches to metadata definition?

3 *How should we map class inheritance hierarchies?* There are several standard strategies. What about polymorphic associations, abstract classes, and interfaces?

4 *How do object identity and equality relate to database (primary key) identity?* How do we map instances of particular classes to particular table rows?

5   *How does the persistence logic interact at runtime with the objects of the business domain?* This is a problem of generic programming, and there are a number of solutions including source generation, runtime reflection, runtime bytecode generation, and buildtime bytecode enhancement. The solution to this problem might affect your build process (but, preferably, shouldn't otherwise affect you as a user).

6   *What is the lifecyle of a persistent object?* Does the lifecycle of some objects depend upon the lifecycle of other associated objects? How do we translate the lifecyle of an object to the lifecycle of a database row?

7   *What facilities are provided for sorting, searching, and aggregating?* The application could do some of these things in memory. But efficient use of relational technology requires that this work sometimes be performed by the database.

8   *How do we efficiently retrieve data with associations?* Efficient access to relational data is usually accomplished via table joins. Object-oriented applications usually access data by navigating an object graph. Two data access patterns should be avoided when possible: the *n+1 selects* problem, and its complement, the *Cartesian product* problem (fetching too much data in a single select).

In addition, two issues are common to any data-access technology. They also impose fundamental constraints on the design and architecture of an ORM:

- Transactions and concurrency
- Cache management (and concurrency)

As you can see, a full object-mapping tool needs to address quite a long list of issues. We discuss the way Hibernate manages these problems and data-access issues in chapters 3, 4, and 5, and we broaden the subject later in the book.

By now, you should be starting to see the value of ORM. In the next section, we look at some of the other benefits you gain when you use an ORM solution.

1.4.3 Why ORM?

An ORM implementation is a complex beast—less complex than an application server, but more complex than a web application framework like Struts or Tapestry. Why should we introduce another new complex infrastructural element into our system? Will it be worth it?

It will take us most of this book to provide a complete answer to those questions. For the impatient, this section provides a quick summary of the most compelling benefits. But first, let's quickly dispose of a non-benefit.

A supposed advantage of ORM is that it "shields" developers from "messy" SQL. This view holds that object-oriented developers can't be expected to understand SQL or relational databases well and that they find SQL somehow offensive. On the contrary, we believe that Java developers must have a sufficient level of familiarity with—and appreciation of—relational modeling and SQL in order to work with ORM. ORM is an advanced technique to be used by developers who have already done it the hard way. To use Hibernate effectively, you must be able to view and interpret the SQL statements it issues and understand the implications for performance.

Let's look at some of the benefits of ORM and Hibernate.

Productivity

Persistence-related code can be perhaps the most tedious code in a Java application. Hibernate eliminates much of the grunt work (more than you'd expect) and lets you concentrate on the business problem. No matter which application development strategy you prefer—top-down, starting with a domain model; or bottom-up, starting with an existing database schema—Hibernate used together with the appropriate tools will significantly reduce development time.

Maintainability

Fewer lines of code (LOC) makes the system more understandable since it emphasizes business logic rather than plumbing. Most important, a system with less code is easier to refactor. Automated object/relational persistence substantially reduces LOC. Of course, counting lines of code is a debatable way of measuring application complexity.

However, there are other reasons that a Hibernate application is more maintainable. In systems with hand-coded persistence, an inevitable tension exists between the relational representation and the object model implementing the domain. Changes to one almost always involve changes to the other. And often the design of one representation is compromised to accommodate the existence of the other. (What almost always happens in practice is that the *object model* of the domain is compromised.) ORM provides a buffer between the two models, allowing more elegant use of object orientation on the Java side, and insulating each model from minor changes to the other.

Performance

A common claim is that hand-coded persistence can always be at least as fast, and can often be faster, than automated persistence. This is true in the same sense that it's true that assembly code can always be at least as fast as Java code, or a hand-written parser can always be at least as fast as a parser generated by YACC or ANTLR—in other words, it's beside the point. The unspoken implication of the claim is that hand-coded persistence *will* perform at least as well in an actual application. But this implication will be true only if the effort required to implement at-least-as-fast hand-coded persistence is similar to the amount of effort involved in utilizing an automated solution. The really interesting question is, what happens when we consider time and budget constraints?

Given a persistence task, many optimizations are possible. Some (such as query hints) are much easier to achieve with hand-coded SQL/JDBC. Most optimizations, however, are much easier to achieve with automated ORM. In a project with time constraints, hand-coded persistence usually allows you to make some optimizations, some of the time. Hibernate allows many more optimizations to be used *all* the time. Furthermore, automated persistence improves developer productivity so much that you can spend more time hand-optimizing the few remaining bottlenecks.

Finally, the people who implemented your ORM software probably had much more time to investigate performance optimizations than you have. Did you know, for instance, that pooling `PreparedStatement` instances results in a significant performance increase for the DB2 JDBC driver but breaks the InterBase JDBC driver? Did you realize that updating only the changed columns of a table can be significantly faster for some databases but potentially slower for others? In your handcrafted solution, how easy is it to experiment with the impact of these various strategies?

Vendor independence

An ORM abstracts your application away from the underlying SQL database and SQL dialect. If the tool supports a number of different databases (most do), then this confers a certain level of portability on your application. You shouldn't necessarily expect write once/run anywhere, since the capabilities of databases differ and achieving full portability would require sacrificing some of the strength of the more powerful platforms. Nevertheless, it's usually much easier to develop a cross-platform application using ORM. Even if you don't require cross-platform operation, an ORM can still help mitigate some of the risks associated with vendor lock-in. In addition, database independence helps in development scenarios where developers use a lightweight local database but deploy for production on a different database.

1.5 *Summary*

In this chapter, we've discussed the concept of object persistence and the importance of ORM as an implementation technique. Object persistence means that individual objects can outlive the application process; they can be saved to a data store and be re-created at a later point in time. The object/relational mismatch comes into play when the data store is an SQL-based relational database management system. For instance, a graph of objects can't simply be saved to a database table; it must be disassembled and persisted to columns of portable SQL data types. A good solution for this problem is ORM, which is especially helpful if we consider richly typed Java domain models.

A domain model represents the business entities used in a Java application. In a layered system architecture, the domain model is used to execute business logic in the business layer (in Java, not in the database). This business layer communicates with the persistence layer beneath in order to load and store the persistent objects of the domain model. ORM is the middleware in the persistence layer that manages the persistence.

ORM isn't a silver bullet for all persistence tasks; its job is to relieve the developer of 95 percent of object persistence work, such as writing complex SQL statements with many table joins and copying values from JDBC result sets to objects or graphs of objects. A full-featured ORM middleware might provide database portability, certain optimization techniques like caching, and other viable functions that aren't easy to hand-code in a limited time with SQL and JDBC.

It's likely that a better solution than ORM will exist some day. We (and many others) may have to rethink everything we know about SQL, persistence API standards, and application integration. The evolution of today's systems into true relational database systems with seamless object-oriented integration remains pure speculation. But we can't wait, and there is no sign that any of these issues will improve soon (a multibillion-dollar industry isn't very agile). ORM is the best solution currently available, and it's a timesaver for developers facing the object/relational mismatch every day.

Introducing and integrating Hibernate

This chapter covers

- Hibernate in action with "Hello World"
- The Hibernate core programming interfaces
- Integration with managed and non-managed environments
- Advanced configuration options

It's good to understand the need for object/relational mapping in Java applications, but you're probably eager to see Hibernate in action. We'll start by showing you a simple example that demonstrates some of its power.

As you're probably aware, it's traditional for a programming book to start with a "Hello World" example. In this chapter, we follow that tradition by introducing Hibernate with a relatively simple "Hello World" program. However, simply printing a message to a console window won't be enough to really demonstrate Hibernate. Instead, our program will store newly created objects in the database, update them, and perform queries to retrieve them from the database.

This chapter will form the basis for the subsequent chapters. In addition to the canonical "Hello World" example, we introduce the core Hibernate APIs and explain how to configure Hibernate in various runtime environments, such as J2EE application servers and stand-alone applications.

2.1 *"Hello World" with Hibernate*

Hibernate applications define *persistent classes* that are "mapped" to database tables. Our "Hello World" example consists of one class and one mapping file. Let's see what a simple persistent class looks like, how the mapping is specified, and some of the things we can do with instances of the persistent class using Hibernate.

The objective of our sample application is to store messages in a database and to retrieve them for display. The application has a simple persistent class, `Message`, which represents these printable messages. Our `Message` class is shown in listing 2.1.

Listing 2.1 `Message.java`: A simple persistent class

```java
package hello;
public class Message {                      Identifier
    private Long id;            ◄──────────  attribute
    private String text;        ◄─────────── Message text
    private Message nextMessage;  ◄────────┐ Reference to
    private Message() {}                    │ another
    public Message(String text) {           │ Message
        this.text = text;
    }
    public Long getId() {
        return id;
    }
    private void setId(Long id) {
        this.id = id;
    }
    public String getText() {
        return text;
```

```
    }
    public void setText(String text) {
        this.text = text;
    }

     public Message getNextMessage() {
         return nextMessage;
     }
     public void setNextMessage(Message nextMessage) {
         this.nextMessage = nextMessage;
     }
}
```

Our Message class has three attributes: the identifier attribute, the text of the message, and a reference to another Message. The identifier attribute allows the application to access the database identity—the primary key value—of a persistent object. If two instances of Message have the same identifier value, they represent the same row in the database. We've chosen Long for the type of our identifier attribute, but this isn't a requirement. Hibernate allows virtually anything for the identifier type, as you'll see later.

You may have noticed that all attributes of the Message class have JavaBean-style property accessor methods. The class also has a constructor with no parameters. The persistent classes we use in our examples will almost always look something like this.

Instances of the Message class may be managed (made persistent) by Hibernate, but they don't *have* to be. Since the Message object doesn't implement any Hibernate-specific classes or interfaces, we can use it like any other Java class:

```
Message message = new Message("Hello World");
System.out.println( message.getText() );
```

This code fragment does exactly what we've come to expect from "Hello World" applications: It prints "Hello World" to the console. It might look like we're trying to be cute here; in fact, we're demonstrating an important feature that distinguishes Hibernate from some other persistence solutions, such as EJB entity beans. Our persistent class can be used in any execution context at all—no special container is needed. Of course, you came here to see Hibernate itself, so let's save a new Message to the database:

```
Session session = getSessionFactory().openSession();
Transaction tx = session.beginTransaction();
Message message = new Message("Hello World");
session.save(message);
```

```
tx.commit();
session.close();
```

This code calls the Hibernate Session and Transaction interfaces. (We'll get to that getSessionFactory() call soon.) It results in the execution of something similar to the following SQL:

```
insert into MESSAGES (MESSAGE_ID, MESSAGE_TEXT, NEXT_MESSAGE_ID)
values (1, 'Hello World', null)
```

Hold on—the MESSAGE_ID column is being initialized to a strange value. We didn't set the id property of message anywhere, so we would expect it to be null, right? Actually, the id property is special: It's an *identifier property*—it holds a generated unique value. (We'll discuss how the value is generated later.) The value is assigned to the Message instance by Hibernate when save() is called.

For this example, we assume that the MESSAGES table already exists. In chapter 9, we'll show you how to use Hibernate to automatically create the tables your application needs, using just the information in the mapping files. (There's some more SQL you won't need to write by hand!) Of course, we want our "Hello World" program to print the message to the console. Now that we have a message in the database, we're ready to demonstrate this. The next example retrieves all messages from the database, in alphabetical order, and prints them:

```
Session newSession = getSessionFactory().openSession();
Transaction newTransaction = newSession.beginTransaction();
List messages =
        newSession.find("from Message as m order by m.text asc");
System.out.println( messages.size() + " message(s) found:" );
for ( Iterator iter = messages.iterator(); iter.hasNext(); ) {
    Message message = (Message) iter.next();
    System.out.println( message.getText() );
}
newTransaction.commit();
newSession.close();
```

The literal string "from Message as m order by m.text asc" is a Hibernate query, expressed in Hibernate's own object-oriented Hibernate Query Language (HQL). This query is internally translated into the following SQL when find() is called:

```
select m.MESSAGE_ID, m.MESSAGE_TEXT, m.NEXT_MESSAGE_ID
from MESSAGES m
order by m.MESSAGE_TEXT asc
```

The code fragment prints

```
1 message(s) found:
Hello World
```

If you've never used an ORM tool like Hibernate before, you were probably expecting to see the SQL statements somewhere in the code or metadata. They aren't there. All SQL is generated at runtime (actually at startup, for all reusable SQL statements).

To allow this magic to occur, Hibernate needs more information about how the Message class should be made persistent. This information is usually provided in an *XML mapping document*. The mapping document defines, among other things, how properties of the Message class map to columns of the MESSAGES table. Let's look at the mapping document in listing 2.2.

Listing 2.2   A simple Hibernate XML mapping

```
<?xml version="1.0"?>
<!DOCTYPE hibernate-mapping PUBLIC
    "-//Hibernate/Hibernate Mapping DTD//EN"
    "http://hibernate.sourceforge.net/hibernate-mapping-2.0.dtd">
<hibernate-mapping>
    <class
        name="hello.Message"
        table="MESSAGES">
        <id
            name="id"
            column="MESSAGE_ID">
            <generator class="increment"/>
        </id>
        <property
            name="text"
            column="MESSAGE_TEXT"/>
        <many-to-one
            name="nextMessage"
            cascade="all"
            column="NEXT_MESSAGE_ID"/>
    </class>
</hibernate-mapping>
```

Note that Hibernate 2.0 and Hibernate 2.1 have the same DTD!

The mapping document tells Hibernate that the Message class is to be persisted to the MESSAGES table, that the identifier property maps to a column named MESSAGE_ID, that the text property maps to a column named MESSAGE_TEXT, and that the property named nextMessage is an association with *many-to-one multiplicity* that maps to a column named NEXT_MESSAGE_ID. (Don't worry about the other details for now.)

As you can see, the XML document isn't difficult to understand. You can easily write and maintain it by hand. In chapter 3, we discuss a way of generating the

XML file from comments embedded in the source code. Whichever method you choose, Hibernate has enough information to completely generate all the SQL statements that would be needed to insert, update, delete, and retrieve instances of the Message class. You no longer need to write these SQL statements by hand.

NOTE   Many Java developers have complained of the "metadata hell" that accompanies J2EE development. Some have suggested a movement away from XML metadata, back to plain Java code. Although we applaud this suggestion for some problems, ORM represents a case where text-based metadata really is necessary. Hibernate has sensible defaults that minimize typing and a mature document type definition that can be used for auto-completion or validation in editors. You can even automatically generate metadata with various tools.

Now, let's change our first message and, while we're at it, create a new message associated with the first, as shown in listing 2.3.

Listing 2.3   Updating a message

```
Session session = getSessionFactory().openSession();
Transaction tx = session.beginTransaction();

// 1 is the generated id of the first message
Message message =
        (Message) session.load( Message.class, new Long(1) );
message.setText("Greetings Earthling");
Message nextMessage = new Message("Take me to your leader (please)");
message.setNextMessage( nextMessage );
tx.commit();
session.close();
```

This code calls three SQL statements inside the same transaction:

```
select m.MESSAGE_ID, m.MESSAGE_TEXT, m.NEXT_MESSAGE_ID
from MESSAGES m
where m.MESSAGE_ID = 1

insert into MESSAGES (MESSAGE_ID, MESSAGE_TEXT, NEXT_MESSAGE_ID)
values (2, 'Take me to your leader (please)', null)

update MESSAGES
set MESSAGE_TEXT = 'Greetings Earthling', NEXT_MESSAGE_ID = 2
where MESSAGE_ID = 1
```

Notice how Hibernate detected the modification to the text and nextMessage properties of the first message and automatically updated the database. We've taken advantage of a Hibernate feature called *automatic dirty checking:* This feature saves us the effort of explicitly asking Hibernate to update the database when we modify the state of an object inside a transaction. Similarly, you can see that the new message was made persistent when a reference was created from the first message. This feature is called *cascading save:* It saves us the effort of explicitly making the new object persistent by calling save(), as long as it's reachable by an already-persistent instance. Also notice that the ordering of the SQL statements isn't the same as the order in which we set property values. Hibernate uses a sophisticated algorithm to determine an efficient ordering that avoids database foreign key constraint violations but is still sufficiently predictable to the user. This feature is called *transactional write-behind.*

If we run "Hello World" again, it prints

```
2 message(s) found:
Greetings Earthling
Take me to your leader (please)
```

This is as far as we'll take the "Hello World" application. Now that we finally have some code under our belt, we'll take a step back and present an overview of Hibernate's main APIs.

2.2 *Understanding the architecture*

The programming interfaces are the first thing you have to learn about Hibernate in order to use it in the persistence layer of your application. A major objective of API design is to keep the interfaces between software components as narrow as possible. In practice, however, ORM APIs aren't especially small. Don't worry, though; you don't have to understand all the Hibernate interfaces at once. Figure 2.1 illustrates the roles of the most important Hibernate interfaces in the business and persistence layers. We show the business layer above the persistence layer, since the business layer acts as a client of the persistence layer in a traditionally layered application. Note that some simple applications might not cleanly separate business logic from persistence logic; that's okay—it merely simplifies the diagram.

The Hibernate interfaces shown in figure 2.1 may be approximately classified as follows:

- Interfaces called by applications to perform basic CRUD and querying operations. These interfaces are the main point of dependency of application business/control logic on Hibernate. They include Session, Transaction, and Query.

- Interfaces called by application infrastructure code to configure Hibernate, most importantly the `Configuration` class.

- *Callback* interfaces that allow the application to react to events occurring inside Hibernate, such as `Interceptor`, `Lifecycle`, and `Validatable`.

- Interfaces that allow extension of Hibernate's powerful mapping functionality, such as `UserType`, `CompositeUserType`, and `IdentifierGenerator`. These interfaces are implemented by application infrastructure code (if necessary).

Hibernate makes use of existing Java APIs, including JDBC), Java Transaction API (JTA, and Java Naming and Directory Interface (JNDI). JDBC provides a rudimentary level of abstraction of functionality common to relational databases, allowing almost any database with a JDBC driver to be supported by Hibernate. JNDI and JTA allow Hibernate to be integrated with J2EE application servers.

In this section, we don't cover the detailed semantics of Hibernate API methods, just the role of each of the primary interfaces. You can find most of these interfaces in the package `net.sf.hibernate`. Let's take a brief look at each interface in turn.

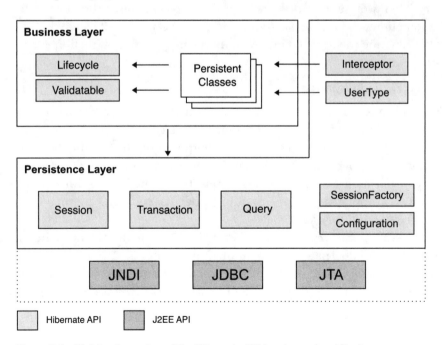

Figure 2.1   High-level overview of the Hibernate API in a layered architecture

2.2.1 *The core interfaces*

The five core interfaces are used in just about every Hibernate application. Using these interfaces, you can store and retrieve persistent objects and control transactions.

Session interface

The Session interface is the primary interface used by Hibernate applications. An instance of Session is lightweight and is inexpensive to create and destroy. This is important because your application will need to create and destroy sessions all the time, perhaps on every request. Hibernate sessions are *not* threadsafe and should by design be used by only one thread at a time.

The Hibernate notion of a *session* is something between *connection* and *transaction*. It may be easier to think of a session as a cache or collection of loaded objects relating to a single unit of work. Hibernate can detect changes to the objects in this unit of work. We sometimes call the Session a *persistence manager* because it's also the interface for persistence-related operations such as storing and retrieving objects. Note that a Hibernate session has nothing to do with the web-tier HttpSession. When we use the word *session* in this book, we mean the Hibernate session. We sometimes use *user session* to refer to the HttpSession object.

We describe the Session interface in detail in chapter 4, section 4.2, "The persistence manager."

SessionFactory interface

The application obtains Session instances from a SessionFactory. Compared to the Session interface, this object is much less exciting.

The SessionFactory is certainly not lightweight! It's intended to be shared among many application threads. There is typically a single SessionFactory for the whole application—created during application initialization, for example. However, if your application accesses multiple databases using Hibernate, you'll need a SessionFactory for each database.

The SessionFactory caches generated SQL statements and other mapping metadata that Hibernate uses at runtime. It also holds cached data that has been read in one unit of work and may be reused in a future unit of work (only if class and collection mappings specify that this *second-level cache* is desirable).

Configuration interface

The Configuration object is used to configure and bootstrap Hibernate. The application uses a Configuration instance to specify the location of mapping documents and Hibernate-specific properties and then create the SessionFactory.

Even though the Configuration interface plays a relatively small part in the total scope of a Hibernate application, it's the first object you'll meet when you begin using Hibernate. Section 2.3 covers the problem of configuring Hibernate in some detail.

Transaction interface

The Transaction interface is an optional API. Hibernate applications may choose not to use this interface, instead managing transactions in their own infrastructure code. A Transaction abstracts application code from the underlying transaction implementation—which might be a JDBC transaction, a JTA UserTransaction, or even a Common Object Request Broker Architecture (CORBA) transaction—allowing the application to control transaction boundaries via a consistent API. This helps to keep Hibernate applications portable between different kinds of execution environments and containers.

We use the Hibernate Transaction API throughout this book. Transactions and the Transaction interface are explained in chapter 5.

Query and Criteria interfaces

The Query interface allows you to perform queries against the database and control how the query is executed. Queries are written in HQL or in the native SQL dialect of your database. A Query instance is used to bind query parameters, limit the number of results returned by the query, and finally to execute the query.

The Criteria interface is very similar; it allows you to create and execute object-oriented criteria queries.

To help make application code less verbose, Hibernate provides some shortcut methods on the Session interface that let you invoke a query in one line of code. We won't use these shortcuts in the book; instead, we'll always use the Query interface.

A Query instance is lightweight and can't be used outside the Session that created it. We describe the features of the Query interface in chapter 7.

2.2.2 *Callback interfaces*

Callback interfaces allow the application to receive a notification when something interesting happens to an object—for example, when an object is loaded, saved, or deleted. Hibernate applications don't need to implement these callbacks, but they're useful for implementing certain kinds of generic functionality, such as creating audit records.

The Lifecycle and Validatable interfaces allow a persistent object to react to events relating to its own *persistence lifecycle*. The persistence lifecycle is encompassed by an object's CRUD operations. The Hibernate team was heavily influenced by other ORM solutions that have similar callback interfaces. Later, they realized that having the persistent classes implement Hibernate-specific interfaces probably isn't a good idea, because doing so pollutes our persistent classes with nonportable code. Since these approaches are no longer favored, we don't discuss them in this book.

The Interceptor interface was introduced to allow the application to process callbacks without forcing the persistent classes to implement Hibernate-specific APIs. Implementations of the Interceptor interface are passed to the persistent instances as parameters. We'll discuss an example in chapter 8.

2.2.3 *Types*

A fundamental and very powerful element of the architecture is Hibernate's notion of a Type. A Hibernate Type object maps a Java type to a database column type (actually, the type may span multiple columns). All persistent properties of persistent classes, including associations, have a corresponding Hibernate type. This design makes Hibernate extremely flexible and extensible.

There is a rich range of built-in types, covering all Java primitives and many JDK classes, including types for java.util.Currency, java.util.Calendar, byte[], and java.io.Serializable.

Even better, Hibernate supports user-defined *custom types*. The interfaces UserType and CompositeUserType are provided to allow you to add your own types. You can use this feature to allow commonly used application classes such as Address, Name, or MonetaryAmount to be handled conveniently and elegantly. Custom types are considered a central feature of Hibernate, and you're encouraged to put them to new and creative uses!

We explain Hibernate types and user-defined types in chapter 6, section 6.1, "Understanding the Hibernate type system."

2.2.4 *Extension interfaces*

Much of the functionality that Hibernate provides is configurable, allowing you to choose between certain built-in strategies. When the built-in strategies are insufficient, Hibernate will usually let you plug in your own custom implementation by implementing an interface. Extension points include:

- Primary key generation (IdentifierGenerator interface)
- SQL dialect support (Dialect abstract class)
- Caching strategies (Cache and CacheProvider interfaces)
- JDBC connection management (ConnectionProvider interface)
- Transaction management (TransactionFactory, Transaction, and TransactionManagerLookup interfaces)
- ORM strategies (ClassPersister interface hierarchy)
- Property access strategies (PropertyAccessor interface)
- Proxy creation (ProxyFactory interface)

Hibernate ships with at least one implementation of each of the listed interfaces, so you don't usually need to start from scratch if you wish to extend the built-in functionality. The source code is available for you to use as an example for your own implementation.

By now you can see that before we can start writing any code that uses Hibernate, we must answer this question: How do we get a Session to work with?

2.3 *Basic configuration*

We've looked at an example application and examined Hibernate's core interfaces. To use Hibernate in an application, you need to know how to configure it. Hibernate can be configured to run in almost any Java application and development environment. Generally, Hibernate is used in two- and three-tiered client/server applications, with Hibernate deployed only on the server. The client application is usually a web browser, but Swing and SWT client applications aren't uncommon. Although we concentrate on multitiered web applications in this book, our explanations apply equally to other architectures, such as command-line applications. It's important to understand the difference in configuring Hibernate for managed and non-managed environments:

- *Managed environment*—Pools resources such as database connections and allows transaction boundaries and security to be specified declaratively (that is, in metadata). A J2EE application server such as JBoss, BEA WebLogic, or IBM WebSphere implements the standard (J2EE-specific) managed environment for Java.

- *Non-managed environment*—Provides basic concurrency management via thread pooling. A servlet container like Jetty or Tomcat provides a non-managed server environment for Java web applications. A stand-alone desktop or command-line application is also considered non-managed. Non-managed environments don't provide automatic transaction or resource management or security infrastructure. The application itself manages database connections and demarcates transaction boundaries.

Hibernate attempts to abstract the environment in which it's deployed. In the case of a non-managed environment, Hibernate handles transactions and JDBC connections (or delegates to application code that handles these concerns). In managed environments, Hibernate integrates with container-managed transactions and datasources. Hibernate can be configured for deployment in both environments.

In both managed and non-managed environments, the first thing you must do is start Hibernate. In practice, doing so is very easy: You have to create a `Session-Factory` from a `Configuration`.

2.3.1 Creating a SessionFactory

In order to create a `SessionFactory`, you first create a single instance of `Configuration` during application initialization and use it to set the location of the mapping files. Once configured, the `Configuration` instance is used to create the `SessionFactory`. After the `SessionFactory` is created, you can discard the `Configuration` class.

The following code starts Hibernate:

```
Configuration cfg = new Configuration();
cfg.addResource("hello/Message.hbm.xml");
cfg.setProperties( System.getProperties() );
SessionFactory sessions = cfg.buildSessionFactory();
```

The location of the mapping file, `Message.hbm.xml`, is relative to the root of the application classpath. For example, if the classpath is the current directory, the `Message.hbm.xml` file must be in the `hello` directory. XML mapping files *must* be placed in the classpath. In this example, we also use the system properties of the virtual machine to set all other configuration options (which might have been set before by application code or as startup options).

METHOD CHAINING *Method chaining* is a programming style supported by many Hibernate interfaces. This style is more popular in Smalltalk than in Java and is considered by some people to be less readable and more difficult to debug than the more accepted Java style. However, it's very convenient in most cases.

Most Java developers declare setter or adder methods to be of type void, meaning they return no value. In Smalltalk, which has no void type, setter or adder methods usually return the receiving object. This would allow us to rewrite the previous code example as follows:

```
SessionFactory sessions = new Configuration()
    .addResource("hello/Message.hbm.xml")
    .setProperties( System.getProperties() )
    .buildSessionFactory();
```

Notice that we didn't need to declare a local variable for the Configuration. We use this style in some code examples; but if you don't like it, you don't need to use it yourself. If you *do* use this coding style, it's better to write each method invocation on a different line. Otherwise, it might be difficult to step through the code in your debugger.

By convention, Hibernate XML mapping files are named with the .hbm.xml extension. Another convention is to have one mapping file per class, rather than have all your mappings listed in one file (which is possible but considered bad style). Our "Hello World" example had only one persistent class, but let's assume we have multiple persistent classes, with an XML mapping file for each. Where should we put these mapping files?

The Hibernate documentation recommends that the mapping file for each persistent class be placed in the same directory as that class. For instance, the mapping file for the Message class would be placed in the hello directory in a file named Message.hbm.xml. If we had another persistent class, it would be defined in its own mapping file. We suggest that you follow this practice. The monolithic metadata files encouraged by some frameworks, such as the struts-config.xml found in Struts, are a major contributor to "metadata hell." You load multiple mapping files by calling addResource() as often as you have to. Alternatively, if you follow the convention just described, you can use the method addClass(), passing a persistent class as the parameter:

```
SessionFactory sessions = new Configuration()
    .addClass(org.hibernate.auction.model.Item.class)
    .addClass(org.hibernate.auction.model.Category.class)
    .addClass(org.hibernate.auction.model.Bid.class)
    .setProperties( System.getProperties() )
    .buildSessionFactory();
```

The `addClass()` method assumes that the name of the mapping file ends with the `.hbm.xml` extension and is deployed along with the mapped class file.

We've demonstrated the creation of a single `SessionFactory`, which is all that most applications need. If another `SessionFactory` is needed—if there are multiple databases, for example—you repeat the process. Each `SessionFactory` is then available for one database and ready to produce `Sessions` to work with that particular database and a set of class mappings.

Of course, there is more to configuring Hibernate than just pointing to mapping documents. You also need to specify how database connections are to be obtained, along with various other settings that affect the behavior of Hibernate at runtime. The multitude of configuration properties may appear overwhelming (a complete list appears in the Hibernate documentation), but don't worry; most define reasonable default values, and only a handful are commonly required.

To specify configuration options, you may use any of the following techniques:

- Pass an instance of `java.util.Properties` to `Configuration.setProperties()`.

- Set system properties using `java -Dproperty=value`.

- Place a file called `hibernate.properties` in the classpath.

- Include `<property>` elements in `hibernate.cfg.xml` in the classpath.

The first and second options are rarely used except for quick testing and prototypes, but most applications need a fixed configuration file. Both the `hibernate.properties` and the `hibernate.cfg.xml` files provide the same function: to configure Hibernate. Which file you choose to use depends on your syntax preference. It's even possible to mix both options and have different settings for development and deployment, as you'll see later in this chapter.

A rarely used alternative option is to allow the application to provide a JDBC Connection when it opens a Hibernate `Session` from the `SessionFactory` (for example, by calling `sessions.openSession(myConnection)`). Using this option means that you don't have to specify any database connection properties. We don't recommend this approach for new applications that can be configured to use the environment's database connection infrastructure (for example, a JDBC connection pool or an application server datasource).

Of all the configuration options, database connection settings are the most important. They differ in managed and non-managed environments, so we deal with the two cases separately. Let's start with non-managed.

2.3.2 *Configuration in non-managed environments*

In a non-managed environment, such as a servlet container, the application is responsible for obtaining JDBC connections. Hibernate is part of the application, so it's responsible for getting these connections. You tell Hibernate how to get (or create new) JDBC connections. Generally, it isn't advisable to create a connection each time you want to interact with the database. Instead, Java applications should use a pool of JDBC connections. There are three reasons for using a pool:

- Acquiring a new connection is expensive.
- Maintaining many idle connections is expensive.
- Creating prepared statements is also expensive for some drivers.

Figure 2.2 shows the role of a JDBC connection pool in a web application runtime environment. Since this non-managed environment doesn't implement connection pooling, the application must implement its own pooling algorithm or rely upon a third-party library such as the open source *C3P0* connection pool. Without Hibernate, the application code usually calls the connection pool to obtain JDBC connections and execute SQL statements.

With Hibernate, the picture changes: It acts as a client of the JDBC connection pool, as shown in figure 2.3. The application code uses the Hibernate `Session` and `Query` APIs for persistence operations and only has to manage database transactions, ideally using the Hibernate `Transaction` API.

Using a connection pool

Hibernate defines a plugin architecture that allows integration with any connection pool. However, support for C3P0 is built in, so we'll use that. Hibernate will set up the connection pool for you with the given properties. An example of a `hibernate.properties` file using C3P0 is shown in listing 2.4.

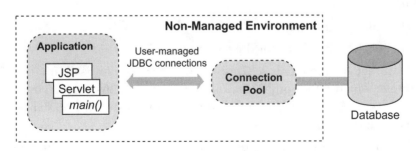

Figure 2.2 **JDBC** connection pooling in a non-managed environment

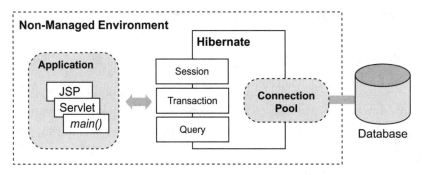

Figure 2.3 Hibernate with a connection pool in a non-managed environment

---

Listing 2.4 Using `hibernate.properties` for C3P0 connection pool settings

```
hibernate.connection.driver_class = org.postgresql.Driver
hibernate.connection.url = jdbc:postgresql://localhost/auctiondb
hibernate.connection.username = auctionuser
hibernate.connection.password = secret
hibernate.dialect = net.sf.hibernate.dialect.PostgreSQLDialect
hibernate.c3p0.min_size=5
hibernate.c3p0.max_size=20
hibernate.c3p0.timeout=300
hibernate.c3p0.max_statements=50
hibernate.c3p0.idle_test_period=3000
```

This code's lines specify the following information, beginning with the first line:

- The name of the Java class implementing the JDBC `Driver` (the driver JAR file must be placed in the application's classpath).

- A JDBC URL that specifies the host and database name for JDBC connections.

- The database user name.

- The database password for the specified user.

- A `Dialect` for the database. Despite the ANSI standardization effort, SQL is implemented differently by various databases vendors. So, you must specify a `Dialect`. Hibernate includes built-in support for all popular SQL databases, and new dialects may be defined easily.

- The minimum number of JDBC connections that C3P0 will keep ready.

- The maximum number of connections in the pool. An exception will be thrown at runtime if this number is exhausted.

- The timeout period (in this case, 5 minutes or 300 seconds) after which an idle connection will be removed from the pool.

- The maximum number of prepared statements that will be cached. Caching of prepared statements is essential for best performance with Hibernate.

- The idle time in seconds before a connection is automatically validated.

Specifying properties of the form `hibernate.c3p0.*` selects C3P0 as Hibernate's connection pool (you don't need any other switch to enable C3P0 support). C3P0 has even more features than we've shown in the previous example, so we refer you to the Hibernate API documentation. The Javadoc for the class `net.sf.hibernate.cfg.Environment` documents every Hibernate configuration property, including all C3P0-related settings and settings for other third-party connection pools directly supported by Hibernate.

The other supported connection pools are Apache DBCP and Proxool. You should try each pool in your own environment before deciding between them. The Hibernate community tends to prefer C3P0 and Proxool.

Hibernate also ships with a default connection pooling mechanism. This connection pool is only suitable for testing and experimenting with Hibernate: You should *not* use this built-in pool in production systems. It isn't designed to scale to an environment with many concurrent requests, and it lacks the fault tolerance features found in specialized connection pools.

Starting Hibernate

How do you start Hibernate with these properties? You declared the properties in a file named `hibernate.properties`, so you need only place this file in the application classpath. It will be automatically detected and read when Hibernate is first initialized when you create a `Configuration` object.

Let's summarize the configuration steps you've learned so far (this is a good time to download and install Hibernate, if you'd like to continue in a non-managed environment):

1   Download and unpack the JDBC driver for your database, which is usually available from the database vendor web site. Place the JAR files in the application classpath; do the same with `hibernate2.jar`.

2   Add Hibernate's dependencies to the classpath; they're distributed along with Hibernate in the `lib/` directory. See also the text file `lib/README.txt` for a list of required and optional libraries.

3   Choose a JDBC connection pool supported by Hibernate and configure it with a properties file. Don't forget to specify the SQL dialect.

4   Let the `Configuration` know about these properties by placing them in a `hibernate.properties` file in the classpath.

5   Create an instance of `Configuration` in your application and load the XML mapping files using either `addResource()` or `addClass()`. Build a `Session-Factory` from the `Configuration` by calling `buildSessionFactory()`.

Unfortunately, you don't have any mapping files yet. If you like, you can run the "Hello World" example or skip the rest of this chapter and start learning about persistent classes and mappings in chapter 3. Or, if you want to know more about using Hibernate in a managed environment, read on.

2.3.3 *Configuration in managed environments*

A managed environment handles certain cross-cutting concerns, such as application security (authorization and authentication), connection pooling, and transaction management. J2EE application servers are typical managed environments. Although application servers are generally designed to support EJBs, you can still take advantage of the other managed services provided, even if you don't use EJB entity beans.

Hibernate is often used with session or message-driven EJBs, as shown in figure 2.4. EJBs call the same Hibernate APIs as servlets, JSPs, or stand-alone applications: `Session`, `Transaction`, and `Query`. The Hibernate-related code is fully portable between non-managed and managed environments. Hibernate handles the different connection and transaction strategies transparently.

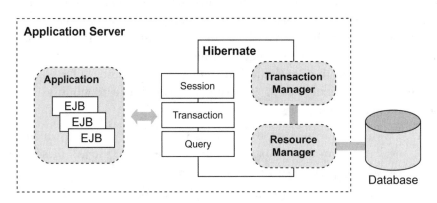

Figure 2.4   Hibernate in a managed environment with an application server

An application server exposes a connection pool as a JNDI-bound *datasource*, an instance of javax.jdbc.Datasource. You need to tell Hibernate where to find the datasource in JNDI, by supplying a fully qualified JNDI name. An example Hibernate configuration file for this scenario is shown in listing 2.5.

Listing 2.5 Sample hibernate.properties for a container-provided datasource

```
hibernate.connection.datasource = java:/comp/env/jdbc/AuctionDB
hibernate.transaction.factory_class = \
    net.sf.hibernate.transaction.JTATransactionFactory
hibernate.transaction.manager_lookup_class = \
    net.sf.hibernate.transaction.JBossTransactionManagerLookup
hibernate.dialect = net.sf.hibernate.dialect.PostgreSQLDialect
```

This file first gives the JNDI name of the datasource. The datasource must be configured in the J2EE enterprise application deployment descriptor; this is a vendor-specific setting. Next, you enable Hibernate integration with JTA. Now Hibernate needs to locate the application server's TransactionManager in order to integrate fully with the container transactions. No standard approach is defined by the J2EE specification, but Hibernate includes support for all popular application servers. Finally, of course, the Hibernate SQL dialect is required.

Now that you've configured everything correctly, using Hibernate in a managed environment isn't much different than using it in a non-managed environment: Just create a Configuration with mappings and build a SessionFactory. However, some of the transaction environment–related settings deserve some extra consideration.

Java already has a standard transaction API, JTA, which is used to control transactions in a managed environment with J2EE. This is called *container-managed transactions* (CMT). If a JTA transaction manager is present, JDBC connections are enlisted with this manager and under its full control. This isn't the case in a non-managed environment, where an application (or the pool) manages the JDBC connections and JDBC transactions directly.

Therefore, managed and non-managed environments can use different transaction methods. Since Hibernate needs to be portable across these environments, it defines an API for controlling transactions. The Hibernate Transaction interface abstracts the underlying JTA or JDBC transaction (or, potentially, even a CORBA transaction). This underlying transaction strategy is set with the property hibernate.transaction.factory_class, and it can take one of the following two values:

- `net.sf.hibernate.transaction.JDBCTransactionFactory` delegates to direct JDBC transactions. This strategy should be used with a connection pool in a non-managed environment and is the default if no strategy is specified.

- `net.sf.hibernate.transaction.JTATransactionFactory` delegates to JTA. This is the correct strategy for CMT, where connections are enlisted with JTA. Note that if a JTA transaction is already in progress when `beginTransaction()` is called, subsequent work takes place in the context of that transaction (otherwise a new JTA transaction is started).

For a more detailed introduction to Hibernate's `Transaction` API and the effects on your specific application scenario, see chapter 5, section 5.1, "Transactions." Just remember the two steps that are necessary if you work with a J2EE application server: Set the factory class for the Hibernate `Transaction` API to JTA as described earlier, and declare the transaction manager lookup specific to your application server. The lookup strategy is required only if you use the second-level caching system in Hibernate, but it doesn't hurt to set it even without using the cache.

HIBERNATE WITH TOMCAT   Tomcat isn't a full application server; it's just a servlet container, albeit a servlet container with some features usually found only in application servers. One of these features may be used with Hibernate: the Tomcat connection pool. Tomcat uses the DBCP connection pool internally but exposes it as a JNDI datasource, just like a real application server. To configure the Tomcat datasource, you'll need to edit `server.xml` according to instructions in the Tomcat JNDI/JDBC documentation. You can configure Hibernate to use this datasource by setting `hibernate.connection.datasource`. Keep in mind that Tomcat doesn't ship with a transaction manager, so this situation is still more like a non-managed environment as described earlier.

You should now have a running Hibernate system, whether you use a simple servlet container or an application server. Create and compile a persistent class (the initial `Message`, for example), copy Hibernate and its required libraries to the classpath together with a `hibernate.properties` file, and build a `SessionFactory`.

The next section covers advanced Hibernate configuration options. Some of them are recommended, such as logging executed SQL statements for debugging or using the convenient XML configuration file instead of plain properties. However, you may safely skip this section and come back later once you have read more about persistent classes in chapter 3.

2.4 Advanced configuration settings

When you finally have a Hibernate application running, it's well worth getting to know all the Hibernate configuration parameters. These parameters let you optimize the runtime behavior of Hibernate, especially by tuning the JDBC interaction (for example, using JDBC batch updates).

We won't bore you with these details now; the best source of information about configuration options is the Hibernate reference documentation. In the previous section, we showed you the options you'll need to get started.

However, there is one parameter that we *must* emphasize at this point. You'll need it continually whenever you develop software with Hibernate. Setting the property `hibernate.show_sql` to the value `true` enables logging of all generated SQL to the console. You'll use it for troubleshooting, performance tuning, and just to see what's going on. It pays to be aware of what your ORM layer is doing—that's why ORM doesn't hide SQL from developers.

So far, we've assumed that you specify configuration parameters using a `hibernate.properties` file or an instance of `java.util.Properties` programmatically. There is a third option you'll probably like: using an XML configuration file.

2.4.1 Using XML-based configuration

You can use an XML configuration file (as demonstrated in listing 2.6) to fully configure a `SessionFactory`. Unlike `hibernate.properties`, which contains only configuration parameters, the `hibernate.cfg.xml` file may also specify the location of mapping documents. Many users prefer to centralize the configuration of Hibernate in this way instead of adding parameters to the `Configuration` in application code.

> **Listing 2.6 Sample `hibernate.cfg.xml` configuration file**

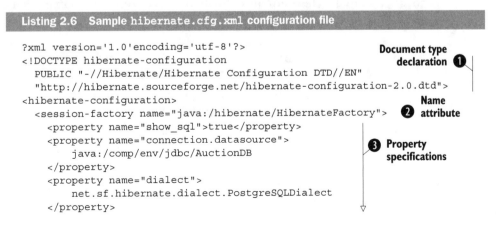

```
?xml version='1.0'encoding='utf-8'?>
<!DOCTYPE hibernate-configuration
    PUBLIC "-//Hibernate/Hibernate Configuration DTD//EN"
    "http://hibernate.sourceforge.net/hibernate-configuration-2.0.dtd">
<hibernate-configuration>
    <session-factory name="java:/hibernate/HibernateFactory">
        <property name="show_sql">true</property>
        <property name="connection.datasource">
            java:/comp/env/jdbc/AuctionDB
        </property>
        <property name="dialect">
            net.sf.hibernate.dialect.PostgreSQLDialect
        </property>
```

Document type declaration ❶

Name attribute ❷

Property specifications ❸

```
        <property name="transaction.manager_lookup_class">
            net.sf.hibernate.transaction.JBossTransactionManagerLookup
        </property>                                                          ③
        <mapping resource="auction/Item.hbm.xml"/>        ④ Mapping
        <mapping resource="auction/Category.hbm.xml"/>      document
        <mapping resource="auction/Bid.hbm.xml"/>           specifications
    </session-factory>
</hibernate-configuration>
```

① The *document type* declaration is used by the XML parser to validate this document against the Hibernate configuration DTD.

② The optional `name` attribute is equivalent to the property `hibernate.session_factory_name` and used for JNDI binding of the `SessionFactory`, discussed in the next section.

③ Hibernate properties may be specified without the `hibernate` prefix. Property names and values are otherwise identical to programmatic configuration properties.

④ Mapping documents may be specified as application resources or even as hard-coded filenames. The files used here are from our online auction application, which we'll introduce in chapter 3.

Now you can initialize Hibernate using

```
SessionFactory sessions = new Configuration()
        .configure().buildSessionFactory();
```

Wait—how did Hibernate know where the configuration file was located?

When `configure()` was called, Hibernate searched for a file named `hibernate.cfg.xml` in the classpath. If you wish to use a different filename or have Hibernate look in a subdirectory, you must pass a path to the `configure()` method:

```
SessionFactory sessions = new Configuration()
        .configure("/hibernate-config/auction.cfg.xml")
            .buildSessionFactory();
```

Using an XML configuration file is certainly more comfortable than a properties file or even programmatic property configuration. The fact that you can have the class mapping files externalized from the application's source (even if it would be only in a startup helper class) is a major benefit of this approach. You can, for example, use different sets of mapping files (and different configuration options), depending on your database and environment (development or production), and switch them programatically.

If you have both `hibernate.properties` and `hibernate.cfg.xml` in the classpath, the settings of the XML configuration file will override the settings used in the properties. This is useful if you keep some base settings in properties and override them for each deployment with an XML configuration file.

You may have noticed that the `SessionFactory` was also given a `name` in the XML configuration file. Hibernate uses this name to automatically bind the `SessionFactory` to JNDI after creation.

2.4.2 *JNDI-bound SessionFactory*

In most Hibernate applications, the `SessionFactory` should be instantiated once during application initialization. The single instance should then be used by all code in a particular process, and any `Sessions` should be created using this single `SessionFactory`. A frequently asked question is where this factory must be placed and how it can be accessed without much hassle.

In a J2EE environment, a `SessionFactory` bound to JNDI is easily shared between different threads and between various Hibernate-aware components. Or course, JNDI isn't the only way that application components might obtain a `SessionFactory`. There are many possible implementations of this Registry pattern, including use of the `ServletContext` or a `static final` variable in a singleton. A particularly elegant approach is to use an application scope IoC (Inversion of Control) framework component. However, JNDI is a popular approach (and is exposed as a JMX service, as you'll see later). We discuss some of the alternatives in chapter 8, section 8.1, "Designing layered applications."

> **NOTE** The Java Naming and Directory Interface (JNDI) API allows objects to be stored to and retrieved from a hierarchical structure (directory tree). JNDI implements the Registry pattern. Infrastructural objects (transaction contexts, datasources), configuration settings (environment settings, user registries), and even application objects (EJB references, object factories) may all be bound to JNDI.

The `SessionFactory` will automatically bind itself to JNDI if the property `hibernate.session_factory_name` is set to the name of the directory node. If your runtime environment doesn't provide a default JNDI context (or if the default JNDI implementation doesn't support instances of `Referenceable`), you need to specify a JNDI initial context using the properties `hibernate.jndi.url` and `hibernate.jndi.class`.

Here is an example Hibernate configuration that binds the `SessionFactory` to the name `hibernate/HibernateFactory` using Sun's (free) file system–based JNDI implementation, `fscontext.jar`:

```
hibernate.connection.datasource = java:/comp/env/jdbc/AuctionDB
hibernate.transaction.factory_class = \
    net.sf.hibernate.transaction.JTATransactionFactory
hibernate.transaction.manager_lookup_class = \
    net.sf.hibernate.transaction.JBossTransactionManagerLookup
hibernate.dialect = net.sf.hibernate.dialect.PostgreSQLDialect
hibernate.session_factory_name = hibernate/HibernateFactory
hibernate.jndi.class = com.sun.jndi.fscontext.RefFSContextFactory
hibernate.jndi.url = file:/auction/jndi
```

Of course, you can also use the XML-based configuration for this task. This example also isn't realistic, since most application servers that provide a connection pool through JNDI also have a JNDI implementation with a writable default context. JBoss certainly has, so you can skip the last two properties and just specify a name for the `SessionFactory`. All you have to do now is call `Configuration.configure().buildSessionFactory()` once to initialize the binding.

> **NOTE** Tomcat comes bundled with a read-only JNDI context, which isn't writable from application-level code after the startup of the servlet container. Hibernate can't bind to this context; you have to either use a full context implementation (like the Sun FS context) or disable JNDI binding of the `SessionFactory` by omitting the `session_factory_name` property in the configuration.

Let's look at some other very important configuration settings that log Hibernate operations.

2.4.3 Logging

Hibernate (and many other ORM implementations) executes SQL statements *asynchronously*. An `INSERT` statement isn't usually executed when the application calls `Session.save()`; an `UPDATE` isn't immediately issued when the application calls `Item.addBid()`. Instead, the SQL statements are usually issued at the end of a transaction. This behavior is called *write-behind*, as we mentioned earlier.

This fact is evidence that tracing and debugging ORM code is sometimes non-trivial. In theory, it's possible for the application to treat Hibernate as a black box and ignore this behavior. Certainly the Hibernate application can't detect this asynchronicity (at least, not without resorting to direct JDBC calls). However, when you find yourself troubleshooting a difficult problem, you need to be able to see *exactly* what's going on inside Hibernate. Since Hibernate is open source, you can easily step into the Hibernate code. Occasionally, doing so helps a great deal! But, especially in the face of asynchronous behavior, debugging Hibernate can quickly get you lost. You can use logging to get a view of Hibernate's internals.

We've already mentioned the `hibernate.show_sql` configuration parameter, which is usually the first port of call when troubleshooting. Sometimes the SQL alone is insufficient; in that case, you must dig a little deeper.

Hibernate logs all interesting events using Apache `commons-logging`, a thin abstraction layer that directs output to either Apache log4j (if you put `log4j.jar` in your classpath) or JDK1.4 logging (if you're running under JDK1.4 or above and log4j isn't present). We recommend log4j, since it's more mature, more popular, and under more active development.

To see any output from log4j, you'll need a file named `log4j.properties` in your classpath (right next to `hibernate.properties` or `hibernate.cfg.xml`). This example directs all log messages to the console:

```
### direct log messages to stdout ###
log4j.appender.stdout=org.apache.log4j.ConsoleAppender
log4j.appender.stdout.Target=System.out
log4j.appender.stdout.layout=org.apache.log4j.PatternLayout
log4j.appender.stdout.layout.ConversionPattern=%d{ABSOLUTE}
⇒ %5p %c{1}:%L - %m%n
### root logger option ###
log4j.rootLogger=warn, stdout
### Hibernate logging options ###
log4j.logger.net.sf.hibernate=info
### log JDBC bind parameters ###
log4j.logger.net.sf.hibernate.type=info
```

With this configuration, you won't see many log messages at runtime. Replacing info with `debug` for the `log4j.logger.net.sf.hibernate` category will reveal the inner workings of Hibernate. Make sure you don't do this in a production environment—writing the log will be much slower than the actual database access.

Finally, you have the `hibernate.properties`, `hibernate.cfg.xml`, and `log4j.properties` configuration files.

There is another way to configure Hibernate, if your application server supports the Java Management Extensions.

2.4.4 *Java Management Extensions (JMX)*

The Java world is full of specifications, standards, and, of course, implementations of these. A relatively new but important standard is in its first version: the *Java*

Management Extensions (JMX). JMX is about the management of systems components or, better, of system services.

Where does Hibernate fit into this new picture? Hibernate, when deployed in an application server, makes use of other services like managed transactions and pooled database transactions. But why not make Hibernate a managed service itself, which others can depend on and use? This is possible with the Hibernate JMX integration, making Hibernate a managed JMX component.

The JMX specification defines the following components:

- *The JMX MBean*—A reusable component (usually infrastructural) that exposes an interface for *management* (administration)
- *The JMX container*—Mediates generic access (local or remote) to the MBean
- *The (usually generic) JMX client*—May be used to administer any MBean via the JMX container

An application server with support for JMX (such as JBoss) acts as a JMX container and allows an MBean to be configured and initialized as part of the application server startup process. It's possible to monitor and administer the MBean using the application server's administration console (which acts as the JMX client).

An MBean may be packaged as a JMX service, which is not only portable between application servers with JMX support but also deployable to a running system (a *hot deploy*).

Hibernate may be packaged and administered as a JMX MBean. The Hibernate JMX service allows Hibernate to be initialized at application server startup and controlled (configured) via a JMX client. However, JMX components aren't automatically integrated with container-managed transactions. So, the configuration options in listing 2.7 (a JBoss service deployment descriptor) look similar to the usual Hibernate settings in a managed environment.

> **Listing 2.7 Hibernate `jboss-service.xml` JMX deployment descriptor**

```
<server>
<mbean
    code="net.sf.hibernate.jmx.HibernateService"
    name="jboss.jca:service=HibernateFactory, name=HibernateFactory">
  <depends>jboss.jca:service=RARDeployer</depends>
  <depends>jboss.jca:service=LocalTxCM,name=DataSource</depends>
  <attribute name="MapResources">
    auction/Item.hbm.xml, auction/Bid.hbm.xml
  </attribute>
```

```
    <attribute name="JndiName">
      java:/hibernate/HibernateFactory
    </attribute>
    <attribute name="Datasource">
      java:/comp/env/jdbc/AuctionDB
    </attribute>
    <attribute name="Dialect">
      net.sf.hibernate.dialect.PostgreSQLDialect
    </attribute>
    <attribute name="TransactionStrategy">
      net.sf.hibernate.transaction.JTATransactionFactory
    </attribute>
    <attribute name="TransactionManagerLookupStrategy">
      net.sf.hibernate.transaction.JBossTransactionManagerLookup
    </attribute>
    <attribute name="UserTransactionName">
      java:/UserTransaction
    </attribute>
  </mbean>
  </server>
```

The `HibernateService` depends on two other JMX services: `service=RARDeployer` and `service=LocalTxCM,name=DataSource`, both in the `jboss.jca` service domain name.

The Hibernate MBean may be found in the package `net.sf.hibernate.jmx`. Unfortunately, lifecycle management methods like starting and stopping the JMX service aren't part of the JMX 1.0 specification. The methods `start()` and `stop()` of the `HibernateService` are therefore specific to the JBoss application server.

NOTE   If you're interested in the advanced usage of JMX, JBoss is a good open source starting point: All services (even the EJB container) in JBoss are implemented as MBeans and can be managed via a supplied console interface.

We recommend that you try to configure Hibernate programmatically (using the `Configuration` object) before you try to run Hibernate as a JMX service. However, some features (like hot-redeployment of Hibernate applications) may be possible only with JMX, once they become available in Hibernate. Right now, the biggest advantage of Hibernate with JMX is the automatic startup; it means you no longer have to create a `Configuration` and build a `SessionFactory` in your application code, but can simply access the `SessionFactory` through JNDI once the `HibernateService` has been deployed and started.

2.5 *Summary*

In this chapter, we took a high-level look at Hibernate and its architecture after running a simple "Hello World" example. You also saw how to configure Hibernate in various environments and with various techniques, even including JMX.

The `Configuration` and `SessionFactory` interfaces are the entry points to Hibernate for applications running in both managed and non-managed environments. Hibernate provides additional APIs, such as the `Transaction` interface, to bridge the differences between environments and allow you to keep your persistence code portable.

Hibernate can be integrated into almost every Java environment, be it a servlet, an applet, or a fully managed three-tiered client/server application. The most important elements of a Hibernate configuration are the database resources (connection configuration), the transaction strategies, and, of course, the XML-based mapping metadata.

Hibernate's configuration interfaces have been designed to cover as many usage scenarios as possible while still being easy to understand. Usually, a single file named `hibernate.cfg.xml` and one line of code are enough to get Hibernate up and running.

None of this is much use without some persistent classes and their XML mapping documents. The next chapter is dedicated to writing and mapping persistent classes. You'll soon be able to store and retrieve persistent objects in a real application with a nontrivial object/relational mapping.

Mapping persistent classes

This chapter covers

- POJO basics for rich domain models
- Mapping POJOs with Hibernate metadata
- Mapping class inheritance and fine-grained models
- An introduction to class association mappings

The "Hello World" example in chapter 2 introduced you to Hibernate; however, it isn't very useful for understanding the requirements of real-world applications with complex data models. For the rest of the book, we'll use a much more sophisticated example application—an online auction system—to demonstrate Hibernate.

In this chapter, we start our discussion of the application by introducing a programming model for persistent classes. Designing and implementing the persistent classes is a multistep process that we'll examine in detail.

First, you'll learn how to identify the *business entities* of a problem domain. We create a conceptual model of these entities and their attributes, called a *domain model*. We implement this domain model in Java by creating a persistent class for each entity. (We'll spend some time exploring exactly what these Java classes should look like.)

We then define *mapping metadata* to tell Hibernate how these classes and their properties relate to database tables and columns. This involves writing or generating XML documents that are eventually deployed along with the compiled Java classes and used by Hibernate at runtime. This discussion of mapping metadata is the core of this chapter, along with the in-depth exploration of the mapping techniques for fine-grained classes, object identity, inheritance, and associations. This chapter therefore provides the beginnings of a solution to the first four generic problems of ORM listed in section 1.4.2, "Generic ORM problems."

We'll start by introducing the example application.

3.1 *The CaveatEmptor application*

The CaveatEmptor online auction application demonstrates ORM techniques and Hibernate functionality; you can download the source code for the entire working application from the web site http://caveatemptor.hibernate.org. The application will have a web-based user interface and run inside a servlet engine like Tomcat. We won't pay much attention to the user interface; we'll concentrate on the data access code. In chapter 8, we discuss the changes that would be necessary if we were to perform all business logic and data access from a separate business-tier implemented as EJB session beans.

But, let's start at the beginning. In order to understand the design issues involved in ORM, let's pretend the CaveatEmptor application doesn't yet exist, and that we're building it from scratch. Our first task would be *analysis*.

3.1.1 Analyzing the business domain

A software development effort begins with analysis of the problem domain (assuming that no legacy code or legacy database already exist).

At this stage, you, with the help of problem domain experts, identify the main *entities* that are relevant to the software system. Entities are usually notions understood by users of the system: Payment, Customer, Order, Item, Bid, and so forth. Some entities might be abstractions of less concrete things the user thinks about (for example, PricingAlgorithm), but even these would usually be understandable to the user. All these entities are found in the conceptual view of the business, which we sometimes call a *business model*. Developers of object-oriented software analyze the business model and create an object model, still at the conceptual level (no Java code).This object model may be as simple as a mental image existing only in the mind of the developer, or it may be as elaborate as a UML class diagram (as in figure 3.1) created by a CASE (Computer-Aided Software Engineering) tool like ArgoUML or TogetherJ.

This simple model contains entities that you're bound to find in any typical auction system: Category, Item, and User. The entities and their relationships (and perhaps their attributes) are all represented by this model of the problem domain. We call this kind of model—an object-oriented model of entities from the problem domain, encompassing only those entities that are of interest to the user—a *domain model*. It's an abstract view of the real world. We refer to this model when we implement our persistent Java classes.

Let's examine the outcome of our analysis of the problem domain of the Caveat-Emptor application.

3.1.2 The CaveatEmptor domain model

The CaveatEmptor site auctions many different kinds of items, from electronic equipment to airline tickets. Auctions proceed according to the "English auction" model: Users continue to place bids on an item until the bid period for that item expires, and the highest bidder wins.

In any store, goods are categorized by type and grouped with similar goods into sections and onto shelves. Clearly, our auction catalog requires some kind of hierarchy of item categories. A buyer may browse these categories or arbitrarily search by category and item attributes. Lists of items appear in the category browser and

Figure 3.1   A class diagram of a typical online auction object model

search result screens. Selecting an item from a list will take the buyer to an item detail view.

An auction consists of a sequence of bids. One particular bid is the winning bid. User details include name, login, address, email address, and billing information.

A *web of trust* is an essential feature of an online auction site. The web of trust allows users to build a reputation for trustworthiness (or untrustworthiness). Buyers may create comments about sellers (and vice versa), and the comments are visible to all other users.

A high-level overview of our domain model is shown in figure 3.2. Let's briefly discuss some interesting features of this model.

Each item may be auctioned only once, so we don't need to make Item distinct from the Auction entities. Instead, we have a single auction item entity named Item. Thus, Bid is associated directly with Item. Users can write Comments about other users only in the context of an auction; hence the association between Item and Comment. The Address information of a User is modeled as a separate class, even though the User may have only one Address. We do allow the user to have multiple BillingDetails. The various billing strategies are represented as subclasses of an abstract class (allowing future extension).

A Category might be nested inside another Category. This is expressed by a *recursive* association, from the Category entity to itself. Note that a single Category may have multiple child categories but at most one parent category. Each Item belongs to at least one Category.

The entities in a domain model should encapsulate state and behavior. For example, the User entity should define the name and address of a customer and the logic required to calculate the shipping costs for items (to this particular customer). Our domain model is a *rich* object model, with complex associations, interactions, and inheritance relationships. An interesting and detailed discussion of object-oriented techniques for working with domain models can be found in *Patterns of Enterprise Application Architecture* [Fowler 2003] or in *Domain-Driven Design* [Evans 2004].

However, in this book, we won't have much to say about business rules or about the *behavior* of our domain model. This is certainly not because we consider this an unimportant concern; rather, this concern is mostly orthogonal to the problem of persistence. It's the *state* of our entities that is persistent. So, we concentrate our discussion on how to best represent state in our domain model, not on how to represent behavior. For example, in this book, we aren't interested in how tax for sold items is calculated or how the system might approve a new user account. We're

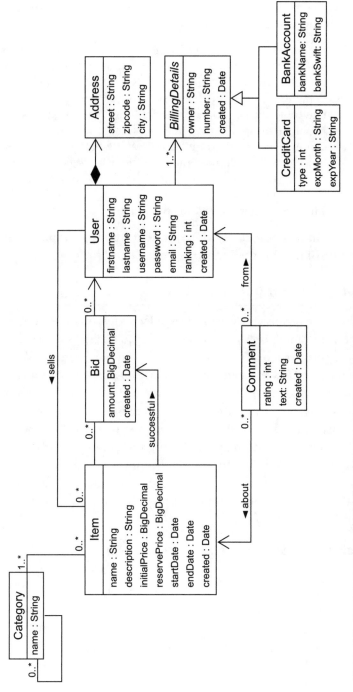

Figure 3.2 Persistent classes of the CaveatEmptor object model and their relationships

more interested in how the relationship between users and the items they sell is represented and made persistent.

> **FAQ** *Can you use ORM without a domain model?* We stress that object persistence with full ORM is most suitable for applications based on a rich domain model. If your application doesn't implement complex business rules or complex interactions between entities (or if you have few entities), you may not need a domain model. Many simple and some not-so-simple problems are perfectly suited to table-oriented solutions, where the application is designed around the database data model instead of around an object-oriented domain model, often with logic executed in the database (stored procedures). However, the more complex and expressive your domain model, the more you will benefit from using Hibernate; it shines when dealing with the full complexity of object/relational persistence.

Now that we have a domain model, our next step is to implement it in Java. Let's look at some of the things we need to consider.

3.2 Implementing the domain model

Several issues typically must be addressed when you implement a domain model in Java. For instance, how do you separate the business concerns from the cross-cutting concerns (such as transactions and even persistence)? What kind of persistence is needed: Do you need *automated* or *transparent* persistence? Do you have to use a specific programming model to achieve this? In this section, we examine these types of issues and how to address them in a typical Hibernate application.

Let's start with an issue that any implementation must deal with: the separation of concerns. The domain model implementation is usually a central, organizing component; it's reused heavily whenever you implement new application functionality. For this reason, you should be prepared to go to some lengths to ensure that concerns other than business aspects don't leak into the domain model implementation.

3.2.1 Addressing leakage of concerns

The domain model implementation is such an important piece of code that it shouldn't depend on other Java APIs. For example, code in the domain model shouldn't perform JNDI lookups or call the database via the JDBC API. This allows you to reuse the domain model implementation virtually anywhere. Most importantly, it makes it easy to *unit test* the domain model (in JUnit, for example) outside of any application server or other managed environment.

We say that the domain model should be "concerned" only with modeling the business domain. However, there are other concerns, such as persistence, transaction management, and authorization. You shouldn't put code that addresses these *cross-cutting concerns* in the classes that implement the domain model. When these concerns start to appear in the domain model classes, we call this an example of *leakage of concerns.*

The EJB standard tries to solve the problem of leaky concerns. Indeed, if we implemented our domain model using entity beans, the container would take care of some concerns for us (or at least externalize those concerns to the deployment descriptor). The EJB container prevents leakage of certain cross-cutting concerns using *interception.* An EJB is a *managed component,* always executed inside the EJB container. The container intercepts calls to your beans and executes its own functionality. For example, it might pass control to the CMP engine, which takes care of persistence. This approach allows the container to implement the predefined cross-cutting concerns—security, concurrency, persistence, transactions, and remoteness—in a generic way.

Unfortunately, the EJB specification imposes many rules and restrictions on how you must implement a domain model. This in itself is a kind of leakage of concerns—in this case, the concerns of the container implementor have leaked! Hibernate isn't an application server, and it doesn't try to implement all the cross-cutting concerns mentioned in the EJB specification. Hibernate is a solution for just one of these concerns: persistence. If you require declarative security and transaction management, you should still access your domain model via a session bean, taking advantage of the EJB container's implementation of these concerns. Hibernate is commonly used together with the well-known session façade J2EE pattern.

Much discussion has gone into the topic of persistence, and both Hibernate and EJB entity beans take care of that concern. However, Hibernate offers something that entity beans don't: *transparent persistence.*

3.2.2 *Transparent and automated persistence*

Your application server's CMP engine implements *automated persistence.* It takes care of the tedious details of JDBC `ResultSet` and `PreparedStatement` handling. So does Hibernate; indeed, Hibernate is a great deal more sophisticated in this respect. But Hibernate does this in a way that is *transparent* to your domain model.

We use *transparent* to mean a complete separation of concerns between the persistent classes of the domain model and the persistence logic itself, where the persistent classes are unaware of—and have no dependency to—the persistence mechanism.

Our `Item` class, for example, will not have any code-level dependency to any Hibernate API. Furthermore:

- Hibernate doesn't require that any special superclasses or interfaces be inherited or implemented by persistent classes. Nor are any special classes used to implement properties or associations. Thus, transparent persistence improves code readability, as you'll soon see.

- Persistent classes may be reused outside the context of persistence, in unit tests or in the user interface (UI) tier, for example. Testability is a basic requirement for applications with rich domain models.

- In a system with transparent persistence, objects aren't aware of the underlying data store; they need not even be aware that they are being persisted or retrieved. Persistence concerns are externalized to a generic *persistence manager* interface —in the case of Hibernate, the `Session` and `Query` interfaces.

Transparent persistence fosters a degree of portability; without special interfaces, the persistent classes are decoupled from any particular persistence solution. Our business logic is fully reusable in any other application context. We could easily change to another transparent persistence mechanism.

By this definition of transparent persistence, you see that certain non-automated persistence layers are transparent (for example, the DAO pattern) because they decouple the persistence-related code with abstract programming interfaces. Only plain Java classes without dependencies are exposed to the business logic. Conversely, some automated persistence layers (including entity beans and some ORM solutions) are non-transparent, because they require special interfaces or intrusive programming models.

We regard transparency as required. In fact, transparent persistence should be one of the primary goals of any ORM solution. However, no automated persistence solution is completely transparent: Every automated persistence layer, including Hibernate, imposes *some* requirements on the persistent classes. For example, Hibernate requires that collection-valued properties be typed to an interface such as `java.util.Set` or `java.util.List` and not to an actual implementation such as `java.util.HashSet` (this is a good practice anyway). (We discuss the reasons for this requirement in appendix B, "ORM implementation strategies.")

You now know why the persistence mechanism should have minimal impact on how you implement a domain model and that transparent and automated persistence are required. EJB isn't transparent, so what kind of programming model should you use? Do you need a special programming model at all? In theory, no;

in practice, you should adopt a disciplined, consistent programming model that is well accepted by the Java community. Let's discuss this programming model and see how it works with Hibernate.

3.2.3 Writing POJOs

Developers have found entity beans to be tedious, unnatural, and unproductive. As a reaction against entity beans, many developers started talking about *Plain Old Java Objects* (POJOs), a back-to-basics approach that essentially revives JavaBeans, a component model for UI development, and reapplies it to the business layer. (Most developers are now using the terms *POJO* and *JavaBean* almost synonymously.)[1]

Hibernate works best with a domain model implemented as POJOs. The few requirements that Hibernate imposes on your domain model are also best practices for the POJO programming model. So, most POJOs are Hibernate-compatible without any changes. The programming model we'll introduce is a non-intrusive mix of JavaBean specification details, POJO best practices, and Hibernate requirements. A POJO declares *business methods*, which define behavior, and *properties*, which represent state. Some properties represent associations to other POJOs.

Listing 3.1 shows a simple POJO class; it's an implementation of the User entity of our domain model.

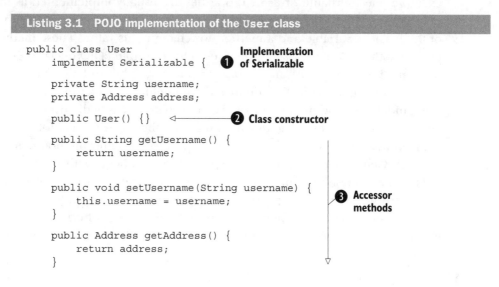

Listing 3.1 POJO implementation of the User class

```
public class User
    implements Serializable {          ❶ Implementation
                                           of Serializable

    private String username;
    private Address address;

    public User() {}      ⟵          ❷ Class constructor

    public String getUsername() {
        return username;
    }

    public void setUsername(String username) {
        this.username = username;          ❸ Accessor
    }                                          methods

    public Address getAddress() {
        return address;
    }
```

---

[1] POJO is sometimes also written as Plain *Ordinary* Java Objects; this term was coined in 2002 by Martin Fowler, Rebecca Parsons, and Josh Mackenzie.

```
public void setAddress(Address address) {
    this.address = address;
}

public MonetaryAmount calcShippingCosts(Address fromLocation) {
    ...
}                                                    Business method ④
}
```

❶ Hibernate doesn't require that persistent classes implement `Serializable`. However, when objects are stored in an `HttpSession` or passed by value using RMI, serialization is necessary. (This is very likely to happen in a Hibernate application.)

❷ Unlike the JavaBeans specification, which requires no specific constructor, Hibernate requires a constructor with no arguments for every persistent class. Hibernate instantiates persistent classes using `Constructor.newInstance()`, a feature of the Java reflection API. The constructor may be non-public, but it should be at least package-visible if runtime-generated proxies will be used for performance optimization (see chapter 4).

❸ The properties of the POJO implement the attributes of our business entities—for example, the username of `User`. Properties are usually implemented as instance variables, together with *property accessor methods*: a method for retrieving the value of the instance variable and a method for changing its value. These methods are known as the *getter* and *setter*, respectively. Our example POJO declares getter and setter methods for the private `username` instance variable and also for `address`.

The JavaBean specification defines the guidelines for naming these methods. The guidelines allow generic tools like Hibernate to easily discover and manipulate the property value. A getter method name begins with `get`, followed by the name of the property (the first letter in uppercase); a setter method name begins with `set`. Getter methods for Boolean properties may begin with `is` instead of `get`.

Hibernate doesn't require that accessor methods be declared public; it can easily use private accessors for property management.

Some getter and setter methods do something more sophisticated than simple instance variables access (validation, for example). Trivial accessor methods are common, however.

❹ This POJO also defines a business method that calculates the cost of shipping an item to a particular user (we left out the implementation of this method).

Now that you understand the value of using POJO persistent classes as the programming model, let's see how you handle the associations between those classes.

3.2.4 *Implementing POJO associations*

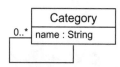

Figure 3.3   Diagram of the `Category` **class with an association**

You use properties to express associations between POJO classes, and you use accessor methods to navigate the object graph at runtime. Let's consider the associations defined by the `Category` class. The first association is shown in figure 3.3.

As with all our diagrams, we left out the association-related attributes (`parentCategory` and `childCategories`) because they would clutter the illustration. These attributes and the methods that manipulate their values are called *scaffolding code*.

Let's implement the scaffolding code for the *one-to-many* self-association of `Category`:

```
public class Category implements Serializable {
    private String name;
    private Category parentCategory;
    private Set childCategories = new HashSet();

    public Category() { }
    ...
}
```

To allow bidirectional navigation of the association, we require two attributes. The `parentCategory` attribute implements the *single-valued end* of the association and is declared to be of type `Category`. The *many-valued end*, implemented by the `child-Categories` attribute, must be of collection type. We choose a `Set`, since duplicates are disallowed, and initialize the instance variable to a new instance of `HashSet`.

Hibernate requires interfaces for collection-typed attributes. You must use `java.util.Set` rather than `HashSet`, for example. At runtime, Hibernate wraps the `HashSet` instance with an instance of one of Hibernate's own classes. (This special class isn't visible to the application code). It is good practice to program to collection interfaces, rather than concrete implementations, so this restriction shouldn't bother you.

We now have some private instance variables but no public interface to allow access from business code or property management by Hibernate. Let's add some accessor methods to the `Category` class:

```
public String getName() {
    return name;
}
```

```
public void setName(String name) {
    this.name = name;
}

public Set getChildCategories() {
    return childCategories;
}

public void setChildCategories(Set childCategories) {
    this.childCategories = childCategories;
}

public Category getParentCategory() {
    return parentCategory;
}

public void setParentCategory(Category parentCategory) {
    this.parentCategory = parentCategory;
}
```

Again, these accessor methods need to be declared `public` only if they're part of the external interface of the persistent class, the public interface used by the application logic.

The basic procedure for adding a child `Category` to a parent `Category` looks like this:

```
Category aParent = new Category();
Category aChild = new Category();
aChild.setParentCategory(aParent);
aParent.getChildCategories().add(aChild);
```

Whenever an association is created between a parent `Category` and a child `Category`, two actions are required:

- The `parentCategory` of the child must be set, effectively breaking the association between the child and its old parent (there can be only one parent for any child).

- The child must be added to the `childCategories` collection of the new parent `Category`.

MANAGED RELATIONSHIPS IN HIBERNATE Hibernate doesn't "manage" persistent associations. If you want to manipulate an association, you must write exactly the same code you would write without Hibernate. If an association is bidirectional, both sides of the relationship must be considered. Programming models like EJB entity beans muddle this behavior by introducing *container-managed relationships*. The container automatically changes the other side of a relationship if one side is modified by the application. This is one of the reasons why code that uses entity beans can't be reused outside the container.

If you ever have problems understanding the behavior of associations in Hibernate, just ask yourself, "What would I do *without* Hibernate?" Hibernate doesn't change the usual Java semantics.

It's a good idea to add a convenience method to the Category class that groups these operations, allowing reuse and helping ensure correctness:

```
public void addChildCategory(Category childCategory) {
    if (childCategory == null)
        throw new IllegalArgumentException("Null child category!");
    if (childCategory.getParentCategory() != null)
      childCategory.getParentCategory().getChildCategories()
                                  .remove(childCategory);
    childCategory.setParentCategory(this);
    childCategories.add(childCategory);

}
```

The addChildCategory() method not only reduces the lines of code when dealing with Category objects, but also enforces the cardinality of the association. Errors that arise from leaving out one of the two required actions are avoided. This kind of *grouping of operations* should always be provided for associations, if possible.

Because we would like the addChildCategory() to be the only externally visible mutator method for the child categories, we make the setChildCategories() method private. Hibernate doesn't care if property accessor methods are private or public, so we can focus on good API design.

A different kind of relationship exists between Category and the Item: a bidirectional *many-to-many association* (see figure 3.4).

In the case of a many-to-many association, both sides are implemented with collection-valued attributes. Let's add the new attributes and methods to access the Item class to our Category class, as shown in listing 3.2.

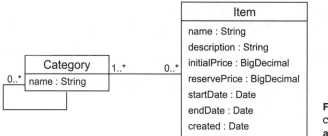

Figure 3.4
Category **and the**
associated Item

Listing 3.2   Category to Item scaffolding code

```
public class Category {

    ...
    private Set items = new HashSet();
    ...

    public Set getItems() {
        return items;
    }

    public void setItems(Set items) {
        this.items = items;
    }
}
```

The code for the Item class (the other end of the many-to-many association) is similar to the code for the Category class. We add the collection attribute, the standard accessor methods, and a method that simplifies relationship management (you can also add this to the Category class, see listing 3.3).

Listing 3.3   Item to Category scaffolding code

```
public class Item {

    private String name;
    private String description;
    ...
    private Set categories = new HashSet();
    ...

    public Set getCategories() {
        return categories;
    }

    private void setCategories(Set categories) {
        this.categories = categories;
    }

    public void addCategory(Category category) {
        if (category == null)
            throw new IllegalArgumentException("Null category");
        category.getItems().add(this);
        categories.add(category);
    }
}
```

The addCategory() of the Item method is similar to the addChildCategory convenience method of the Category class. It's used by a client to manipulate the relationship between Item and a Category. For the sake of readability, we won't show convenience methods in future code samples and assume you'll add them according to your own taste.

Convenience methods for association handling is however not the only way to improve a domain model implementation. You can also add logic to your accessor methods.

3.2.5 *Adding logic to accessor methods*

One of the reasons we like to use JavaBeans-style accessor methods is that they provide encapsulation: The hidden internal implementation of a property can be changed without any changes to the public interface. This allows you to abstract the internal data structure of a class—the instance variables—from the design of the database.

For example, if your database stores a name of the user as a single NAME column, but your User class has firstname and lastname properties, you can add the following persistent name property to your class:

```
public class User {
    private String firstname;
    private String lastname;
    ...

    public String getName() {
        return firstname + ' ' + lastname;
    }
    public void setName(String name) {
        StringTokenizer t = new StringTokenizer(name);
        firstname = t.nextToken();
        lastname = t.nextToken();
    )
    ...

}
```

Later, you'll see that a Hibernate *custom type* is probably a better way to handle many of these kinds of situations. However, it helps to have several options.

Accessor methods can also perform validation. For instance, in the following example, the setFirstName() method verifies that the name is capitalized:

```
public class User {
    private String firstname;
    ...
```

```
public String getFirstname() {
    return firstname;
}

public void setFirstname(String firstname)
  throws InvalidNameException {
    if ( !StringUtil.isCapitalizedName(firstname) )
        throw new InvalidNameException(firstname);
    this.firstname = firstname;
)
  ...

}
```

However, Hibernate will later use our accessor methods to populate the state of an object when loading the object from the database. Sometimes we would prefer that this validation *not* occur when Hibernate is initializing a newly loaded object. In that case, it might make sense to tell Hibernate to directly access the instance variables (we map the property with `access="field"` in Hibernate metadata), forcing Hibernate to bypass the setter method and access the instance variable directly. Another issue to consider is *dirty checking*. Hibernate automatically detects object state changes in order to synchronize the updated state with the database. It's usually completely safe to return a different object from the getter method to the object passed by Hibernate to the setter. Hibernate will compare the objects by value—not by object identity—to determine if the property's persistent state needs to be updated. For example, the following getter method won't result in unnecessary SQL UPDATEs:

```
public String getFirstname() {
    return new String(firstname);
}
```

However, there is one very important exception. Collections are compared by identity!

For a property mapped as a persistent collection, you should return *exactly* the same collection instance from the getter method as Hibernate passed to the setter method. If you don't, Hibernate will update the database, even if no update is necessary, *every time* the session synchronizes state held in memory with the database. This kind of code should almost always be avoided in accessor methods:

```
public void setNames(List namesList) {
    names = (String[]) namesList.toArray();
}

public List getNames() {
    return Arrays.asList(names);
}
```

You can see that Hibernate doesn't unnecessarily restrict the JavaBeans (POJO) programming model. You're free to implement whatever logic you need in accessor methods (as long as you keep the same collection instance in both getter and setter). If absolutely necessary, you can tell Hibernate to use a different access strategy to read and set the state of a property (for example, direct instance field access), as you'll see later. This kind of transparency guarantees an independent and reusable domain model implementation.

Now that we've implemented some persistent classes of our domain model, we need to define the ORM.

3.3 *Defining the mapping metadata*

ORM tools require a metadata format for the application to specify the mapping between classes and tables, properties and columns, associations and foreign keys, Java types and SQL types. This information is called the *object/relational mapping metadata*. It defines the transformation between the different data type systems and relationship representations.

It's our job as developers to define and maintain this metadata. We discuss various approaches in this section.

3.3.1 *Metadata in XML*

Any ORM solution should provide a human-readable, easily hand-editable mapping format, not only a GUI mapping tool. Currently, the most popular object/relational metadata format is XML. Mapping documents written in and with XML are lightweight, are human readable, are easily manipulated by version-control systems and text editors, and may be customized at deployment time (or even at runtime, with programmatic XML generation).

But is XML-based metadata really the best approach? A certain backlash against the overuse of XML can be seen in the Java community. Every framework and application server seems to require its own XML descriptors.

In our view, there are three main reasons for this backlash:

- Many existing metadata formats weren't designed to be readable and easy to edit by hand. In particular, a major cause of pain is the lack of sensible defaults for attribute and element values, requiring significantly more typing than should be necessary.

- Metadata-based solutions were often used inappropriately. Metadata is not, by nature, more flexible or maintainable than plain Java code.

- Good XML editors, especially in IDEs, aren't as common as good Java coding environments. Worst, and most easily fixable, a document type declaration (DTD) often isn't provided, preventing auto-completion and validation. Another problem are DTDs that are too generic, where every declaration is wrapped in a generic "extension" of "meta" element.

There is no getting around the need for text-based metadata in ORM. However, Hibernate was designed with full awareness of the typical metadata problems. The metadata format is extremely readable and defines useful default values. When attribute values are missing, Hibernate uses reflection on the mapped class to help determine the defaults. Hibernate comes with a documented and complete DTD. Finally, IDE support for XML has improved lately, and modern IDEs provide dynamic XML validation and even an auto-complete feature. If that's not enough for you, in chapter 9 we demonstrate some tools that may be used to generate Hibernate XML mappings.

Let's look at the way you can use XML metadata in Hibernate. We created the `Category` class in the previous section; now we need to map it to the `CATEGORY` table in the database. To do that, we use the XML mapping document in listing 3.4.

Listing 3.4   Hibernate XML mapping of the `Category` class

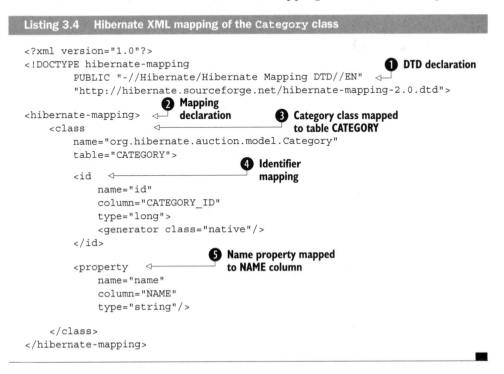

```xml
<?xml version="1.0"?>
<!DOCTYPE hibernate-mapping                              ❶ DTD declaration
        PUBLIC "-//Hibernate/Hibernate Mapping DTD//EN"
        "http://hibernate.sourceforge.net/hibernate-mapping-2.0.dtd">
                                        ❷ Mapping
<hibernate-mapping>                       declaration    ❸ Category class mapped
    <class                                                 to table CATEGORY
        name="org.hibernate.auction.model.Category"
        table="CATEGORY">
                                        ❹ Identifier
        <id                               mapping
            name="id"
            column="CATEGORY_ID"
            type="long">
            <generator class="native"/>
        </id>
                                        ❺ Name property mapped
        <property                           to NAME column
            name="name"
            column="NAME"
            type="string"/>

    </class>
</hibernate-mapping>
```

❶ The Hibernate mapping DTD should be declared in every mapping file; it's required for syntactic validation of the XML.

❷ Mappings are declared inside a `<hibernate-mapping>` element. You can include as many class mappings as you like, along with certain other special declarations that we'll mention later in the book.

❸ The class `Category` (in the package `org.hibernate.auction.model`) is mapped to the table `CATEGORY`. Every row in this table represents one instance of type `Category`.

❹ We haven't discussed the concept of *object identity*, so you may be surprised by this mapping element. This complex topic is covered in section 3.4. To understand this mapping, it's sufficient to know that every record in the `CATEGORY` table will have a primary key value that matches the object identity of the instance in memory. The `<id>` mapping element is used to define the details of object identity.

❺ The property name of type `String` is mapped to a database column `NAME`. Note that the type declared in the mapping is a built-in Hibernate type (`string`), not the type of the Java property or the SQL column type. Think about this as the "mapping data type." We take a closer look at these types in chapter 6, section 6.1, "Understanding the Hibernate type system."

We've intentionally left the association mappings out of this example. Association mappings are more complex, so we'll return to them in section 3.7.

TRY IT *Starting Hibernate with your first persistent class*—After you've written the POJO code for the `Category` and saved its Hibernate mapping to an XML file, you can start up Hibernate with this mapping and try some operations. However, the POJO code for `Category` shown earlier wasn't complete: You have to add an additional property named `id` of type `java.lang.Long` and its accessor methods to enable Hibernate identity management, as discussed later in this chapter. Creating the database schema with its tables for such a simple class should be no problem for you. Observe the log of your application to check for a successful startup and creation of a new `SessionFactory` from the `Configuration` shown in chapter 2.

If you can't wait any longer, check out the `save()`, `load()`, and `delete()` methods of the `Session` you can obtain from the `SessionFactory`. Make sure you correctly deal with transactions; the easiest way is to get a new `Transaction` object with `Session.beginTransaction()` and commit it with its `commit()` method after you've made your calls. See the code in section 2.1, "Hello World with Hibernate," if you'd like to copy some example code for your first test.

Although it's possible to declare mappings for multiple classes in one mapping file by using multiple `<class>` elements, the recommended practice (and the practice expected by some Hibernate tools) is to use one mapping file per persistent class. The convention is to give the file the same name as the mapped class, appending an `hbm` suffix: for example, `Category.hbm.xml`.

Let's discuss basic class and property mappings in Hibernate. Keep in mind that we still need to come back later in this chapter to the problem of mapping associations between persistent classes.

3.3.2 *Basic property and class mappings*

A typical Hibernate property mapping defines a JavaBeans property name, a database column name, and the name of a Hibernate type. It maps a JavaBean style property to a table column. The basic declaration provides many variations and optional settings. It's often possible to omit the type name. So, if `description` is a property of (Java) type `java.lang.String`, Hibernate will use the Hibernate type `string` by default (we discuss the Hibernate type system in chapter 6). Hibernate uses reflection to determine the Java type of the property. Thus, the following mappings are equivalent:

```
<property name="description" column="DESCRIPTION" type="string"/>

<property name="description" column="DESCRIPTION"/>
```

You can even omit the column name if it's the same as the property name, ignoring case. (This is one of the sensible defaults we mentioned earlier.)

For some cases you might need to use a `<column>` element instead of the `column` attribute. The `<column>` element provides more flexibility; it has more optional attributes and may appear more than once. The following two property mappings are equivalent:

```
<property name="description" column="DESCRIPTION" type="string"/>

<property name="description" type="string">
    <column name="DESCRIPTION"/>
</property>
```

The `<property>` element (and especially the `<column>` element) also defines certain attributes that apply mainly to automatic database schema generation. If you aren't using the `hbm2ddl` tool (see section 9.2, "Automatic schema generation") to generate the database schema, you can safely omit these. However, it's still preferable to include at least the `not-null` attribute, since Hibernate will then be able to report illegal null property values without going to the database:

```
<property name="initialPrice" column="INITIAL_PRICE" not-null="true"/>
```

Detection of illegal null values is mainly useful for providing sensible exceptions at development time. It isn't intended for true data validation, which is outside the scope of Hibernate.

Some properties don't map to a column at all. In particular, a *derived* property takes its value from an SQL expression.

Using derived properties

The value of a derived property is calculated at runtime by evaluation of an expression. You define the expression using the formula attribute. For example, we might map a totalIncludingTax property without having a single column with the total price in the database:

```
<property name="totalIncludingTax"
          formula="TOTAL + TAX_RATE * TOTAL"
          type="big_decimal"/>
```

The given SQL formula is evaluated every time the entity is retrieved from the database. The property doesn't have a column attribute (or sub-element) and never appears in an SQL INSERT or UPDATE, only in SELECTs. Formulas may refer to columns of the database table, call SQL functions, and include SQL subselects.

This example, mapping a derived property of item, uses a correlated subselect to calculate the average amount of all bids for an item:

```
<property
    name="averageBidAmount"
    formula="( select AVG(b.AMOUNT) from BID b
⇒where b.ITEM_ID = ITEM_ID )"
    type="big_decimal"/>
```

Notice that unqualified column names refer to table columns of the class to which the derived property belongs.

As we mentioned earlier, Hibernate doesn't require property accessor methods on POJO classes, if you define a new property access strategy.

Property access strategies

The access attribute allows you to specify how Hibernate should access property values of the POJO. The default strategy, property, uses the property accessors (get/set method pair). The field strategy uses reflection to access the instance variable directly. The following "property" mapping doesn't require a get/set pair:

```
<property name="name"
          column="NAME"
```

```
        type="string"
        access="field"/>
```

Access to properties via accessor methods is considered best practice by the Hibernate community. It provides an extra level of abstraction between the Java domain model and the data model, beyond what is already provided by Hibernate. Properties are more flexible; for example, property definitions may be overridden by persistent subclasses.

If neither accessor methods nor direct instance variable access is appropriate, you can define your own customized property access strategy by implementing the interface net.sf.hibernate.property.PropertyAccessor and name it in the access attribute.

Controlling insertion and updates

For properties that map to columns, you can control whether they appear in the INSERT statement by using the insert attribute and whether they appear in the UPDATE statement by using the update attribute.

The following property never has its state written to the database:

```
<property name="name"
        column="NAME"
        type="string"
        insert="false"
        update="false"/>
```

The property name of the JavaBean is therefore *immutable* and can be read from the database but not modified in any way. If the complete class is immutable, set the mutable="false" in the class mapping

In addition, the dynamic-insert attribute tells Hibernate whether to include unmodified property values in an SQL INSERT, and the dynamic-update attribute tells Hibernate whether to include unmodified properties in the SQL UPDATE:

```
<class name="org.hibernate.auction.model.User"
        dynamic-insert="true"
        dynamic-update="true">
        ...
</class>
```

These are both class-level settings. Enabling either of these settings will cause Hibernate to generate some SQL at runtime, instead of using the SQL cached at startup time. The performance cost is usually small. Furthermore, leaving out columns in an insert (and especially in an update) can occasionally improve performance if your tables define many columns.

Using quoted SQL identifiers

By default, Hibernate doesn't quote table and column names in the generated SQL. This makes the SQL slightly more readable and also allows us to take advantage of the fact that most SQL databases are case insensitive when comparing unquoted identifiers. From time to time, especially in legacy databases, you'll encounter identifiers with strange characters or whitespace, or you may wish to force case-sensitivity.

If you quote a table or column name with backticks in the mapping document, Hibernate will always quote this identifier in the generated SQL. The following property declaration forces Hibernate to generate SQL with the quoted column name "Item Description". Hibernate will also know that Microsoft SQL Server needs the variation [Item Description] and that MySQL requires `Item Description`.

```
<property name="description"
        column=""`Item Description`"/>
```

There is no way, apart from quoting all table and column names in backticks, to force Hibernate to use quoted identifiers everywhere.

Naming conventions

You'll often encounter organizations with strict conventions for database table and column names. Hibernate provides a feature that allows you to enforce naming standards automatically.

Suppose that all table names in CaveatEmptor should follow the pattern CE_<table name>.

One solution is to manually specify a table attribute on all <class> and collection elements in our mapping files. This approach is time-consuming and easily forgotten. Instead, we can implement Hibernate's NamingStrategy interface, as in listing 3.5

Listing 3.5 NamingStrategy implementation

```
public class CENamingStrategy implements NamingStrategy {

    public String classToTableName(String className) {
        return tableName(
            StringHelper.unqualify(className).toUpperCase() );
    }

    public String propertyToColumnName(String propertyName) {
        return propertyName.toUpperCase();
    }
```

```
public String tableName(String tableName) {
    return "CE_" + tableName;
}

public String columnName(String columnName) {
    return columnName;
}

public String propertyToTableName(String className,
    String propertyName) {
    return classToTableName(className) + '_' +
        propertyToColumnName(propertyName);
}

}
```

The classToTableName() method is called only if a <class> mapping doesn't specify an explicit table name. The propertyToColumnName() method is called if a property has no explicit column name. The tableName() and columnName() methods are called when an explicit name *is* declared.

If we enable our CENamingStrategy, this class mapping declaration

```
<class name="BankAccount">
```

will result in CE_BANKACCOUNT as the name of the table. The classToTableName() method was called with the fully qualified class name as the argument.

However, if a table name is specified

```
<class name="BankAccount" table="BANK_ACCOUNT">
```

then CE_BANK_ACCOUNT will be the name of the table. In this case, BANK_ACCOUNT was passed to the tableName() method.

The best feature of the NamingStrategy is the potential for dynamic behavior. To activate a specific naming strategy, we can pass an instance to the Hibernate Configuration at runtime:

```
Configuration cfg = new Configuration();
cfg.setNamingStrategy( new CENamingStrategy() );
SessionFactory sessionFactory =
    cfg.configure().buildSessionFactory();
```

This will allow us to have multiple SessionFactory instances based on the same mapping documents, each using a different NamingStrategy. This is extremely useful in a multiclient installation where unique table names (but the same data model) are required for each client.

However, a better way to handle this kind of requirement is to use the concept of an SQL *schema* (a kind of namespace).

SQL schemas

You can specify a default schema using the `hibernate.default_schema` configuration option. Alternatively, you can specify a schema in the mapping document. A schema may be specified for a particular class or collection mapping:

```
<hibernate-mapping>
    <class
        name="org.hibernate.auction.model.Category"
        table="CATEGORY"
        schema="AUCTION">
        ...
    </class>
</hibernate-mapping>
```

It can even be declared for the whole document:

```
<hibernate-mapping
    default-schema="AUCTION">
    ..
</hibernate-mapping>
```

This isn't the only thing the root `<hibernate-mapping>` element is useful for.

Declaring class names

All the persistent classes of the CaveatEmptor application are declared in the Java package `org.hibernate.auction.model`. It would become tedious to specify this package name every time we named a class in our mapping documents.

Let's reconsider our mapping for the `Category` class (the file `Category.hbm.xml`):

```
<?xml version="1.0"?>
<!DOCTYPE hibernate-mapping
        PUBLIC "-//Hibernate/Hibernate Mapping DTD//EN"
        "http://hibernate.sourceforge.net/hibernate-mapping-2.0.dtd">

<hibernate-mapping>
    <class
        name="org.hibernate.auction.model.Category"
        table="CATEGORY">
        ...
    </class>
</hibernate-mapping>
```

We don't want to repeat the full package name whenever this or any other class is named in an association, subclass, or component mapping. So, instead, we'll specify a package:

```
<?xml version="1.0"?>
<!DOCTYPE hibernate-mapping
        PUBLIC "-//Hibernate/Hibernate Mapping DTD//EN"
        "http://hibernate.sourceforge.net/hibernate-mapping-2.0.dtd">

<hibernate-mapping
    package="org.hibernate.auction.model">
    <class
        name="Category"
        table="CATEGORY">
        ...
    </class>
</hibernate-mapping>
```

Now all unqualified class names that appear in this mapping document will be prefixed with the declared package name. We assume this setting in all mapping examples in this book.

If writing XML files by hand (using the DTD for auto-completion, of course) still seems like too much work, *attribute-oriented programming* might be a good choice. Hibernate mapping files can be automatically generated from attributes directly embedded in the Java source code.

3.3.3 *Attribute-oriented programming*

The innovative XDoclet project has brought the notion of attribute-oriented programming to Java. Until JDK 1.5, the Java language had no support for annotations; so XDoclet leverages the Javadoc tag format (@attribute) to specify class-, field-, or method-level metadata attributes. (There is a book about XDoclet from Manning Publications: *XDoclet in Action* [Walls/Richards, 2004].)

XDoclet is implemented as an Ant task that generates code or XML metadata as part of the build process. Creating the Hibernate XML mapping document with XDoclet is straightforward; instead of writing it by hand, we mark up the Java source code of our persistent class with custom Javadoc tags, as shown in listing 3.6.

Listing 3.6 Using XDoclet tags to mark up Java properties with mapping metadata

```
/**
 * The Category class of the CaveatEmptor auction site domain model.
 *
 * @hibernate.class
 * table="CATEGORY"
 */
```

```
public class Category {
    ...

    /**
     * @hibernate.id
     * generator-class="native"
     * column="CATEGORY_ID"
     */
    public Long getId() {
        return id;
    }

    ...

    /**
     * @hibernate.property
     */
    public String getName() {
        return name;
    }

    ...

}
```

With the annotated class in place and an Ant task ready, we can automatically generate the same XML document shown in the previous section (listing 3.4).

The downside to XDoclet is the requirement for another build step. Most large Java projects are using Ant already, so this is usually a non-issue. Arguably, XDoclet mappings are less configurable at deployment time. However, nothing is stopping you from hand-editing the generated XML before deployment, so this probably isn't a significant objection. Finally, support for XDoclet tag validation may not be available in your development environment. However, JetBrains IntelliJ IDEA and Eclipse both support at least auto-completion of tag names. (We look at the use of XDoclet with Hibernate in chapter 9, section 9.5, "XDoclet.")

NOTE   XDoclet isn't a standard approach to attribute-oriented metadata. A new Java specification, JSR 175, defines *annotations* as extensions to the Java language. JSR 175 is already implemented in JDK 1.5, so projects like XDoclet and Hibernate will probably provide support for JSR 175 annotations in the near future.

Both of the approaches we have described so far, XML and XDoclet attributes, assume that all mapping information is known at deployment time. Suppose that some information isn't known before the application starts. Can you programmatically manipulate the mapping metadata at runtime?

3.3.4 *Manipulating metadata at runtime*

It's sometimes useful for an application to browse, manipulate, or build new mappings at runtime. XML APIs like DOM, dom4j, and JDOM allow direct runtime manipulation of XML documents. So, you could create or manipulate an XML document at runtime, before feeding it to the Configuration object.

However, Hibernate also exposes a configuration-time metamodel. The metamodel contains all the information declared in your XML mapping documents. Direct programmatic manipulation of this metamodel is sometimes useful, especially for applications that allow for extension by user-written code.

For example, the following code adds a new property, motto, to the User class mapping:

```
// Get the existing mapping for User from Configuration
PersistentClass userMapping = cfg.getClassMapping(User.class);

// Define a new column for the USER table
Column column = new Column();
column.setType(Hibernate.STRING);
column.setName("MOTTO");
column.setNullable(false);
column.setUnique(true);
userMapping.getTable().addColumn(column);

// Wrap the column in a Value
SimpleValue value = new SimpleValue();
value.setTable( userMapping.getTable() );
value.addColumn(column);
value.setType(Hibernate.STRING);

// Define a new property of the User class
Property prop = new Property();
prop.setValue(value);
prop.setName("motto");
userMapping.addProperty(prop);

// Build a new session factory, using the new mapping
SessionFactory sf = cfg.buildSessionFactory();
```

A PersistentClass object represents the metamodel for a single persistent class; we retrieve it from the Configuration. Column, SimpleValue, and Property are all classes of the Hibernate metamodel and are available in the package net.sf.hibernate.mapping. Keep in mind that adding a property to an existing persistent class mapping as shown here is easy, but programmatically creating a new mapping for a previously unmapped class is quite a bit more involved.

Once a SessionFactory is created, its mappings are immutable. In fact, the SessionFactory uses a different metamodel internally than the one used at configuration time. There is no way to get back to the original `Configuration` from the `SessionFactory` or `Session`. However, the application may read the `SessionFactory`'s metamodel by calling `getClassMetadata()` or `getCollectionMetadata()`. For example:

```
Category category = ...;
ClassMetadata meta = sessionFactory.getClassMetadata(Category.class);
String[] metaPropertyNames = meta.getPropertyNames();
Object[] propertyValues = meta.getPropertyValues(category);
```

This code snippet retrieves the names of persistent properties of the `Category` class and the values of those properties for a particular instance. This helps you write generic code. For example, you might use this feature to label UI components or improve log output.

Now let's turn to a special mapping element you've seen in most of our previous examples: the *identifier property mapping*. We'll begin by discussing the notion of *object identity*.

3.4 *Understanding object identity*

It's vital to understand the difference between *object identity* and *object equality* before we discuss terms like *database identity* and how Hibernate manages identity. We need these concepts if we want to finish mapping our CaveatEmptor persistent classes and their associations with Hibernate.

3.4.1 *Identity versus equality*

Java developers understand the difference between Java object *identity* and *equality*. Object identity, `==`, is a notion defined by the Java virtual machine. Two object references are identical if they point to the same memory location.

On the other hand, object equality is a notion defined by classes that implement the `equals()` method, sometimes also referred to as *equivalence*. Equivalence means that two different (non-identical) objects have the same value. Two different instances of `String` are equal if they represent the same sequence of characters, even though they each have their own location in the memory space of the virtual machine. (We admit that this is not entirely true for `String`s, but you get the idea.)

Persistence complicates this picture. With object/relational persistence, a persistent object is an in-memory representation of a particular row of a database table. So, along with Java identity (memory location) and object equality, we pick up *database identity* (location in the persistent data store). We now have three methods for identifying objects:

- *Object identity*—Objects are identical if they occupy the same memory location in the JVM. This can be checked by using the == operator.

- *Object equality*—Objects are equal if they have the same value, as defined by the equals(Object o) method. Classes that don't explicitly override this method inherit the implementation defined by java.lang.Object, which compares object identity.

- *Database identity*—Objects stored in a relational database are identical if they represent the same row or, equivalently, share the same table and primary key value.

You need to understand how database identity relates to object identity in Hibernate.

3.4.2 *Database identity with Hibernate*

Hibernate exposes database identity to the application in two ways:

- The value of the *identifier property* of a persistent instance
- The value returned by Session.getIdentifier(Object o)

The identifier property is special: Its value is the primary key value of the database row represented by the persistent instance. We don't usually show the identifier property in our domain model—it's a persistence-related concern, not part of our business problem. In our examples, the identifier property is always named id. So if myCategory is an instance of Category, calling myCategory.getId() returns the primary key value of the row represented by myCategory in the database.

Should you make the accessor methods for the identifier property private scope or public? Well, database identifiers are often used by the application as a convenient handle to a particular instance, even outside the persistence layer. For example, web applications often display the results of a search screen to the user as a list of summary information. When the user selects a particular element, the application might need to retrieve the selected object. It's common to use a lookup by identifier for this purpose—you've probably already used identifiers this way, even in applications using direct JDBC. It's therefore usually appropriate to fully expose the database identity with a public identifier property accessor.

On the other hand, we usually declare the setId() method private and let Hibernate generate and set the identifier value. The exceptions to this rule are classes with natural keys, where the value of the identifier is assigned by the application before the object is made persistent, instead of being generated by Hibernate. (We discuss natural keys in the next section.) Hibernate doesn't allow you to change the identifier value of a persistent instance after it's first assigned.

Remember, part of the definition of a primary key is that its value should never change. Let's implement an identifier property for the Category class:

```
public class Category {
    private Long id;
    ...
    public Long getId() {
        return this.id;
    }

    private void setId(Long id) {
        this.id = id;
    }
    ...
}
```

The property type depends on the primary key type of the CATEGORY table and the Hibernate mapping type. This information is determined by the <id> element in the mapping document:

```
<class name="Category" table="CATEGORY">
    <id name="id" column="CATEGORY_ID" type="long">
        <generator class="native"/>
    </id>
    ...
</class>
```

The identifier property is mapped to the primary key column CATEGORY_ID of the table CATEGORY. The Hibernate type for this property is long, which maps to a BIG-INT column type in most databases and which has also been chosen to match the type of the identity value produced by the native identifier generator. (We discuss identifier generation strategies in the next section.) So, in addition to operations for testing Java object identity (a == b) and object equality (a.equals(b)), you may now use a.getId().equals(b.getId()) to test database identity.

An alternative approach to handling database identity is to not implement any identifier property, and let Hibernate manage database identity internally. In this case, you omit the name attribute in the mapping declaration:

```
<id column="CATEGORY_ID">
    <generator class="native"/>
</id>
```

Hibernate will now manage the identifier values internally. You may obtain the identifier value of a persistent instance as follows:

```
Long catId = (Long) session.getIdentifier(category);
```

This technique has a serious drawback: You can no longer use Hibernate to manipulate *detached objects* effectively (see chapter 4, section 4.1.6, "Outside the identity scope"). So, you should always use identifier properties in Hibernate. (If you don't like them being visible to the rest of your application, make the accessor methods private.)

Using database identifiers in Hibernate is easy and straightforward. Choosing a good primary key (and key generation strategy) might be more difficult. We discuss these issues next.

3.4.3 *Choosing primary keys*

You have to tell Hibernate about your preferred primary key generation strategy. But first, let's define *primary key*.

The *candidate key* is a column or set of columns that uniquely identifies a specific row of the table. A candidate key must satisfy the following properties:

- The value or values are never null.
- Each row has a unique value or values.
- The value or values of a particular row never change.

For a given table, several columns or combinations of columns might satisfy these properties. If a table has only one identifying attribute, it is by definition the *primary key*. If there are multiple candidate keys, you need to choose between them (candidate keys not chosen as the primary key should be declared as unique keys in the database). If there are *no* unique columns or unique combinations of columns, and hence no candidate keys, then the table is by definition not a relation as defined by the relational model (it permits duplicate rows), and you should rethink your data model.

Many legacy SQL data models use *natural* primary keys. A natural key is a key with business meaning: an attribute or combination of attributes that is unique by virtue of its business semantics. Examples of natural keys might be a U.S. Social Security Number or Australian Tax File Number. Distinguishing natural keys is simple: If a candidate key attribute has meaning outside the database context, it's a natural key, whether or not it's automatically generated.

Experience has shown that natural keys almost always cause problems in the long run. A good primary key must be unique, constant, and required (never null or unknown). Very few entity attributes satisfy these requirements, and some that do aren't efficiently indexable by SQL databases. In addition, you should make absolutely certain that a candidate key definition could never change throughout the lifetime of the database before promoting it to a primary key. Changing the definition of a primary key and all foreign keys that refer to it is a frustrating task.

For these reasons, we strongly recommend that new applications use synthetic identifiers (also called *surrogate keys*). Surrogate keys have no business meaning—they are unique values generated by the database or application. There are a number of well-known approaches to surrogate key generation.

Hibernate has several built-in identifier generation strategies. We list the most useful options in table 3.1.

Table 3.1 Hibernate's built-in identifier generator modules

Generator name	Description
native	The `native` identity generator picks other identity generators like `identity`, `sequence`, or `hilo` depending on the capabilities of the underlying database.
identity	This generator supports identity columns in DB2, MySQL, MS SQL Server, Sybase, HSQLDB, Informix, and HypersonicSQL. The returned identifier is of type `long`, `short`, or `int`.
sequence	A sequence in DB2, PostgreSQL, Oracle, SAP DB, McKoi, Firebird, or a generator in InterBase is used. The returned identifier is of type `long`, `short`, or `int`.
increment	At Hibernate startup, this generator reads the maximum primary key column value of the table and increments the value by one each time a new row is inserted. The generated identifier is of type `long`, `short`, or `int`. This generator is especially efficient if the single-server Hibernate application has exclusive access to the database but shouldn't be used in any other scenario.
hilo	A *high/low algorithm* is an efficient way to generate identifiers of type `long`, `short`, or `int`, given a table and column (by default `hibernate_unique_key` and `next_hi`, respectively) as a source of hi values. The high/low algorithm generates identifiers that are unique only for a particular database. See [Ambler 2002] for more information about the high/low approach to unique identifiers.
uuid.hex	This generator uses a 128-bit UUID (an algorithm that generates identifiers of type `string`, unique within a network). The IP address is used in combination with a unique timestamp. The UUID is encoded as a string of hexadecimal digits of length 32. This generation strategy isn't popular, since `CHAR` primary keys consume more database space than numeric keys and are marginally slower.

You aren't limited to these built-in strategies; you may create your own identifier generator by implementing Hibernate's `IdentifierGenerator` interface. It's even possible to mix identifier generators for persistent classes in a single domain model, but for non-legacy data we recommend using the same generator for all classes.

The special `assigned` identifier generator strategy is most useful for entities with natural primary keys. This strategy lets the application assign identifier values by setting the identifier property before making the object persistent by calling save(). This strategy has some serious disadvantages when you're working with detached objects and transitive persistence (both of these concepts are discussed in the next chapter). Don't use assigned identifiers if you can avoid them; it's much easier to use a surrogate primary key generated by one of the strategies listed in table 3.1.

For legacy data, the picture is more complicated. In this case, we're often stuck with natural keys and especially *composite keys* (natural keys composed of multiple table columns). Because composite identifiers can be more difficult to work with, we only discuss them in the context of chapter 8, section 8.3.1, "Legacy schemas and composite keys."

The next step is to add identifier properties to the classes of the CaveatEmptor application. Do *all* persistent classes have their own database identity? To answer this question, we must explore the distinction between *entities* and *value types* in Hibernate. These concepts are required for fine-grained object modeling.

3.5 *Fine-grained object models*

A major objective of the Hibernate project is support for *fine-grained* object models, which we isolated as the most important requirement for a rich domain model. It's one reason we've chosen POJOs.

In crude terms, *fine-grained* means "more classes than tables." For example, a user might have both a billing address and a home address. In the database, we might have a single USER table with the columns BILLING_STREET, BILLING_CITY, and BILLING_ZIPCODE along with HOME_STREET, HOME_CITY, and HOME_ZIPCODE. There are good reasons to use this somewhat denormalized relational model (performance, for one).

In our object model, we could use the same approach, representing the two addresses as six string-valued properties of the User class. But we would much rather model this using an Address class, where User has the billingAddress and homeAddress properties.

This object model achieves improved cohesion and greater code reuse and is more understandable. In the past, many ORM solutions haven't provided good support for this kind of mapping.

Hibernate emphasizes the usefulness of fine-grained classes for implementing type-safety and behavior. For example, many people would model an email address as a string-valued property of User. We suggest that a more sophisticated approach is to define an actual `EmailAddress` class that could add higher level semantics and behavior. For example, it might provide a `sendEmail()` method.

3.5.1 *Entity and value types*

This leads us to a distinction of central importance in ORM. In Java, all classes are of equal standing: All objects have their own identity and lifecycle, and all class instances are passed by reference. Only primitive types are passed by value.

We're advocating a design in which there are more persistent classes than tables. One row represents multiple objects. Because database identity is implemented by primary key value, some persistent objects won't have their own identity. In effect, the persistence mechanism implements pass-by-value semantics for some classes. One of the objects represented in the row has its own identity, and others depend on that.

Hibernate makes the following essential distinction:

- An object of *entity* type has its own database identity (primary key value). An object reference to an entity is persisted as a reference in the database (a foreign key value). An entity has its own lifecycle; it may exist independently of any other entity.

- An object of *value type* has no database identity; it belongs to an entity, and its persistent state is embedded in the table row of the owning entity (except in the case of collections, which are also considered value types, as you'll see in chapter 6). Value types don't have identifiers or identifier properties. The lifespan of a value-type instance is bounded by the lifespan of the owning entity.

The most obvious value types are simple objects like `Strings` and `Integers`. Hibernate also lets you treat a user-defined class as a value type, as you'll see next. (We also come back to this important concept in chapter 6, section 6.1, "Understanding the Hibernate type system.")

3.5.2 *Using components*

So far, the classes of our object model have all been entity classes with their own lifecycle and identity. The `User` class, however, has a special kind of association with the `Address` class, as shown in figure 3.5.

In object modeling terms, this association is a kind of *aggregation*—a "part of" relationship. Aggregation is a strong form of association: It has additional semantics with regard to the lifecycle of objects. In our case, we have an even stronger

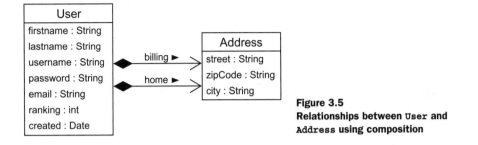

Figure 3.5
Relationships between User and Address using composition

form, *composition,* where the lifecycle of the part is dependent on the lifecycle of the whole.

Object modeling experts and UML designers will claim that there is no difference between this composition and other weaker styles of association when it comes to the Java implementation. But in the context of ORM, there is a big difference: a composed class is often a candidate value type.

We now map Address as a value type and User as an entity. Does this affect the implementation of our POJO classes?

Java itself has no concept of composition—a class or attribute can't be marked as a component or composition. The only difference is the object identifier: A component has no identity, hence the persistent component class requires no identifier property or identifier mapping. The composition between User and Address is a metadata-level notion; we only have to tell Hibernate that the Address is a value type in the mapping document.

Hibernate uses the term *component* for a user-defined class that is persisted to the same table as the owning entity, as shown in listing 3.7. (The use of the word *component* here has nothing to do with the architecture-level concept, as in *software component.*)

Listing 3.7   Mapping the User class with a component Address

```
<class
    name="User"
    table="USER">

<id
    name="id"
    column="USER_ID"
    type="long">
    <generator class="native"/>
</id>

<property
```

```
              name="username"
              column="USERNAME"
              type="string"/>

      <component                        Declare persistent
          name="homeAddress"      ❶   attributes
          class="Address">

          <property name="street"
                    type="string"
                    column="HOME_STREET"
                    notnull="true"/>
          <property name="city"
                    type="string"
                    column="HOME_CITY"
                    not-null="true"/>
          <property name="zipcode"
                    type="short"
                    column="HOME_ZIPCODE"
                    not-null="true"/>

      </component>

      <component                        Reuse
          name="billingAddress"   ❷   component class
          class="Address">

          <property name="street"
                    type="string"
                    column="BILLING_STREET"
                    notnull="true"/>
          <property name="city"
                    type="string"
                    column="BILLING_CITY"
                    not-null="true"/>
          <property name="zipcode"
                    type="short"
                    column="BILLING_ZIPCODE"
                    not-null="true"/>

      </component>

      . . .

  </class>
```

❶ We declare the persistent attributes of Address inside the <component> element. The property of the User class is named homeAddress.

❷ We reuse the same component class to map another property of this type to the same table.

Figure 3.6 shows how the attributes of the
`Address` class are persisted to the same table as
the `User` entity.

Notice that in this example, we have modeled
the composition association as *unidirectional*. We
can't navigate from `Address` to `User`. Hibernate
supports both unidirectional and bidirectional
compositions; however, unidirectional composition is far more common. Here's an example of a
bidirectional mapping:

```
<component
    name="homeAddress"
    class="Address">
    <parent name="user"/>
    <property name="street" type="string" column="HOME_STREET"/>
    <property name="city" type="string" column="HOME_CITY"/>
    <property name="zipcode" type="short" column="HOME_ZIPCODE"/>
</component>
```

**Figure 3.6   Table attributes of `User`
with `Address` component**

The `<parent>` element maps a property of type `User` to the owning entity, in this
example, the property is named `user`. We then call `Address.getUser()` to navigate
in the other direction.

A Hibernate component may own other components and even associations to
other entities. This flexibility is the foundation of Hibernate's support for fine-
grained object models. (We'll discuss various component mappings in chapter 6.)

However, there are two important limitations to classes mapped as components:

- Shared references aren't possible. The component `Address` doesn't have its
  own database identity (primary key) and so a particular `Address` object can't
  be referred to by any object other than the containing instance of `User`.

- There is no elegant way to represent a null reference to an `Address`. In lieu
  of an elegant approach, Hibernate represents null components as null values in all mapped columns of the component. This means that if you store a
  component object with all null property values, Hibernate will return a null
  component when the owning entity object is retrieved from the database.

Support for fine-grained classes isn't the only ingredient of a rich domain model.
Class inheritance and polymorphism are defining features of object-oriented
models.

3.6 *Mapping class inheritance*

A simple strategy for mapping classes to database tables might be "one table for every class." This approach sounds simple, and it works well until you encounter inheritance.

Inheritance is the most visible feature of the structural mismatch between the object-oriented and relational worlds. Object-oriented systems model both "is a" and "has a" relationships. SQL-based models provide only "has a" relationships between entities.

There are three different approaches to representing an inheritance hierarchy. These were catalogued by Scott Ambler [Ambler 2002] in his widely read paper "Mapping Objects to Relational Databases":

- *Table per concrete class*—Discard polymorphism and inheritance relationships completely from the relational model
- *Table per class hierarchy*—Enable polymorphism by denormalizing the relational model and using a type discriminator column to hold type information
- *Table per subclass*—Represent "is a" (inheritance) relationships as "has a" (foreign key) relationships

This section takes a *top down* approach; it assumes that we're starting with a domain model and trying to derive a new SQL schema. However, the mapping strategies described are just as relevant if we're working *bottom up*, starting with existing database tables.

3.6.1 *Table per concrete class*

Suppose we stick with the simplest approach: We could use exactly one table for each (non-abstract) class. All properties of a class, including inherited properties, could be mapped to columns of this table, as shown in figure 3.7.

The main problem with this approach is that it doesn't support polymorphic associations very well. In the database, associations are usually represented as foreign key relationships. In figure 3.7, if the subclasses are all mapped to different tables, a polymorphic association to their superclass (abstract BillingDetails in this example) can't be represented as a simple foreign key relationship. This would be problematic in our domain model, because BillingDetails is associated with User; hence both tables would need a foreign key reference to the USER table.

Polymorphic queries (queries that return objects of all classes that match the interface of the queried class) are also problematic. A query against the superclass must

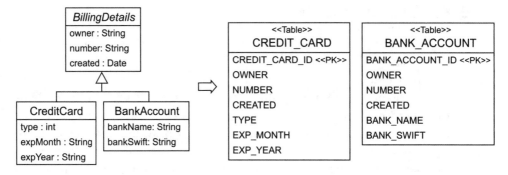

Figure 3.7 Mapping a composition bidirectional

be executed as several SQL SELECTs, one for each concrete subclass. We might be able to use an SQL UNION to improve performance by avoiding multiple round trips to the database. However, unions are somewhat nonportable and otherwise difficult to work with. Hibernate doesn't support the use of unions at the time of writing, and will always use multiple SQL queries. For a query against the BillingDetails class (for example, restricting to a certain date of creation), Hibernate would use the following SQL:

```
select CREDIT_CARD_ID, OWNER, NUMBER, CREATED, TYPE, ...
from CREDIT_CARD
where CREATED = ?

select BANK_ACCOUNT_ID, OWNER, NUMBER, CREATED, BANK_NAME, ...
from BANK_ACCOUNT
where CREATED = ?
```

Notice that a separate query is needed for each concrete subclass.

On the other hand, queries against the concrete classes are trivial and perform well:

```
select CREDIT_CARD_ID, TYPE, EXP_MONTH, EXP_YEAR
  from CREDIT_CARD where CREATED = ?
```

(Note that here, and in other places in this book, we show SQL that is *conceptually* identical to the SQL executed by Hibernate. The actual SQL might look superficially different.)

A further conceptual problem with this mapping strategy is that several different columns of different tables share the same semantics. This makes schema evolution more complex. For example, a change to a superclass property type results in changes to multiple columns. It also makes it much more difficult to implement database integrity constraints that apply to all subclasses.

This mapping strategy doesn't require any special Hibernate mapping declaration: Simply create a new `<class>` declaration for each concrete class, specifying a different `table` attribute for each. We recommend this approach (only) for the top level of your class hierarchy, where polymorphism isn't usually required.

3.6.2 *Table per class hierarchy*

Alternatively, an entire class hierarchy could be mapped to a single table. This table would include columns for all properties of all classes in the hierarchy. The concrete subclass represented by a particular row is identified by the value of a *type discriminator* column. This approach is shown in figure 3.8.

This mapping strategy is a winner in terms of both performance and simplicity. It's the best-performing way to represent polymorphism—both polymorphic and nonpolymorphic queries perform well—and it's even easy to implement by hand. Ad hoc reporting is possible without complex joins or unions, and schema evolution is straightforward.

There is one major problem: Columns for properties declared by subclasses must be declared to be nullable. If your subclasses each define several non-nullable properties, the loss of NOT NULL constraints could be a serious problem from the point of view of data integrity.

In Hibernate, we use the `<subclass>` element to indicate a table-per-class hierarchy mapping, as in listing 3.8.

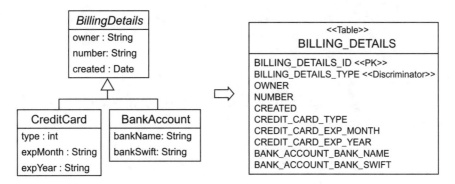

Figure 3.8   Table per class hierarchy mapping

Listing 3.8   Hibernate `<subclass>` mapping

```
<hibernate-mapping>        ❶ Root class, mapped to table
    <class     ◁────────────┘
        name="BillingDetails"
        table="BILLING_DETAILS" discriminator-value="BD">

        <id
            name="id"
            column="BILLING_DETAILS_ID"
            type="long">
            <generator class="native"/>
        </id>
                               ❷ Discriminator column
        <discriminator   ◁──────────┘
            column="BILLING_DETAILS_TYPE"
            type="string"/>
                           ❸ Property mappings
        <property   ◁───────────────┘
            name="name"
            column="OWNER"
            type="string"/>

            . . .
                           ❹ CreditCard subclass
        <subclass   ◁───────────────┘
            name="CreditCard"
            discriminator-value="CC">

            <property
                name="type"
                column="CREDIT_CARD_TYPE"/>
            . . .

        </subclass>

        . . .

    </class>
</hibernate-mapping>
```

❶ The root class `BusinessDetails` of the inheritance hierarchy is mapped to the table `BUSINESS_DETAILS`.

❷ We have to use a special column to distinguish between persistent classes: the *discriminator*. This isn't a property of the persistent class; it's used internally by Hibernate. The column name is `BILLING_DETAILS_TYPE`, and the values will be strings—in this case, `"CC"` or `"BA"`. Hibernate will automatically set and retrieve the discriminator values.

❸ Properties of the superclass are mapped as always, with a `<property>` element.

❹ Every subclass has its own `<subclass>` element. Properties of a subclass are mapped to columns in the BILLING_DETAILS table. Remember that `not-null` constraints aren't allowed, because a `CreditCard` instance won't have a `bankSwift` property and the BANK_ACCOUNT_BANK_SWIFT field must be null for that row.

The `<subclass>` element can in turn contain other `<subclass>` elements, until the whole hierarchy is mapped to the table. A `<subclass>` element can't contain a `<joined-subclass>` element. (The `<joined-subclass>` element is used in the specification of the third mapping option: one table per subclass. This option is discussed in the next section.) The mapping strategy can't be switched anymore at this point.

Hibernate would use the following SQL when querying the `BillingDetails` class:

```
select BILLING_DETAILS_ID, BILLING_DETAILS_TYPE,
       OWNER, ..., CREDIT_CARD_TYPE,
from BILLING_DETAILS
where CREATED = ?
```

To query the `CreditCard` subclass, Hibernate would use a condition on the discriminator:

```
select BILLING_DETAILS_ID,
       CREDIT_CARD_TYPE, CREDIT_CARD_EXP_MONTH, ...
from BILLING_DETAILS
where BILLING_DETAILS_TYPE='CC' and CREATED = ?
```

How could it be any simpler than that?

3.6.3 *Table per subclass*

The third option is to represent inheritance relationships as relational foreign key associations. *Every* subclass that declares persistent properties—including abstract classes and even interfaces—has its own table.

Unlike the strategy that uses a table per concrete class, the table here contains columns only for each *non-inherited* property (each property declared by the subclass itself) along with a primary key that is also a foreign key of the superclass table. This approach is shown in figure 3.9.

If an instance of the `CreditCard` subclass is made persistent, the values of properties declared by the `BillingDetails` superclass are persisted to a new row of the BILLING_DETAILS table. Only the values of properties declared by the subclass are persisted to the new row of the CREDIT_CARD table. The two rows are linked together by their shared primary key value. Later, the subclass instance may be retrieved from the database by joining the subclass table with the superclass table.

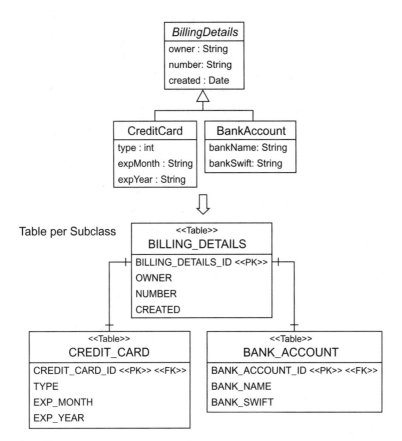

Figure 3.9   Table per subclass mapping

The primary advantage of this strategy is that the relational model is completely normalized. Schema evolution and integrity constraint definition are straightforward. A polymorphic association to a particular subclass may be represented as a foreign key pointing to the table of that subclass.

In Hibernate, we use the `<joined-subclass>` element to indicate a table-per-subclass mapping (see listing 3.9).

Listing 3.9   Hibernate `<joined-subclass>` mapping

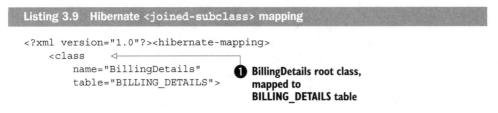

```
<?xml version="1.0"?><hibernate-mapping>
    <class
        name="BillingDetails"
        table="BILLING_DETAILS">
```

① BillingDetails root class, mapped to BILLING_DETAILS table

```
<id
    name="id"
    column="BILLING_DETAILS_ID"
    type="long">
    <generator class="native"/>
</id>

<property
    name="owner"
    column="OWNER"
    type="string"/>

    ...

<joined-subclass                    ❷ <joined-subclass>
    name="CreditCard"                    element
    table="CREDIT_CARD">

    <key column="CREDIT_CARD_ID">       ❸ Primary/foreign key

    <property
        name="type"
        column="TYPE"/>

    ...

</joined-subclass>

    ...

    </class>
</hibernate-mapping>
```

 Again, the root class `BillingDetails` is mapped to the table `BILLING_DETAILS`. Note that no discriminator is required with this strategy.

❷ The new `<joined-subclass>` element is used to map a subclass to a new table (in this example, `CREDIT_CARD`). All properties declared in the joined subclass will be mapped to this table. Note that we intentionally left out the mapping example for `BankAccount`, which is similar to `CreditCard`.

❸ A primary key is required for the `CREDIT_CARD` table; it will also have a foreign key constraint to the primary key of the `BILLING_DETAILS` table. A `CreditCard` object lookup will require a join of both tables.

A `<joined-subclass>` element may contain other `<joined-subclass>` elements but not a `<subclass>` element. Hibernate doesn't support mixing of these two mapping strategies.

Hibernate will use an outer join when querying the `BillingDetails` class:

```
select BD.BILLING_DETAILS_ID, BD.OWNER, BD.NUMER, BD.CREATED,
       CC.TYPE, ..., BA.BANK_SWIFT, ...
    case
        when CC.CREDIT_CARD_ID is not null then 1
        when BA.BANK_ACCOUNT_ID is not null then 2
        when BD.BILLING_DETAILS_ID is not null then 0
    end as TYPE
from BILLING_DETAILS BD
    left join CREDIT_CARD CC on
            BD.BILLING_DETAILS_ID = CC.CREDIT_CARD_ID
    left join BANK_ACCOUNT BA on
            BD.BILLING_DETAILS_ID = BA.BANK_ACCOUNT_ID
where BD.CREATED = ?
```

The SQL case statement uses the existence (or nonexistence) of rows in the subclass tables CREDIT_CARD and BANK_ACCOUNT to determine the concrete subclass for a particular row of the BILLING_DETAILS table.

To narrow the query to the subclass, Hibernate uses an inner join instead:

```
select BD.BILLING_DETAILS_ID, BD.OWNER, BD.CREATED, CC.TYPE, ...
from CREDIT_CARD CC
    inner join BILLING_DETAILS BD on
            BD.BILLING_DETAILS_ID = CC.CREDIT_CARD_ID
where CC.CREATED = ?
```

As you can see, this mapping strategy is more difficult to implement by hand—even ad hoc reporting will be more complex. This is an important consideration if you plan to mix Hibernate code with handwritten SQL/JDBC. (For ad hoc reporting, database views provide a way to offset the complexity of the table-per-subclass strategy. A view may be used to transform the table-per-subclass model into the much simpler table-per-hierarchy model.)

Furthermore, even though this mapping strategy is deceptively simple, our experience is that performance may be unacceptable for complex class hierarchies. Queries always require either a join across many tables or many sequential reads. Our problem should be recast as how to choose an appropriate *combination* of mapping strategies for our application's class hierarchies. A typical domain model design has a mix of interfaces and abstract classes.

3.6.4 *Choosing a strategy*

You can apply all mapping strategies to abstract classes and interfaces. Interfaces may have no state but may contain accessor method declarations, so they can be treated like abstract classes. You can map an interface using <class>, <subclass>, or <joined-subclass>; and you can map any declared or inherited property using

`<property>`. Hibernate won't try to instantiate an abstract class, however, even if you query or load it.

Here are some rules of thumb:

- If you don't require polymorphic associations or queries, lean toward the table-per-concrete-class strategy. If you require polymorphic associations (an association to a superclass, hence to all classes in the hierarchy with dynamic resolution of the concrete class at runtime) or queries, and subclasses declare relatively few properties (particularly if the main difference between subclasses is in their behavior), lean toward the table-per-class-hierarchy model.

- If you require polymorphic associations or queries, and subclasses declare many properties (subclasses differ mainly by the data they hold), lean toward the table-per-subclass approach.

By default, choose table-per-class-hierarchy for simple problems. For more complex cases (or when you're overruled by a data modeler insisting upon the importance of nullability constraints), you should consider the table-per-subclass strategy. But at that point, ask yourself whether it might be better to remodel inheritance as delegation in the object model. Complex inheritance is often best avoided for all sorts of reasons unrelated to persistence or ORM. Hibernate acts as a buffer between the object and relational models, but that doesn't mean you can completely ignore persistence concerns when designing your object model.

Note that you may also use `<subclass>` and `<joined-subclass>` mapping elements in a separate mapping file (as a top-level element, instead of `<class>`). You then have to declare the class that is extended (for example, `<subclass name="CreditCard" extends="BillingDetails">`), and the superclass mapping must be loaded before the subclass mapping file. This technique allows you to extend a class hierarchy without modifying the mapping file of the superclass.

You have now seen the intricacies of mapping an entity in isolation. In the next section, we turn to the problem of mapping associations between entities, which is another major issue arising from the object/relational paradigm mismatch.

3.7 Introducing associations

Managing the associations between classes and the relationships between tables is the soul of ORM. Most of the difficult problems involved in implementing an ORM solution relate to association management.

The Hibernate association model is extremely rich but is not without pitfalls, especially for new users. In this section, we won't try to cover all the possible combinations. What we'll do is examine certain cases that are extremely common. We return to the subject of association mappings in chapter 6, for a more complete treatment.

But first, there's something we need to explain up front.

3.7.1 Managed associations?

If you've used CMP 2.0/2.1, you're familiar with the concept of a *managed association* (or managed relationship). CMP associations are called container-managed relationships (CMRs) for a reason. Associations in CMP are inherently bidirectional: A change made to one side of an association is instantly reflected at the other side. For example, if we call `bid.setItem(item)`, the container automatically calls `item.getBids().add(item)`.

Transparent POJO-oriented persistence implementations such as Hibernate do *not* implement managed associations. Contrary to CMR, Hibernate associations are all inherently *unidirectional*. As far as Hibernate is concerned, the association from `Bid` to `Item` is a *different association* than the association from `Item` to `Bid`.

To some people, this seems strange; to others, it feels completely natural. After all, associations at the Java language level are always unidirectional—and Hibernate claims to implement persistence for plain Java objects. We'll merely observe that this decision was made because Hibernate objects, unlike entity beans, are *not* assumed to be always under the control of a container. In Hibernate applications, the behavior of a non-persistent instance is the same as the behavior of a persistent instance.

Because associations are so important, we need a very precise language for classifying them.

3.7.2 Multiplicity

In describing and classifying associations, we'll almost always use the association *multiplicity*. Look at figure 3.10.

For us, the multiplicity is just two bits of information:

- Can there be more than one `Bid` for a particular `Item`?
- Can there be more than one `Item` for a particular `Bid`?

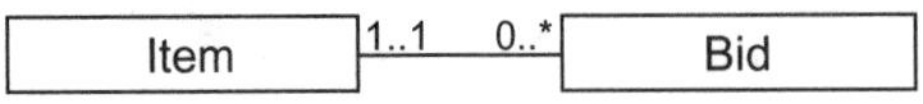

Figure 3.10
Relationship between `Item` and `Bid`

After glancing at the object model, we conclude that the association from `Bid` to `Item` is a *many-to-one* association. Recalling that associations are directional, we would also call the inverse association from `Item` to `Bid` a *one-to-many* association.

(Clearly, there are two more possibilities: *many-to-many* and *one-to-one*; we'll get back to these possibilities in chapter 6.)

In the context of object persistence, we aren't interested in whether "many" really means "two" or "maximum of five" or "unrestricted."

3.7.3 *The simplest possible association*

The association from `Bid` to `Item` is an example of the simplest possible kind of association in ORM. The object reference returned by `getItem()` is easily mapped to a foreign key column in the `BID` table. First, here's the Java class implementation of `Bid`:

```
public class Bid {
    ...

    private Item item;

    public void setItem(Item item) {
        this.item = item;
    }

    public Item getItem() {
        return item;
    }

    ...

}
```

Next, here's the Hibernate mapping for this association:

```
<class
    name="Bid"
    table="BID">
    ...
    <many-to-one
        name="item"
        column="ITEM_ID"
        class="Item"
        not-null="true"/>

</class>
```

This mapping is called a *unidirectional many-to-one association*. The column `ITEM_ID` in the `BID` table is a foreign key to the primary key of the `ITEM` table.

We have explicitly specified the class, `Item`, that the association refers to. This specification is usually optional, since Hibernate can determine this using reflection.

We specified the `not-null` attribute because we can't have a bid without an item. The `not-null` attribute doesn't affect the runtime behavior of Hibernate in this case; it exists mainly to control automatic data definition language (DDL) generation (see chapter 9).

3.7.4 *Making the association bidirectional*

So far so good. But we also need to be able to easily fetch all the bids for a particular item. We need a bidirectional association here, so we have to add scaffolding code to the `Item` class:

```
public class Item {
    ...

    private Set bids = new HashSet();

    public void setBids(Set bids) {
        this.bids = bids;
    }

    public Set getBids() {
        return bids;
    }

    public void addBid(Bid bid) {
        bid.setItem(this);
        bids.add(bid);
    }

    ...

}
```

You can think of the code in `addBid()` (a convenience method) as implementing a managed association in the object model.

A basic mapping for this *one-to-many association* would look like this:

```
<class
    name="Item"
    table="ITEM">
    ...

    <set name="bids">
        <key column="ITEM_ID"/>
        <one-to-many class="Bid"/>
    </set>

</class>
```

The column mapping defined by the `<key>` element is a foreign key column of the associated `BID` table. Notice that we specify the same foreign key column in this collection mapping that we specified in the mapping for the many-to-one association. The table structure for this association mapping is shown in figure 3.11.

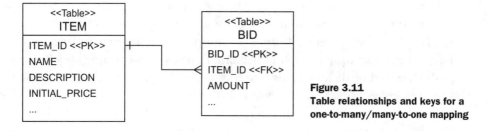

Figure 3.11
Table relationships and keys for a one-to-many/many-to-one mapping

Now we have two different unidirectional associations mapped to the same foreign key, which poses a problem. At runtime, there are two different in-memory representations of the same foreign key value: the `item` property of `Bid` and an element of the `bids` collection held by an `Item`. Suppose our application modifies the association by, for example, adding a bid to an item in this fragment of the `addBid()` method:

```
bid.setItem(item);
bids.add(bid);
```

This code is fine, but in this situation, Hibernate detects two different changes to the in-memory persistent instances. From the point of view of the database, just one value must be updated to reflect these changes: the `ITEM_ID` column of the `BID` table. *Hibernate doesn't transparently detect the fact that the two changes refer to the same database column, since at this point we've done nothing to indicate that this is a bidirectional association.*

We need one more thing in our association mapping to tell Hibernate to treat this as a bidirectional association: The `inverse` attribute tells Hibernate that the collection is a mirror image of the many-to-one association on the other side:

```
<class
    name="Item"
    table="ITEM">

    ...

    <set
        name="bids"
        inverse="true">

        <key column="ITEM_ID"/>
```

```
        <one-to-many class="Bid"/>

    </set>

</class>
```

Without the `inverse` attribute, Hibernate would try to execute two different SQL statements, both updating the same foreign key column, when we manipulate the association between the two instances. By specifying `inverse="true"`, we explicitly tell Hibernate which end of the association it should synchronize with the database. In this example, we tell Hibernate that it should propagate changes made at the `Bid` end of the association to the database, ignoring changes made only to the `bids` collection. Thus if we only call `item.getBids().add(bid)`, no changes will be made persistent. This is consistent with the behavior in Java without Hibernate: If an association is bidirectional, you have to create the link on two sides, not just one.

We now have a working *bidirectional many-to-one association* (which could also be called a bidirectional one-to-many association, of course).

One final piece is missing. We explore the notion of *transitive persistence* in much greater detail in the next chapter. For now, we'll introduce the concepts of *cascading save* and *cascading delete*, which we need in order to finish our mapping of this association.

When we instantiate a new `Bid` and add it to an `Item`, the bid should become persistent immediately. We would like to avoid the need to explicitly make a `Bid` persistent by calling `save()` on the `Session` interface.

We make one final tweak to the mapping document to enable cascading save:

```
<class
    name="Item"
    table="ITEM">
    ...

    <set
        name="bids"
        inverse="true"
        cascade="save-update">

        <key column="ITEM_ID"/>
        <one-to-many class="Bid"/>

    </set>

</class>
```

The `cascade` attribute tells Hibernate to make any new `Bid` instance persistent (that is, save it in the database) if the `Bid` is referenced by a persistent `Item`.

The `cascade` attribute is directional: It applies to only one end of the association. We could also specify `cascade="save-update"` for the many-to-one association declared in the mapping for `Bid`, but doing so would make no sense in this case because `Bid`s are created after `Item`s.

Are we finished? Not quite. We still need to define the lifecycle for both entities in our association.

3.7.5 *A parent/child relationship*

With the previous mapping, the association between `Bid` and `Item` is fairly loose. We would use this mapping in a real system if both entities had their own lifecycle and were created and removed in unrelated business processes. Certain associations are much stronger than this; some entities are bound together so that their lifecycles aren't truly independent. In our example, it seems reasonable that deletion of an item implies deletion of all bids for the item. A particular bid instance references only one item instance for its entire lifetime. In this case, cascading both saves and deletions makes sense.

If we enable cascading delete, the association between `Item` and `Bid` is called a *parent/child relationship*. In a parent/child relationship, the parent entity is responsible for the lifecycle of its associated child entities. This is the same semantics as a composition (using Hibernate components), but in this case only entities are involved; `Bid` isn't a value type. The advantage of using a parent/child relationship is that the child may be loaded individually or referenced directly by another entity. A bid, for example, may be loaded and manipulated without retrieving the owning item. It may be stored without storing the owning item at the same time. Furthermore, we reference the same `Bid` instance in a second property of `Item`, the single `successfulBid` (see figure 3.2, page 63). Objects of value type can't be shared.

To remodel the `Item` to `Bid` association as a parent/child relationship, the only change we need to make is to the `cascade` attribute:

```
<class
    name="Item"
    table="ITEM">

    ...

    <set
        name="bids"
        inverse="true"
        cascade="all-delete-orphan">

        <key column="ITEM_ID"/>
        <one-to-many class="Bid"/>

    </set>

</class>
```

We used `cascade="all-delete-orphan"` to indicate the following:

- Any newly instantiated `Bid` becomes persistent if the `Bid` is referenced by a persistent `Item` (as was also the case with `cascade="save-update"`). Any persistent `Bid` should be deleted if it's referenced by an `Item` when the item is deleted.

- Any persistent `Bid` should be deleted if it's removed from the `bids` collection of a persistent `Item`. (Hibernate will assume that it was only referenced by this item and consider it an orphan.)

We have achieved with the following with this mapping: A `Bid` is removed from the database if it's removed from the collection of `Bids` of the `Item` (or it's removed if the `Item` itself is removed).

The cascading of operations to associated entities is Hibernate's implementation of *transitive persistence*. We look more closely at this concept in chapter 4, section 4.3, "Using transitive persistence in Hibernate."

We have covered only a tiny subset of the association options available in Hibernate. However, you already have enough knowledge to be able to build entire applications. The remaining options are either rare or are variations of the associations we have described.

We recommend keeping your association mappings simple, using Hibernate queries for more complex tasks.

3.8 Summary

In this chapter, we have focused on the structural aspect of the object/relational paradigm mismatch and have discussed the first four generic ORM problems. We discussed the programming model for persistent classes and the Hibernate ORM metadata for fine-grained classes, object identity, inheritance, and associations.

You now understand that persistent classes in a domain model should be free of cross-cutting concerns such as transactions and security. Even persistence-related concerns shouldn't leak into the domain model. We no longer entertain the use of restrictive programming models such as EJB entity beans for our domain model. Instead, we use transparent persistence, together with the unrestrictive POJO programming model—which is really a set of best practices for the creation of properly encapsulated Java types.

Hibernate requires you to provide metadata in XML text format. You use this metadata to define the mapping strategy for all your persistent classes (and tables). We created mappings for classes and properties and looked at class association mappings. You saw how to implement the three well-known inheritance-mapping strategies in Hibernate.

You also learned about the important differences between *entities* and *value-typed* objects in Hibernate. Entities have their own identity and lifecycle, whereas value-typed objects are dependent on an entity and are persisted with by-value semantics. Hibernate allows fine-grained object models with fewer tables than persistent classes.

Finally, we have implemented and mapped our first parent/child association between persistent classes, using database foreign key fields and the cascading of operations full stop.

In the next chapter, we investigate the dynamic aspects of the object/relational mismatch, including a much deeper study of the cascaded operations we introduced and the lifecycle of persistent objects.

Working with
persistent objects

4

You now have an understanding of how Hibernate and ORM solve the static aspects of the object/relational mismatch. With what you know so far, it's possible to solve the structural mismatch problem, but an *efficient* solution to the problem requires something more. We must investigate strategies for runtime data access, since they're crucial to the performance of our applications. You need to learn how to efficiently store and load objects.

This chapter covers the *behavioral* aspect of the object/relational mismatch, listed in chapter 1 as the last four O/R mapping problems described in section 1.4.2. We consider these problems to be at least as important as the structural problems discussed in chapter 3. In our experience, many developers are only aware of the structural mismatch and rarely pay attention to the more dynamic behavioral aspects of the mismatch.

In this chapter, we discuss the lifecycle of objects—how an object becomes persistent, and how it stops being considered persistent—and the method calls and other actions that trigger these transitions. The Hibernate persistence manager, the `Session`, is responsible for managing object state, so you'll learn how to use this important API.

Retrieving object graphs efficiently is another central concern, so we introduce the basic strategies in this chapter. Hibernate provides several ways to specify queries that return objects without losing much of the power inherent to SQL. Because network latency caused by remote access to the database can be an important limiting factor in the overall performance of Java applications, you must learn how to retrieve a graph of objects with a minimal number of database hits.

Let's start by discussing objects, their lifecycle, and the events that trigger a change of persistent state. These basics will give you the background you need when working with your object graph, so you'll know when and how to load and save your objects. The material might be formal, but a solid understanding of the *persistence lifecycle* is essential.

4.1 *The persistence lifecycle*

Since Hibernate is a transparent persistence mechanism—classes are unaware of their own persistence capability—it's possible to write application logic that is unaware of whether the objects it operates on represent persistent state or temporary state that exists only in memory. The application shouldn't necessarily need to care that an object is persistent when invoking its methods.

However, in any application with persistent state, the application must interact with the persistence layer whenever it needs to propagate state held in memory to the database (or vice versa). To do this, you call Hibernate's persistence manager and query interfaces. When interacting with the persistence mechanism that way, it's necessary for the application to concern itself with the state and lifecycle of an object with respect to persistence. We'll refer to this as the *persistence lifecycle*.

Different ORM implementations use different terminology and define different states and state transitions for the persistence lifecycle. Moreover, the object states used internally might be different from those exposed to the client application. Hibernate defines only three states, hiding the complexity of its internal implementation from the client code. In this section, we explain these three states: *transient, persistent,* and *detached*.

Let's look at these states and their transitions in a state chart, shown in figure 4.1. You can also see the method calls to the persistence manager that trigger transitions. We discuss this chart in this section; refer to it later whenever you need an overview.

In its lifecycle, an object can transition from a transient object to a persistent object to a detached object. Let's take a closer look at each of these states.

4.1.1 *Transient objects*

In Hibernate, objects instantiated using the new operator aren't immediately persistent. Their state is *transient*, which means they aren't associated with any database table row, and so their state is lost as soon as they're dereferenced (no longer referenced by any other object) by the application. These objects have a lifespan that

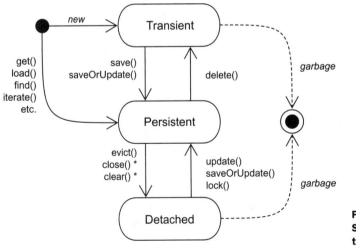

Figure 4.1
States of an object and transitions in a Hibernate application

* affects all instances in a Session

effectively ends at that time, and they become inaccessible and available for garbage collection.

Hibernate considers all transient instances to be nontransactional; a modification to the state of a transient instance isn't made in the context of any transaction. This means Hibernate doesn't provide any rollback functionality for transient objects. (In fact, Hibernate doesn't roll back any object changes, as you'll see later.)

Objects that are referenced only by other transient instances are, by default, also transient. For an instance to transition from transient to persistent state requires either a save() call to the persistence manager or the creation of a reference from an already persistent instance.

4.1.2 *Persistent objects*

A persistent instance is any instance with a *database identity*, as defined in chapter 3, section 3.4, "Understanding object identity." That means a persistent instance has a primary key value set as its database identifier.

Persistent instances might be objects instantiated by the application and then made persistent by calling the save() method of the persistence manager (the Hibernate Session, discussed in more detail later in this chapter). Persistent instances are then associated with the persistence manager. They might even be objects that became persistent when a reference was created from another persistent object already associated with a persistence manager. Alternatively, a persistent instance might be an instance retrieved from the database by execution of a query, by an identifier lookup, or by navigating the object graph starting from another persistent instance. In other words, persistent instances are always associated with a Session and are *transactional*.

Persistent instances participate in transactions—their state is synchronized with the database at the end of the transaction. When a transaction commits, state held in memory is propagated to the database by the execution of SQL INSERT, UPDATE, and DELETE statements. This procedure might also occur at other times. For example, Hibernate might synchronize with the database before execution of a query. This ensures that queries will be aware of changes made earlier during the transaction.

We call a persistent instance *new* if it has been allocated a primary key value but has not yet been inserted into the database. The new persistent instance will remain "new" until synchronization occurs.

Of course, you don't update the database row of every persistent object in memory at the end of the transaction. ORM software must have a strategy for detecting which persistent objects have been modified by the application in the transaction.

We call this *automatic dirty checking* (an object with modifications that haven't yet been propagated to the database is considered *dirty*). Again, this state isn't visible to the application. We call this feature *transparent transaction-level write-behind*, meaning that Hibernate propagates state changes to the database as late as possible but hides this detail from the application.

Hibernate can detect exactly which attributes have been modified, so it's possible to include only the columns that need updating in the SQL UPDATE statement. This might bring performance gains, particularly with certain databases. However, it isn't usually a significant difference, and, in theory, it could harm performance in some environments. So, by default, Hibernate includes all columns in the SQL UPDATE statement (hence, Hibernate can generate this basic SQL at startup, not at runtime). If you only want to update modified columns, you can enable dynamic SQL generation by setting dynamic-update="true" in a class mapping. (Note that this feature is extremely difficult to implement in a handcoded persistence layer.) We talk about Hibernate's transaction semantics and the synchronization process (known as *flushing*) in more detail in the next chapter.

Finally, a persistent instance may be made transient via a delete() call to the persistence manager API, resulting in deletion of the corresponding row of the database table.

4.1.3 Detached objects

When a transaction completes, the persistent instances associated with the persistence manager still exist. (If the transaction were successful, their in-memory state will have been synchronized with the database.) In ORM implementations with *process-scoped identity* (see the following sections), the instances retain their association to the persistence manager and are still considered persistent.

In the case of Hibernate, however, these instances lose their association with the persistence manager when you close() the Session. We refer to these objects as *detached*, indicating that their state is no longer guaranteed to be synchronized with database state; they're no longer under the management of Hibernate. However, they still contain persistent data (that may possibly soon be stale). It's possible (and common) for the application to retain a reference to a detached object outside of a transaction (and persistence manager). Hibernate lets you reuse these instances in a new transaction by reassociating them with a new persistence manager. (After reassociation, they're considered persistent.) This feature has a deep impact on how multitiered applications may be designed. The ability to return objects from one transaction to the presentation layer and later reuse them in a new transaction is one of Hibernate's main selling points. We discuss this usage in the next chapter as an implementation technique for long-running *application transactions.* We also show you how to avoid the DTO (anti-) pattern by using detached objects in chapter 8, in the section "Rethinking data transfer objects."

Hibernate also provides an explicit detachment operation: the `evict()` method of the `Session`. However, this method is typically used only for cache management (a performance consideration). It's *not* normal to perform detachment explicitly. Rather, all objects retrieved in a transaction become detached when the `Session` is closed or when they're serialized (if they're passed remotely, for example). So, Hibernate doesn't need to provide functionality for controlling detachment of *subgraphs.* Instead, the application can control the depth of the fetched subgraph (the instances that are currently loaded in memory) using the query language or explicit graph navigation. Then, when the `Session` is closed, this entire subgraph (all objects associated with a persistence manager) becomes detached.

Let's look at the different states again but this time consider the *scope of object identity.*

4.1.4 *The scope of object identity*

As application developers, we identify an object using Java object identity (`a==b`). So, if an object changes state, is its Java identity guaranteed to be the same in the new state? In a layered application, that might not be the case.

In order to explore this topic, it's important to understand the relationship between Java identity, `a==b`, and database identity, `a.getId().equals( b.getId() )`. Sometimes both are equivalent; sometimes they aren't. We refer to the conditions under which Java identity is equivalent to database identity as the *scope of object identity.*

For this scope, there are three common choices:

- A primitive persistence layer with *no identity scope* makes no guarantees that if a row is accessed twice, the same Java object instance will be returned to the application. This becomes problematic if the application modifies two different instances that both represent the same row in a single transaction (how do you decide which state should be propagated to the database?).

- A persistence layer using *transaction-scoped identity* guarantees that, in the context of a single transaction, there is only one object instance that represents a particular database row. This avoids the previous problem and also allows for some caching to be done at the transaction level.

- *Process-scoped identity* goes one step further and guarantees that there is only one object instance representing the row in the whole process (JVM).

For a typical web or enterprise application, transaction-scoped identity is preferred. Process-scoped identity offers some potential advantages in terms of cache utilization and the programming model for reuse of instances across multiple transactions; however, in a pervasively multithreaded application, the cost of always synchronizing shared access to persistent objects in the global identity map is too high a price to pay. It's simpler, and more scalable, to have each thread work with a distinct set of persistent instances in each transaction scope.

Speaking loosely, we would say that Hibernate implements transaction-scoped identity. Actually, the Hibernate identity scope is the Session instance, so identical objects are guaranteed if the same persistence manager (the Session) is used for several operations. But a Session isn't the same as a (database) transaction—it's a much more flexible element. We'll explore the differences and the consequences of this concept in the next chapter. Let's focus on the persistence lifecycle and identity scope again.

If you request two objects using the same database identifier value in the same Session, the result will be two references to the same in-memory object. The following code example demonstrates this behavior, with several load() operations in two Sessions:

```
Session session1 = sessions.openSession();
Transaction tx1 = session1.beginTransaction();

// Load Category with identifier value "1234"
Object a = session1.load(Category.class, new Long(1234) );
Object b = session1.load(Category.class, new Long(1234) );

if ( a==b ) {
    System.out.println("a and b are identical.");
}

tx1.commit();
session1.close();

Session session2 = sessions.openSession();
Transaction tx2 = session2.beginTransaction();

Object b2 = session2.load(Category.class, new Long(1234) );

if ( a!=b2 ) {
    System.out.println("a and b2 are not identical.");
}

tx2.commit();
session2.close();
```

Object references a and b not only have the same database identity, they also have the same Java identity since they were loaded in the same Session. Once outside this boundary, however, Hibernate doesn't guarantee Java identity, so a and b2 aren't identical and the message is printed on the console. Of course, a test for database identity—a.getId().equals (b2.getId())—would still return true.

To further complicate our discussion of identity scopes, we need to consider how the persistence layer handles a reference to an object outside its identity scope. For example, for a persistence layer with transaction-scoped identity such as Hibernate, is a reference to a detached object (that is, an instance persisted or loaded in a previous, completed session) tolerated?

4.1.5 *Outside the identity scope*

If an object reference leaves the scope of guaranteed identity, we call it a *reference to a detached object*. Why is this concept useful?

In web applications, you usually don't maintain a database transaction across a user interaction. Users take a long time to think about modifications, but for scalability reasons, you must keep database transactions short and release database resources as soon as possible. In this environment, it's useful to be able to reuse a reference to a detached instance. For example, you might want to send an object retrieved in one unit of work to the presentation tier and later reuse it in a second unit of work, after it's been modified by the user.

You don't usually wish to reattach the entire object graph in the second unit of of work; for performance (and other) reasons, it's important that reassociation of detached instances be selective. Hibernate supports *selective reassociation of detached instances.* This means the application can efficiently reattach a *subgraph* of a graph of detached objects with the current ("second") Hibernate Session. Once a detached object has been reattached to a new Hibernate persistence manager, it may be considered a persistent instance, and its state will be synchronized with the database at the end of the transaction (due to Hibernate's automatic dirty checking of persistent instances).

Reattachment might result in the creation of new rows in the database when a reference is created from a detached instance to a new transient instance. For example, a new Bid might have been added to a detached Item while it was on the presentation tier. Hibernate can detect that the Bid is new and must be inserted in the database. For this to work, Hibernate must be able to distinguish between a "new" transient instance and an "old" detached instance. Transient instances (such as the Bid) might need to be saved; detached instances (such as the Item) might need to be reattached (and later updated in the database). There are several ways to distinguish between transient and detached instances, but the nicest approach is to look at the value of the identifier property. Hibernate can examine the identifier of a transient or detached object on reattachment and treat the object (and the associated graph of objects) appropriately. We discuss this important issue further in section 4.3.4, "Distinguishing between transient and detached instances."

If you want to take advantage of Hibernate's support for reassociation of detached instances in your own applications, you need to be aware of Hibernate's identity scope when designing your application—that is, the Session scope that guarantees identical instances. As soon as you leave that scope and have detached instances, another interesting concept comes into play.

We need to discuss the relationship between Java *equality* (see chapter 3, section 3.4.1, "Identity versus equality") and database identity. Equality is an identity concept that you, as a class developer, control and that you can (and sometimes have to) use for classes that have detached instances. Java equality is defined by the implementation of the equals() and hashCode() methods in the persistent classes of the domain model.

4.1.6 *Implementing equals() and hashCode()*

The equals() method is called by application code or, more importantly, by the Java collections. A Set collection, for example, calls equals() on each object you put in the Set, to determine (and prevent) duplicate elements.

First let's consider the default implementation of equals(), defined by java.lang.Object, which uses a comparison by Java identity. Hibernate guarantees that there is a unique instance for each row of the database inside a Session. Therefore, the default identity equals() is appropriate if you never mix instances—that is, if you never put detached instances from different sessions into the same Set. (Actually, the issue we're exploring is also visible if detached instances are from the same session but have been serialized and deserialized in different scopes.) As soon as you have instances from multiple sessions, however, it becomes possible to have a Set containing two Items that each represent the same row of the database table but don't have the same Java identity. This would almost always be semantically wrong. Nevertheless, it's possible to build a complex application with identity (default) equals as long as you exercise discipline when dealing with detached objects from different sessions (and keep an eye on serialization and deserialization). One nice thing about this approach is that you don't have to write extra code to implement your own notion of equality.

However, if this concept of equality isn't what you want, you have to override equals() in your persistent classes. Keep in mind that when you override equals(), you always need to also override hashCode() so the two methods are *consistent* (if two objects are equal, they must have the same hashcode). Let's look at some of the ways you can override equals() and hashCode() in persistent classes.

Using database identifier equality

A clever approach is to implement `equals()` to compare just the database identifier property (usually a surrogate primary key) value:

```
public class User {
    ...

    public boolean equals(Object other) {
        if (this==other) return true;
        if (id==null) return false;
        if ( !(other instanceof User) ) return false;
        final User that = (User) other;
        return this.id.equals( that.getId() );
    }
    public int hashCode() {
        return id==null ?
            System.identityHashCode(this) :
            id.hashCode();
    }

}
```

Notice how this `equals()` method falls back to Java identity for transient instances (if `id==null`) that don't have a database identifier value assigned yet. This is reasonable, since they can't have the same persistent identity as another instance.

Unfortunately, this solution has one huge problem: Hibernate doesn't assign identifier values until an entity is saved. So, if the object is added to a `Set` before being saved, its hash code changes while it's contained by the `Set`, contrary to the contract of `java.util.Set`. In particular, this problem makes cascade save (discussed later in this chapter) useless for sets. We strongly discourage this solution (database identifier equality).

Comparing by value

A better way is to include all persistent properties of the persistent class, apart from any database identifier property, in the `equals()` comparison. This is how most people perceive the meaning of `equals()`; we call it *by value* equality.

When we say "all properties," we don't mean to include collections. Collection state is associated with a different table, so it seems wrong to include it. More important, you don't want to force the entire object graph to be retrieved just to perform `equals()`. In the case of `User`, this means you shouldn't include the `items` collection (the items sold by this user) in the comparison. So, this is the implementation you could use:

```
public class User {
    ...

    public boolean equals(Object other) {
        if (this==other) return true;
        if ( !(other instanceof User) ) return false;
        final User that = (User) other;
        if ( !this.getUsername().equals( that.getUsername() )
            return false;
        if ( !this.getPassword().equals( that.getPassword() )
            return false;
        return true;
    }
    public int hashCode() {
        int result = 14;
        result = 29 * result + getUsername().hashCode();
        result = 29 * result + getPassword().hashCode();
        return result;
    }

}
```

However, there are again two problems with this approach:

- Instances from different sessions are no longer equal if one is modified (for example, if the user changes his password).

- Instances with different database identity (instances that represent different rows of the database table) could be considered equal, unless there is some combination of properties that are guaranteed to be unique (the database columns have a unique constraint). In the case of User, there is a unique property: username.

To get to the solution we recommend, you need to understand the notion of a *business key*.

Using business key equality

A *business key* is a property, or some combination of properties, that is unique for each instance with the same database identity. Essentially, it's the natural key you'd use if you weren't using a surrogate key. Unlike a natural primary key, it isn't an absolute requirement that the business key never change—as long as it changes rarely, that's enough.

We argue that every entity should have a business key, even if it includes all properties of the class (this would be appropriate for some immutable classes). The business key is what the user thinks of as uniquely identifying a particular record, whereas the surrogate key is what the application and database use.

Business key equality means that the equals() method compares only the properties that form the business key. This is a perfect solution that avoids all the problems described earlier. The only downside is that it requires extra thought to identify the correct business key in the first place. But this effort is required anyway; it's important to identify any unique keys if you want your database to help ensure data integrity via constraint checking.

For the User class, username is a great candidate business key. It's never null, it's unique, and it changes rarely (if ever):

```
public class User {
    ...

    public boolean equals(Object other) {
        if (this==other) return true;
        if ( !(other instanceof User) ) return false;
        final User that = (User) other;
        return this.username.equals( that.getUsername() );
    }

    public int hashCode() {
        return username.hashCode();
    }

}
```

For some other classes, the business key might be more complex, consisting of a combination of properties. For example, candidate business keys for the Bid class are the item ID together with the bid amount, or the item ID together with the date and time of the bid. A good business key for the BillingDetails abstract class is the number together with the type (subclass) of billing details. Notice that it's almost never correct to override equals() on a subclass and include another property in the comparison. It's tricky to satisfy the requirements that equality be both symmetric and transitive in this case; and, more important, the business key wouldn't correspond to any well-defined candidate natural key in the database (subclass properties may be mapped to a different table).

You might have noticed that the equals() and hashCode() methods always access the properties of the other object via the getter methods. This is important, since the object instance passed as other might be a proxy object, not the actual instance that holds the persistent state. This is one point where Hibernate isn't completely transparent, but it's a good practice to use accessor methods instead of direct instance variable access anyway.

Finally, take care when modifying the value of the business key properties; don't change the value while the domain object is in a set.

We've talked about the persistence manager in this section. It's time to take a closer look at the persistence manager and explore the Hibernate Session API in greater detail. We'll come back to detached objects with more details in the next chapter.)

4.2 *The persistence manager*

Any transparent persistence tool includes a *persistence manager* API, which usually provides services for

- Basic CRUD operations
- Query execution
- Control of transactions
- Management of the transaction-level cache

The persistence manager can be exposed by several different interfaces (in the case of Hibernate, Session, Query, Criteria, and Transaction). Under the covers, the implementations of these interfaces are coupled tightly.

The central interface between the application and Hibernate is Session; it's your starting point for all the operations just listed. For most of the rest of this book, we'll refer to the *persistence manager* and the *session* interchangeably; this is consistent with usage in the Hibernate community.

So, how do you start using the session? At the beginning of a unit of work, a thread obtains an instance of Session from the application's SessionFactory. The application might have multiple SessionFactorys if it accesses multiple datasources. But you should never create a new SessionFactory just to service a particular request—creation of a SessionFactory is extremely expensive. On the other hand, Session creation is extremely *inexpensive*; the Session doesn't even obtain a JDBC Connection until a connection is required.

After opening a new session, you use it to load and save objects.

4.2.1 *Making an object persistent*

The first thing you want to do with a Session is make a new transient object persistent. To do so, you use the save() method:

```
User user = new User();
user.getName().setFirstname("John");
user.getName().setLastname("Doe");
```

```
Session session = sessions.openSession();
Transaction tx = session.beginTransaction();

session.save(user);

tx.commit();
session.close();
```

First, we instantiate a new transient object user as usual. Of course, we might also instantiate it after opening a Session; they aren't related yet. We open a new Session using the SessionFactory referred to by sessions, and then we start a new database transaction.

A call to save() makes the transient instance of User persistent. It's now associated with the current Session. However, no SQL INSERT has yet been executed. The Hibernate Session never executes any SQL statement until absolutely necessary.

The changes made to persistent objects have to be synchronized with the database at some point. This happens when we commit() the Hibernate Transaction. In this case, Hibernate obtains a JDBC connection and issues a single SQL INSERT statement. Finally, the Session is closed and the JDBC connection is released.

Note that it's better (but not required) to fully initialize the User instance before associating it with the Session. The SQL INSERT statement contains the values that were held by the object *at the point when save() was called.* You can, of course, modify the object after calling save(), and your changes will be propagated to the database as an SQL UPDATE.

Everything between session.beginTransaction() and tx.commit() occurs in one database transaction. We haven't discussed transactions in detail yet; we'll leave that topic for the next chapter. But keep in mind that all database operations in a transaction scope either completely succeed or completely fail. If one of the UPDATE or INSERT statements made on tx.commit() fails, all changes made to persistent objects in this transaction will be rolled back at the database level. However, Hibernate does *not* roll back in-memory changes to persistent objects; this is reasonable since a failure of a database transaction is normally nonrecoverable and you have to discard the failed Session immediately.

4.2.2 *Updating the persistent state of a detached instance*

Modifying the user after the session is closed will have no effect on its persistent representation in the database. When the session is closed, user becomes a *detached* instance. It may be reassociated with a new Session by calling update() or lock().

The update() method forces an update to the persistent state of the object in the database, scheduling an SQL UPDATE. Here's an example of detached object handling:

```
user.setPassword("secret");

Session sessionTwo = sessions.openSession();
Transaction tx = sessionTwo.beginTransaction();

sessionTwo.update(user);

user.setUsername("jonny");

tx.commit();
sessionTwo.close();
```

It doesn't matter if the object is modified before or after it's passed to update(). The important thing is that the call to update() is used to reassociate the detached instance to the new Session (and current transaction) and tells Hibernate to treat the object as dirty (unless select-before-update is enabled for the persistent class mapping, in which case Hibernate will determine if the object is dirty by executing a SELECT statement and comparing the object's current state to the current database state).

A call to lock() associates the object with the Session without forcing an update, as shown here:

```
Session sessionTwo = sessions.openSession();
Transaction tx = sessionTwo.beginTransaction();

sessionTwo.lock(user, LockMode.NONE);

user.setPassword("secret");
user.setLoginName("jonny");

tx.commit();
sessionTwo.close();
```

In this case, it *does* matter whether changes are made before or after the object is associated with the session. Changes made before the call to lock() aren't propagated to the database; you only use lock() if you're sure that the detached instance hasn't been modified.

We discuss Hibernate lock modes in the next chapter. By specifying Lock-Mode.NONE here, we tell Hibernate not to perform a version check or obtain any database-level locks when reassociating the object with the Session. If we specified LockMode.READ or LockMode.UPGRADE, Hibernate would execute a SELECT statement in order to perform a version check (and to set an upgrade lock).

4.2.3 *Retrieving a persistent object*

The `Session` is also used to query the database and retrieve existing persistent objects. Hibernate is especially powerful in this area, as you'll see later in this chapter and in chapter 7. However, special methods are provided on the `Session` API for the simplest kind of query: retrieval by identifier. One of these methods is `get()`, demonstrated here:

```
Session session = sessions.openSession();
Transaction tx = session.beginTransaction();

int userID = 1234;
User user = (User) session.get(User.class, new Long(userID));

tx.commit();
session.close();
```

The retrieved object `user` may now be passed to the presentation layer for use outside the transaction as a detached instance (after the session has been closed). If no row with the given identifier value exists in the database, the `get()` returns `null`.

4.2.4 *Updating a persistent object*

Any persistent object returned by `get()` or any other kind of query is already associated with the current `Session` and transaction context. It can be modified, and its state will be synchronized with the database. This mechanism is called *automatic dirty checking*, which means Hibernate will track and save the changes you make to an object inside a session:

```
Session session = sessions.openSession();
Transaction tx = session.beginTransaction();

int userID = 1234;
User user = (User) session.get(User.class, new Long(userID));

user.setPassword("secret");

tx.commit();
session.close();
```

First we retrieve the object from the database with the given identifier. We modify the object, and these modifications are propagated to the database when `tx.commit()` is called. Of course, as soon as we close the `Session`, the instance is considered detached.

4.2.5 *Making a persistent object transient*

You can easily make a persistent object transient, removing its persistent state from the database, using the `delete()` method:

```
Session session = sessions.openSession();
Transaction tx = session.beginTransaction();

int userID = 1234;
User user = (User) session.get(User.class, new Long(userID));

session.delete(user);

tx.commit();
session.close();
```

The SQL DELETE will be executed only when the Session is synchronized with the database at the end of the transaction.

After the Session is closed, the user object is considered an ordinary transient instance. The transient instance will be destroyed by the garbage collector if it's no longer referenced by any other object. Both the in-memory object instance and the persistent database row will have been removed.

4.2.6 *Making a detached object transient*

Finally, you can make a detached instance transient, deleting its persistent state from the database. This means you don't have to reattach (with update() or lock()) a detached instance to delete it from the database; you can directly delete a detached instance:

```
Session session = sessions.openSession();
Transaction tx = session.beginTransaction();

session.delete(user);

tx.commit();
session.close();
```

In this case, the call to delete() does two things: It associates the object with the Session and then schedules the object for deletion, executed on tx.commit().

You now know the persistence lifecycle and the basic operations of the persistence manager. Together with the persistent class mappings we discussed in chapter 3, you can create your own small Hibernate application. (If you like, you can jump to chapter 8 and read about a handy Hibernate helper class for SessionFactory and Session management.) Keep in mind that we didn't show you any exception-handling code so far, but you should be able to figure out the try/catch blocks yourself. Map some simple entity classes and components, and then store and load objects in a stand-alone application (you don't need a web container or application server, just write a main method). However, as soon as you try to store associated entity objects—that is, when you deal with a more complex object graph—you'll see that calling `save()` or `delete()` on each object of the graph isn't an efficient way to write applications.

You'd like to make as few calls to the `Session` as possible. *Transitive persistence* provides a more natural way to force object state changes and to control the persistence lifecycle.

4.3 *Using transitive persistence in Hibernate*

Real, nontrivial applications work not with single objects but rather with graphs of objects. When the application manipulates a graph of persistent objects, the result may be an object graph consisting of persistent, detached, and transient instances. *Transitive persistence* is a technique that allows you to propagate persistence to transient and detached subgraphs automatically.

For example, if we add a newly instantiated `Category` to the already persistent hierarchy of categories, it should automatically become persistent without a call to `Session.save()`. We gave a slightly different example in chapter 3 when we mapped a parent/child relationship between `Bid` and `Item`. In that case, not only were bids automatically made persistent when they were added to an item, but they were also automatically deleted when the owning item was deleted.

There is more than one model for transitive persistence. The best known is *persistence by reachability,* which we'll discuss first. Although some basic principles are the same, Hibernate uses its own, more powerful model, as you'll see later.

4.3.1 *Persistence by reachability*

An object persistence layer is said to implement *persistence by reachability* if any instance becomes persistent when the application creates an object reference to the instance from another instance that is already persistent. This behavior is illustrated by the object diagram (note that this isn't a class diagram) in figure 4.2.

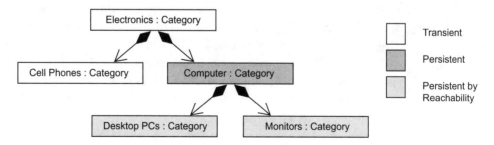

Figure 4.2   Persistence by reachability with a root persistent object

In this example, "Computer" is a persistent object. The objects "Desktop PCs" and "Monitors" are also persistent; they're reachable from the "Computer" `Category` instance. "Electronics" and "Cell Phones" are transient. Note that we assume navigation is only possible to child categories, and not to the parent—for example, we can call `computer.getChildCategories()`. Persistence by reachability is a recursive algorithm: All objects reachable from a persistent instance become persistent either when the original instance is made persistent or just before in-memory state is synchronized with the data store.

Persistence by reachability guarantees referential integrity; any object graph can be completely re-created by loading the persistent root object. An application may walk the object graph from association to association without worrying about the persistent state of the instances. (SQL databases have a different approach to referential integrity, relying on foreign key and other constraints to detect a misbehaving application.)

In the purest form of persistence by reachability, the database has some top-level, or *root*, object from which all persistent objects are reachable. Ideally, an instance should become transient and be deleted from the database if it isn't reachable via references from the root persistent object.

Neither Hibernate nor other ORM solutions implement this form; there is no analog of the root persistent object in an SQL database and no persistent garbage collector that can detect unreferenced instances. Object-oriented data stores might implement a garbage-collection algorithm similar to the one implemented for in-memory objects by the JVM, but this option isn't available in the ORM world; scanning all tables for unreferenced rows won't perform acceptably.

So, persistence by reachability is at best a halfway solution. It helps you make transient objects persistent and propagate their state to the database without many calls to the persistence manager. But (at least, in the context of SQL databases and ORM) it isn't a full solution to the problem of making persistent objects transient and removing their state from the database. This turns out to be a much more difficult problem. You can't simply remove all reachable instances when you remove an object; other persistent instances may hold references to them (remember that entities can be shared). You can't even safely remove instances that aren't referenced by any persistent object in memory; the instances in memory are only a small subset of all objects represented in the database. Let's look at Hibernate's more flexible transitive persistence model.

4.3.2 *Cascading persistence with Hibernate*

Hibernate's transitive persistence model uses the same basic concept as persistence by reachability—that is, object associations are examined to determine transitive state. However, Hibernate allows you to specify a *cascade style* for each association mapping, which offers more flexibility and fine-grained control for all state transitions. Hibernate reads the declared style and cascades operations to associated objects automatically.

By default, Hibernate does *not* navigate an association when searching for transient or detached objects, so saving, deleting, or reattaching a `Category` won't affect the child category objects. This is the opposite of the persistence-by-reachability default behavior. If, for a particular association, you wish to enable transitive persistence, you must override this default in the mapping metadata.

You can map entity associations in metadata with the following attributes:

- `cascade="none"`, the default, tells Hibernate to ignore the association.

- `cascade="save-update"` tells Hibernate to navigate the association when the transaction is committed and when an object is passed to `save()` or `update()` and save newly instantiated transient instances and persist changes to detached instances.

- `cascade="delete"` tells Hibernate to navigate the association and delete persistent instances when an object is passed to `delete()`.

- `cascade="all"` means to cascade both save-update and delete, as well as calls to `evict` and `lock`.

- `cascade="all-delete-orphan"` means the same as `cascade="all"` but, in addition, Hibernate deletes any persistent entity instance that has been removed (dereferenced) from the association (for example, from a collection).

- `cascade="delete-orphan"` Hibernate will delete any persistent entity instance that has been removed (dereferenced) from the association (for example, from a collection).

This *association-level cascade style* model is both richer and less safe than persistence by reachability. Hibernate doesn't make the same strong guarantees of referential integrity that persistence by reachability provides. Instead, Hibernate partially delegates referential integrity concerns to the foreign key constraints of the underlying relational database. Of course, there is a good reason for this design decision: It allows Hibernate applications to use *detached* objects efficiently, because you can control reattachment of a detached object graph at the association level.

Let's elaborate on the cascading concept with some example association mappings. We recommend that you read the next section in one turn, because each example builds on the previous one. Our first example is straightforward; it lets you save newly added categories efficiently.

4.3.3 *Managing auction categories*

System administrators can create new categories, rename categories, and move subcategories around in the category hierarchy. This structure can be seen in figure 4.3.

Now, we map this class and the association:

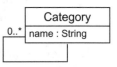

Figure 4.3
Category class with association to itself

```
<class name="Category" table="CATEGORY">
    ...
    <property name="name" column="CATEGORY_NAME"/>

    <many-to-one
        name="parentCategory"
        class="Category"
        column="PARENT_CATEGORY_ID"
        cascade="none"/>

    <set
        name="childCategories"
        table="CATEGORY"
        cascade="save-update"
        inverse="true">
        <key column="PARENT_CATEGORY_ID"/>
        <one-to-many class="Category"/>

    </set>
    ...
</class>
```

This is a recursive, bidirectional, one-to-many association, as briefly discussed in chapter 3. The one-valued end is mapped with the <many-to-one> element and the Set typed property with the <set>. Both refer to the same foreign key column: PARENT_CATEGORY_ID.

Suppose we create a new Category as a child category of "Computer" (see figure 4.4).

We have several ways to create this new "Laptops" object and save it in the database. We could go back to the database and retrieve the "Computer" category to which our new "Laptops" category will belong, add the new category, and commit the transaction:

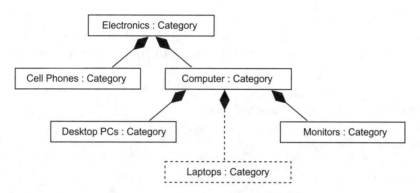

Figure 4.4 Adding a new `Category` to the object graph

```
Session session = sessions.openSession();
Transaction tx = session.beginTransaction();

Category computer = (Category) session.get(Category.class, computerId);
Category laptops = new Category("Laptops");

computer.getChildCategories().add(laptops);
laptops.setParentCategory(computer);

tx.commit();
session.close();
```

The `computer` instance is persistent (attached to a session), and the `childCategories` association has cascade save enabled. Hence, this code results in the new `laptops` category becoming persistent when `tx.commit()` is called, because Hibernate cascades the dirty-checking operation to the children of `computer`. Hibernate executes an `INSERT` statement.

Let's do the same thing again, but this time create the link between "Computer" and "Laptops" outside of any transaction (in a real application, it's useful to manipulate an object graph in a presentation tier—for example, before passing the graph back to the persistence layer to make the changes persistent):

```
Category computer = ... // Loaded in a previous session

Category laptops = new Category("Laptops");

computer.getChildCategories().add(laptops);
laptops.setParentCategory(computer);
```

The detached computer object and any other detached objects it refers to are now associated with the new transient laptops object (and vice versa). We make this change to the object graph persistent by saving the new object in a second Hibernate session:

```
Session session = sessions.openSession();
Transaction tx = session.beginTransaction();

// Persist one new category and the link to its parent category
session.save(laptops);

tx.commit();
session.close();
```

Hibernate will inspect the database identifier property of the parent category of laptops and correctly create the relationship to the "Computer" category in the database. Hibernate inserts the identifier value of the parent into the foreign key field of the new "Laptops" row in CATEGORY.

Since cascade="none" is defined for the parentCategory association, Hibernate ignores changes to any of the other categories in the hierarchy ("Computer", "Electronics"). It doesn't cascade the call to save() to entities referred to by this association. If we had enabled cascade="save-update" on the <many-to-one> mapping of parentCategory, Hibernate would have had to navigate the whole graph of objects in memory, synchronizing all instances with the database. This process would perform badly, because a lot of useless data access would be required. In this case, we neither needed nor wanted transitive persistence for the parentCategory association.

Why do we have cascading operations? We could have saved the laptop object, as shown in the previous example, without any cascade mapping being used. Well, consider the following case:

```
Category computer = ... // Loaded in a previous Session

Category laptops = new Category("Laptops");
Category laptopAccessories = new Category("Laptop Accessories");
Category laptopTabletPCs = new Category("Tablet PCs")

laptops.addChildCategory(laptopAccessories);
laptops.addChildCategory(laptopTabletPCs);

computer.addChildCategory(laptops);
```

(Notice that we use the convenience method addChildCategory() to set both ends of the association link in one call, as described in chapter 3.)

It would be undesirable to have to save each of the three new categories individually. Fortunately, because we mapped the childCategories association with cascade="save-update", we don't need to. The same code we used before to save the single "Laptops" category will save all three new categories in a new session:

```
Session session = sessions.openSession();
Transaction tx = session.beginTransaction();

// Persist all three new Category instances
session.save(laptops);

tx.commit();
session.close();
```

You're probably wondering why the cascade style is called cascade="save-update" rather than cascade="save". Having just made all three categories persistent previously, suppose we made the following changes to the category hierarchy in a subsequent request (outside of a session and transaction):

```
laptops.setName("Laptop Computers");
laptopAccessories.setName("Accessories & Parts");
laptopTabletPCs.setName("Tablet Computers");

Category laptopBags = new Category("Laptop Bags");
laptops.addChildCategory(laptopBags);
```

We have added a new category as a child of the "Laptops" category and modified all three existing categories. The following code propagates these changes to the database:

```
Session session = sessions.openSession();
Transaction tx = session.beginTransaction();

// Update three old Category instances and insert the new one
session.update(laptops);

tx.commit();
session.close();
```

Specifying cascade="save-update" on the childCategories association accurately reflects the fact that Hibernate determines what is needed to persist the objects to the database. In this case, it will reattach/update the three detached categories (laptops, laptopAccessories, and laptopTabletPCs) and save the new child category (laptopBags).

Notice that the last code example differs from the previous two session examples only in a single method call. The last example uses update() instead of save() because laptops was already persistent.

We can rewrite all the examples to use the saveOrUpdate() method. Then the three code snippets are identical:

```
Session session = sessions.openSession();
Transaction tx = session.beginTransaction();

// Let Hibernate decide what's new and what's detached
session.saveOrUpdate(laptops);

tx.commit();
session.close();
```

The saveOrUpdate() method tells Hibernate to propagate the state of an instance to the database by creating a new database row if the instance is a new transient instance or updating the existing row if the instance is a detached instance. In other words, it does exactly the same thing with the laptops category as cascade="save-update" did with the child categories of laptops.

One final question: How did Hibernate know which children were detached and which were new transient instances?

4.3.4 *Distinguishing between transient and detached instances*

Since Hibernate doesn't keep a reference to a detached instance, you have to let Hibernate know how to distinguish between a detached instance like laptops (if it was created in a previous session) and a new transient instance like laptopBags.

A range of options is available. Hibernate will assume that an instance is an unsaved transient instance if:

- The identifier property (if it exists) is null.
- The version property (if it exists) is null.
- You supply an unsaved-value in the mapping document for the class, and the value of the identifier property matches.
- You supply an unsaved-value in the mapping document for the version property, and the value of the version property matches.
- You supply a Hibernate Interceptor and return Boolean.TRUE from Interceptor.isUnsaved() after checking the instance in your code.

In our domain model, we have used the nullable type java.lang.Long as our identifier property type everywhere. Since we're using generated, synthetic identifiers, this solves the problem. New instances have a null identifier property value, so Hibernate treats them as transient. Detached instances have a non-null identifier value, so Hibernate treats them properly too.

However, if we had used the primitive type long in our persistent classes, we would have needed to use the following identifier mapping in all our classes:

```
<class name="Category" table="CATEGORY">

    <id name="id" unsaved-value="0">
        <generator class="native"/>
    </id>

    ....

</class>
```

The unsaved-value attribute tells Hibernate to treat instances of Category with an identifier value of 0 as newly instantiated transient instances. The default value for the attribute unsaved-value is null; so, since we've chosen Long as our identifier property type, we can omit the unsaved-value attribute in our auction application classes (we use the same identifier type everywhere).

UNSAVED ASSIGNED IDENTIFIERS This approach works nicely for synthetic identifiers, but it breaks down in the case of keys assigned by the application, including composite keys in legacy systems. We discuss this issue in chapter 8, section 8.3.1, "Legacy schemas and composite keys." Avoid application-assigned (and composite) keys in new applications if possible.

You now have the knowledge to optimize your Hibernate application and reduce the number of calls to the persistence manager if you want to save and delete objects. Check the unsaved-value attributes of all your classes and experiment with detached objects to get a feeling for the Hibernate transitive persistence model.

We'll now switch perspectives and look at another important concept: how to get a graph of persistent objects out of the database (that is, how to load objects).

4.4 *Retrieving objects*

Retrieving persistent objects from the database is one of the most interesting (and complex) parts of working with Hibernate. Hibernate provides the following ways to get objects out of the database:

- Navigating the object graph, starting from an already loaded object, by accessing the associated objects through property accessor methods such as aUser.getAddress().getCity(). Hibernate will automatically load (or preload) nodes of the graph while you navigate the graph if the Session is open.

- Retrieving by identifier, which is the most convenient and performant method when the unique identifier value of an object is known.

- Using the Hibernate Query Language (HQL), which is a full object-oriented query language.

- Using the Hibernate `Criteria` API, which provides a type-safe and object-oriented way to perform queries without the need for string manipulation. This facility includes queries based on an example object.

- Using native SQL queries, where Hibernate takes care of mapping the JDBC result sets to graphs of persistent objects.

In your Hibernate applications, you'll use a combination of these techniques. Each retrieval method may use a different fetching strategy—that is, a strategy that defines what part of the persistent object graph should be retrieved. The goal is to find the best retrieval method and fetching strategy for every use case in your application while at the same time minimizing the number of SQL queries for best performance.

We won't discuss each retrieval method in much detail in this section; instead we'll focus on the basic fetching strategies and how to tune Hibernate mapping files for best default fetching performance for all methods. Before we look at the fetching strategies, we'll give an overview of the retrieval methods. (We mention the Hibernate caching system but fully explore it in the next chapter.)

Let's start with the simplest case, retrieval of an object by giving its identifier value (navigating the object graph should be self-explanatory). You saw a simple retrieval by identifier earlier in this chapter, but there is more to know about it.

4.4.1 *Retrieving objects by identifier*

The following Hibernate code snippet retrieves a `User` object from the database:

```
User user = (User) session.get(User.class, userID);
```

The `get()` method is special because the identifier uniquely identifies a single instance of a class. Hence it's common for applications to use the identifier as a convenient handle to a persistent object. Retrieval by identifier can use the cache when retrieving an object, avoiding a database hit if the object is already cached.

Hibernate also provides a `load()` method:

```
User user = (User) session.load(User.class, userID);
```

The `load()` method is older; `get()` was added to Hibernate's API due to user request. The difference is trivial:

- If `load()` can't find the object in the cache or database, an exception is thrown. The `load()` method never returns `null`. The `get()` method returns `null` if the object can't be found.

- The load() method may return a proxy instead of a real persistent instance. A proxy is a placeholder that triggers the loading of the real object when it's accessed for the first time; we discuss proxies later in this section. On the other hand, get() never returns a proxy.

Choosing between get() and load() is easy: If you're certain the persistent object exists, and nonexistence would be considered exceptional, load() is a good option. If you aren't certain there is a persistent instance with the given identifier, use get() and test the return value to see if it's null. Using load() has a further implication: The application may retrieve a valid *reference* (a proxy) to a persistent instance without hitting the database to retrieve its persistent state. So load() might not throw an exception when it doesn't find the persistent object in the cache or database; the exception would be thrown later, when the proxy is accessed.

Of course, retrieving an object by identifier isn't as flexible as using arbitrary queries.

4.4.2 *Introducing HQL*

The Hibernate Query Language is an object-oriented dialect of the familiar relational query language SQL. HQL bears close resemblances to ODMG OQL and EJB-QL; but unlike OQL, it's adapted for use with SQL databases, and it's much more powerful and elegant than EJB-QL (However, EJB-QL 3.0 will be very similar to HQL.) HQL is easy to learn with basic knowledge of SQL.

HQL isn't a data-manipulation language like SQL. It's used only for object retrieval, not for updating, inserting, or deleting data. Object state synchronization is the job of the persistence manager, not the developer.

Most of the time, you'll only need to retrieve objects of a particular class and restrict by the properties of that class. For example, the following query retrieves a user by first name:

```
Query q = session.createQuery("from User u where u.firstname = :fname");
q.setString("fname", "Max");
List result = q.list();
```

After preparing query q, we bind the identifier value to a named parameter, fname. The result is returned as a List of User objects.

HQL is powerful, and even though you may not use the advanced features all the time, you'll need them for some difficult problems. For example, HQL supports the following:

- The ability to apply restrictions to properties of associated objects related by reference or held in collections (to navigate the object graph using query language).

- The ability to retrieve only properties of an entity or entities, without the overhead of loading the entity itself in a transactional scope. This is sometimes called a *report query*; it's more correctly called *projection*.

- The ability to order the results of the query.

- The ability to paginate the results.

- Aggregation with `group by`, `having`, and aggregate functions like `sum`, `min`, and `max`.

- Outer joins when retrieving multiple objects per row.

- The ability to call user-defined SQL functions.

- Subqueries (nested queries).

We discuss all these features in chapter 7, together with the optional native SQL query mechanism.

4.4.3 *Query by criteria*

The Hibernate *query by criteria* (QBC) API lets you build a query by manipulating criteria objects at runtime. This approach lets you specify constraints dynamically without direct string manipulations, but it doesn't lose much of the flexibility or power of HQL. On the other hand, queries expressed as criteria are often less readable than queries expressed in HQL.

Retrieving a user by first name is easy using a `Criteria` object:

```
Criteria criteria = session.createCriteria(User.class);
criteria.add( Expression.like("firstname", "Max") );
List result = criteria.list();
```

A `Criteria` is a tree of `Criterion` instances. The `Expression` class provides static factory methods that return `Criterion` instances. Once the desired criteria tree is built, it's executed against the database.

Many developers prefer QBC, considering it a more object-oriented approach. They also like the fact that the query syntax may be parsed and validated at compile time, whereas HQL expressions aren't parsed until runtime.

The nice thing about the Hibernate `Criteria` API is the `Criterion` framework. This framework allows extension by the user, which is difficult in the case of a query language like HQL.

4.4.4 *Query by example*

As part of the QBC facility, Hibernate supports *query by example* (QBE). The idea behind QBE is that the application supplies an instance of the queried class with certain property values set (to nondefault values). The query returns all persistent instances with matching property values. QBE isn't a particularly powerful approach, but it can be convenient for some applications. The following code snippet demonstrates a Hibernate QBE:

```
User exampleUser = new User();
exampleUser.setFirstname("Max");
Criteria criteria = session.createCriteria(User.class);
criteria.add( Example.create(exampleUser) );
List result = criteria.list();
```

A typical use case for QBE is a search screen that allows users to specify a range of property values to be matched by the returned result set. This kind of functionality can be difficult to express cleanly in a query language; string manipulations would be required to specify a dynamic set of constraints.

Both the QBC API and the example query mechanism are discussed in more detail in chapter 7.

You now know the basic retrieval options in Hibernate. We focus on the strategies for fetching object graphs in the rest of this section. A fetching strategy defines what part of the object graph (or, what subgraph) is retrieved with a query or load operation.

4.4.5 *Fetching strategies*

In traditional relational data access, you'd fetch all the data required for a particular computation with a single SQL query, taking advantage of inner and outer joins to retrieve related entities. Some primitive ORM implementations fetch data piecemeal, with many requests for small chunks of data in response to the application's navigating a graph of persistent objects. This approach doesn't make efficient use of the relational database's join capabilities. In fact, this data access strategy scales poorly by nature. One of the most difficult problems in ORM—probably *the* most difficult—is providing for efficient access to relational data, given an application that prefers to treat the data as a graph of objects.

For the kinds of applications we've often worked with (multi-user, distributed, web, and enterprise applications), object retrieval using many round trips to/from the database is unacceptable. Hence we argue that tools should emphasize the *R* in ORM to a much greater extent than has been traditional.

The problem of fetching object graphs efficiently (with minimal access to the database) has often been addressed by providing association-level fetching strategies specified in metadata of the association mapping. The trouble with this approach is that each piece of code that uses an entity requires a *different* set of associated objects. But this isn't enough. We argue that what is needed is support for fine-grained *runtime* association fetching strategies. Hibernate supports both, it lets you specify a default fetching strategy in the mapping file and then override it at runtime in code.

Hibernate allows you to choose among four fetching strategies for any association, in association metadata and at runtime:

- *Immediate fetching*—The associated object is fetched immediately, using a sequential database read (or cache lookup).

- *Lazy fetching*—The associated object or collection is fetched "lazily," when it's first accessed. This results in a new request to the database (unless the associated object is cached).

- *Eager fetching*—The associated object or collection is fetched together with the owning object, using an SQL outer join, and no further database request is required.

- *Batch fetching*—This approach may be used to improve the performance of lazy fetching by retrieving a batch of objects or collections when a lazy association is accessed. (Batch fetching may also be used to improve the performance of immediate fetching.)

Let's look more closely at each fetching strategy.

Immediate fetching

Immediate association fetching occurs when you retrieve an entity from the database and then immediately retrieve another associated entity or entities in a further request to the database or cache. Immediate fetching isn't usually an efficient fetching strategy unless you expect the associated entities to almost always be cached already.

Lazy fetching

When a client requests an entity and its associated graph of objects from the database, it isn't usually necessary to retrieve the whole graph of every (indirectly) associated object. You wouldn't want to load the whole database into memory at once; for example, loading a single Category shouldn't trigger the loading of all Items in that category.

Lazy fetching lets you decide how much of the object graph is loaded in the first database hit and which associations should be loaded only when they're first accessed. Lazy fetching is a foundational concept in object persistence and the first step to attaining acceptable performance.

We recommend that, to start with, all associations be configured for lazy (or perhaps batched lazy) fetching in the mapping file. This strategy may then be overridden at runtime by queries that force eager fetching to occur.

Eager (outer join) fetching

Lazy association fetching can help reduce database load and is often a good default strategy. However, it's a bit like a blind guess as far as performance optimization goes.

Eager fetching lets you explicitly specify which associated objects should be loaded together with the referencing object. Hibernate can then return the associated objects in a single database request, utilizing an SQL OUTER JOIN. Performance optimization in Hibernate often involves judicious use of eager fetching for particular transactions. Hence, even though default eager fetching may be declared in the mapping file, it's more common to specify the use of this strategy at runtime for a particular HQL or criteria query.

Batch fetching

Batch fetching isn't strictly an association fetching strategy; it's a technique that may help improve the performance of lazy (or immediate) fetching. Usually, when you load an object or collection, your SQL WHERE clause specifies the identifier of the object or object that owns the collection. If batch fetching is enabled, Hibernate looks to see what other proxied instances or uninitialized collections are referenced in the current session and tries to load them at the same time by specifying multiple identifier values in the WHERE clause.

We aren't great fans of this approach; eager fetching is almost always faster. Batch fetching is useful for inexperienced users who wish to achieve acceptable performance in Hibernate without having to think too hard about the SQL that will be executed. (Note that batch fetching may be familiar to you, since it's used by many EJB2 engines.)

We'll now declare the fetching strategy for some associations in our mapping metadata.

4.4.6 Selecting a fetching strategy in mappings

Hibernate lets you select default association fetching strategies by specifying attributes in the mapping metadata. You can override the default strategy using features of Hibernate's query methods, as you'll see in chapter 7. A minor caveat: You don't have to understand every option presented in this section immediately; we recommend that you get an overview first and use this section as a reference when you're optimizing the default fetching strategies in your application.

A wrinkle in Hibernate's mapping format means that collection mappings function slightly differently than single-point associations; so, we'll cover the two cases separately. Let's first consider both ends of the bidirectional association between Bid and Item.

Single point associations

For a `<many-to-one>` or `<one-to-one>` association, lazy fetching is possible only if the associated class mapping enables proxying. For the Item class, we enable proxying by specifying lazy="true":

```
<class name="Item" lazy="true">
```

Now, remember the association from Bid to Item:

```
<many-to-one name="item" class="Item">
```

When we retrieve a Bid from the database, the association property may hold an instance of a Hibernate *generated subclass* of Item that delegates all method invocations to a different instance of Item that is fetched lazily from the database (this is the more elaborate definition of a Hibernate proxy).

Hibernate uses two different instances so that even polymorphic associations can be proxied—when the proxied object is fetched, it may be an instance of a mapped subclass of Item (if there were any subclasses of Item, that is). We can even choose any interface implemented by the Item class as the type of the proxy. To do so, we declare it using the proxy attribute, instead of specifying lazy="true":

```
<class name="Item" proxy="ItemInterface">
```

As soon as we declare the proxy or lazy attribute on Item, any single-point association to Item is proxied and fetched lazily, unless that association overrides the fetching strategy by declaring the outer-join attribute.

There are three possible values for outer-join:

- `outer-join="auto"`—The default. When the attribute isn't specified; Hibernate fetches the associated object lazily if the associated class has proxying enabled, or eagerly using an outer join if proxying is disabled (default).

- `outer-join="true"`—Hibernate always fetches the association eagerly using an outer join, even if proxying is enabled. This allows you to choose different fetching strategies for different associations to the same proxied class.

- `outer-join="false"`—Hibernate never fetches the association using an outer join, even if proxying is disabled. This is useful if you expect the associated object to exist in the second-level cache (see chapter 5). If it isn't available in the second-level cache, the object is fetched immediately using an extra SQL SELECT.

So, if we wanted to reenable eager fetching for the association, now that proxying is enabled, we would specify

```
<many-to-one name="item" class="Item" outer-join="true">
```

For a one-to-one association (discussed in more detail in chapter 6), lazy fetching is conceptually possible only when the associated object always exists. We indicate this by specifying `constrained="true"`. For example, if an item can have only one bid, the mapping for the Bid is

```
<one-to-one name="item" class="Item" constrained="true">
```

The `constrained` attribute has a slightly similar interpretation to the `not-null` attribute of a `<many-to-one>` mapping. It tells Hibernate that the associated object is *required* and thus cannot be `null`.

To enable batch fetching, we specify the `batch-size` in the mapping for Item:

```
<class name="Item" lazy="true" batch-size="9">
```

The batch size limits the number of items that may be retrieved in a single batch. Choose a reasonably small number here.

You'll meet the same attributes (`outer-join`, `batch-size`, and `lazy`) when we consider collections, but the interpretation is slightly different.

Collections

In the case of collections, fetching strategies apply not just to entity associations, but also to collections of values (for example, a collection of strings could be fetched by outer join).

Just like classes, collections have their own proxies, which we usually call *collection wrappers*. Unlike classes, the collection wrapper is always there, even if lazy fetching is disabled (Hibernate needs the wrapper to detect collection modifications).

Collection mappings may declare a `lazy` attribute, an `outer-join` attribute, neither, or both (specifying both isn't meaningful). The meaningful options are as follows:

- *Neither attribute specified*—This option is equivalent to `outer-join="false"` `lazy="false"`. The collection is fetched from the second-level cache or by an immediate extra SQL `SELECT`. This option is the default and is most useful when the second-level cache is enabled for this collection.

- `outer-join="true"`—Hibernate fetches the association eagerly using an outer join. At the time of this writing, Hibernate is able to fetch only one collection per SQL `SELECT`, so it isn't possible to declare multiple collections belonging to the same persistent class with `outer-join="true"`.

- `lazy="true"`—Hibernate fetches the collection lazily, when it's first accessed.

We don't recommend eager fetching for collections, so we'll map the item's collection of bids with `lazy="true"`. This option is almost always used for collection mappings (it should be the default, and we recommend that you consider it as a default for all your collection mappings):

```
<set name="bids" lazy="true">
    <key column="ITEM_ID"/>
    <one-to-many class="Bid"/>
</set>
```

We can even enable batch fetching for the collection. In this case, the batch size doesn't refer to the number of bids in the batch; it refers to the number of collections of bids:

```
<set name="bids" lazy="true" batch-size="9">
    <key column="ITEM_ID"/>
    <one-to-many class="Bid"/>
</set>
```

This mapping tells Hibernate to load up to nine collections of bids in one batch, depending on how many uninitialized collections of bids are currently present in the items associated with the session. In other words, if there are five `Item` instances with persistent state in a `Session`, and all have an uninitialized `bids` collection, Hibernate will automatically load all five collections in a single SQL query if one is accessed. If there are 11 items, only 9 collections will be fetched. Batch fetching can significantly reduce the number of queries required for hierarchies of objects (for example, when loading the tree of parent and child Category objects).

Let's talk about a special case: many-to-many associations (we discuss this mapping in more detail in chapter 6). You usually use a *link table* (some developers also call it *relationship table* or *association table*) that holds only the key values of the two associated tables and therefore allows a many-to-many multiplicity. This additional table has to be considered if you decide to use eager fetching. Look at the following straightforward many-to-many example, which maps the association from Category to Item:

```
<set name="items" outer-join="true" table="CATEGORY_ITEM">
    <key column="CATEGORY_ID"/>
    <many-to-many column="ITEM_ID" class="Item"/>
</set>
```

In this case, the eager fetching strategy refers only to the association table CATEGORY_ITEM. If we load a Category with this fetching strategy, Hibernate will automatically fetch all link entries from CATEGORY_ITEM in a single outer join SQL query, but not the item instances from ITEM!

The entities contained in the many-to-many association can of course also be fetched eagerly with the same SQL query. The <many-to-many> element allows this behavior to be customized:

```
<set name="items" outer-join="true" table="CATEGORY_ITEM">
    <key column="CATEGORY_ID"/>
    <many-to-many column="ITEM_ID" outer-join="true" class="Item"/>
</set>
```

Hibernate will now fetch all Items in a Category with a single outer join query when the Category is loaded. However, keep in mind that we usually recommend lazy loading as the default fetching strategy and that Hibernate is limited to one eagerly fetched collection per mapped persistent class.

Setting the fetch depth

We'll now discuss a global fetching strategy setting: the *maximum fetch depth*. This setting controls the number of outer-joined tables Hibernate will use in a single SQL query. Consider the complete association chain from Category to Item, and from Item to Bid. The first is a many-to-many association and the second is a one-to-many; hence both associations are mapped with collection elements. If we declare outer-join="true" for both associations (don't forget the special <many-to-many> declaration) and load a single Category, how many queries will Hibernate execute? Will only the Items be eagerly fetched, or also all the Bids of each Item?

You probably expect a single query, with an outer join operation including the CATEGORY, CATEGORY_ITEM, ITEM, and BID tables. However, this isn't the case by default.

Hibernate's outer join fetch behavior is controlled with the global configuration option hibernate.max_fetch_depth. If you set this to 1 (also the default), Hibernate will fetch only the Category and the link entries from the CATEGORY_ITEM association table. If you set it to 2, Hibernate executes an outer join that also includes the Items in the same SQL query. Setting this option to 3 joins all four tables in one SQL statement and also loads all Bids.

Recommended values for the fetch depth depend on the join performance and the size of the database tables; test your applications with low values (less than 4) first, and decrease or increase the number while tuning your application. The global maximum fetch depth also applies to single-ended association (<many-to-one>, <one-to-one>) mapped with an eager fetching strategy.

Keep in mind that eager fetching strategies declared in the mapping metadata are effective only if you use retrieval by identifier, use the criteria query API, or navigate through the object graph manually. Any HQL query may specify its own fetching strategy at runtime, thus ignoring the mapping defaults. You can also override the defaults (that is, not ignore them) with criteria queries. This is an important difference, and we cover it in more detail in chapter 7, section 7.3.2, "Fetching associations."

However, you may sometimes simply like to initialize a proxy or a collection wrapper manually with a simple API call.

Initializing lazy associations

A proxy or collection wrapper is automatically initialized when any of its methods are invoked (except the identifier property getter, which may return the identifier value without fetching the underlying persistent object). However, it's only possible to initialize a proxy or collection wrapper if it's currently associated with an open Session. If you close the session and try to access an uninitialized proxy or collection, Hibernate throws a runtime exception.

Because of this behavior, it's sometimes useful to explicitly initialize an object before closing the session. This approach isn't as flexible as retrieving the complete required object subgraph with an HQL query, using arbitrary fetching strategies at runtime.

We use the static method Hibernate.initialize() for manual initialization:

```
Session session = sessions.openSession();
Transaction tx = session.beginTransaction();
```

```
Category cat = (Category) session.get(Category.class, id);
Hibernate.initialize( cat.getItems() );

tx.commit();
session.close();

Iterator iter = cat.getItems().iterator();
...
```

`Hibernate.initialize()` may be passed a collection wrapper, as in this example, or a proxy. You may also, in similar rare cases, check the current state of a property by calling `Hibernate.isInitialized()`. (Note that `initialize()` doesn't cascade to any associated objects.)

Another solution for this problem is to keep the session open until the application thread finishes, so you can navigate the object graph whenever you like and have Hibernate automatically initialize all lazy references. This is a problem of application design and transaction demarcation; we discuss it again in chapter 8, section 8.1, "Designing layered applications." However, your first choice should be to fetch the complete required graph in the first place, using HQL or criteria queries, with a sensible and optimized default fetching strategy in the mapping metadata for all other cases.

4.4.7 *Tuning object retrieval*

Let's look at the steps involved when you're tuning the object retrieval operations in your application:

1 Enable the Hibernate SQL log, as described in chapter 2. You should also be prepared to read, understand, and evaluate SQL queries and their performance characteristics for your specific relational model: Will a single join operation be faster than two selects? Are all the indexes used properly, and what is the cache hit ratio inside the database? Get your DBA to help you with the performance evaluation; only she will have the knowledge to decide which SQL execution plan is the best.

2 Step through your application use case by use case and note how many and what SQL statements Hibernate executes. A use case can be a single screen in your web application or a sequence of user dialogs. This step also involves collecting the object-retrieval methods you use in each use case: walking the graph, retrieval by identifier, HQL, and criteria queries. Your goal is to bring down the number (and complexity) of SQL queries for each use case by tuning the default fetching strategies in metadata.

3 You may encounter two common issues:

- If the SQL statements use join operations that are too complex and slow, set `outer-join` to false for `<many-to-one>` associations (this is enabled by default). Also try to tune with the global `hibernate.max_fetch_depth` configuration option, but keep in mind that this is best left at a value between 1 and 4.

- If too many SQL statements are executed, use `lazy="true"` for all collection mappings; by default, Hibernate will execute an immediate additional fetch for the collection elements (which, if they're entities, can cascade further into the graph). In rare cases, if you're sure, enable `outer-join="true"` and disable lazy loading for particular collections. Keep in mind that only one collection property per persistent class may be fetched eagerly. Use batch fetching with values between 3 and 10 to further optimize collection fetching if the given unit of work involves several "of the same" collections or if you're accessing a tree of parent and child objects.

4 After you set a new fetching strategy, rerun the use case and check the generated SQL again. Note the SQL statements, and go to the next use case.

5 After you optimize all use cases, check every one again and see if any optimizations had side effects for others. With some experience, you'll be able to avoid any negative effects and get it right the first time.

This optimization technique isn't only practical for the default fetching strategies; you can also use it to tune HQL and criteria queries, which can ignore and override the default fetching for specific use cases and units of work. We discuss runtime fetching in chapter 7.

In this section, we've started to think about performance issues, especially issues related to association fetching. Of course, the quickest way to fetch a graph of objects is to fetch it from the cache in memory, as shown in the next chapter.

4.5 *Summary*

The dynamic aspects of the object/relational mismatch are just as important as the better known and better understood structural mismatch problems. In this chapter, we were primarily concerned with the lifecycle of objects with respect to the persistence mechanism. Now you understand the three object states defined by Hibernate: persistent, detached, and transient. Objects transition between states when you invoke methods of the `Session` interface or create and remove references from a graph of already persistent instances. This latter behavior is governed by the configurable cascade styles, Hibernate's model for transitive persistence. This model lets you declare the cascading of operations (such as saving or deletion) on an association basis, which is more powerful and flexible than the traditional *persistence by reachability* model. Your goal is to find the best cascading style for each association and therefore minimize the number of persistence manager calls you have to make when storing objects.

Retrieving objects from the database is equally important: You can walk the graph of domain objects by accessing properties and let Hibernate transparently fetch objects. You can also load objects by identifier, write arbitrary queries in the HQL, or create an object-oriented representation of your query using the query by criteria API. In addition, you can use native SQL queries in special cases.

Most of these object-retrieval methods use the default fetching strategies we defined in mapping metadata (HQL ignores them; criteria queries can override them). The correct fetching strategy minimizes the number of SQL statements that have to be executed by lazily, eagerly, or batch-fetching objects. You optimize your Hibernate application by analyzing the SQL executed in each use case and tuning the default and runtime fetching strategies.

Next we explore the closely related topics of *transactions* and *caching*.

5

*Transactions,
concurrency,
and caching*

This chapter covers

- Database transactions and locking
- Long-running application transactions
- The Hibernate first- and second-level caches
- The caching system in practice with CaveatEmptor

Now that you understand the basics of object/relational mapping with Hibernate, let's take a closer look at one of the core issues in database application design: *transaction management.* In this chapter, we examine how you use Hibernate to manage transactions, how concurrency is handled, and how caching is related to both aspects. Let's look at our example application.

Some application functionality requires that several different things be done together. For example, when an auction finishes, our CaveatEmptor application has to perform four different tasks:

1. Mark the winning (highest amount) bid.
2. Charge the seller the cost of the auction.
3. Charge the successful bidder the price of the winning bid.
4. Notify the seller and the successful bidder.

What happens if we can't bill the auction costs because of a failure in the external credit card system? Our business requirements might state that either all listed actions must succeed or none must succeed. If so, we call these steps collectively a *transaction* or *unit of work.* If only one step fails, the whole unit of work must fail. We say that the transaction is *atomic:* Several operations are grouped together as a single indivisible unit.

Furthermore, transactions allow multiple users to work concurrently with the same data without compromising the integrity and correctness of the data; a particular transaction shouldn't be visible to and shouldn't influence other concurrently running transactions. Several different strategies are used to implement this behavior, which is called *isolation.* We'll explore them in this chapter.

Transactions are also said to exhibit *consistency* and *durability.* Consistency means that any transaction works with a consistent set of data and leaves the data in a consistent state when the transaction completes. Durability guarantees that once a transaction completes, all changes made during that transaction become persistent and aren't lost even if the system subsequently fails. Atomicity, consistency, isolation, and durability are together known as the *ACID* criteria.

We begin this chapter with a discussion of system-level *database transactions,* where the database guarantees ACID behavior. We'll look at the JDBC and JTA APIs and see how Hibernate, working as a client of these APIs, is used to control database transactions.

In an online application, database transactions must have extremely short lifespans. A database transaction should span a single batch of database operations, interleaved with business logic. It should certainly not span interaction with the user. We'll augment your understanding of transactions with the notion of a long-running *application transaction*, where database operations occur in several batches, alternating with user interaction. There are several ways to implement application transactions in Hibernate applications, all of which are discussed in this chapter. Finally, the subject of caching is much more closely related to transactions than it might appear at first sight. In the second half of this chapter, armed with an understanding of transactions, we explore Hibernate's sophisticated cache architecture. You'll learn which data is a good candidate for caching and how to handle concurrency of the cache. We'll then enable caching in the CaveatEmptor application.

Let's begin with the basics and see how transactions work at the lowest level, the database.

5.1 *Understanding database transactions*

Databases implement the notion of a unit of work as a *database transaction* (sometimes called a *system transaction*).

A database transaction groups data-access operations. A transaction is guaranteed to end in one of two ways: it's either *committed* or *rolled back*. Hence, database transactions are always truly *atomic*. In figure 5.1, you can see this graphically.

If several database operations should be executed inside a transaction, you must mark the boundaries of the unit of work. You must start the transaction and, at some point, commit the changes. If an error occurs (either while executing operations or when committing the changes), you have to roll back the transaction to leave the data in a consistent state. This is known as *transaction demarcation,* and (depending on the API you use) it involves more or less manual intervention.

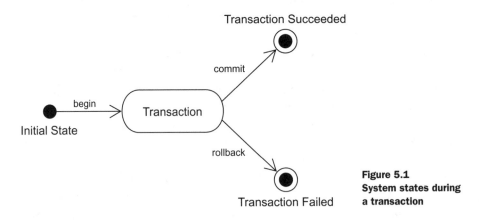

**Figure 5.1
System states during
a transaction**

You may already have experience with two transaction-handling programming interfaces: the JDBC API and the JTA.

5.1.1 *JDBC and JTA transactions*

In a non-managed environment, the JDBC API is used to mark transaction boundaries. You begin a transaction by calling `setAutoCommit(false)` on a JDBC connection and end it by calling `commit()`. You may, at any time, force an immediate rollback by calling `rollback()`. (Easy, huh?)

> **FAQ** *What auto commit mode should you use?* A magical setting that is often a source of confusion is the JDBC connection's *auto commit* mode. If a database connection is in auto commit mode, the database transaction will be committed immediately after each SQL statement, and a new transaction will be started. This can be useful for ad hoc database queries and ad hoc data updates.
>
> Auto commit mode is almost always inappropriate in an application, however. An application doesn't perform ad hoc or any unplanned queries; instead, it executes a preplanned sequence of related operations (which are, by definition, never ad hoc). Therefore, Hibernate automatically disables auto commit mode as soon as it fetches a connection (from a connection provider—that is, a connection pool). If you supply your own connection when you open the `Session`, it's your responsibility to turn off auto commit!
>
> Note that some database systems enable auto commit by default for each new connection, but others don't. You might want to disable auto commit in your global database system configuration to ensure that you never run into any problems. You may then enable auto commit only when you execute ad hoc queries (for example, in your database SQL query tool).

In a system that stores data in multiple databases, a particular unit of work may involve access to more than one data store. In this case, you can't achieve atomicity using JDBC alone. You require a *transaction manager* with support for distributed transactions (two-phase commit). You communicate with the transaction manager using the JTA.

In a managed environment, JTA is used not only for distributed transactions, but also for declarative *container managed transactions* (CMT). CMT allows you to avoid explicit transaction demarcation calls in your application source code; rather, transaction demarcation is controlled by a deployment-specific descriptor. This descriptor defines how a transaction context *propagates* when a single thread passes through several different EJBs.

We aren't interested in the details of direct JDBC or JTA transaction demarcation. You'll be using these APIs only indirectly.

Hibernate communicates with the database via a JDBC Connection; hence it must support both APIs. In a stand-alone (or web-based) application, only the JDBC transaction handling is available; in an application server, Hibernate can use JTA. Since we would like Hibernate application code to look the same in both managed and non-managed environments, Hibernate provides its own abstraction layer, hiding the underlying transaction API. Hibernate allows user extension, so you could even plug in an adaptor for the CORBA transaction service.

Transaction management is exposed to the application developer via the Hibernate Transaction interface. You aren't forced to use this API—Hibernate lets you control JTA or JDBC transactions directly, but this usage is discouraged, and we won't discuss this option.

5.1.2 *The Hibernate Transaction API*

The Transaction interface provides methods for declaring the boundaries of a database transaction. See listing 5.1 for an example of the basic usage of Transaction.

Listing 5.1 Using the Hibernate Transaction API

```
Session session = sessions.openSession();
Transaction tx = null;
try {
    tx = session.beginTransaction();

    concludeAuction();

    tx.commit();
} catch (Exception e) {
    if (tx != null) {
        try {
            tx.rollback();
        } catch (HibernateException he) {
            //log he and rethrow e
        }
    }
    throw e;
} finally {
    try {
        session.close();
    } catch (HibernateException he) {
        throw he;
    }
}
```

The call to `session.beginTransaction()` marks the beginning of a database transaction. In the case of a non-managed environment, this starts a JDBC transaction on the JDBC connection. In the case of a managed environment, it starts a new JTA transaction if there is no current JTA transaction, or joins the existing current JTA transaction. This is all handled by Hibernate—you shouldn't need to care about the implementation.

The call to `tx.commit()` synchronizes the `Session` state with the database. Hibernate then commits the underlying transaction if and only if `beginTransaction()` started a new transaction (in both managed and non-managed cases). If `begin-Transaction()` did *not* start an underlying database transaction, `commit()` only synchronizes the `Session` state with the database; it's left to the responsible party (the code that started the transaction in the first place) to end the transaction. This is consistent with the behavior defined by JTA.

If `concludeAuction()` threw an exception, we must force the transaction to roll back by calling `tx.rollback()`. This method either rolls back the transaction immediately or marks the transaction for "rollback only" (if you're using CMTs).

FAQ   *Is it faster to roll back read-only transactions?*   If code in a transaction reads data but doesn't modify it, should you roll back the transaction instead of committing it? Would this be faster?

Apparently some developers found this approach to be faster in some special circumstances, and this belief has now spread through the community. We tested this with the more popular database systems and found no difference. We also failed to discover any source of real numbers showing a performance difference. There is also no reason why a database system should be implemented suboptimally—that is, why it shouldn't use the fastest transaction cleanup algorithm internally. Always commit your transaction and roll back if the commit fails.

It's critically important to close the Session in a finally block in order to ensure that the JDBC connection is released and returned to the connection pool. (This step is the responsibility of the application, even in a managed environment.)

NOTE   The example in listing 5.1 is the standard idiom for a Hibernate unit of work; therefore, it includes all exception-handling code for the checked `HibernateException`. As you can see, even rolling back a `Transaction` and closing the `Session` can throw an exception. You don't want to use this example as a template in your own application, since you'd rather hide the exception handling with generic infrastructure code. You can, for example, use a utility class to convert the `HibernateException` to an unchecked runtime exception and hide the details of rolling back a transaction and closing the session. We discuss this question of application design in more detail in chapter 8, section 8.1, "Designing layered applications."

However, there is one important aspect you must be aware of: the Session has to be immediately closed and discarded (not reused) when an exception occurs. Hibernate can't retry failed transactions. This is no problem in practice, because database exceptions are usually fatal (constraint violations, for example) and there is no well-defined state to continue after a failed transaction. An application in production shouldn't throw any database exceptions either.

We've noted that the call to commit() synchronizes the Session state with the database. This is called *flushing*, a process you automatically trigger when you use the Hibernate Transaction API.

5.1.3 *Flushing the Session*

The Hibernate Session implements *transparent write behind*. Changes to the domain model made in the scope of a Session aren't immediately propagated to the database. This allows Hibernate to coalesce many changes into a minimal number of database requests, helping minimize the impact of network latency.

For example, if a single property of an object is changed twice in the same Transaction, Hibernate only needs to execute one SQL UPDATE. Another example of the usefulness of transparent write behind is that Hibernate can take advantage of the JDBC batch API when executing multiple UPDATE, INSERT, or DELETE statements.

Hibernate flushes occur only at the following times:

- When a Transaction is committed
- Sometimes before a query is executed
- When the application calls Session.flush() explicitly

Flushing the Session state to the database at the end of a database transaction is required in order to make the changes durable and is the common case. Hibernate doesn't flush before every query. However, if there are changes held in memory that would affect the results of the query, Hibernate will, by default, synchronize first.

You can control this behavior by explicitly setting the Hibernate FlushMode via a call to session.setFlushMode(). The flush modes are as follows:

- FlushMode.AUTO—The default. Enables the behavior just described.
- FlushMode.COMMIT—Specifies that the session won't be flushed before query execution (it will be flushed only at the end of the database transaction). Be

aware that this setting may expose you to stale data: modifications you made to objects only in memory may conflict with the results of the query.

- `FlushMode.NEVER`—Lets you specify that only explicit calls to `flush()` result in synchronization of session state with the database.

We don't recommend that you change this setting from the default. It's provided to allow performance optimization in rare cases. Likewise, most applications rarely need to call `flush()` explicitly. This functionality is useful when you're working with triggers, mixing Hibernate with direct JDBC, or working with buggy JDBC drivers. You should be aware of the option but not necessarily look out for use cases.

Now that you understand the basic usage of database transactions with the Hibernate `Transaction` interface, let's turn our attention more closely to the subject of concurrent data access.

It seems as though you shouldn't have to care about transaction isolation—the term implies that something either is or is not isolated. This is misleading. *Complete* isolation of concurrent transactions is extremely expensive in terms of application scalability, so databases provide several degrees of isolation. For most applications, incomplete transaction isolation is acceptable. It's important to understand the degree of isolation you should choose for an application that uses Hibernate and how Hibernate integrates with the transaction capabilities of the database.

5.1.4 *Understanding isolation levels*

Databases (and other transactional systems) attempt to ensure *transaction isolation*, meaning that, from the point of view of each concurrent transaction, it appears that no other transactions are in progress.

Traditionally, this has been implemented using locking. A transaction may place a lock on a particular item of data, temporarily preventing access to that item by other transactions. Some modern databases such as Oracle and PostgreSQL implement transaction isolation using *multiversion concurrency control*, which is generally considered more scalable. We'll discuss isolation assuming a locking model (most of our observations are also applicable to multiversion concurrency).

This discussion is about database transactions and the isolation level provided by the database. Hibernate doesn't add additional semantics; it uses whatever is available with a given database. If you consider the many years of experience that database vendors have had with implementing concurrency control, you'll clearly see the advantage of this approach. Your part, as a Hibernate application developer, is to understand the capabilities of your database and how to change the database isolation behavior if needed in your particular scenario (and by your data integrity requirements).

Isolation issues

First, let's look at several phenomena that break full transaction isolation. The ANSI SQL standard defines the standard transaction isolation levels in terms of which of these phenomena are permissible:

- *Lost update*—Two transactions both update a row and then the second transaction aborts, causing both changes to be lost. This occurs in systems that don't implement any locking. The concurrent transactions aren't isolated.

- *Dirty read*—One transaction reads changes made by another transaction that hasn't yet been committed. This is very dangerous, because those changes might later be rolled back.

- *Unrepeatable read*—A transaction reads a row twice and reads different state each time. For example, another transaction may have written to the row, and committed, between the two reads.

- *Second lost updates problem*—A special case of an unrepeatable read. Imagine that two concurrent transactions both read a row, one writes to it and commits, and then the second writes to it and commits. The changes made by the first writer are lost.

- *Phantom read*—A transaction executes a query twice, and the second result set includes rows that weren't visible in the first result set. (It need not necessarily be *exactly* the same query.) This situation is caused by another transaction inserting new rows between the execution of the two queries.

Now that you understand all the bad things that could occur, we can define the various *transaction isolation levels* and see what problems they prevent.

Isolation levels

The standard isolation levels are defined by the ANSI SQL standard but aren't particular to SQL databases. JTA defines the same isolation levels, and you'll use these levels to declare your desired transaction isolation later:

- *Read uncommitted*—Permits dirty reads but not lost updates. One transaction may not write to a row if another uncommitted transaction has already written to it. Any transaction may read any row, however. This isolation level may be implemented using exclusive write locks.

- *Read committed*—Permits unrepeatable reads but not dirty reads. This may be achieved using momentary shared read locks and exclusive write locks. Reading transactions don't block other transactions from accessing a row.

However, an uncommitted writing transaction blocks all other transactions from accessing the row.

- *Repeatable read*—Permits neither unrepeatable reads nor dirty reads. Phantom reads may occur. This may be achieved using shared read locks and exclusive write locks. Reading transactions block writing transactions (but not other reading transactions), and writing transactions block all other transactions.

- *Serializable*—Provides the strictest transaction isolation. It emulates serial transaction execution, as if transactions had been executed one after another, serially, rather than concurrently. Serializability may not be implemented using only row-level locks; there must be another mechanism that prevents a newly inserted row from becoming visible to a transaction that has already executed a query that would return the row.

It's nice to know how all these technical terms are defined, but how does that help you choose an isolation level for your application?

5.1.5 *Choosing an isolation level*

Developers (ourselves included) are often unsure about what transaction isolation level to use in a production application. Too great a degree of isolation will harm performance of a highly concurrent application. Insufficient isolation may cause subtle bugs in our application that can't be reproduced and that we'll never find out about until the system is working under heavy load in the deployed environment.

Note that we refer to *caching* and *optimistic locking* (using versioning) in the following explanation, two concepts explained later in this chapter. You might want to skip this section and come back when it's time to make the decision for an isolation level in your application. Picking the right isolation level is, after all, highly dependent on your particular scenario. The following discussion contains recommendations; nothing is carved in stone.

Hibernate tries hard to be as transparent as possible regarding the transactional semantics of the database. Nevertheless, caching and optimistic locking affect these semantics. So, what is a sensible database isolation level to choose in a Hibernate application?

First, you eliminate the *read uncommitted* isolation level. It's extremely dangerous to use one transaction's uncommitted changes in a different transaction. The rollback or failure of one transaction would affect other concurrent transactions. Rollback of the first transaction could bring other transactions down with it, or perhaps even cause them to leave the database in an inconsistent state. It's possible that changes made by a transaction that ends up being rolled back could be committed anyway, since they could be read and then propagated by another transaction that *is* successful!

Second, most applications don't need *serializable* isolation (phantom reads aren't usually a problem), and this isolation level tends to scale poorly. Few existing applications use serializable isolation in production; rather, they use pessimistic locks (see section 5.1.7, "Using pessimistic locking"), which effectively forces a serialized execution of operations in certain situations.

This leaves you a choice between read committed and repeatable read. Let's first consider repeatable read. This isolation level eliminates the possibility that one transaction could overwrite changes made by another concurrent transaction (the second lost updates problem) if all data access is performed in a single atomic database transaction. This is an important issue, but using repeatable read isn't the only way to resolve it.

Let's assume you're using versioned data, something that Hibernate can do for you automatically. The combination of the (mandatory) Hibernate first-level session cache and versioning already gives you most of the features of repeatable read isolation. In particular, versioning prevents the second lost update problem, and the first-level session cache ensures that the state of the persistent instances loaded by one transaction is isolated from changes made by other transactions. So, read committed isolation for all database transactions would be acceptable if you use versioned data.

Repeatable read provides a bit more reproducibility for query result sets (only for the duration of the database transaction), but since phantom reads are still possible, there isn't much value in that. (It's also not common for web applications to query the same table twice in a single database transaction.)

You also have to consider the (optional) second-level Hibernate cache. It can provide the same transaction isolation as the underlying database transaction, but it might even weaken isolation. If you're heavily using a cache concurrency strategy for the second-level cache that doesn't preserve repeatable read semantics (for example, the read-write and especially the nonstrict-read-write strategies, both discussed later in this chapter), the choice for a default isolation level is easy: You can't achieve repeatable read anyway, so there's no point slowing down the database. On the other hand, you might not be using second-level caching for critical classes, or you might be using a fully transactional cache that provides repeatable read isolation. Should you use repeatable read in this case? You can if you like, but it's probably not worth the performance cost.

Setting the transaction isolation level allows you to choose a good default locking strategy for all your database transactions. How do you set the isolation level?

5.1.6 Setting an isolation level

Every JDBC connection to a database uses the database's default isolation level, usually read committed or repeatable read. This default can be changed in the database configuration. You may also set the transaction isolation for JDBC connections using a Hibernate configuration option:

```
hibernate.connection.isolation = 4
```

Hibernate will then set this isolation level on every JDBC connection obtained from a connection pool before starting a transaction. The sensible values for this option are as follows (you can also find them as constants in `java.sql.Connection`):

- 1—Read uncommitted isolation
- 2—Read committed isolation
- 4—Repeatable read isolation
- 8—Serializable isolation

Note that Hibernate never changes the isolation level of connections obtained from a datasource provided by the application server in a managed environment. You may change the default isolation using the configuration of your application server.

As you can see, setting the isolation level is a global option that affects all connections and transactions. From time to time, it's useful to specify a more restrictive lock for a particular transaction. Hibernate allows you to explicitly specify the use of a *pessimistic* lock.

5.1.7 Using pessimistic locking

Locking is a mechanism that prevents concurrent access to a particular item of data. When one transaction holds a lock on an item, no concurrent transaction can read and/or modify this item. A lock might be just a momentary lock, held while the item is being read, or it might be held until the completion of the transaction. A *pessimistic lock* is a lock that is acquired when an item of data is read and that is held until transaction completion.

In read-committed mode (our preferred transaction isolation level), the database never acquires pessimistic locks unless explicitly requested by the application. Usually, pessimistic locks aren't the most scalable approach to concurrency. However, in certain special circumstances, they may be used to prevent database-level deadlocks, which result in transaction failure. Some databases (Oracle and PostgreSQL, for example) provide the SQL SELECT. . . FOR UPDATE syntax to allow the use of explicit pessimistic locks. You can check the Hibernate Dialects to find out if your database supports this feature. If your database isn't supported, Hibernate will always execute a normal SELECT without the FOR UPDATE clause.

The Hibernate LockMode class lets you request a pessimistic lock on a particular item. In addition, you can use the LockMode to force Hibernate to bypass the cache layer or to execute a simple version check. You'll see the benefit of these operations when we discuss versioning and caching.

Let's see how to use LockMode. If you have a transaction that looks like this

```
Transaction tx = session.beginTransaction();
Category cat = (Category) session.get(Category.class, catId);
cat.setName("New Name");
tx.commit();
```

then you can obtain a pessimistic lock as follows:

```
Transaction tx = session.beginTransaction();
Category cat =
    (Category) session.get(Category.class, catId, LockMode.UPGRADE);
cat.setName("New Name");
tx.commit();
```

With this mode, Hibernate will load the Category using a SELECT. . . FOR UPDATE, thus locking the retrieved rows in the database until they're released when the transaction ends.

Hibernate defines several lock modes:

- LockMode.NONE—Don't go to the database unless the object isn't in either cache.

- LockMode.READ—Bypass both levels of the cache, and perform a version check to verify that the object in memory is the same version that currently exists in the database.

- LockMode.UPDGRADE—Bypass both levels of the cache, do a version check (if applicable), and obtain a database-level pessimistic upgrade lock, if that is supported.

- LockMode.UPDGRADE_NOWAIT—The same as UPGRADE, but use a SELECT. . . FOR UPDATE NOWAIT on Oracle. This disables waiting for concurrent lock releases, thus throwing a locking exception immediately if the lock can't be obtained.

- LockMode.WRITE—Is obtained automatically when Hibernate has written to a row in the current transaction (this is an internal mode; you can't specify it explicitly).

By default, load() and get() use LockMode.NONE. LockMode.READ is most useful with Session.lock() and a detached object. For example:

```
Item item = ... ;
Bid bid = new Bid();
item.addBid(bid);
...
Transaction tx = session.beginTransaction();
session.lock(item, LockMode.READ);
tx.commit();
```

This code performs a version check on the detached Item instance to verify that the database row wasn't updated by another transaction since it was retrieved, before saving the new Bid by cascade (assuming that the association from Item to Bid has cascading enabled).

By specifying an explicit LockMode other than LockMode.NONE, you force Hibernate to bypass both levels of the cache and go all the way to the database. We think that most of the time caching is more useful than pessimistic locking, so we don't use an explicit LockMode unless we really need it. Our advice is that if you have a professional DBA on your project, let the DBA decide which transactions require pessimistic locking once the application is up and running. This decision should depend on subtle details of the interactions between different transactions and can't be guessed up front.

Let's consider another aspect of concurrent data access. We think that most Java developers are familiar with the notion of a database transaction and that is what they usually mean by *transaction*. In this book, we consider this to be a *fine-grained* transaction, but we also consider a more coarse-grained notion. Our coarse-grained transactions will correspond to what *the user of the application* considers a single unit of work. Why should this be any different than the fine-grained database transaction?

The database *isolates* the effects of concurrent database transactions. It should appear to the application that each transaction is the only transaction currently accessing the database (even when it isn't). Isolation is expensive. The database must allocate significant resources to each transaction for the duration of the transaction. In particular, as we've discussed, many databases lock rows that have been read or updated by a transaction, preventing access by any other transaction, until the first transaction completes. In highly concurrent systems, these locks can prevent scalability if they're held for longer than absolutely necessary. For this reason, you shouldn't hold the database transaction (or even the JDBC connection) open while waiting for user input. (All this, of course, also applies to a Hibernate `Transaction`, since it's merely an adaptor to the underlying database transaction mechanism.)

If you want to handle long user think time while still taking advantage of the ACID attributes of transactions, simple database transactions aren't sufficient. You need a new concept, long-running *application transactions*.

5.2 *Working with application transactions*

Business processes, which might be considered a single unit of work *from the point of view of the user*, necessarily span multiple user client requests. This is especially true when a user makes a decision to update data on the basis of the current state of that data.

In an extreme example, suppose you collect data entered by the user on multiple screens, perhaps using wizard-style step-by-step navigation. You must read and write related items of data in several requests (hence several database transactions) until the user clicks Finish on the last screen. Throughout this process, the data must remain consistent and the user must be informed of any change to the data made by any concurrent transaction. We call this coarse-grained transaction concept an *application transaction*, a broader notion of the unit of work.

We'll now restate this definition more precisely. Most web applications include several examples of the following type of functionality:

1   Data is retrieved and displayed on the screen in a first database transaction.

2   The user has an opportunity to view and then modify the data, outside of any database transaction.

3   The modifications are made persistent in a second database transaction.

In more complicated applications, there may be several such interactions with the user before a particular business process is complete. This leads to the notion of an application transaction (sometimes called a *long transaction, user transaction* or *business transaction*). We prefer application transaction or user transaction, since these terms are less vague and emphasize the transaction aspect from the point of view of the user.

Since you can't rely on the database to enforce isolation (or even atomicity) of concurrent application transactions, isolation becomes a concern of the application itself—perhaps even a concern of the user.

Let's discuss application transactions with an example.

In our CaveatEmptor application, both the user who posted a comment and any system administrator can open an Edit Comment screen to delete or edit the text of a comment. Suppose two different administrators open the edit screen to view the same comment simultaneously. Both edit the comment text and submit their changes. At this point, we have three ways to handle the concurrent attempts to write to the database:

- *Last commit wins*—Both updates succeed, and the second update overwrites the changes of the first. No error message is shown.

- *First commit wins*—The first modification is persisted, and the user submitting the second change receives an error message. The user must restart the business process by retrieving the updated comment. This option is often called *optimistic locking*.

- *Merge conflicting updates*—The first modification is persisted, and the second modification may be applied selectively by the user.

The first option, last commit wins, is problematic; the second user overwrites the changes of the first user without seeing the changes made by the first user or even knowing that they existed. In our example, this probably wouldn't matter, but it would be unacceptable for some other kinds of data. The second and third options are usually acceptable for most kinds of data. From our point of view, the third option is just a variation of the second—instead of showing an error message, we show the message and then allow the user to manually merge changes. There is no single best solution. You must investigate your own business requirements to decide among these three options.

The first option happens by default if you don't do anything special in your application; so, this option requires no work on your part (or on the part of Hibernate). You'll have two database transactions: The comment data is loaded in the first database transaction, and the second database transaction saves the changes without checking for updates that could have happened in between.

On the other hand, Hibernate can help you implement the second and third strategies, using *managed versioning* for *optimistic locking*.

5.2.1 Using managed versioning

Managed versioning relies on either a version number that is incremented or a timestamp that is updated to the current time, every time an object is modified. For Hibernate managed versioning, we must add a new property to our Comment class and map it as a version number using the `<version>` tag. First, let's look at the changes to the `Comment` class:

```
public class Comment {
    ...
    private int version;
    ...
    void setVersion(int version) {
        this.version = version;
    }
    int getVersion() {
        return version;
    }
}
```

You can also use a public scope for the setter and getter methods. The `<version>` property mapping must come immediately after the identifier property mapping in the mapping file for the `Comment` class:

```
<class name="Comment" table="COMMENTS">
    <id ...
    <version name="version" column="VERSION"/>
    ...
</class>
```

The version number is just a counter value—it doesn't have any useful semantic value. Some people prefer to use a timestamp instead:

```
public class Comment {
    ...
    private Date lastUpdatedDatetime;
    ...
    void setLastUpdatedDatetime(Date lastUpdatedDatetime) {
        this.lastUpdatedDatetime = lastUpdatedDatetime;
    }
    public Date getLastUpdatedDatetime() {
        return lastUpdatedDatetime;
    }
}
<class name="Comment" table="COMMENTS">
    <id ...../>
    <timestamp name="lastUpdatedDatetime" column="LAST_UPDATED"/>
    ...
</class>
```

In theory, a timestamp is slightly less safe, since two concurrent transactions might both load and update the same item all in the same millisecond; in practice, this is unlikely to occur. However, we recommend that new projects use a numeric version and not a timestamp.

You don't need to set the value of the version or timestamp property yourself; Hibernate will initialize the value when you first save a `Comment`, and increment or reset it whenever the object is modified.

FAQ   *Is the version of the parent updated if a child is modified?*   For example, if a single bid in the collection `bids` of an `Item` is modified, is the version number of the `Item` also increased by one or not? The answer to that and similar questions is simple: Hibernate will increment the version number whenever an object is dirty. This includes all dirty properties, whether they're single-valued or collections. Think about the relationship between `Item` and `Bid`: If a `Bid` is modified, the version of the related `Item` isn't incremented. If we add or remove a `Bid` from the collection of bids, the version of the `Item` will be updated. (Of course, we would make `Bid` an immutable class, since it doesn't make sense to modify bids.)

Whenever Hibernate updates a comment, it uses the version column in the SQL `WHERE` clause:

```
update COMMENTS set COMMENT_TEXT='New comment text', VERSION=3
where COMMENT_ID=123 and VERSION=2
```

If another application transaction would have updated the same item since it was read by the current application transaction, the `VERSION` column would not contain the value 2, and the row would not be updated. Hibernate would check the row count returned by the JDBC driver—which in this case would be the number of rows updated, zero—and throw a `StaleObjectStateException`.

Using this exception, we might show the user of the second application transaction an error message ("You have been working with stale data because another user modified it!") and let the *first commit win*. Alternatively, we could catch the exception and show the second user a new screen, allowing the user to manually *merge changes* between the two versions.

As you can see, Hibernate makes it easy to use managed versioning to implement optimistic locking. Can you use optimistic locking and pessimistic locking together, or do you have to make a decision for one? And why is it called *optimistic*?

An optimistic approach always assumes that everything will be OK and that conflicting data modifications are rare. Instead of being pessimistic and blocking concurrent data access immediately (and forcing execution to be serialized), optimistic concurrency control will only block at the end of a unit of work and raise an error.

Both strategies have their place and uses, of course. Multiuser applications usually default to optimistic concurrency control and use pessimistic locks when appropriate. Note that the duration of a pessimistic lock in Hibernate is a single database transaction! This means you can't use an exclusive lock to block concurrent access longer than a single database transaction. We consider this a good thing, because the only solution would be an extremely expensive lock held in memory (or a so called *lock table* in the database) for the duration of, for example, an application transaction. This is almost always a performance bottleneck; every data access involves additional lock checks to a synchronized lock manager. You may, if absolutely required in your particular application, implement a simple long pessimistic lock yourself, using Hibernate to manage the lock table. Patterns for this can be found on the Hibernate website; however, we definitely don't recommend this approach. You have to carefully examine the performance implications of this exceptional case.

Let's get back to application transactions. You now know the basics of managed versioning and optimistic locking. In previous chapters (and earlier in this chapter), we have talked about the Hibernate `Session` as not being the same as a transaction. In fact, a `Session` has a flexible scope, and you can use it in different ways with database and application transactions. This means that the *granularity* of a `Session` is flexible; it can be any unit of work you want it to be.

5.2.2 *Granularity of a Session*

To understand how you can use the Hibernate `Session`, let's consider its relationship with transactions. Previously, we have discussed two related concepts:

- The scope of object identity (see section 4.1.4)
- The granularity of database and application transactions

The Hibernate `Session` instance defines the scope of object identity. The Hibernate `Transaction` instance matches the scope of a database transaction.

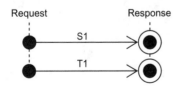

Figure 5.2 Using one to one `Session` and `Transaction` per request/response cycle

What is the relationship between a `Session` and application transaction? Let's start this discussion with the most common usage of the `Session`.

Usually, we open a new `Session` for each client request (for example, a web browser request) and begin a new `Transaction`. After executing the business logic, we commit the database transaction and close the `Session`, before sending the response to the client (see figure 5.2).

The session (S1) and the database transaction (T1) therefore have the same granularity. If you're not working with the concept of application transactions, this simple approach is all you need in your application. We also like to call this approach *session-per-request*.

If you need a long-running application transaction, you might, thanks to detached objects (and Hibernate's support for optimistic locking as discussed in the previous section), implement it using the same approach (see figure 5.3).

Suppose your application transaction spans two client request/response cycles—for example, two HTTP requests in a web application. You could load the interesting objects in a first Session and later reattach them to a new Session after they've been modified by the user. Hibernate will automatically perform a version check. The time between (S1, T1) and (S2, T2) can be "long," as long as your user needs to make his changes. This approach is also known as *session-per-request-with-detached-objects*.

Alternatively, you might prefer to use a single Session that spans multiple requests to implement your application transaction. In this case, you don't need to worry about reattaching detached objects, since the objects remain persistent within the context of the one long-running Session (see figure 5.4). Of course, Hibernate is still responsible for performing optimistic locking.

A Session is serializable and may be safely stored in the servlet HttpSession, for example. The underlying JDBC connection has to be closed, of course, and a new connection must be obtained on a subsequent request. You use the disconnect() and reconnect() methods of the Session interface to release the connection and later obtain a new connection. This approach is known as *session-per-application-transaction* or *long Session*.

Usually, your first choice should be to keep the Hibernate Session open no longer than a single database transaction (session-per-request). Once the initial database transaction is complete, the longer the session remains open, the greater

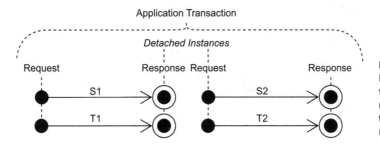

Figure 5.3
Implementing application transactions with multiple Sessions, one for each request/response cycle

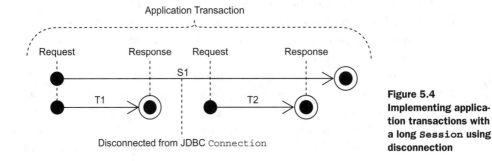

**Figure 5.4
Implementing application transactions with a long Session using disconnection**

the chance that it holds stale data in its cache of persistent objects (the session is the mandatory first-level cache). Certainly, you should never reuse a single session for longer than it takes to complete a single application transaction.

The question of application transactions and the scope of the Session is a matter of application design. We discuss implementation strategies with examples in chapter 8, section 8.2, "Implementing application transactions."

Finally, there is an important issue you might be concerned about. If you work with a legacy database schema, you probably can't add version or timestamp columns for Hibernate's optimistic locking.

5.2.3 *Other ways to implement optimistic locking*

If you don't have version or timestamp columns, Hibernate can still perform optimistic locking, but only for objects that are retrieved and modified in the same Session. If you need optimistic locking for detached objects, you *must* use a version number or timestamp.

This alternative implementation of optimistic locking checks the current database state against the unmodified values of persistent properties at the time the object was retrieved (or the last time the session was flushed). You can enable this functionality by setting the optimistic-lock attribute on the class mapping:

```
<class name="Comment" table="COMMENT" optimistic-lock="all">
    <id ...../>
    ...
</class>
```

Now, Hibernate will include all properties in the WHERE clause:

```
update COMMENTS set COMMENT_TEXT='New text'
where COMMENT_ID=123
and    COMMENT_TEXT='Old Text'
and    RATING=5
and    ITEM_ID=3
and    FROM_USER_ID=45
```

Alternatively, Hibernate will include only the modified properties (only `COMMENT_TEXT`, in this example) if you set `optimistic-lock="dirty"`. (Note that this setting also requires you to set the class mapping to `dynamic-update="true"`.)

We don't recommend this approach; it's slower, more complex, and less reliable than version numbers and doesn't work if your application transaction spans multiple sessions (which is the case if you're using detached objects).

We'll now again switch perspective and consider a new Hibernate aspect. We already mentioned the close relationship between transactions and caching in the introduction of this chapter. The fundamentals of transactions and locking, and also the session granularity concepts, are of central importance when we consider caching data in the application tier.

5.3 Caching theory and practice

A major justification for our claim that applications using an object/relational persistence layer are expected to outperform applications built using direct JDBC is the potential for caching. Although we'll argue passionately that most applications should be designed so that it's possible to achieve acceptable performance *without* the use of a cache, there is no doubt that for some kinds of applications—especially read-mostly applications or applications that keep significant metadata in the database—caching can have an enormous impact on performance.

We start our exploration of caching with some background information. This includes an explanation of the different caching and identity scopes and the impact of caching on transaction isolation. This information and these rules can be applied to caching in general; they aren't only valid for Hibernate applications. This discussion gives you the background to understand why the Hibernate caching system is like it is. We'll then introduce the Hibernate caching system and show you how to enable, tune, and manage the first- and second-level Hibernate cache. We recommend that you carefully study the fundamentals laid out in this section before you start using the cache. Without the basics, you might quickly run into hard-to-debug concurrency problems and risk the integrity of your data.

A cache keeps a representation of current database state close to the application, either in memory or on disk of the application server machine. The cache is a local copy of the data. The cache sits between your application and the database. The cache may be used to avoid a database hit whenever

- The application performs a lookup by identifier (primary key)
- The persistence layer resolves an association lazily

It's also possible to cache the results of queries. As you'll see in chapter 7, the performance gain of caching query results is minimal in most cases, so this functionality is used much less often.

Before we look at how Hibernate's cache works, let's walk through the different caching options and see how they're related to identity and concurrency.

5.3.1 Caching strategies and scopes

Caching is such a fundamental concept in object/relational persistence that you can't understand the performance, scalability, or transactional semantics of an ORM implementation without first knowing what kind of caching strategy (or strategies) it uses. There are three main types of cache:

- *Transaction scope*—Attached to the current unit of work, which may be an actual database transaction or an application transaction. It's valid and used as long as the unit of work runs. Every unit of work has its own cache.

- *Process scope*—Shared among many (possibly concurrent) units of work or transactions. This means that data in the process scope cache is accessed by concurrently running transactions, obviously with implications on transaction isolation. A process scope cache might store the persistent instances themselves in the cache, or it might store just their persistent state in a disassembled format.

- *Cluster scope*—Shared among multiple processes on the same machine or among multiple machines in a cluster. It requires some kind of *remote process communication* to maintain consistency. Caching information has to be replicated to all nodes in the cluster. For many (not all) applications, cluster scope caching is of dubious value, since reading and updating the cache might be only marginally faster than going straight to the database.

Persistence layers might provide multiple levels of caching. For example, a *cache miss* (a cache lookup for an item that isn't contained in the cache) at the transaction scope might be followed by a lookup at the process scope. A database request would be the last resort.

The type of cache used by a persistence layer affects the scope of object identity (the relationship between Java object identity and database identity).

Caching and object identity

Consider a transaction scope cache. It seems natural that this cache is also used as the identity scope of persistent objects. This means the transaction scope cache implements identity handling: two lookups for objects using the same database identifier return the same actual Java instance in a particular unit of work. A transaction scope cache is therefore ideal if a persistence mechanism also provides transaction-scoped object identity.

Persistence mechanisms with a process scope cache might choose to implement process-scoped identity. In this case, object identity is equivalent to database identity for the whole process. Two lookups using the same database identifier in two concurrently running units of work result in the same Java instance. Alternatively, objects retrieved from the process scope cache might be returned *by value*. The cache contains tuples of data, not persistent instances. In this case, each unit of work retrieves its own copy of the state (a tuple) and constructs its own persistent instance. The scope of the cache and the scope of object identity are no longer the same.

A cluster scope cache always requires remote communication, and in the case of POJO-oriented persistence solutions like Hibernate, objects are always passed remotely by value. A cluster scope cache can't guarantee identity across a cluster. You have to choose between transaction- or process-scoped object identity.

For typical web or enterprise application architectures, it's most convenient that the scope of object identity be limited to a single unit of work. In other words, it's neither necessary nor desirable to have identical objects in two concurrent threads. There are other kinds of applications (including some desktop or fat-client architectures) where it might be appropriate to use process-scoped object identity. This is particularly true where memory is extremely limited—the memory consumption of a transaction scope cache is proportional to the number of concurrent units of work.

The real downside to process-scoped identity is the need to synchronize access to persistent instances in the cache, resulting in a high likelihood of deadlocks.

Caching and concurrency

Any ORM implementation that allows multiple units of work to share the same persistent instances must provide some form of object-level locking to ensure synchronization of concurrent access. Usually this is implemented using read and write locks (held in memory) together with deadlock detection. Implementations like Hibernate, which maintain a distinct set of instances for each unit of work (transaction-scoped identity), avoid these issues to a great extent.

It's our opinion that locks held in memory are to be avoided, at least for web and enterprise applications where multiuser scalability is an overriding concern. In these applications, it's usually not required to compare object identity across *concurrent* units of work; each user should be completely isolated from other users.

There is quite a strong case for this view when the underlying relational database implements a multiversion concurrency model (Oracle or PostgreSQL, for example). It's somewhat undesirable for the object/relational persistence cache to redefine the transactional semantics or concurrency model of the underlying database.

Let's consider the options again. A transaction scope cache is preferred if you also use transaction-scoped object identity and is the best strategy for highly concurrent multiuser systems. This first-level cache would be mandatory, because it also guarantees identical objects. However, this isn't the only cache you can use. For some data, a second-level cache scoped to the process (or cluster) that returns data by value can be useful. This scenario therefore has two cache layers; you'll later see that Hibernate uses this approach.

Let's discuss which data benefits from second-level caching—or, in other words, when to turn on the process (or cluster) scope second-level cache in addition to the mandatory first-level transaction scope cache.

Caching and transaction isolation

A process or cluster scope cache makes data retrieved from the database in one unit of work visible to another unit of work. This may have some very nasty side-effects upon transaction isolation.

First, if an application has non-exclusive access to the database, process scope caching shouldn't be used, except for data which changes rarely and may be safely refreshed by a cache expiry. This type of data occurs frequently in content management-type applications but rarely in financial applications.

You need to look out for two main scenarios involving non-exclusive access:

- Clustered applications
- Shared legacy data

Any application that is designed to scale must support clustered operation. A process scope cache doesn't maintain consistency between the different caches on different machines in the cluster. In this case, you should use a cluster scope (distributed) cache instead of the process scope cache.

Many Java applications share access to their database with other (legacy) applications. In this case, you shouldn't use any kind of cache beyond a transaction scope cache. There is no way for a cache system to know when the legacy application updated the shared data. Actually, it's *possible* to implement application-level functionality to trigger an invalidation of the process (or cluster) scope cache when changes are made to the database, but we don't know of any standard or best way to achieve this. Certainly, it will never be a built-in feature of Hibernate. If you implement such a solution, you'll most likely be on your own, because it's extremely specific to the environment and products used.

After considering non-exclusive data access, you should establish what isolation level is required for the application data. Not every cache implementation respects all transaction isolation levels, and it's critical to find out what is required. Let's look at data that benefits most from a process (or cluster) scoped cache.

A full ORM solution will let you configure second-level caching separately for each class. Good candidate classes for caching are classes that represent

- Data that changes rarely
- Non-critical data (for example, content-management data)
- Data that is local to the application and not shared

Bad candidates for second-level caching are

- Data that is updated often
- Financial data
- Data that is shared with a legacy application

However, these aren't the only rules we usually apply. Many applications have a number of classes with the following properties:

- A small number of instances
- Each instance referenced by many instances of another class or classes
- Instances rarely (or never) updated

This kind of data is sometimes called *reference data*. Reference data is an excellent candidate for caching with a process or cluster scope, and any application that uses reference data heavily will benefit greatly if that data is cached. You allow the data to be refreshed when the cache timeout period expires.

We've shaped a picture of a dual layer caching system in the previous sections, with a transaction scope first-level and an optional second-level process or cluster scope cache. This is close to the Hibernate caching system.

5.3.2 *The Hibernate cache architecture*

As we said earlier, Hibernate has a two-level cache architecture. The various elements of this system can be seen in figure 5.5.

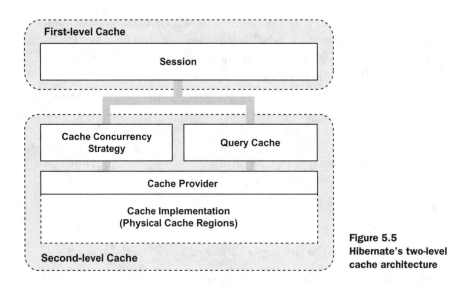

Figure 5.5
Hibernate's two-level cache architecture

The first-level cache is the `Session` itself. A session lifespan corresponds to either a database transaction or an application transaction (as explained earlier in this chapter). We consider the cache associated with the `Session` to be a transaction scope cache. The first-level cache is mandatory and can't be turned off; it also guarantees object identity inside a transaction.

The second-level cache in Hibernate is pluggable and might be scoped to the process or cluster. This is a cache of state (returned by value), not of persistent instances. A cache concurrency strategy defines the transaction isolation details for a particular item of data, whereas the cache provider represents the physical, actual cache implementation. Use of the second-level cache is optional and can be configured on a per-class and per-association basis.

Hibernate also implements a cache for query result sets that integrates closely with the second-level cache. This is an optional feature. We discuss the query cache in chapter 7, since its usage is closely tied to the actual query being executed.

Let's start with using the first-level cache, also called the session cache.

Using the first-level cache

The session cache ensures that when the application requests the same persistent object twice in a particular session, it gets back the same (identical) Java instance. This sometimes helps avoid unnecessary database traffic. More important, it ensures the following:

- The persistence layer isn't vulnerable to stack overflows in the case of circular references in a graph of objects.

- There can never be conflicting representations of the same database row at the end of a database transaction. There is at most a single object representing any database row. All changes made to that object may be safely written to the database (flushed).

- Changes made in a particular unit of work are always immediately visible to all other code executed inside that unit of work.

You don't have to do anything special to enable the session cache. It's always on and, for the reasons shown, can't be turned off.

Whenever you pass an object to save(), update(), or saveOrUpdate(), and whenever you retrieve an object using load(), find(), list(), iterate(), or filter(), that object is added to the session cache. When flush() is subsequently called, the state of that object will be synchronized with the database.

If you don't want this synchronization to occur, or if you're processing a huge number of objects and need to manage memory efficiently, you can use the evict() method of the Session to remove the object and its collections from the first-level cache. There are several scenarios where this can be useful.

Managing the first-level cache

Consider this frequently asked question: "I get an OutOfMemoryException when I try to load 100,000 objects and manipulate all of them. How can I do mass updates with Hibernate?"

It's our view that ORM isn't suitable for mass update (or mass delete) operations. If you have a use case like this, a different strategy is almost always better: call a stored procedure in the database or use direct SQL UPDATE and DELETE statements. Don't transfer all the data to main memory for a simple operation if it can be performed more efficiently by the database. If your application is *mostly* mass operation use cases, ORM isn't the right tool for the job!

If you insist on using Hibernate even for mass operations, you can immediately evict() each object after it has been processed (while iterating through a query result), and thus prevent memory exhaustion.

To completely evict all objects from the session cache, call Session.clear(). We aren't trying to convince you that evicting objects from the first-level cache is a bad thing in general, but that good use cases are rare. Sometimes, using projection and a report query, as discussed in chapter 7, section 7.4.5, "Improving performance with report queries," might be a better solution.

Note that eviction, like save or delete operations, can be automatically applied to associated objects. Hibernate will evict associated instances from the `Session` if the mapping attribute `cascade` is set to `all` or `all-delete-orphan` for a particular association.

When a first-level cache miss occurs, Hibernate tries again with the second-level cache if it's enabled for a particular class or association.

The Hibernate second-level cache

The Hibernate second-level cache has process or cluster scope; all sessions share the same second-level cache. The second-level cache actually has the scope of a `SessionFactory`.

Persistent instances are stored in the second-level cache in a *disassembled* form. Think of disassembly as a process a bit like serialization (the algorithm is much, much faster than Java serialization, however).

The internal implementation of this process/cluster scope cache isn't of much interest; more important is the correct usage of the *cache policies*—that is, caching strategies and physical cache providers.

Different kinds of data require different cache policies: the ratio of reads to writes varies, the size of the database tables varies, and some tables are shared with other external applications. So the second-level cache is configurable at the granularity of an individual class or collection role. This lets you, for example, enable the second-level cache for reference data classes and disable it for classes that represent financial records. The cache policy involves setting the following:

- Whether the second-level cache is enabled
- The Hibernate concurrency strategy
- The cache expiration policies (such as timeout, LRU, memory-sensitive)
- The physical format of the cache (memory, indexed files, cluster-replicated)

Not all classes benefit from caching, so it's extremely important to be able to disable the second-level cache. To repeat, the cache is usually useful only for read-mostly classes. If you have data that is updated more often than it's read, don't enable the second-level cache, even if all other conditions for caching are true! Furthermore, the second-level cache can be dangerous in systems that share the database with other writing applications. As we explained in earlier sections, you must exercise careful judgment here.

The Hibernate second-level cache is set up in two steps. First, you have to decide which *concurrency strategy* to use. After that, you configure cache expiration and physical cache attributes using the *cache provider.*

Built-in concurrency strategies

A concurrency strategy is a mediator; it's responsible for storing items of data in the cache and retrieving them from the cache. This is an important role, because it also defines the transaction isolation semantics for that particular item. You'll have to decide, for each persistent class, which cache concurrency strategy to use, if you want to enable the second-level cache.

There are four built-in concurrency strategies, representing decreasing levels of strictness in terms of transaction isolation:

- *transactional*—Available in a managed environment only. It guarantees full transactional isolation up to *repeatable read*, if required. Use this strategy for read-mostly data where it's critical to prevent stale data in concurrent transactions, in the rare case of an update.

- *read-write*—Maintains *read committed* isolation, using a timestamping mechanism. It's available only in non-clustered environments. Again, use this strategy for read-mostly data where it's critical to prevent stale data in concurrent transactions, in the rare case of an update.

- *nonstrict-read-write*—Makes no guarantee of consistency between the cache and the database. If there is a possibility of concurrent access to the same entity, you should configure a sufficiently short expiry timeout. Otherwise, you may read stale data in the cache. Use this strategy if data rarely changes (many hours, days or even a week) and a small likelihood of stale data isn't of critical concern. Hibernate invalidates the cached element if a modified object is flushed, but this is an asynchronous operation, without any cache locking or guarantee that the retrieved data is the latest version.

- *read-only*—A concurrency strategy suitable for data which never changes. Use it for reference data only.

Note that with decreasing strictness comes increasing performance. You have to carefully evaluate the performance of a clustered cache with full transaction isolation before using it in production. In many cases, you might be better off disabling the second-level cache for a particular class if stale data isn't an option. First benchmark your application with the second-level cache disabled. Then enable it for good candidate classes, one at a time, while continuously testing the performance of your system and evaluating concurrency strategies.

It's possible to define your own concurrency strategy by implementing `net.sf.hibernate.cache.CacheConcurrencyStrategy`, but this is a relatively difficult task and only appropriate for extremely rare cases of optimization.

Your next step after considering the concurrency strategies you'll use for your cache candidate classes is to pick a *cache provider*. The provider is a plugin, the physical implementation of a cache system.

Choosing a cache provider

For now, Hibernate forces you to choose a single cache provider for the whole application. Providers for the following products are built into Hibernate:

- *EHCache* is intended for a simple process scope cache in a single JVM. It can cache in memory or on disk, and it supports the optional Hibernate query result cache.

- *OpenSymphony OSCache* is a library that supports caching to memory and disk in a single JVM, with a rich set of expiration policies and query cache support.

- *SwarmCache* is a cluster cache based on JGroups. It uses clustered invalidation but doesn't support the Hibernate query cache.

- *JBossCache* is a fully transactional replicated clustered cache also based on the JGroups multicast library. The Hibernate query cache is supported, assuming that clocks are synchronized in the cluster.

It's easy to write an adaptor for other products by implementing `net.sf.hibernate.cache.CacheProvider`.

Not every cache provider is compatible with every concurrency strategy. The compatibility matrix in table 5.1 will help you choose an appropriate combination.

Table 5.1 Cache concurrency strategy support

Cache Provider	read-only	nonstrict-read-write	read-write	transactional
EHCache	X	X	X	
OSCache	X	X	X	
SwarmCache	X	X		
JBossCache	X			X

Setting up caching therefore involves two steps:

1 Look at the mapping files for your persistent classes and decide which cache concurrency strategy you'd like to use for each class and each association.

2 Enable your preferred cache provider in the global Hibernate configuration and customize the provider-specific settings.

For example, if you're using OSCache, you should edit `oscache.properties`, or for EHCache, `ehcache.xml` in your classpath.

Let's add caching to our CaveatEmptor `Category` and `Item` classes.

5.3.3 *Caching in practice*

Remember that you don't have to explicitly enable the first-level cache. So, let's declare caching policies and set up cache providers for the second-level cache in our CaveatEmptor application.

The `Category` has a small number of instances and is updated rarely, and instances are shared among many users, so it's a great candidate for use of the second-level cache. We start by adding the mapping element required to tell Hibernate to cache `Category` instances:

```
<class
        name="Category"
        table="CATEGORY">
        <cache usage="read-write"/>

        <id ....
    </class>
```

The `usage="read-write"` attribute tells Hibernate to use a read-write concurrency strategy for the `Category` cache. Hibernate will now try the second-level cache whenever we navigate to a `Category` or when we load a `Category` by identifier.

We have chosen `read-write` instead of `nonstrict-read-write`, since `Category` is a highly concurrent class, shared among many concurrent transactions, and it's clear that a read-committed isolation level is good enough. However, `nonstrict-read-write` would probably be an acceptable alternative, since a small probability of inconsistency between the cache and database is acceptable (the category hierarchy has little financial significance).

This mapping was enough to tell Hibernate to cache all simple `Category` property values but not the state of associated entities or collections. Collections require their own `<cache>` element. For the `items` collection, we'll use a `read-write` concurrency strategy:

```
<class
        name="Category"
        table="CATEGORY">
        <cache usage="read-write"/>

        <id ....

        <set name="items" lazy="true">
          <cache usage="read-write"/>
          <key ....
    </set>

</class>
```

This cache will be used when we call `category.getItems().iterate()`, for example.

Now, a collection cache holds only the identifiers of the associated item instances. So, if we require the instances themselves to be cached, we must enable caching of the `Item` class. A read-write strategy is especially appropriate here. Our users don't want to make decisions (placing a `Bid`) based on possibly stale data. Let's go a step further and consider the collection of `Bids`. A particular `Bid` in the `bids` collection is immutable, but we have to map the collection using `read-write`, since new bids may be made at any time (and it's critical that we be immediately aware of new bids):

```
<class
        name="Item"
        table="ITEM">
        <cache usage="read-write"/>

        <id ....

        <set name="bids" lazy="true">
            <cache usage="read-write"/>
            <key ....
        </set>
    </class>
```

To the immutable `Bid` class, we apply a read-only strategy:

```
<class
        name="Bid"
        table="BID">
        <cache usage="read-only"/>

        <id ....

    </class>
```

Cached `Bid` data is valid indefinitely, because bids are never updated. No cache invalidation is required. (Instances may be evicted by the cache provider—for example, if the maximum number of objects in the cache is reached.)

User is an example of a class that could be cached with the nonstrict-read-write strategy, but we aren't certain that it makes sense to cache users at all.

Let's set the cache provider, expiration policies, and physical properties of our cache. We use *cache regions* to configure class and collection caching individually.

Understanding cache regions

Hibernate keeps different classes/collections in different cache *regions*. A region is a named cache: a handle by which you can reference classes and collections in the cache provider configuration and set the expiration policies applicable to that region.

The name of the region is the class name, in the case of a class cache; or the class name together with the property name, in the case of a collection cache. Category instances are cached in a region named org.hibernate.auction.Category, and the items collection is cached in a region named org.hibernate.auction.Category.items.

You can use the Hibernate configuration property hibernate.cache.region_prefix to specify a root region name for a particular SessionFactory. For example, if the prefix was set to node1, Category would be cached in a region named node1.org.hibernate.auction.Category. This setting is useful if your application includes multiple SessionFactory instances.

Now that you know about cache regions, let's configure the expiry policies for the Category cache. First we'll choose a cache provider. Assume that we're running our auction application in a single JVM, so we don't need a cluster-safe implementation (which would limit our options).

Setting up a local cache provider

We need to set the property that selects a cache provider:

```
hibernate.cache.provider_class=net.sf.ehcache.hibernate.Provider
```

We've chosen EHCache as our second-level cache.

Now, we need to specify the expiry policies for the cache regions. EHCache has its own configuration file, ehcache.xml, in the classpath of the application. The Hibernate distribution comes bundled with example configuration files for all built-in cache providers, so we recommend the usage comments in those files for detailed configuration and assume the defaults for all options we don't mention explicitly.

A cache configuration in ehcache.xml for the Category class might look like this:

```
<cache name="org.hibernate.auction.model.Category"
       maxElementsInMemory="500"
```

```
        eternal="true"
        timeToIdleSeconds="0"
        timeToLiveSeconds="0"
        overflowToDisk="false"
/>
```

There are a small number of `Category` instances, and they're all shared among many concurrent transactions. We therefore disable eviction by timeout by choosing a cache size limit greater than the number of categories in our system and setting `eternal="true"`. There is no need to expire cached data by timeout because the `Category` cache concurrency strategy is read-write and because there are no other applications changing category data. We also disable disk-based caching, since we know that there are few instances of `Category` and so memory consumption won't be a problem.

`Bids`, on the other hand, are small and immutable, but there are many of them; so we must configure EHCache to carefully manage the cache memory consumption. We use both an expiry timeout and a maximum cache size limit:

```
<cache name="org.hibernate.auction.model.Bid"
        maxElementsInMemory="5000"
        eternal="false"
        timeToIdleSeconds="1800"
        timeToLiveSeconds="100000"
        overflowToDisk="false"
/>
```

The `timeToIdleSeconds` attribute defines the expiry time in seconds since an element was last accessed in the cache. We must set a sensible value here, since we don't want unused bids to consume memory. The `timeToLiveSeconds` attribute defines the maximum expiry time in seconds since the element was added to the cache. Since bids are immutable, we don't need them to be removed from the cache if they're being accessed regularly. Hence, `timeToLiveSeconds` is set to a high number.

The result is that cached bids are removed from the cache if they have not been used in the past 30 minutes or if they're the least recently used item when the total size of the cache has reached its maximum limit of 5000 elements.

We've disabled the disk-based cache in this example, since we anticipate that the application server will be deployed to the same machine as the database. If the expected physical architecture were different, we might enable the disk-based cache.

Optimal cache eviction policies are, as you can see, specific to the particular data and particular application. You must consider many external factors, including available memory on the application server machine, expected load on the database machine, network latency, existence of legacy applications, and so on. Some of these factors can't possibly be known at development time, so you'll often need to iteratively test the performance impact of different settings in the production environment or a simulation of it.

This is especially true in a more complex scenario, with a replicated cache deployed to a cluster of server machines.

Setting up a replicated cache

EHCache is an excellent cache provider if your application is deployed on a single virtual machine. However, enterprise applications supporting thousands of concurrent users might require more computing power, and scaling your application might be critical to the success of your project. Hibernate applications are naturally scalable—that is, Hibernate behaves the same whether it's deployed to a single machine or to many machines. The only feature of Hibernate that must be configured specifically for clustered operation is the second-level cache. With a few changes to our cache configuration, we're able to use a clustered caching system.

It isn't necessarily wrong to use a purely local (non–cluster-aware) cache provider in a cluster. Some data—especially immutable data, or data that can be refreshed by cache timeout—doesn't require clustered invalidation and may safely be cached locally, even in a clustered environment. We might be able to have each node in the cluster use a local instance of EHCache, and carefully choose sufficiently short `timeToLiveSeconds` timeouts.

However, if you require strict cache consistency in a clustered environment, you must use a more sophisticated cache provider. We recommend JBossCache, a fully transactional, cluster-safe caching system based on the JGroups multicast library. JBossCache is extremely performant, and cluster communication may be tuned in almost any way imaginable.

We'll now step through a setup of JBossCache for CaveatEmptor for a small cluster of two nodes: node *A* and node *B*. However, we only scratch the surface of the topic; cluster configurations are by nature complex, and many settings depend on the particular scenario.

First, we have to check that all our mapping files use read-only or transactional as a cache concurrency strategy. These are the only strategies supported by the JBossCache provider. A nice trick can help us avoid this search-and-replace problem in the future: Instead of placing `<cache>` elements in our mapping files, we can centralize cache configuration in `hibernate.cfg.xml`:

```
<hibernate-configuration>
    <session-factory>
        <property .../>
        <mapping .../>

        <class-cache
                class="org.hibernate.auction.model.Item"
                usage="transactional"/>

        <collection-cache
                collection="org.hibernate.auction.model.Item.bids"
                usage="transactional"/>

    </session-factory>

</hibernate-configuration>
```

We enabled transactional caching for Item and the bids collection in this example. However, there is one important caveat: at the time of this writing, Hibernate will run into a conflict if we also have <cache> elements in the mapping file for Item. We therefore can't use the global configuration to override the mapping file settings. We recommend that you use the centralized cache configuration from the start, especially if you aren't sure how your application might be deployed. It's also easier to tune cache settings with a centralized configuration.

The next step in our cluster setup is the configuration of the JBossCache provider. First, we enable it in the Hibernate configuration—for example, if we aren't using properties, in hibernate.cfg.xml:

```
<property name="cache.provider_class">
    net.sf.hibernate.cache.TreeCacheProvider
</property>
```

JBossCache has its own configuration file, treecache.xml, which is expected in the classpath of your application. In most scenarios, you need a different configuration for each node in your cluster, and you have to make sure the correct file is copied to the classpath on deployment. Let's look at a typical configuration file. In our two-node cluster (named MyCluster), this file is used on the node *A*:

```
<?xml version="1.0" encoding="UTF-8"?>

<server>

    <classpath codebase="./lib"
                archives="jboss-cache.jar, jgroups.jar"/>

    <mbean code="org.jboss.cache.TreeCache"
            name="jboss.cache:service=TreeCache">

        <depends>jboss:service=Naming</depends>
        <depends>jboss:service=TransactionManager</depends>
```

```xml
<attribute name="ClusterName">MyCluster</attribute>

<attribute name="CacheMode">REPL_SYNC</attribute>
<attribute name="SyncReplTimeout">10000</attribute>
<attribute name="LockAcquisitionTimeout">15000</attribute>
<attribute name="FetchStateOnStartup">true</attribute>

<attribute name="EvictionPolicyClass">
    org.jboss.cache.eviction.LRUPolicy
</attribute>

<attribute name="EvictionPolicyConfig">
  <config>
    <attribute name="wakeUpIntervalSeconds">5</attribute>
    <!-- Cache wide default -->
    <region name="/_default_">
        <attribute name="maxNodes">5000</attribute>
        <attribute name="timeToIdleSeconds">1000</attribute>
    </region>
    <region name="/org/hibernate/auction/model/Category">
        <attribute name="maxNodes">500</attribute>
        <attribute name="timeToIdleSeconds">5000</attribute>
    </region>
    <region name="/org/hibernate/auction/model/Bid">
        <attribute name="maxNodes">5000</attribute>
        <attribute name="timeToIdleSeconds">1800</attribute>
    </region>
  </config>
</attribute>

<attribute name="ClusterConfig">
    <config>
        <UDP bind_addr="192.168.0.1"
            ip_mcast="true"
            loopback="false"/>

        <PING timeout="2000"
            num_initial_members="3"
            up_thread="false"
            down_thread="false"/>

        <FD_SOCK/>

        <pbcast.NAKACK gc_lag="50"
                retransmit_timeout="600,1200,2400,4800"
                max_xmit_size="8192"
                up_thread="false" down_thread="false"/>

        <UNICAST timeout="600,1200,2400"
            window_size="100"
            min_threshold="10"
            down_thread="false"/>

        <pbcast.STABLE desired_avg_gossip="20000"
```

```
                              up_thread="false"
                              down_thread="false"/>

              <FRAG frag_size="8192"
                    down_thread="false"
                    up_thread="false"/>

              <pbcast.GMS join_timeout="5000"
                          join_retry_timeout="2000"
                          shun="true" print_local_addr="true"/>

              <pbcast.STATE_TRANSFER up_thread="true"
                                     down_thread="true"/>

          </config>
        </attribute>

      </mbean>
    </server>
```

Granted, this configuration file might look scary at first, but it's easy to understand. You have to know that it isn't only a configuration file for JBossCache, it's many things in one: a JMX service configuration for JBoss deployment, a configuration file for TreeCache, and a fine-grained configuration of JGroups, the communication library.

Let's ignore the first few lines relating to JBoss deployment (they will be ignored when running JBossCache outside a JBoss application server) and look at the Tree-Cache configuration attributes. These settings define a replicated cache that uses *synchronized* communication. This means that a node sending a replication message waits until all nodes in the group acknowledge the message. This is a good choice for use in a true replicated cache. Asynchronous non-blocking communication might be more appropriate if node *B* was a *hot standby* (a node that immediately takes over if node *A* fails) instead of a live partner. A hot standby is used when the purpose of the cluster is failover rather than throughput. The other configuration attributes are self explanatory, dealing with issues such as timeouts and population of the cache when a new node joins the cluster.

JBossCache provides pluggable eviction policies. In this case, we've selected the built-in policy, org.jboss.cache.eviction.LRUPolicy. We then configure eviction for each cache region, just as we did with EHCache.

Finally, let's look at the JGroups cluster communication configuration. The order of communication protocols is extremely important, so don't change or add lines randomly. Most interesting is the first protocol, <UDP>. We declare a binding of the communication socket to the IP interface 192.168.0.1 (the IP address of node *A* in our network) and enable multicast communication. The `loopback` attribute has to be set to true if node *A* would be a Microsoft Windows machine (it isn't).

The other JGroups attributes are more complex and can be found in the JGroups documentation. They deal with the discovery algorithms used to detect new nodes in a group, failure detection, and in general, the management of the group communication.

So, after changing the cache concurrency strategy of your persistent classes to transactional (or read-only) and creating a `treecache.xml` file for node *A*, you can start up your application and check the log output. We recommend enabling DEBUG logging for the `org.jboss.cache` class; you'll see how JBossCache reads the configuration and node *A* is reported as the first node in the cluster. To deploy node *B*, change the IP address in the configuration file and repeat the deployment procedure with this new file. You should see join messages on both nodes as soon as the cache is started. Your Hibernate application will now use fully transactional caching in a cluster: each element put into the cache will be replicated, and updated elements will be invalidated.

There is one final optional setting to consider. For cluster cache providers, it might be better to set the Hibernate configuration option `hibernate.cache.use_minimal_puts` to `true`. When this setting is enabled, Hibernate will only add an item to the cache after checking to ensure that the item isn't already cached. This strategy performs better if cache writes (puts) are much more expensive than cache reads (gets). This is the case for a replicated cache in a cluster, but not for a local cache (the default is `false`, optimized for a local cache). Whether you're using a cluster or a local cache, you sometimes need to control it programmatically for testing or tuning purposes.

Controlling the second-level cache

Hibernate has some useful methods that will help you test and tune your cache. You may wonder how to disable the second-level cache completely. Hibernate will only load the cache provider and start using the second-level cache if you have any cache declarations in your mapping files or XML configuration file. If you comment them out, the cache is disabled. This is another good reason to prefer centralized cache configuration in `hibernate.cfg.xml`.

Just as the `Session` provides methods for controlling the first-level cache programmatically, so does the `SessionFactory` for the second-level cache.

You can call `evict()` to remove an element from the cache, by specifying the class and the object identifier value:

```
SessionFactory.evict( Category.class, new Long(123) );
```

You can also evict all elements of a certain class or only evict a particular collection role:

```
SessionFactory.evict("org.hibernate.auction.model.Category");
```

You'll rarely need these control mechanisms.

5.4 Summary

This chapter was dedicated to concurrency control and data caching.

You learned that for a single unit of work, either all operations should be completely successful or the whole unit of work should fail (and changes made to persistent state should be rolled back). This led us to the notion of a transaction and the ACID attributes. A transaction is atomic, leaves data in a consistent state, and is isolated from concurrently running transactions, and you have the guarantee that data changed by a transaction is durable.

You use two transaction concepts in Hibernate applications: short database transactions and long-running application transactions. Usually, you use read committed isolation for database transactions, together with optimistic concurrency control (version and timestamp checking) for long application transactions. Hibernate greatly simplifies the implementation of application transactions because it manages version numbers and timestamps for you.

Finally, we discussed the fundamentals of caching, and you learned how to use caching effectively in Hibernate applications.

Hibernate provides a dual-layer caching system with a first-level object cache (the `Session`) and a pluggable second-level data cache. The first-level cache is always active—it's used to resolve circular references in your object graph and to optimize performance in a single unit of work. The (process or cluster scope) second-level cache on the other hand is optional and works best for read-mostly candidate classes. You can configure a non-volatile second-level cache for reference (read-only) data or even a second-level cache with full transaction isolation for critical data. However, you have to carefully examine whether the performance gain is worth the effort. The second-level cache can be customized fine-grained, for each persistent class and even for each collection and class association. Used correctly and thoroughly tested, caching in Hibernate gives you a level of performance that is almost unachievable in a hand-coded data access layer.

Advanced mapping concepts

This chapter covers

- The Hibernate type system
- Custom mapping types
- Collection mappings
- One-to-one and many-to-many associations

In chapter 3, we introduced the most important ORM features provided by Hibernate. You've met basic class and property mappings, inheritance mappings, component mappings, and one-to-many association mappings. We now continue exploring these topics by turning to the more exotic collection and association mappings. At various places, we'll warn you against using a feature without careful consideration. For example, it's usually possible to implement any domain model using only component mappings and one-to-many (occasionally one-to-one) associations. The exotic mapping features should be used with care, perhaps even *avoided* most of the time.

Before we start to talk about the exotic features, you need a more rigorous understanding of Hibernate's type system—particularly of the distinction between entity and value types.

6.1 *Understanding the Hibernate type system*

In chapter 3, section 3.5.1, "Entity and value types," we first distinguished between entity and value types, a central concept of ORM in Java. We must elaborate that distinction in order for you to fully understand the Hibernate type system of entities, value types, and mapping types.

Entities are the coarse-grained classes in a system. You usually define the features of a system in terms of the entities involved: "the user places a bid for an item" is a typical feature definition that mentions three entities. Classes of value type often don't appear in the business requirements—they're usually the fine-grained classes representing strings, numbers, and monetary amounts. Occasionally, value types *do* appear in feature definitions: "the user changes billing address" is one example, assuming that Address is a value type, but this is atypical.

More formally, an *entity* is any class whose instances have their own persistent identity. A *value type* is a class that doesn't define some kind of persistent identity. In practice, this means entity types are classes with identifier properties, and value-type classes depend on an entity.

At runtime, you have a graph of entity instances interleaved with value type instances. The entity instances may be in any of the three persistent lifecycle states: transient, detached, or persistent. We don't consider these lifecycle states to apply to the value type instances.

Therefore, entities have their own lifecycle. The save() and delete() methods of the Hibernate Session interface apply to instances of entity classes, never to value type instances. The persistence lifecycle of a value type instance is completely tied to the lifecycle of the owning entity instance. For example, the username becomes persistent when the user is saved; it never becomes persistent independently of the user.

In Hibernate, a value type may define associations; it's possible to navigate from a value type instance to some other entity. However, it's *never* possible to navigate from the other entity back to the value type instance. Associations *always* point to entities. This means that a value type instance is owned by exactly one entity when it's retrieved from the database—it's never shared.

At the level of the database, any table is considered an entity. However, Hibernate provides certain constructs to hide the existence of a database-level entity from the Java code. For example, a many-to-many association mapping hides the intermediate association table from the application. A collection of strings (more accurately, a collection of value-typed instances) behaves like a value type from the point of view of the application; however, it's mapped to its own table. Although these features seem nice at first (they simplify the Java code), we have over time become suspicious of them. Inevitably, these hidden entities end up needing to be exposed to the application as business requirements evolve. The many-to-many association table, for example, often has additional columns that are added when the application is maturing. We're almost prepared to recommend that every database-level entity be exposed to the application as an entity class. For example, we'd be inclined to model the many-to-many association as two one-to-many associations to an intervening entity class. We'll leave the final decision to you, however, and return to the topic of many-to-many entity associations later in this chapter.

So, entity classes are always mapped to the database using `<class>`, `<subclass>`, and `<joined-subclass>` mapping elements. How are value types mapped?

Consider this mapping of the CaveatEmptor `User` and email address:

```
<property
        name="email"
        column="EMAIL"
        type="string"/>
```

Let's focus on the `type="string"` attribute. In ORM, you have to deal with Java types and SQL data types. The two different type systems must be bridged. This is the job of the Hibernate *mapping types*, and `string` is the name of a built-in Hibernate mapping type.

The `string` mapping type isn't the only one built into Hibernate; Hibernate comes with various mapping types that define default persistence strategies for primitive Java types and certain JDK classes.

6.1.1 Built-in mapping types

Hibernate's built-in mapping types usually share the name of the Java type they map; however, there may be more than one Hibernate mapping type for a particular Java type. Furthermore, the built-in types may *not* be used to perform arbitrary conversions, such as mapping a VARCHAR field value to a Java Integer property value. You may define your own *custom value types* to do this kind of thing, as discussed later in this chapter.

We'll now discuss the basic, date and time, large object, and various other built-in mapping types and show you what Java and SQL data types they handle.

Java primitive mapping types

The basic mapping types in table 6.1 map Java primitive types (or their wrapper types) to appropriate built-in SQL standard types.

Table 6.1 Primitive types

Mapping type	Java type	Standard SQL built-in type
integer	int or java.lang.Integer	INTEGER
long	long or java.lang.Long	BIGINT
short	short or java.lang.Short	SMALLINT
float	float or java.lang.Float	FLOAT
double	double or java.lang.Double	DOUBLE
big_decimal	java.math.BigDecimal	NUMERIC
character	java.lang.String	CHAR(1)
string	java.lang.String	VARCHAR
byte	byte or java.lang.Byte	TINYINT
boolean	boolean or java.lang.Boolean	BIT
yes_no	boolean or java.lang.Boolean	CHAR(1) ('Y' or 'N')
true_false	boolean or java.lang.Boolean	CHAR(1) ('T' or 'F')

You've probably noticed that your database doesn't support some of the SQL types listed in table 6.1. The listed names are ANSI-standard data types. Most database vendors ignore this part of the SQL standard (because their type systems sometimes predate the standard). However, the JDBC driver provides a partial abstraction of vendor-specific SQL data types, allowing Hibernate to work with ANSI-standard types when executing data manipulation language (DML). For database-specific DDL generation, Hibernate translates from the ANSI-standard type to an appropriate vendor-specific type, using the built-in support for specific SQL dialects. (You usually don't have to worry about SQL data types if you're using Hibernate for data access and data schema definition.)

Date and time mapping types

Table 6.2 lists Hibernate types associated with dates, times, and timestamps. In your domain model, you may choose to represent date and time data using either `java.util.Date`, `java.util.Calendar`, or the subclasses of `java.util.Date` defined in the `java.sql` package. This is a matter of taste, and we leave the decision to you—make sure you're consistent, however!

Table 6.2 Date and time types

Mapping type	Java type	Standard SQL built-in type
date	java.util.Date or java.sql.Date	DATE
time	java.util.Date or java.sql.Time	TIME
timestamp	java.util.Date or java.sql.Timestamp	TIMESTAMP
calendar	java.util.Calendar	TIMESTAMP
calendar_date	java.util.Calendar	DATE

Large object mapping types

Table 6.3 lists Hibernate types for handling binary data and large objects. Note that none of these types may be used as the type of an identifier property.

Table 6.3 Binary and large object types

Mapping type	Java type	Standard SQL built-in type
binary	byte[]	VARBINARY (or BLOB)
text	java.lang.String	CLOB
serializable	any Java class that implements java.io.Serializable	VARBINARY (or BLOB)
clob	java.sql.Clob	CLOB
blob	java.sql.Blob	BLOB

`java.sql.Blob` and `java.sql.Clob` are the most efficient way to handle large objects in Java. Unfortunately, an instance of `Blob` or `Clob` is only useable until the JDBC transaction completes. So if your persistent class defines a property of `java.sql.Clob` or `java.sql.Blob` (not a good idea anyway), you'll be restricted in how instances of the class may be used. In particular, you won't be able to use instances of that class as detached objects. Furthermore, many JDBC drivers don't feature working support for `java.sql.Blob` and `java.sql.Clob`. Therefore, it makes more sense to map large objects using the `binary` or `text` mapping type, assuming retrieval of the entire large object into memory isn't a performance killer.

Note you can find up-to-date design patterns and tips for large object usage on the Hibernate website, with tricks for particular platforms.

Various JDK mapping types

Table 6.4 lists Hibernate types for various other Java types of the JDK that may be represented as VARCHARs in the database.

Table 6.4   Other JDK-related types

Mapping type	Java type	Standard SQL built-in type
class	java.lang.Class	VARCHAR
locale	java.util.Locale	VARCHAR
timezone	java.util.TimeZone	VARCHAR
currency	java.util.Currency	VARCHAR

Certainly, `<property>` isn't the only Hibernate mapping element that has a `type` attribute.

6.1.2 Using mapping types

All of the basic mapping types may appear almost anywhere in the Hibernate mapping document, on normal property, identifier property, and other mapping elements.

The `<id>`, `<property>`, `<version>`, `<discriminator>`, `<index>`, and `<element>` elements all define an attribute named `type`. (There are certain limitations on which mapping basic types may function as an identifier or discriminator type, however.)

You can see how useful the built-in mapping types are in this mapping for the `BillingDetails` class:

```
<class name="BillingDetails"
       table="BILLING_DETAILS"
       discriminator-value="null">

    <id name="id" type="long" column="BILLING_DETAILS_ID">
        <generator class="native"/>
    </id>

    <discriminator type="character" column="TYPE"/>

    <property name="number" type="string"/>
    ...
</class>
```

The `BillingDetails` class is mapped as an entity. Its `discriminator`, identifier, and `number` properties are value typed, and we use the built-in Hibernate mapping types to specify the conversion strategy.

It's often not necessary to explicitly specify a built-in mapping type in the XML mapping document. For instance, if you have a property of Java type `java.lang.String`, Hibernate will discover this using reflection and select `string` by default. We can easily simplify the previous mapping example:

```
<class name="BillingDetails"
       table="BILLING_DETAILS"
       discriminator-value="null">

    <id name="id" column="BILLING_DETAILS_ID">
        <generator class="native"/>
    </id>

    <discriminator type="character" column="TYPE"/>

    <property name="number"/>
    ....
</class>
```

The most important case where this approach doesn't work well is a `java.util.Date` property. By default, Hibernate interprets a `Date` as a `timestamp` mapping. You'd need to explicitly specify `type="time"` or `type="date"` if you didn't wish to persist both date and time information.

For each of the built-in mapping types, a constant is defined by the class `net.sf.hibernate.Hibernate`. For example, `Hibernate.STRING` represents the `string` mapping type. These constants are useful for query parameter binding, as discussed in more detail in chapter 7:

```
session.createQuery("from Item i where i.description like :desc")
    .setParameter("desc", desc, Hibernate.STRING)
    .list();
```

These constants are also useful for programmatic manipulation of the Hibernate mapping metamodel, as discussed in chapter 3.

Of course, Hibernate isn't limited to the built-in mapping types. We consider the extensible mapping type system one of the core features and an important aspect that makes Hibernate so flexible.

Creating custom mapping types

Object-oriented languages like Java make it easy to define new types by writing new classes. Indeed, this is a fundamental part of the definition of object orientation. If you were limited to the predefined built-in Hibernate mapping types when declaring properties of persistent classes, you'd lose much of Java's expressiveness. Furthermore, your domain model implementation would be tightly coupled to the physical data model, since new type conversions would be impossible.

Most ORM solutions that we've seen provide some kind of support for user-defined strategies for performing type conversions. These are often called *converters*. For example, the user would be able to create a new strategy for persisting a property of JDK type `Integer` to a `VARCHAR` column. Hibernate provides a similar, much more powerful, feature called *custom mapping types*.

Hibernate provides two user-friendly interfaces that applications may use when defining new mapping types. These interfaces reduce the work involved in defining custom mapping types and insulate the custom type from changes to the Hibernate core. This allows you to easily upgrade Hibernate and keep your existing custom mapping types. You can find many examples of useful Hibernate mapping types on the Hibernate community website.

The first of the programming interfaces is `net.sf.hibernate.UserType`. `UserType` is suitable for most simple cases and even for some more complex problems. Let's use it in a simple scenario.

Our `Bid` class defines an `amount` property; our `Item` class defines an `initialPrice` property, both monetary values. So far, we've only used a simple `BigDecimal` to represent the value, mapped with `big_decimal` to a single `NUMERIC` column.

Suppose we wanted to support multiple currencies in our auction application and that we had to refactor the existing domain model for this (customer-driven) change. One way to implement this change would be to add new properties to `Bid` and `Item`: `amountCurrency` and `initialPriceCurrency`. We would then map these new properties to additional `VARCHAR` columns with the built-in `currency` mapping type. We hope you *never* use this approach!

Creating a UserType

Instead, we should create a MonetaryAmount class that encapsulates both currency and amount. Note that this is a class of the domain model; it doesn't have any dependency on Hibernate interfaces:

```
public class MonetaryAmount implements Serializable {

    private final BigDecimal value;
    private final Currency currency;

    public MonetaryAmount(BigDecimal value, Currency currency) {
        this.value = value;
        this.currency = currency;
    }

    public BigDecimal getValue() { return value; }

    public Currency getCurrency() { return currency; }

    public boolean equals(Object o) { ... }
    public int hashCode() { ...}
}
```

We've made MonetaryAmount an immutable class. This is a good practice in Java. Note that we have to implement equals() and hashCode() to finish the class (there is nothing special to consider here). We use this new MonetaryAmount to replace the BigDecimal of the initialPrice property in Item. Of course, we can, and should use it for all other BigDecimal prices in our persistent classes (such as the Bid.amount) and even in business logic (for example, in the billing system).

Let's map this refactored property of Item to the database. Suppose we're working with a legacy database that contains all monetary amounts in USD. Our application is no longer restricted to a single currency (the point of the refactoring), but it takes time to get the changes done by the database team. We need to convert the amount to USD when we persist the MonetaryAmount and convert it back to USD when we are loading objects.

For this, we create a MonetaryAmountUserType class that implements the Hibernate interface UserType. Our custom mapping type, is shown in listing 6.1.

Listing 6.1 Custom mapping type for monetary amounts in USD

```
package auction.customtypes;

import ...;

public class MonetaryAmountUserType implements UserType {

    private static final int[] SQL_TYPES = {Types.NUMERIC};
```

```
    public int[] sqlTypes() { return SQL_TYPES; }      ❶

    public Class returnedClass() { return MonetaryAmount.class; }      ❷

    public boolean equals(Object x, Object y) {      ❸
        if (x == y) return true;
        if (x == null || y == null) return false;
        return x.equals(y);
            }

    public Object deepCopy(Object value) { return value; }      ❹

    public boolean isMutable() { return false; }      ❺

    public Object nullSafeGet(ResultSet resultSet,      ❻
                              String[] names,
                              Object owner)
            throws HibernateException, SQLException {

        if (resultSet.wasNull()) return null;
        BigDecimal valueInUSD = resultSet.getBigDecimal(names[0]);

        return new MonetaryAmount(valueInUSD, Currency.getInstance)"USD"));
    }

    public void nullSafeSet(PreparedStatement statement,      ❼
                            Object value,
                            int index)
            throws HibernateException, SQLException {
        if (value == null) {
            statement.setNull(index, Types.NUMERIC);
        } else {
            MonetaryAmount anyCurrency = (MonetaryAmount)value;
            MonetaryAmount amountInUSD =
              MonetaryAmount.convert( anyCurrency,
                                      Currency.getInstance("USD") );
            // The convert() method isn't shown in our examples
            statement.setBigDecimal(index, amountInUSD.getValue());
        }
      }
    }
```

❶ The `sqlTypes()` method tells Hibernate what SQL column types to use for DDL schema generation. The type codes are defined by `java.sql.Types`. Notice that this method returns an array of type codes. A `UserType` may map a single property to *multiple* columns, but our legacy data model only has a single `NUMERIC`.

❷ `returnedClass()` tells Hibernate what Java type is mapped by this `UserType`.

❸ The `UserType` is responsible for dirty-checking property values. The `equals()` method compares the current property value to a previous snapshot and determines whether the property is dirty and must by saved to the database.

❹ The `UserType` is also partially responsible for creating the snapshot in the first place. Since `MonetaryAmount` is an immutable class, the `deepCopy()` method returns its argument. In the case of a mutable type, it would need to return a copy of the argument to be used as the snapshot value. This method is also called when an instance of the type is written to or read from the second-level cache.

❺ Hibernate can make some minor performance optimizations for immutable types like this one. The `isMutable()` method tells Hibernate that this type is immutable.

❻ The `nullSafeGet()` method retrieves the property value from the JDBC `ResultSet`. You can also access the `owner` of the component if you need it for the conversion. All database values are in USD, so you have to convert the `MonetaryAmount` returned by this method before you show it to the user.

❼ The `nullSafeSet()` method writes the property value to the JDBC `PreparedStatement`. This method takes whatever currency is set and converts it to a simple `BigDecimal` USD value before saving.

We now map the `initialPrice` property of `Item` as follows:

```
<property name="initialPrice"
          column="INITIAL_PRICE"
          type="auction.customtypes.MonetaryAmountUserType"/>
```

This is the simplest kind of transformation that a `UserType` could perform. *Much more sophisticated things are possible.* A custom mapping type could perform validation; it could read and write data to and from an LDAP directory; it could even retrieve persistent objects from a different Hibernate `Session` for a different database. You're limited mainly by your imagination!

We'd prefer to represent both the amount and currency of our monetary amounts in the database, especially if the schema isn't legacy but can be defined (or updated quickly). We could still use a `UserType`, but then we wouldn't be able to use the amount (or currency) in object queries. The Hibernate query engine (discussed in more detail in the next chapter) wouldn't know anything about the individual properties of `MonetaryAmount`. You can access the properties in your Java code (`MonetaryAmount` is just a regular class of the domain model, after all), but not in Hibernate queries.

Instead, we should use a CompositeUserType if we need the full power of Hibernate queries. This (slightly more complex) interface exposes the properties of our MonetaryAmount to Hibernate.

Creating a CompositeUserType

To demonstrate the flexibility of custom mapping types, we don't change our MonetaryAmount class (and other persistent classes) at all—we change only the custom mapping type, as shown in listing 6.2.

Listing 6.2 Custom mapping type for monetary amounts in new database schemas

```
package auction.customtypes;

import ...;

public class MonetaryAmountCompositeUserType
        implements CompositeUserType {

    public Class returnedClass() { return MonetaryAmount.class; }

    public boolean equals(Object x, Object y) {
        if (x == y) return true;
        if (x == null || y == null) return false;
        return x.equals(y);
    }

    public Object deepCopy(Object value) {
        return value; // MonetaryAmount is immutable
    }

    public boolean isMutable() { return false; }

    public Object nullSafeGet(ResultSet resultSet,
                              String[] names,
                              SessionImplementor session,
                              Object owner)
        throws HibernateException, SQLException {

        if (resultSet.wasNull()) return null;
        BigDecimal value = resultSet.getBigDecimal( names[0] );
        Currency currency =
           Currency.getInstance(resultSet.getString( names[1] ));
        return new MonetaryAmount(value, currency);
    }

    public void nullSafeSet(PreparedStatement statement,
                            Object value,
                            int index,
                            SessionImplementor session)
        throws HibernateException, SQLException {
```

```
        if (value==null) {
            statement.setNull(index, Types.NUMERIC);
            statement.setNull(index+1, Types.VARCHAR);
        } else {
            MonetaryAmount amount = (MonetaryAmount) value;
            String currencyCode =
                        amount.getCurrency().getCurrencyCode();
            statement.setBigDecimal( index, amount.getValue() );
            statement.setString( index+1, currencyCode );
        }
    }
    public String[] getPropertyNames() {   ❶
        return new String[] { "value", "currency" };
    }

    public Type[] getPropertyTypes() {   ❷
        return new Type[] { Hibernate.BIG_DECIMAL, Hibernate.CURRENCY };
    }

    public Object getPropertyValue(Object component,   ❸
                                    int property)
            throws HibernateException {
        MonetaryAmount MonetaryAmount = (MonetaryAmount) component;
        if (property == 0)
            return MonetaryAmount.getValue()();
        else
            return MonetaryAmount.getCurrency();
    }

    public void setPropertyValue(Object component,   ❹
                                    int property,
                                    Object value) throws HibernateException {
        throw new UnsupportedOperationException("Immutable!");
    }

    public Object assemble(Serializable cached,   ❺
                            SessionImplementor session,
                            Object owner)
            throws HibernateException {
        return cached;
    }

    public Serializable disassemble(Object value,   ❻
                                    SessionImplementor session)
            throws HibernateException {
        return (Serializable) value;
    }

}
```

A `CompositeUserType` has its own properties, defined by `getPropertyNames()`.

❷ The properties each have their own type, as defined by `getPropertyTypes()`.

❸ The `getPropertyValue()` method returns the value of an individual property of the `MonetaryAmount`.

❹ Since `MonetaryAmount` is immutable, we can't set property values individually (no problem; this method is optional).

❺ The `assemble()` method is called when an instance of the type is read from the second-level cache.

❻ The `disassemble()` method is called when an instance of the type is written to the second-level cache.

The order of properties must be the same in the `getPropertyNames()`, `getPropertyTypes()`, and `getPropertyValues()` methods. The `initialPrice` property now maps to two columns, so we declare both in the mapping file. The first column stores the value; the second stores the currency of the `MonetaryAmount` (the order of columns must match the order of properties in your type implementation):

```
<property name="initialPrice"
          type="auction.customtypes.MonetaryAmountCompositeUserType">
    <column name="INITIAL_PRICE"/>
    <column name="INITIAL_PRICE_CURRENCY"/>
</property>
```

In a query, we can now refer to the `amount` and `currency` properties of the custom type, even though they don't appear anywhere in the mapping document as individual properties:

```
from Item i
where i.initialPrice.value > 100.0
  and i.initialPrice.currency = 'AUD'
```

We've expanded the buffer between the Java object model and the SQL database schema with our custom composite type. Both representations can now handle changes more robustly.

If implementing custom types seems complex, relax; you rarely need to use a custom mapping type. An alternative way to represent the `MonetaryAmount` class is to use a component mapping, as in section 3.5.2, "Using components." The decision to use a custom mapping type is often a matter of taste.

Let's look at an extremely important, application of custom mapping types. The *type-safe enumeration* design pattern is found in almost all enterprise applications.

Using enumerated types

An *enumerated type* is a common Java idiom where a class has a constant (small) number of immutable instances.

For example, the Comment class (users giving comments about other users in CaveatEmptor) defines a rating. In our current model, we have a simple int property. A typesafe (and much better) way to implement different ratings (after all, we probably don't want arbitrary integer values) is to create a Rating class as follows:

```
package auction;

public class Rating implements Serializable {

    private String name;

    public static final Rating EXCELLENT = new Rating("Excellent");
    public static final Rating OK = new Rating("OK");
    public static final Rating LOW = new Rating("Low");
    private static final Map INSTANCES = new HashMap();

    static {
        INSTANCES.put(EXCELLENT.toString(), EXCELLENT);
        INSTANCES.put(OK.toString(), OK);
        INSTANCES.put(LOW.toString(), LOW);
    }
    private Rating(String name) {
        this.name=name;
    }

    public String toString() {
        return name;
    }

    Object readResolve() {
        return getInstance(name);
    }

    public static Rating getInstance(String name) {
        return (Rating) INSTANCES.get(name);
    }
}
```

We then change the rating property of our Comment class to use this new type. In the database, ratings would be represented as VARCHAR values. Creating a UserType for Rating-valued properties is straightforward:

```
package auction.customtypes;

import ...;
public class RatingUserType implements UserType {

    private static final int[] SQL_TYPES = {Types.VARCHAR};
```

```
public int[] sqlTypes() { return SQL_TYPES; }
public Class returnedClass() { return Rating.class; }
public boolean equals(Object x, Object y) { return x == y; }
public Object deepCopy(Object value) { return value; }
public boolean isMutable() { return false; }

public Object nullSafeGet(ResultSet resultSet,
                          String[] names,
                          Object owner)
        throws HibernateException, SQLException {

  String name = resultSet.getString(names[0]);
  return resultSet.wasNull() ? null : Rating.getInstance(name);
}

public void nullSafeSet(PreparedStatement statement,
                        Object value,
                        int index)
        throws HibernateException, SQLException {

    if (value == null) {
        statement.setNull(index, Types.VARCHAR);
    } else {
        statement.setString(index, value.toString());
    }
  }
}
}
```

This code is basically the same as the `UserType` implemented earlier. The implementation of `nullSafeGet()` and `nullSafeSet()` is again the most interesting part, containing the logic for the conversion.

One problem you might run into is using enumerated types in Hibernate queries. Consider the following query in HQL that retrieves all comments rated "Low":

```
Query q =
    session.createQuery("from Comment c where c.rating = Rating.LOW");
```

This query doesn't work, because Hibernate doesn't know what to do with `Rating.LOW` and will try to use it as a literal. We have to use a `bind` parameter and set the rating value for the comparison dynamically (which is what we need for other reasons most of the time):

```
Query q =
    session.createQuery("from Comment c where c.rating = :rating");
q.setParameter("rating",
               Rating.LOW,
               Hibernate.custom(RatingUserType.class));
```

The last line in this example uses the static helper method `Hibernate.custom()` to convert the custom mapping type to a Hibernate `Type`, a simple way to tell Hibernate about our enumeration mapping and how to deal with the `Rating.LOW` value.

If you use enumerated types in many places in your application, you may want to take this example `UserType` and make it more generic. JDK 1.5 introduces a new language feature for defining enumerated types, and we recommend using a custom mapping type until Hibernate gets native support for JDK 1.5 features. (Note that the Hibernate2 `PersistentEnum` is considered deprecated and shouldn't be used.)

We've now discussed all kinds of Hibernate mapping types: built-in mapping types, user-defined custom types, and even components (chapter 3). They're all considered value types, because they map objects of value type (not entities) to the database. We're now ready to explore *collections* of value typed instances.

6.2 *Mapping collections of value types*

You've already seen collections in the context of entity relationships in chapter 3. In this section, we discuss collections that contain instances of a value type, including collections of components. Along the way, you'll meet some of the more advanced features of Hibernate collection mappings, which can also be used for collections that represent entity associations, as discussed later in this chapter.

6.2.1 *Sets, bags, lists, and maps*

Suppose that our sellers can attach images to `Items`. An image is accessible only via the containing item; it doesn't need to support associations to any other entity in our system. In this case, it isn't unreasonable to model the image as a value type. `Item` would have a collection of images that Hibernate would consider to be part of the `Item`, without its own lifecycle.

We'll run through several ways to implement this behavior using Hibernate. For now, let's assume that the image is stored somewhere on the filesystem and that we keep just the filename in the database. How images are stored and loaded with this approach isn't discussed.

Using a set

The simplest implementation is a `Set` of `String` filenames. We add a collection property to the `Item` class:

```
private Set images = new HashSet();
...
public Set getImages() {
    return this.images;
}
public void setImages(Set images) {
    this.images = images;
}
```

We use the following mapping in the `Item`:

```
<set name="images" lazy="true" table="ITEM_IMAGE">
    <key column="ITEM_ID"/>
    <element type="string" column="FILENAME" not-null="true"/>
</set>
```

The image filenames are stored in a table named ITEM_IMAGE. From the database's point of view, this table is separate from the ITEM table; but Hibernate hides this fact from us, creating the illusion that there is a single entity. The `<key>` element declares the foreign key, ITEM_ID of the parent entity. The `<element>` tag declares this collection as a collection of value type instances: in this case, of strings.

A set can't contain duplicate elements, so the primary key of the ITEM_IMAGE table consists of both columns in the `<set>` declaration: ITEM_ID and FILENAME. See figure 6.1 for a table schema example.

It doesn't seem likely that we would allow the user to attach the same image more than once, but suppose we did. What kind of mapping would be appropriate?

Using a bag

An unordered collection that permits duplicate elements is called a *bag*. Curiously, the Java `Collections` framework doesn't define a `Bag` interface. Hibernate lets you use a `List` in Java to simulate bag behavior; this is consistent with common usage in the Java community. Note, however, that the `List` contract specifies that a list is an ordered collection; Hibernate won't preserve the ordering when persisting a `List` with bag semantics. To use a bag, change the type of `images` in `Item` from `Set` to `List`, probably using `ArrayList` as an implementation. (You could also use a `Collection` as the type of the property.)

ITEM

ITEM_ID	NAME
1	Foo
2	Bar
3	Baz

ITEM_IMAGE

ITEM_ID	FILENAME
1	fooimage1.jpg
1	fooimage2.jpg
2	barimage1.jpg

Figure 6.1
Table structure and example data for a collection of strings

ITEM

ITEM_ID	NAME
1	Foo
2	Bar
3	Baz

ITEM_IMAGE

ITEM_IMAGE_ID	ITEM_ID	FILENAME
1	1	fooimage1.jpg
2	1	fooimage1.jpg
3	2	barimage1.jpg

Figure 6.2
Table structure using a bag with a surrogate primary key

Changing the table definition from the previous section to permit duplicate FILE-NAMEs requires another primary key. An <idbag> mapping lets us attach a surrogate key column to the collection table, much like the synthetic identifiers we use for entity classes:

```
<idbag name="images" lazy="true" table="ITEM_IMAGE">
    <collection-id type="long" column="ITEM_IMAGE_ID">
        <generator class="sequence"/>
    </collection-id>
    <key column="ITEM_ID"/>
    <element type="string" column="FILENAME" not-null="true"/>
</idbag>
```

In this case, the primary key is the generated ITEM_IMAGE_ID. You can see a graphical view of the database tables in figure 6.2.

You might be wondering why the Hibernate mapping was <idbag> and if there is also a <bag> mapping. You'll soon learn more about bags, but a more likely scenario involves preserving the order in which images were attached to the Item. There are a number of good ways to do this; one way is to use a real list instead of a bag.

Using a list

A <list> mapping requires the addition of an *index column* to the database table. The index column defines the position of the element in the collection. Thus, Hibernate can preserve the ordering of the collection elements when retrieving the collection from the database if we map the collection as a <list>:

```
<list name="images" lazy="true" table="ITEM_IMAGE">
    <key column="ITEM_ID"/>
    <index column="POSITION"/>
    <element type="string" column="FILENAME" not-null="true"/>
</list>
```

The primary key consists of the ITEM_ID and POSITION columns. Notice that duplicate elements (FILENAME) are allowed, which is consistent with the semantics of a

ITEM

ITEM_ID	NAME
1	Foo
2	Bar
3	Baz

ITEM_IMAGE

ITEM_ID	POSITION	FILENAME
1	0	fooimage1.jpg
1	1	fooimage1.jpg
1	2	fooimage2.jpg

Figure 6.3
Tables for a list with positional elements

list. (We don't have to change the Item class; the types we used earlier for the bag are the same.)

If the collection is [fooimage1.jpg, fooimage1.jpg, fooimage2.jpg], the POSI-TION column contains the values 0, 1, and 2, as shown in figure 6.3.

Alternatively, we could use a Java array instead of a list. Hibernate supports this usage; indeed, the details of an array mapping are virtually identical to those of a list. However, we very strongly recommend against the use of arrays, since arrays can't be lazily initialized (there is no way to proxy an array at the virtual machine level).

Now, suppose that our images have user-entered names in addition to the file-names. One way to model this in Java would be to use a Map, with names as keys and filenames as values.

Using a map

Mapping a <map> (pardon us) is similar to mapping a list:

```
<map name="images" lazy="true" table="ITEM_IMAGE">
    <key column="ITEM_ID"/>
    <index column="IMAGE_NAME" type="string"/>
    <element type="string" column="FILENAME" not-null="true"/>
</map>
```

The primary key consists of the ITEM_ID and IMAGE_NAME columns. The IMAGE_NAME column stores the keys of the map. Again, duplicate elements are allowed; see fig-ure 6.4 for a graphical view of the tables.

This Map is unordered. What if we want to always sort our map by the name of the image?

ITEM

ITEM_ID	NAME
1	Foo
2	Bar
3	Baz

ITEM_IMAGE

ITEM_ID	IMAGE_NAME	FILENAME
1	Foo Image 1	fooimage1.jpg
1	Foo Image One	fooimage1.jpg
1	Foo Image 2	fooimage2.jpg

Figure 6.4
Tables for a map, using strings as indexes and elements

Sorted and ordered collections

In a startling abuse of the English language, the words *sorted* and *ordered* mean different things when it comes to Hibernate persistent collections. A *sorted collection* is sorted in memory using a Java comparator. An *ordered collection* is ordered at the database level using an SQL query with an order by clause.

Let's make our map of images a sorted map. This is a simple change to the mapping document:

```
<map name="images"
        lazy="true"
        table="ITEM_IMAGE"
        sort="natural">
    <key column="ITEM_ID"/>
    <index column="IMAGE_NAME" type="string"/>
    <element type="string" column="FILENAME" not-null="true"/>
</map>
```

By specifying sort="natural", we tell Hibernate to use a SortedMap, sorting the image names according to the compareTo() method of java.lang.String. If you want some other sorted order—for example, reverse alphabetical order—you can specify the name of a class that implements java.util.Comparator in the sort attribute. For example:

```
<map name="images"
        lazy="true"
        table="ITEM_IMAGE"
        sort="auction.util.comparator.ReverseStringComparator">

    <key column="ITEM_ID"/>
    <index column="IMAGE_NAME" type="string"/>
    <element type="string" column="FILENAME" not-null="true"/>
</map>
```

The behavior of a Hibernate sorted map is identical to java.util.TreeMap. A sorted set (which behaves like java.util.TreeSet) is mapped in a similar way:

```
<set name="images"
        lazy="true"
        table="ITEM_IMAGE"
        sort="natural">
    <key column="ITEM_ID"/>
    <element type="string" column="FILENAME" not-null="true"/>
</set>
```

Bags can't be sorted (there is no TreeBag, unfortunately), nor may lists; the order of list elements is defined by the list index.

Alternatively, you might choose to use an ordered map, using the sorting capabilities of the database instead of (probably less efficient) in-memory sorting:

```
<map name="images"
     lazy="true"
     table="ITEM_IMAGE"
     order-by="IMAGE_NAME asc">
  <key column="ITEM_ID"/>
  <index column="IMAGE_NAME" type="string"/>
  <element type="string" column="FILENAME" not-null="true"/>
</map>
```

The expression in the `order-by` attribute is a fragment of an SQL `order by` clause. In this case, we order by the `IMAGE_NAME` column, in ascending order. You can even write SQL function calls in the `order-by` attribute:

```
<map name="images"
     lazy="true"
     table="ITEM_IMAGE"
     order-by="lower(FILENAME) asc">
  <key column="ITEM_ID"/>
  <index column="IMAGE_NAME" type="string"/>
  <element type="string" column="FILENAME" not-null="true"/>
</map>
```

Notice that you can order by any column of the collection table. Both sets and bags accept the `order-by` attribute; but again, lists don't. This example uses a bag:

```
<idbag name="images"
       lazy="true"
       table="ITEM_IMAGE"
       order-by="ITEM_IMAGE_ID desc">
  <collection-id type="long" column="ITEM_IMAGE_ID">
      <generator class="sequence"/>
  </collection-id>
  <key column="ITEM_ID"/>
  <element type="string" column="FILENAME" not-null="true"/>
</idbag>
```

Under the covers, Hibernate uses a `LinkedHashSet` and a `LinkedHashMap` to implement ordered sets and maps, so this functionality is only available in JDK 1.4 or later. Ordered bags are possible in all JDK versions.

In a real system, it's likely that we'd need to keep more than just the image name and filename; we'd probably need to create an `Image` class for this extra information. We could map `Image` as an entity class; but since we've already concluded that this isn't absolutely necessary, let's see how much further we can get without an `Image` entity (which would require an association mapping and more complex life-cycle handling).

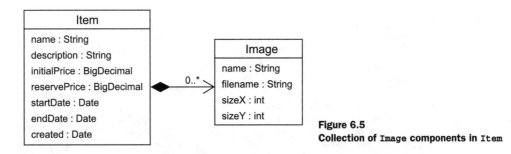

Figure 6.5
Collection of `Image` components in `Item`

In chapter 3, you saw that Hibernate lets you map user-defined classes as components, which are considered to be value types. This is still true even when component instances are collection elements.

Collections of components

Our `Image` class defines the properties `name`, `filename`, `sizeX`, and `sizeY`. It has a single association, with its parent `Item` class, as shown in figure 6.5.

As you can see from the aggregation association style (the black diamond), `Image` is a component of `Item`, and `Item` is the entity that is responsible for the lifecycle of `Image`. References to images aren't shared, so our first choice is a Hibernate component mapping. The multiplicity of the association further declares this association as many-valued—that is, many (or zero) `Images` for the same `Item`.

Writing the component class

First, we implement the `Image` class. This is just a POJO, with nothing special to consider. As you know from chapter 3, component classes don't have an identifier property. However, we must implement `equals()` (and `hashCode()`) to compare the `name`, `filename`, `sizeX`, and `sizeY` properties, to allow Hibernate's dirty checking to function correctly. Strictly speaking, implementing `equals()` and `hashCode()` isn't required for all component classes. However, we recommend it for any component class because the implementation is straightforward and "better safe than sorry" is a good motto.

The `Item` class hasn't changed: it still has a `Set` of images. Of course, the objects in this collection are no longer `Strings`. Let's map this to the database.

Mapping the collection

Collections of components are mapped similarly to other collections of value type instances. The only difference is the use of `<composite-element>` in place of the familiar `<element>` tag. An ordered set of images could be mapped like this:

```
<set name="images"
        lazy="true"
        table="ITEM_IMAGE"
        order-by="IMAGE_NAME asc">
    <key column="ITEM_ID"/>
    <composite-element class="Image">
        <property name="name" column="IMAGE_NAME" not-null="true"/>
        <property name="filename" column="FILENAME" not-null="true"/>
        <property name="sizeX" column="SIZEX" not-null="true"/>
        <property name="sizeY" column="SIZEY" not-null="true"/>
    </composite-element>
</set>
```

This is a set, so the primary key consists of the key column and all element columns: ITEM_ID, IMAGE_NAME, FILENAME, SIZEX, and SIZEY. Since these columns all appear in the primary key, we declare them with not-null="true". (This is clearly a disadvantage of this particular mapping.)

Bidirectional navigation

The association from Item to Image is unidirectional. If the Image class also declared a property named item, holding a reference back to the owning Item, we'd add a <parent> tag to the mapping:

```
<set name="images"
        lazy="true"
        table="ITEM_IMAGE"
        order-by="IMAGE_NAME asc">
    <key column="ITEM_ID"/>
    <composite-element class="Image">
        <parent name="item"/>
        <property name="name" column="IMAGE_NAME" not-null="true"/>
        <property name="filename" column="FILENAME" not-null="true"/>
        <property name="sizeX" column="SIZEX" not-null="true"/>
        <property name="sizeY" column="SIZEY" not-null="true"/>
    </composite-element>
</set>
```

True bidirectional navigation is impossible, however. You can't retrieve an Image independently and then navigate back to its parent Item. This is an important issue: You'll be able to load Image instances by querying for them, but components, like all value types, are retrieved by value. The Image objects won't have a reference to the parent (the property is null). You should use a full parent/child entity association, as described in chapter 3, if you need this kind of functionality.

Still, declaring all properties as not-null is something you should probably avoid. We need a better primary key for the IMAGE table.

Avoiding not-null columns

If a set of Images isn't what we need, other collection styles are possible. For example, an <idbag> offers a surrogate collection key:

```
<idbag name="images"
       lazy="true"
       table="ITEM_IMAGE"
       order-by="IMAGE_NAME asc">
    <collection-id type="long" column="ITEM_IMAGE_ID">
        <generator class="sequence"/>
    </collection-id>
    <key column="ITEM_ID"/>
    <composite-element class="Image">
        <property name="name" column="IMAGE_NAME"/>
        <property name="filename" column="FILENAME" not-null="true"/>
        <property name="sizeX" column="SIZEX"/>
        <property name="sizeY" column="SIZEY"/>
    </composite-element>
</idbag>
```

This time, the primary key is the ITEM_IMAGE_ID column, and it isn't important that we implement equals() and hashCode() (at least, Hibernate doesn't require it). Nor do we need to declare the properties with not-null="true". They may be nullable in the case of an idbag, as shown in figure 6.6.

ITEM_IMAGE

ITEM_IMAGE_ID	ITEM_ID	IMAGE_NAME	FILENAME
1	1	Foo Image 1	fooimage1.jpg
2	1	Foo Image 1	fooimage1.jpg
3	2	Bar Image 1	barimage1.jpg

Figure 6.6
Collection of Image components using a bag with a surrogate key

We should point out that there isn't a great deal of difference between this bag mapping and a standard parent/child entity relationship. The tables are identical, and even the Java code is extremely similar; the choice is mainly a matter of taste. Of course, a parent/child relationship supports shared references to the child entity and true bidirectional navigation.

We could even remove the name property from the Image class and again use the image name as the key of a map:

```
<map name="images"
     lazy="true"
     table="ITEM_IMAGE"
     order-by="IMAGE_NAME asc">
    <key column="ITEM_ID"/>
```

```
<index type="string" column="IMAGE_NAME"/>
<composite-element class="Image">
    <property name="filename" column="FILENAME" not-null="true"/>
    <property name="sizeX" column="SIZEX"/>
    <property name="sizeY" column="SIZEY"/>
</composite-element>
</map>
```

As before, the primary key is composed of IMAGE_ID and IMAGE_NAME.

A composite element class like Image isn't limited to simple properties of basic type like filename. It may contain components, using the `<nested-composite-element>` declaration, and even `<many-to-one>` associations to entities. It may not own collections, however. A composite element with a many-to-one association is useful, and we'll come back to this kind of mapping later in this chapter.

We're finally finished with value types; we'll continue with entity association mapping techniques. The simple parent/child association we mapped in chapter 3 is just one of many possible association mapping styles. Most of them are considered exotic and are rare in practice.

6.3 Mapping entity associations

When we use the word *associations,* we're always referring to relationships between entities. In chapter 3, we demonstrated a unidirectional many-to-one association, made it bidirectional, and finally turned it into a parent/child relationship (one-to-many and many-to-one).

One-to-many associations are easily the most important kind of association. In fact, we go so far as to discourage the use of more exotic association styles when a simple bidirectional many-to-one/one-to-many will do the job. In particular, a many-to-many association may always be represented as two many-to-one associations to an intervening class. This model is usually more easily extensible, so we tend not to use many-to-many associations in our applications.

Armed with this disclaimer, let's investigate Hibernate's rich association mappings starting with one-to-one associations.

6.3.1 One-to-one associations

We argued in chapter 3 that the relationships between User and Address (the user has both a billingAddress and a homeAddress) were best represented using `<component>` mappings. This is usually the simplest way to represent one-to-one relationships, since the lifecycle of one class is almost always dependent on the lifecycle of the other class, and the association is a composition.

But what if we want a dedicated table for `Address` and to map both `User` and `Address` as entities? Then, the classes have a true one-to-one association. In this case, we start with the following mapping for `Address`:

```
<class name="Address" table="ADDRESS">
    <id name="id" column="ADDRESS_ID">
        <generator class="native"/>
    </id>
    <property name="street"/>
    <property name="city"/>
    <property name="zipcode"/>
</class>
```

Note that `Address` now requires an identifier property; it's no longer a component class. There are two different ways to represent a one-to-one association to this `Address` in Hibernate. The first approach adds a foreign key column to the `USER` table.

Using a foreign key association

The easiest way to represent the association from `User` to its `billingAddress` is to use a `<many-to-one>` mapping with a unique constraint on the foreign key. This may surprise you, since *many* doesn't seem to be a good description of either end of a one-to-one association! However, from Hibernate's point of view, there isn't much difference between the two kinds of foreign key associations. So, we add a foreign key column named `BILLING_ADDRESS_ID` to the `USER` table and map it as follows:

```
<many-to-one name="billingAddress"
    class="Address"
    column="BILLING_ADDRESS_ID"
    cascade="save-update"/>
```

Note that we've chosen `save-update` as the cascade style. This means the `Address` will become persistent when we create an association from a persistent `User`. Probably, `cascade="all"` makes sense for this association, since deletion of the `User` should result in deletion of the `Address`. (Remember that `Address` now has its own entity lifecycle.)

Our database schema still allows duplicate values in the `BILLING_ADDRESS_ID` column of the `USER` table, so two users could have a reference to the same address. To make this association truly one-to-one, we add `unique="true"` to the `<many-to-one>` element, constraining the relational model so that there can be only one user per address:

```
<many-to-one name="billingAddress"
    class="Address"
```

```
column="BILLING_ADDRESS_ID"
cascade="all"
unique="true"/>
```

This change adds a unique constraint to the BILLING_ADDRESS_ID column in the DDL generated by Hibernate—resulting in the table structure illustrated by figure 6.7.

But what if we want this association to be navigable from Address to User in Java? From chapter 3, you know how to turn it into a bidirectional one-to-many collection—but we've decided that each Address has just one User, so this can't be the right solution. We don't want a collection of users in the Address class. Instead, we add a property named user (of type User) to the Address class, and map it like so in the mapping of Address:

```
<one-to-one name="user"
    class="User"
    property-ref="billingAddress"/>
```

This mapping tells Hibernate that the user association in Address is the reverse direction of the billingAddress association in User.

In code, we create the association between the two objects as follows:

```
Address address = new Address();
address.setStreet("646 Toorak Rd");
address.setCity("Toorak");
address.setZipcode("3000");

Transaction tx = session.beginTransaction();
User user = (User) session.get(User.class, userId);
address.setUser(user);
user.setBillingAddress(address);
tx.commit();
```

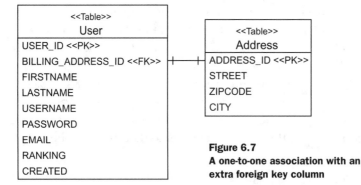

Figure 6.7
A one-to-one association with an extra foreign key column

To finish the mapping, we have to map the `homeAddress` property of `User`. This is easy enough: we add another `<many-to-one>` element to the `User` metadata, mapping a new foreign key column, `HOME_ADDRESS_ID`:

```
<many-to-one name="homeAddress"
    class="Address"
    column="HOME_ADDRESS_ID"
    cascade="save-update"
    unique="true"/>
```

The `USER` table now defines two foreign keys referencing the primary key of the `ADDRESS` table: `HOME_ADDRESS_ID` and `BILLING_ADDRESS_ID`.

Unfortunately, we can't make both the `billingAddress` and `homeAddress` associations bidirectional, since we don't know if a particular address is a billing address or a home address. (We can't decide which property name—`billingAddress` or `homeAddress`—to use for the `property-ref` attribute in the mapping of the user property.) We *could* try making `Address` an abstract class with subclasses `HomeAddress` and `BillingAddress` and mapping the associations to the subclasses. This approach would work, but it's complex and probably not sensible in this case.

Our advice is to avoid defining more than one one-to-one association between any two classes. If you must, leave the associations unidirectional. If you don't have more than one—if there really is exactly one instance of `Address` per `User`—there is an alternative approach to the one we've just shown. Instead of defining a foreign key column in the `USER` table, you can use a *primary key association*.

Using a primary key association

Two tables related by a primary key association share the same primary key values. The primary key of one table is also a foreign key of the other. The main difficulty with this approach is ensuring that associated instances are assigned the same primary key value when the objects are saved. Before we try to solve this problem, let's see how we would map the primary key association.

For a primary key association, *both* ends of the association are mapped using the `<one-to-one>` declaration. This also means that we can no longer map both the billing and home address, only one property. Each row in the `USER` table has a corresponding row in the `ADDRESS` table. Two addresses would require an additional table, and this mapping style therefore wouldn't be adequate. Let's call this single address property `address` and map it with the `User`:

```
<one-to-one name="address"
    class="Address"
    cascade="save-update"/>
```

Next, here's the user of Address:

```
<one-to-one name="user"
    class="User"
    constrained="true"/>
```

The most interesting thing here is the use of constrained="true". It tells Hibernate that there is a foreign key constraint on the primary key of ADDRESS that refers to the primary key of USER.

Now we must ensure that newly saved instances of Address are assigned the same identifier value as their User. We use a special Hibernate identifier-generation strategy called foreign:

```
<class name="Address" table="ADDRESS">
    <id name="id" column="ADDRESS_ID">
        <generator class="foreign">
            <param name="property">user</param>
        </generator>
    </id>
    ...
    <one-to-one name="user"
                class="User"
                constrained="true"/>
</class>
```

The <param> named property of the foreign generator allows us to name a one-to-one association of the Address class—in this case, the user association. The foreign generator inspects the associated object (the User) and uses its identifier as the identifier of the new Address. Look at the table structure in figure 6.8.

The code to create the object association is unchanged for a primary key association; it's the same code we used earlier for the many-to-one mapping style.

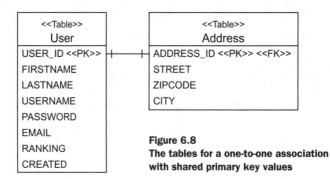

Figure 6.8
The tables for a one-to-one association with shared primary key values

There is now just one remaining entity association multiplicity we haven't discussed: many-to-many.

6.3.2 *Many-to-many associations*

The association between `Category` and `Item` is a many-to-many association, as you can see in figure 6.9.

In a real system, we might not use a many-to-many association. In our experience, there is almost always other information that must be attached to each link between associated instances (for example, the date and time when an item was set in a category), and the best way to represent this information is via an intermediate *association class.* In Hibernate, we could map the association class as an entity and use two one-to-many associations for either side. Perhaps more conveniently, we could also use a composite element class, a technique we'll show you later.

Nevertheless, it's the purpose of this section to implement a real many-to-many entity association. Let's start with a unidirectional example.

A *unidirectional many-to-many association*

If you only require unidirectional navigation, the mapping is straightforward. Unidirectional many-to-many associations are no more difficult than the collections of value type instances we covered previously. For example, if the `Category` has a set of `Items`, we can use this mapping:

```
<set name="items"
     table="CATEGORY_ITEM"
     lazy="true"
     cascade="save-update">
  <key column="CATEGORY_ID"/>
  <many-to-many class="Item" column="ITEM_ID"/>
</set>
```

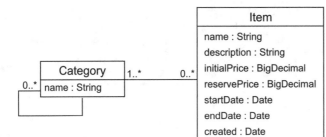

Figure 6.9
A many-to-many valued association between `Category` **and** `Item`

Just like a collection of value type instances, a many-to-many association has its own table, the *link table* or *association table*. In this case, the link table has two columns: the foreign keys of the CATEGORY and ITEM tables. The primary key is composed of both columns. The full table structure is shown in figure 6.10.

We can also use a bag with a separate primary key column:

```
<idbag name="items"
        table="CATEGORY_ITEM"
        lazy="true"
        cascade="save-update">
    <collection-id type="long" column="CATEGORY_ITEM_ID">
        <generator class="sequence"/>
    </collection-id>
    <key column="CATEGORY_ID"/>
    <many-to-many class="Item" column="ITEM_ID"/>
</idbag>
```

As usual with an <idbag> mapping, the primary key is a surrogate key column, CATEGORY_ITEM_ID. Duplicate links are therefore allowed; the same Item can be added twice to a particular Category. (This doesn't seem to be a very useful feature.)

We can even use an indexed collection (a map or list). The following example uses a list:

```
<list name="items"
        table="CATEGORY_ITEM"
        lazy="true"
        cascade="save-update">
    <key column="CATEGORY_ID"/>
    <index column="DISPLAY_POSITION"/>
    <many-to-many class="Item" column="ITEM_ID"/>
</list>
```

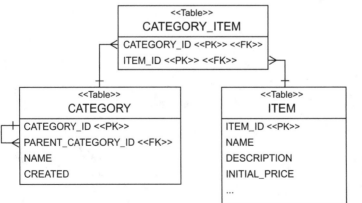

**Figure 6.10
Many-to-many entity
association mapped to
an association table**

The primary key consists of the CATEGORY_ID and DISPLAY_POSITION columns. This mapping guarantees that every Item knows its position in the Category.

Creating an object association is easy:

```
Transaction tx = session.beginTransaction();
Category cat = (Category) session.get(Category.class, categoryId);
Item item = (Item) session.get(Item.class, itemId);

cat.getItems().add(item);

tx.commit();
```

Bidirectional many-to-many associations are slightly more difficult.

A bidirectional many-to-many association

When we mapped a bidirectional one-to-many association in chapter 3 (section 3.7, "Introducing associations"), we explained why one end of the association must be mapped with inverse="true". We encourage you to review that explanation now.

The same principle applies to bidirectional many-to-many associations: each row of the link table is represented by two collection elements, one element at each end of the association. An association between an Item and a Category is represented in memory by the Item instance belonging to the items collection of the Category but also by the Category instance belonging to the categories collection of the Item.

Before we discuss the mapping of this bidirectional case, you must be aware that the code to create the object association also changes:

```
cat.getItems.add(item);
item.getCategories().add(category);
```

As always, a bidirectional association (no matter of what multiplicity) requires that you set both ends of the association.

When you map a bidirectional many-to-many association, you must declare one end of the association using inverse="true" to define which side's state is used to update the link table. You can choose for yourself which end that should be.

Recall this mapping for the items collection from the previous section:

```
<class name="Category" table="CATEGORY">
    ... <
    set name="items"
          table="CATEGORY_ITEM"
          lazy="true"
          cascade="save-update">
      <key column="CATEGORY_ID"/>
```

```
            <many-to-many class="Item" column="ITEM_ID"/>
        </set>
    </class>
```

We can reuse this mapping for the `Category` end of the bidirectional association. We map the `Item` end as follows:

```
<class name="Item" table="ITEM">
    ...
    <set name="categories"
            table="CATEGORY_ITEM"
            lazy="true"
            inverse="true"
            cascade="save-update">
        <key column="ITEM_ID"/>
        <many-to-many class="Category" column="CATEGORY_ID"/>
    </set>
</class>
```

Note the use of `inverse="true"`. Once again, this setting tells Hibernate to ignore changes made to the `categories` collection and use the other end of the association (the `items` collection) as the representation that should be synchronized with the database if we manipulate the association in Java code.

We've chosen `cascade="save-update"` for both ends of the collection; this isn't unreasonable. On the other hand, `cascade="all"`, `cascade="delete"`, and `cascade="all-delete-orphans"` aren't meaningful for many-to-many associations, since an instance with potentially many parents shouldn't be deleted when just one parent is deleted.

What kinds of collections may be used for bidirectional many-to-many associations? Do you need to use the same type of collection at each end? It's reasonable to use, for example, a list at the end not marked `inverse="true"` (or explicitly set false) and a bag at the end that is marked `inverse="true"`.

You can use any of the mappings we've shown for unidirectional many-to-many associations for the noninverse end of the bidirectional association. `<set>`, `<idbag>`, `<list>`, and `<map>` are all possible, and the mappings are identical to those shown previously.

For the inverse end, `<set>` is acceptable, as is the following bag mapping:

```
<class name="Item" table="ITEM">
    ...
    <bag name="categories"
            table="CATEGORY_ITEM"
            lazy="true"
            inverse="true" cascade="save-update">
```

```
            <key column="ITEM_ID"/>
            <many-to-many class="Category" column="CATEGORY_ID"/>
        </bag>
    </class>
```

This is the first time we've shown the `<bag>` declaration: It's similar to an `<idbag>` mapping, but it doesn't involve a surrogate key column. It lets you use a `List` (with bag semantics) in a persistent class instead of a `Set`. Thus it's preferred if the non-inverse side of a many-to-many association mapping is using a map, list, or bag (which all permit duplicates). Remember that a bag doesn't preserve the order of elements, despite the `List` type in the Java property definition.

No other mappings should be used for the inverse end of a many-to-many association. Indexed collections (lists and maps) can't be used, since Hibernate won't initialize or maintain the index column if `inverse="true"`. This is also true and important to remember for all other association mappings involving collections: an indexed collection (or even arrays) can't be set to `inverse="true"`.

We already frowned at the use of a many-to-many association and suggested the use of composite element mappings as an alternative. Let's see how this works.

Using a collection of components for a many-to-many association

Suppose we need to record some information each time we add an `Item` to a `Category`. For example, we might need to store the date and the name of the user who added the item to this category. We need a Java class to represent this information:

```
public class CategorizedItem {
    private String username;
    private Date dateAdded;
    private Item item;
    private Category category;
    ....
}
```

(We omitted the accessors and `equals()` and `hashCode()` methods, but they would be necessary for this component class.)

We map the `items` collection on `Category` as follows:

```
<set name="items" lazy="true" table="CATEGORY_ITEMS">
    <key column="CATEGORY_ID"/>
    <composite-element class="CategorizedItem">
        <parent name="category"/>
        <many-to-one name="item"
                    class="Item"
                    column="ITEM_ID"
                    not-null="true"/>
        <property name="username" column="USERNAME" not-null="true"/>
```

```
            <property name="dateAdded" column="DATE_ADDED" not-null="true"/>
        </composite-element>
    </set>
```

We use the `<many-to-one>` element to declare the association to `Item`, and we use the `<property>` mappings to declare the extra association-related information. The link table now has four columns: `CATEGORY_ID`, `ITEM_ID`, `USERNAME`, and `DATE_ADDED`. The columns of the `CategorizedItem` properties should never be `null`: otherwise we can't identify a single link entry, because they're all part of the table's primary key. You can see the table structure in figure 6.11.

In fact, rather than mapping just the `username`, we might like to keep an actual reference to the `User` object. In this case, we have the following *ternary association* mapping:

```
<set name="items" lazy="true" table="CATEGORY_ITEMS">
    <key column="CATEGORY_ID"/>
    <composite-element class="CategorizedItem">
        <parent name="category"/>
        <many-to-one name="item"
                     class="Item"
                     column="ITEM_ID"
                     not-null="true"/>
        <many-to-one name="user"
                     class="User"
                     column="USER_ID"
                     not-null="true"/>
        <property name="dateAdded" column="DATE_ADDED" not-null="true"/>
    </composite-element>
</set>
```

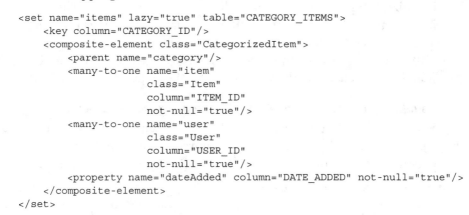

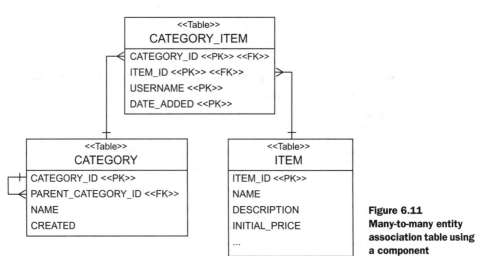

Figure 6.11
Many-to-many entity association table using a component

This is a fairly exotic beast! If you find yourself with a mapping like this, you should ask whether it might be better to map `CategorizedItem` as an entity class and use two one-to-many associations. Furthermore, there is no way to make this mapping bidirectional: a component (such as `CategorizedItem`) can't, by definition, have shared references. You can't navigate from `Item` to `CategorizedItem`.

We talked about some limitations of many-to-many mappings in the previous section. One of them, the restriction to nonindexed collections for the inverse end of an association, also applies to one-to-many associations, if they're bidirectional. Let's take a closer look at one-to-many and many-to-one again, to refresh your memory and elaborate on what we discussed in chapter 3.

One-to-many associations

You already know most of what you need to know about one-to-many associations from chapter 3. We mapped a typical parent/child relationship between two entity persistent classes, `Item` and `Bid`. This was a bidirectional association, using a `<one-to-many>` and a `<many-to-one>` mapping. The "many" end of this association was implemented in Java with a `Set`; we had a collection of bids in the `Item` class. Let's reconsider this mapping and walk through some special cases.

Using a bag with set semantics

For example, if you absolutely need a `List` of children in your parent Java class, it's possible to use a `<bag>` mapping in place of a set. In our example, first we have to replace the type of the `bids` collection in the `Item` persistent class with a `List`. The mapping for the association between `Item` and `Bid` is then left essentially unchanged:

```
<class
    name="Bid"
    table="BID">
    ...
    <many-to-one
        name="item"
        column="ITEM_ID"
        class="Item"
        not-null="true"/>

</class>

<class
    name="Item"
    table="ITEM">
    ...
    <bag
        name="bids"
```

```
            inverse="true"
            cascade="all-delete-orphan">

            <key column="ITEM_ID"/>
            <one-to-many class="Bid"/>
        </bag>

    </class>
```

We renamed the `<set>` element to `<bag>`, making no other changes. Note, however, that this change isn't useful: the underlying table structure doesn't support duplicates, so the `<bag>` mapping results in an association with set semantics. Some tastes prefer the use of `Lists` even for associations with set semantics, but ours doesn't, so we recommend using `<set>` mappings for typical parent/child relationships.

The obvious (and wrong) solution would be to use a real `<list>` mapping for the `bids` with an additional column holding the position of the elements. Remember the Hibernate limitation we introduced earlier in this chapter: you can't use indexed collections on an *inverse* side of an association. The `inverse="true"` side of the association isn't considered when Hibernate saves the object state, so Hibernate will ignore the index of the elements and not update the position column.

However, if your parent/child relationship will only be unidirectional (navigation is only possible from parent to child), you could even use an indexed collection type (because the "many" end would no longer be inverse). Good uses for unidirectional one-to-many associations are uncommon in practice, and we don't have one in our auction application. You may remember that we started with the `Item` and `Bid` mapping in chapter 3, making it first unidirectional, but we quickly introduced the other side of the mapping.

Let's find a different example to implement a unidirectional one-to-many association with an indexed collection.

Unidirectional mapping

For the sake of this section, we now suppose that the association between `Category` and `Item` is to be remodeled as a one-to-many association (an item now belongs to at most one category) and further that the `Item` doesn't own a reference to its current category. In Java code, we model this as a collection named `items` in the `Category` class; we don't have to change anything if we don't use an indexed collection. If `items` is implemented as a `Set`, we use the following mapping:

```
<set name="items" lazy="true">
    <key column="CATEGORY_ID"/>
    <one-to-many class="Item"/>
</set>
```

Remember that one-to-many association mappings don't need to declare a table name. Hibernate already knows that the column names in the collection mapping (in this case, only CATEGORY_ID) belong to the ITEM table. The table structure is shown in figure 6.12.

The other side of the association, the Item class, has no mapping reference to Category. We can now also use an indexed collection in the Category—for example, after we change the items property to List:

```
<list name="items" lazy="true">
    <key>
        <column name="CATEGORY_ID" not-null="false"/>
    </key>
    <index column="DISPLAY_POSITION/>
    <one-to-many class="Item"/>
</list>
```

Note the new DISPLAY_POSITION column in the ITEM table, which holds the position of the Item elements in the collection.

There is an important issue to consider, which, in our experience, puzzles many Hibernate users at first. In a unidirectional one-to-many association, the foreign key column CATEGORY_ID in the ITEM must be nullable. An Item could be saved without knowing anything about a Category—it's a stand-alone entity! This is a consistent model and mapping, and you might have to think about it twice if you deal with a not-null foreign key and a parent/child relationship. Using a bidirectional association (and a Set) is the correct solution.

Now that you know about all the association mapping techniques for normal entities, we still have to consider inheritance and associations to the various levels of an inheritance hierarchy. What we really want is *polymorphic* behavior. Let's see how Hibernate deals with polymorphic entity associations.

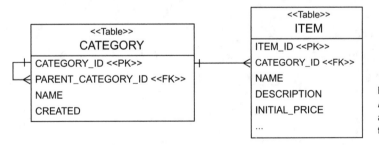

Figure 6.12
A standard one-to-many association using a foreign key column

6.4 *Mapping polymorphic associations*

Polymorphism is a defining feature of object-oriented languages like Java. Support for polymorphic associations and polymorphic queries is a basic feature of an ORM solution like Hibernate. Surprisingly, we've managed to get this far without needing to talk much about polymorphism. Even more surprisingly, there isn't much to say on the topic—polymorphism is so easy to use in Hibernate that we don't need to spend a lot of effort explaining this feature.

To get an overview, we'll first consider a many-to-one association to a class that might have subclasses. In this case, Hibernate guarantees that you can create links to any subclass instance just as you would to instances of the superclass.

6.4.1 *Polymorphic many-to-one associations*

A *polymorphic association* is an association that may refer to instances of a subclass of the class that was explicitly specified in the mapping metadata. For this example, imagine that we don't have many `BillingDetails` per `User`, but only one, as shown in figure 6.13.

We map this association to the abstract class `BillingDetails` as follows:

```
<many-to-one name="billingDetails"
    class="BillingDetails"
    column="BILLING_DETAILS_ID"
    cascade="save-update"/>
```

But since `BillingDetails` is abstract, the association must refer to an instance of one of its subclasses—`CreditCard` or `BankAccount`—at runtime.

All the association mappings we've introduced so far in this chapter support polymorphism. You don't have to do anything special to use polymorphic associations in Hibernate; specify the name of any mapped persistent class in your

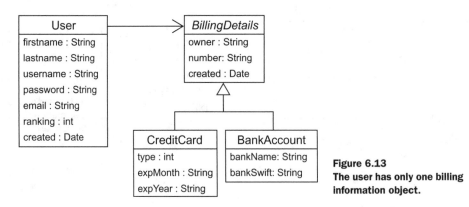

Figure 6.13
The user has only one billing information object.

association mapping (or let Hibernate discover it using reflection); then, if that class declares any `<subclass>` or `<joined-subclass>` elements, the association is naturally polymorphic.

The following code demonstrates the creation of an association to an instance of the `CreditCard` subclass:

```
CreditCard cc = new CreditCard();
cc.setNumber(ccNumber);
cc.setType(ccType);
cc.setExpiryDate(ccExpiryDate);

Session session = sessions.openSession();
Transaction tx = session.beginTransaction();

User user = (User) session.get(User.class, uid);
user.setBillingDetails(cc);

tx.commit();
session.close();
```

Now, when we navigate the association in a second transaction, Hibernate automatically retrieves the `CreditCard` instance:

```
Session session = sessions.openSession();
Transaction tx = session.beginTransaction();

User user = (User) session.get(User.class, uid);
// Invoke the pay() method on the actual subclass
user.getBillingDetails().pay(paymentAmount);

tx.commit();
session.close();
```

There is one thing to watch out for: if `BillingDetails` was mapped with `lazy="true"`, Hibernate would proxy the `billingDetails` association. In this case, we wouldn't be able to perform a typecast to the concrete class `CreditCard` at runtime, and even the `instanceof` operator would behave strangely:

```
User user = (User) session.get(User.class, uid);
BillingDetails bd = user.getBillingDetails();
System.out.println( bd instanceof CreditCard ); // prints "false"
CreditCard cc = (CreditCard) bd; // ClassCastException!
```

In this code, the typecast fails because `bd` is a proxy instance. When a method is invoked on the proxy, the call is delegated to an instance of `CreditCard` that is fetched lazily. To perform a proxysafe typecast, use `Session.load()`:

```
User user = (User) session.get(User.class, uid);
BillingDetails bd = user.getBillingDetails();
// Get a proxy of the subclass, doesn't hit the database
CreditCard cc =
```

```
    (CreditCard) session.load( CreditCard.class, bd.getId() );
expiryDate = cc.getExpiryDate();
```

After the call to load, bd and cc refer to two different proxy instances, which both delegate to the same underlying CreditCard instance.

Note that you can avoid these issues by avoiding lazy fetching, as in the following code, using a query technique discussed in the next chapter:

```
User user = (User) session.createCriteria(User.class)
    .add( Expression.eq("id", uid) )
    .setFetchMode("billingDetails", FetchMode.EAGER)
    .uniqueResult();
// The user's billingDetails were fetched eagerly
CreditCard cc = (CreditCard) user.getBillingDetails();
expiryDate = cc.getExpiryDate();
```

Truly object-oriented code shouldn't use instanceof or numerous typecasts. If you find yourself running into problems with proxies, you should question your design, asking whether there is a more polymorphic approach.

One-to-one associations are handled the same way. What about many-valued associations?

6.4.2 *Polymorphic collections*

Let's refactor the previous example to its original form in CaveatEmptor. If User owns many BillingDetails, we use a bidirectional one-to-many. In Billing-Details, we have the following:

```
<many-to-one name="user"
    class="User"
    column="USER_ID"/>
```

In the Users mapping, we have this:

```
<set name="billingDetails"
      lazy="true"
      cascade="save-update"
      inverse="true">
    <key column="USER_ID"/>
    <one-to-many class="BillingDetails"/>
</set>
```

Adding a CreditCard is easy:

```
CreditCard cc = new CreditCard();
cc.setNumber(ccNumber);
cc.setType(ccType);
cc.setExpiryDate(ccExpiryDate);

Session session = sessions.openSession();
```

```
Transaction tx = session.beginTransaction();

User user = (User) session.get(User.class, uid);
// Call convenience method that sets both "ends"
user.addBillingDetails(cc);

tx.commit();
session.close();
```

As usual, `addBillingDetails()` calls `getBillingDetails().add(cc)` and `cc.set-User(this)`.

We can iterate over the collection and handle instances of `CreditCard` and `BankAccount` polymorphically (we don't want to bill users multiple times in our final system, though):

```
Session session = sessions.openSession();
Transaction tx = session.beginTransaction();

User user = (User) session.get(User.class, uid);
Iterator iter = user.getBillingDetails().iterator();
while ( iter.hasNext() ) {
    BillingDetails bd = (BillingDetails) iter.next();
    // Invoke CreditCard.pay() or BankAccount.pay()
    bd.pay(ccPaymentAmount);
}

tx.commit();
session.close();
```

In the examples so far, we've assumed that `BillingDetails` is a class mapped explicitly in the Hibernate mapping document, and that the inheritance mapping strategy is table-per-hierarchy or table-per-subclass. We haven't yet considered the case of a table-per-concrete-class mapping strategy, where `BillingDetails` wouldn't be mentioned explicitly in the mapping file (only in the Java definition of the subclasses).

6.4.3 *Polymorphic associations and table-per-concrete-class*

In section 3.6.1, "Table per concrete class," we defined the *table-per-concrete-class* mapping strategy and observed that this mapping strategy makes it difficult to represent a polymorphic association, because you can't map a foreign key relationship to the table of the abstract superclass. There is no table for the superclass with this strategy; you only have tables for concrete classes.

Suppose that we want to represent a polymorphic many-to-one association from `User` to `BillingDetails`, where the `BillingDetails` class hierarchy is mapped using this table-per-concrete-class strategy. There is a `CREDIT_CARD` table and a

BANK_ACCOUNT table, but no BILLING_DETAILS table. We need two pieces of information in the USER table to uniquely identify the associated CreditCard or BankAccount:

- The name of the table in which the associated instance resides
- The identifier of the associated instance

The USER table requires the addition of a BILLING_DETAILS_TYPE column, in addition to the BILLING_DETAILS_ID. We use a Hibernate <any> element to map this association:

```
<any name="billingDetails"
     meta-type="string"
     id-type="long"
     cascade="save-update">
  <meta-value value="CREDIT_CARD" class="CreditCard"/>
  <meta-value value="BANK_ACCOUNT"class="BankAccount"/>
  <column name="BILLING_DETAILS_TYPE"/>
  <column name="BILLING_DETAILS_ID"/>
</any>
```

The meta-type attribute specifies the Hibernate type of the BILLING_DETAILS_TYPE column; the id-type attribute specifies the type of the BILLING_DETAILS_ID column (CreditCard and BankAccount must have the same identifier type). Note that the order of the columns is important: first the type, then the identifier.

The <meta-value> elements tell Hibernate how to interpret the value of the BILLING_DETAILS_TYPE column. We don't need to use the full table name here—we can use any value we like as a type discriminator. For example, we can encode the information in two characters:

```
<any name="billingDetails"
     meta-type="string"
     id-type="long"
     cascade="save-update">
  <meta-value value="CC" class="CreditCard"/>
  <meta-value value="CA" class="BankAccount"/>
  <column name="BILLING_DETAILS_TYPE"/>
  <column name="BILLING_DETAILS_ID"/>
</any>
```

An example of this table structure is shown in figure 6.14.

Here is the first major problem with this kind of association: we can't add a foreign key constraint to the BILLING_DETAILS_ID column, since some values refer to the BANK_ACCOUNT table and others to the CREDIT_CARD table. Thus, we need to come up with some other way to ensure integrity (a trigger, for example).

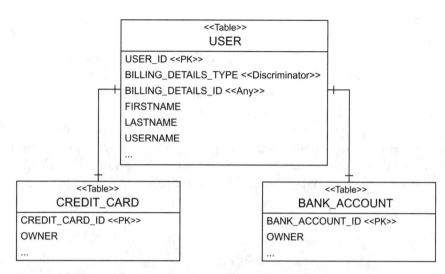

Figure 6.14 Using a discriminator column with an *any* association

Furthermore, it's difficult to write SQL table joins for this association. In particular, the Hibernate query facilities don't support this kind of association mapping, nor may this association be fetched using an outer join. We discourage the use of `<any>` associations for all but the most special cases.

As you can see, polymorphism is messier in the case of a table-per-concrete-class inheritance mapping strategy. We don't usually use this mapping strategy when polymorphic associations are required. As long as you stick to the other inheritance-mapping strategies, polymorphism is straightforward, and you don't usually need to think about it.

6.5 *Summary*

This chapter covered the finer points of ORM and techniques needed to solve the structural mismatch problem. We can now fully map all the entities and associations in the CaveatEmptor domain model.

The Hibernate type system distinguishes *entities* from *value types*. An entity instance has its own lifecycle and persistent identity; an instance of a value type is completely dependant on an owning entity.

Hibernate defines a rich variety of built-in value mapping types. When the predefined types are insufficient, you can easily extend them using custom types or component mappings and even implement arbitrary conversions from Java to SQL data types.

Collection-valued properties are considered to be of value type. A collection doesn't have its own persistent identity and belongs to a single owning entity. You've seen how to map collections, including collections of value-typed instances and many-valued entity associations.

Hibernate supports one-to-one, one-to-many, and many-to-many associations between entities. In practice, we recommend against the overuse of many-to-many associations. Associations in Hibernate are naturally polymorphic. We also talked about bidirectional behavior of such relationships.

Retrieving objects efficiently

7

This chapter covers

- Hibernate query features
- HQL, criteria, and native SQL queries
- Advanced, reporting, and dynamic queries
- Runtime fetching and query optimization

Queries are the most interesting part of writing good data access code. A complex query may require a long time to get right, and its impact on the performance of an application can be tremendous. On the other hand, writing queries becomes much easier with more experience, and what seemed difficult at first may only be a matter of knowing some of the more advanced features of Hibernate.

If you've been using handwritten SQL for a number of years, you might be concerned that ORM will take away some of the expressiveness and flexibility that you're used to. This isn't the case with Hibernate.

Hibernate's powerful query facilities allow you to express almost everything you commonly (or even uncommonly) need to express in SQL, but in object-oriented terms—using classes and properties of classes. Of course, some things don't make sense in an object-oriented query. For example, the Hibernate query language doesn't support database-specific query hints. For these (rare) cases, Hibernate makes it easy for you to fall back to the native SQL dialect of your database.

In chapter 4, we mentioned that there are three ways to express queries in Hibernate. First is the HQL:

```
session.createQuery("from Category c where c.name like 'Laptop%'");
```

Next is the `Criteria` API for *query by criteria* (QBC) and *query by example* (QBE)):

```
session.createCriteria(Category.class)
        .add( Expression.like("name", "Laptop%") );
```

Next, there is direct SQL with automatic mapping of result sets to objects:

```
session.createSQLQuery(
        "select {c.*} from CATEGORY {c} where NAME like 'Laptop%'",
        "c",
        Category.class);
```

This chapter covers query techniques using all three methods. You may also use this chapter as a reference; hence some sections are written in a less verbose style but show many small code examples for different use cases. We also sometimes skip optimizations in our CaveatEmptor application for better readability. For example, instead of referring to the `MonetaryAmount` class, we use a `BigDecimal` amount in comparisons.

First, we show you how queries are executed. Don't let yourself be distracted by the queries themselves; we discuss them soon.

7.1 *Executing queries*

The `Query` and `Criteria` interfaces both define several methods for controlling execution of a query. In addition, `Query` provides methods for binding concrete values to query parameters. To execute a query in your application, you need to obtain an instance of one of these interfaces, using the `Session`.

7.1.1 *The query interfaces*

To create a new `Query` instance, call either `createQuery()` or `createSQLQuery()`. The `createQuery()` method prepares an HQL query:

```
Query hqlQuery = session.createQuery("from User");
```

The `createSQLQuery()` is used to create a SQL query, using the native syntax of the underlying database:

```
Query sqlQuery = session.createSQLQuery(
        "select {u.*} from USERS {u}", "u",
        User.class
        );
```

In both cases, Hibernate returns a newly instantiated `Query` object that may be used to specify exactly how a particular query should be executed, and to execute the query.

To obtain a `Criteria` instance, call `createCriteria()`, passing the class of the objects you want the query to return. This is also called the *root entity* of the criteria query, the `User` in this example:

```
Criteria crit = session.createCriteria(User.class);
```

The `Criteria` instance may be used in the same way as a `Query` object—but it's also used to construct the object-oriented representation of the query by adding `Criterion` instances and navigating associations to new `Criterias`. We discuss this in much more detail later; for now, let's continue with query execution.

Paging the result

Pagination is a commonly used technique. Users might see the result of their search request (for example, for specific `Items`) as a page. This page shows only a limited subset (say, 10 `Items`) at a time, and users can navigate to the next and previous pages manually. Both the `Query` and `Criteria` interfaces support this pagination of the query result:

```
Query query =
        session.createQuery("from User u order by u.name asc");
query.setFirstResult(0);
query.setMaxResults(10);
```

The call to `setMaxResults(10)` limits the query result set to the first 10 objects selected by the database. In this criteria query, the requested page starts in the "middle" of the result set:

```
Criteria crit = session.createCriteria(User.class);
crit.addOrder( Order.asc("name") );
crit.setFirstResult(40);
crit.setMaxResults(20);
List results = crit.list();
```

Starting from the fortieth object, we retrieve the next 20 objects. Note that there is no standard way to express pagination in SQL—but Hibernate knows the tricks to make this work efficiently on your particular database.

You can use the *method-chaining* coding style (methods return the receiving object instead of `void`) with both the `Query` and `Criteria` interfaces, rewriting the two previous examples as follows:

```
List results =
        session.createQuery("from User u order by u.name asc")
                .setFirstResult(0)
                .setMaxResults(10)
                .list();

List results =
        session.createCriteria(User.class)
                .addOrder( Order.asc("name") )
                .setFirstResult(40)
                .setMaxResults(20)
                .list();
```

Chaining method calls is less verbose and is supported by many Hibernate APIs.

Listing and iterating results

The `list()` method executes the query and returns the results as a list:

```
List result = session.createQuery("from User").list();
```

With some queries, we know the result will be only a single instance—for example, if we want only the highest bid. In this case, we can read it from the result list by index: `result.get(0)` or `setMaxResult(1)`. We then execute the query with the `uniqueResult()` method, because we know only one object will be returned:

```
Bid maxBid =
    (Bid) session.createQuery("from Bid b order by b.amount desc")
                .setMaxResults(1)
                .uniqueResult();
Bid bid = (Bid) session.createCriteria(Bid.class)
                    .add( Expression.eq("id", id) )
                    .uniqueResult();
```

If the query returns more than one object, an exception will be thrown.

The `Query` and `Session` interfaces also provide the `iterate()` method, which returns the same result as `list()` (or `find()`) but uses a different strategy for retrieving the results. When you use `iterate()` to execute a query, Hibernate retrieves only the primary key (identifier) values in the first SQL select; it tries to find the rest of the state of the objects in the cache, before querying again for the rest of the property values. This technique can be used to optimize loading in specific cases, as discussed in section 7.6, "Optimizing object retrieval."

> **FAQ** *Is `Session.find()` faster than `Query.list()`?* The `Session` API provides shortcut methods for simple queries. Instead of creating a `Query`, you can also call `Session.find("from User")`. The result is the same as from `Query.list()`; one isn't faster than the other. The same is true for `iterate()`: You're free to choose the API. However, it's highly likely that the query shortcut methods on the `Session` API will be removed in the future to reduce the bloat of session methods. We recommend the `Query` API.

Finally, the `Query` interface lets you bind values to query parameters.

7.1.2 Binding parameters

Here's some code that you should never write:

```
String queryString =
    "from Item i where i.description like '" + searchString + "'";
List result = session.createQuery(queryString).list();
```

One reason you should never write this code is that a malicious user could search for the following item description by entering the value of `searchString` in a search dialog box:

```
foo' and callSomeStoredProcedure() and 'bar' = 'bar
```

As you can see, the original `queryString` would no longer be a simple search for a string, but would also execute a stored procedure in the database! The quote characters aren't escaped; hence the call to the stored procedure would be just another

valid expression in the query. If you write a query like this, you open a major
security hole in your application by allowing the execution of arbitrary code on
your database. Users might even (accidentally) crash your application just by put-
ting a single quote in the search string. Never pass unchecked values from user
input to the database! Fortunately, a simple mechanism prevents this mistake.

The JDBC driver includes functionality for safely binding values to SQL parameters. It knows exactly which characters in the parameter value to escape, so the previous vulnerability doesn't exist. For example, the quote characters in the given
searchString are escaped; they're no longer treated as control characters but
rather as a part of the search string value.

Furthermore, when you use parameters, the database can efficiently cache pre-
compiled prepared statements, improving performance significantly.

There are two approaches to *parameter binding*: using positional parameters or
using named parameters. Hibernate supports JDBC-style positional parameters
(indicated by ? in the query string) as well as named parameters (indicated by
the : prefix).

Using named parameters

Using named parameters, we can rewrite the query as

```
String queryString =
    "from Item item where item.description like :searchString";
```

The colon followed by a parameter name indicates a named parameter. Then, we
can use the Query interface to bind a value to the searchString parameter:

```
List result = session.createQuery(queryString)
                    .setString("searchString", searchString)
                    .list();
```

Because searchString is a user-supplied string variable, we use the setString()
method of the Query interface to bind it to the named parameter (searchString).
This code is cleaner, much safer, and performs better, because a single compiled
SQL statement can be reused if only bind parameters change.

Often, you'll need multiple parameters:

```
String queryString = "from Item item "
                    + "where item.description like :searchString "
                    + "and item.date > :minDate";

List result = session.createQuery(queryString)
                    .setString("searchString", searchString)
                    .setDate("minDate", minDate)
                    .list();
```

Using positional parameters

If you prefer, you can use positional parameters:

```
String queryString = "from Item item "
                   + "where item.description like ? "
                   + "and item.date > ?";

List result = session.createQuery(queryString)
                     .setString(0, searchString)
                     .setDate(1, minDate)
                     .list();
```

Not only is this code much less self-documenting than the alternative with named parameters, it's also much more vulnerable to easy breakage if we change the query string slightly:

```
String queryString = "from Item item "
                   + "where item.date > ? "
                   + "and item.description like ?";
```

Every change of the position of the bind parameters requires a change to the parameter-binding code. This leads to fragile and maintenance-intensive code. We recommend that you avoid positional parameters.

Last, a named parameter may appear multiple times in the query string:

```
String userSearch =
         "from User u where u.username like :searchString"
       + " or u.email like :searchString";

List result = session.createQuery(userSearch)
                     .setString("searchString", searchString)
                     .list();
```

Binding arbitrary arguments

We've used `setString()` and `setDate()` to bind arguments to query parameters. The `Query` interface provides similar convenience methods for binding arguments of most of the Hibernate built-in types: everything from `setInteger()` to `setTimestamp()` and `setLocale()`.

A particularly useful method is `setEntity()`, which lets you bind a persistent entity:

```
session.createQuery("from Item item where item.seller = :seller")
        .setEntity("seller", seller)
        .list();
```

However, there is also a generic method that allows you to bind an argument of any Hibernate type:

```
String queryString = "from Item item "
                    + "where item.seller=:seller and "
                    + "item.description like :desc";

session.createQuery(queryString)
          .setParameter( "seller", seller, Hibernate.entity(User.class) )
          .setParameter( "desc", description, Hibernate.STRING )
          .list();
```

This even works for custom user-defined types like `MonetaryAmount`:

```
Query q =
    session.createQuery("from Bid bid where bid.amount > :amount");
q.setParameter( "amount",
                givenAmount,
                Hibernate.custom(MonetaryAmountUserType.class) );
List result = q.list();
```

For some parameter types, it's possible to guess the Hibernate type from the class of the parameter value. In this case, you don't need to specify the Hibernate type explicitly:

```
String queryString = "from Item item "
                    + "where item.seller = :seller and "
                    + "item.description like :desc";

session.createQuery(queryString)
          .setParameter("seller", seller)
          .setParameter("desc", description)
          .list();
```

As you can see, it even works with entities, such as `seller`. This approach works nicely for `String`, `Integer`, and `Boolean` parameters, for example, but not so well for `Date`, where the Hibernate type might be `timestamp`, `date`, or `time`. In that case, you have to use the appropriate binding method or explicitly use `Hibernate.TIME` (or any other Hibernate type) as the third argument to `setParameter()`.

If we had a JavaBean with `seller` and `description` properties, we could use the `setProperties()` method to bind the query parameters. For example, we could pass query parameters in an instance of the `Item` class:

```
Item item = new Item();
item.setSeller(seller);
item.setDescription(description);

String queryString = "from Item item "
                    + "where item.seller=:seller and "
                    + "item.description like :desc";

session.createQuery(queryString).setProperties(item).list();
```

`setProperties()` matches the names of JavaBean properties to named parameters in the query string, using `setParameter()` to guess the Hibernate type and bind the value. In practice, this turns out to be less useful than it sounds, since some common Hibernate types aren't guessable (`date`, in particular).

The parameter-binding methods of `Query` are null-safe, making this code legal:

```
session.createQuery("from User as u where u.username = :name")
        .setString("name", null)
        .list();
```

However, the result of this code is almost certainly not what we intended. The resulting SQL will contain a comparison like `username = null`, which always evaluates to null in SQL ternary logic. Instead, we must use the `is null` operator:

```
session.createQuery("from User as u where u.email is null").list();
```

So far, the HQL code examples we've shown all use embedded HQL query string literals. This isn't unreasonable for simple queries, but once we start considering complex queries that must be split over multiple lines, it starts to get a bit unwieldy.

7.1.3 *Using named queries*

We don't like to see HQL string literals scattered all over the Java code unless they're necessary. Hibernate lets you externalize query strings to the mapping metadata, a technique that is called *named queries*. This allows you to store all queries related to a particular persistent class (or a set of classes) encapsulated with the other metadata of that class in an XML mapping file. The name of the query is used to call it from the application.

The `getNamedQuery()` method obtains a `Query` instance for a named query:

```
session.getNamedQuery("findItemsByDescription")
        .setString("description", description)
        .list();
```

In this example, we execute the named query `findItemsByDescription` after binding a string argument to a named parameter. The named query is defined in mapping metadata, e.g. in `Item.hbm.xml`, using the `<query>` element:

```
<query name="findItemsByDescription"><![CDATA[
        from Item item where item.description like :description
]]></query>
```

Named queries don't have to be HQL strings; they might even be native SQL queries—and your Java code doesn't need to know the difference:

```
<sql-query name="findItemsByDescription"><![CDATA[
      select {i.*} from ITEM {i} where DESCRIPTION like :description
   ]]>
      <return alias="i" class="Item"/>
</sql-query>
```

This is useful if you think you might want to optimize your queries later by fine-tuning the SQL. It's also a good solution if you have to port a legacy application to Hibernate, where SQL code was isolated from the handcoded JDBC routines. With named queries, you can easily port the queries one by one to mapping files.

We come back to native SQL queries later in this chapter, but now let's continue with basic HQL and criteria queries.

7.2   Basic queries for objects

Let's start with simple queries to become familiar with the HQL syntax and semantics. Although we show the criteria alternative for most HQL queries, keep in mind that HQL is the preferred approach for complex queries. Usually, the criteria can be derived if you know the HQL equivalent, it's much more difficult the other way around.

NOTE   *Testing Hibernate queries*—You can use two tools to execute Hibernate queries ad hoc: *Hibern8IDE*, a Java Swing application; and an Eclipse plugin called *Hibernator*. Both tools let you select Hibernate mapping documents, connect to the database, and then view the result of HQL queries you type interactively. Hibern8IDE even lets you prototype criteria queries by providing a Java BeanShell. You can find links to both tools on the Hibernate project web site.

7.2.1   The simplest query

The simplest query retrieves all instances of a particular persistent class. In HQL, it looks like this:

```
from Bid
```

Using a criteria query, it looks like this:

```
session.createCriteria(Bid.class);
```

Both these queries generate the following SQL:

```
select B.BID_ID, B.AMOUNT, B.ITEM_ID, B.CREATED from BID B
```

Even for this simple case, you can see that HQL is less verbose than SQL.

7.2.2 *Using aliases*

Usually, when you query a class using HQL, you need to assign an *alias* to the queried class to use as reference in other parts of the query:

```
from Bid as bid
```

The as keyword is always optional. The following is equivalent:

```
from Bid bid
```

Think of this as being a bit like the temporary variable declaration in the following Java code:

```
for ( Iterator i = allQueriedBids.iterator(); i.hasNext(); ) {
    Bid bid = (Bid) i.next();
    ...
}
```

We assign the alias bid to queried instances of the Bid class, allowing us to refer to their property values later in the code (or query). To remind yourself of the similarity, we recommend that you use the same naming convention for aliases that you use for temporary variables (camelCase, usually). However, we use shorter aliases in some of the examples in this book (for example, i instead of item) to keep the printed code readable.

> **NOTE** We never write HQL keywords in uppercase; we never write SQL keywords in uppercase either. It looks ugly and antiquated—most modern terminals can display both uppercase and lowercase characters. However, HQL isn't case-sensitive for keywords, so you can write FROM Bid AS bid if you like shouting.

By contrast, a criteria query defines an implicit alias. The root entity in a criteria query is always assigned the alias this. We discuss this topic in more detail later, when we're joining associations with criteria queries. You don't have to think much about aliases when using the Criteria API.

7.2.3 *Polymorphic queries*

We described HQL as an object-oriented query language, so it should support *polymorphic queries*—that is, queries for instances of a class and all instances of its subclasses, respectively. You already know enough HQL that we can demonstrate this. Consider the following query:

```
from BillingDetails
```

This query returns objects of the type `BillingDetails`, which is an abstract class. So, in this case, the concrete objects are of the subtypes of `BillingDetails`: `CreditCard` and `BankAccount`. If we only want instances of a particular subclass, we may use

```
from CreditCard
```

The class named in the `from` clause doesn't need to be a mapped persistent class; any class will do. The following query returns all persistent objects:

```
from java.lang.Object
```

Of course, this also works for interfaces—this query returns all serializable persistent objects:

```
from java.io.Serializable
```

Criteria queries also support polymorphism:

```
session.createCriteria(BillingDetails.class).list();
```

This query returns instances of `BillingDetails` and its subclasses. Likewise, the following criteria query returns all persistent objects:

```
session.createCriteria(java.lang.Object.class).list();
```

Polymorphism applies not only to classes named explicitly in the `from` clause, but also to polymorphic associations, as you'll see later.

We've discussed the `from` clause; now let's move on to the other parts of HQL.

7.2.4 Restriction

Usually, you don't want to retrieve all instances of a class. You must be able to express constraints on the property values of objects returned by the query. Doing so is called *restriction*. The `where` clause is used to express a restriction in both SQL and HQL; these expressions may be of arbitrary complexity. Let's start simple, using HQL:

```
from User u where u.email = 'foo@hibernate.org'
```

Notice that the constraint is expressed in terms of a property, `email`, of the `User` class, and that we use an object-oriented notion: Just as in Java, `u.email` may not be abbreviated to plain `email`.

For a criteria query, we must construct a `Criterion` object to express the constraint. The `Expression` class provides factory methods for built-in `Criterion` types. Let's create the same query using criteria and immediately execute it:

```
Criterion emailEq = Expression.eq("email", "foo@hibernate.org");
Criteria crit = session.createCriteria(User.class);
crit.add(emailEq);
User user = (User) crit.uniqueResult();
```

We create a `Criterion` holding the simple `Expression` for an equality comparison and add it to the `Criteria`. The `uniqueResult()` method executes the query and returns exactly one object as a result.

Usually, we would write this a bit less verbosely, using method chaining:

```
User user = (User) session.createCriteria(User.class)
            .add( Expression.eq("email", "foo@hibernate.org") )
            .uniqueResult();
```

A new feature of JDK 1.5 is *static imports*. Hibernate has some use cases for static imports, so we're looking forward to the new version. For example, by adding

```
static import net.sf.hibernate.Expression.*;
```

we'll be able to abbreviate the criteria query restriction code to

```
User user = (User) session.createCriteria(User.class)
            .add( eq("email", "foo@hibernate.org") )
            .uniqueResult();
```

The SQL generated by these queries is

```
select U.USER_ID, U.FIRSTNAME, U.LASTNAME, U.USERNAME, U.EMAIL
from USER U
where U.EMAIL = 'foo@hibernate.org'
```

You can of course use various other comparison operators in HQL.

7.2.5 *Comparison operators*

A restriction is expressed using ternary logic. The `where` clause is a logical expression that evaluates to true, false, or null for each tuple of objects. You construct logical expressions by comparing properties of objects to other properties or literal values using HQL's built-in comparison operators.

> **FAQ** *What is ternary logic?* A row is included in an SQL result set if and only if the `where` clause evaluates to true. In Java, `notNullObject==null` evaluates to false and `null==null` evaluates to true. In SQL, `NOT_NULL_COLUMN=null` and `null=null` both evaluate to null, not true. Thus, SQL needs a special operator, `IS NULL`, to test whether a value is null. This ternary logic is a way of handling expressions that may be applied to null column values. It is a (debatable) SQL extension to the familiar binary logic of the relational model and of typical programming languages such as Java.

HQL supports the same basic operators as SQL: =, <>, <, >, >=, <=, between, not between, in, and not in. For example:

```
from Bid bid where bid.amount between 1 and 10

from Bid bid where bid.amount > 100

from User u where u.email in ( "foo@hibernate.org", "bar@hibernate.org" )
```

In the case of criteria queries, all the same operators are available via the Expression class:

```
session.createCriteria(Bid.class)
        .add( Expression.between("amount",
                                 new BigDecimal(1),
                                 new BigDecimal(10))
            ).list();


session.createCriteria(Bid.class)
        .add( Expression.gt("amount", new BigDecimal(100) ) )
        .list();

String[] emails = { "foo@hibernate.org", "bar@hibernate.org" };
session.createCriteria(User.class)
        .add( Expression.in("email", emails) )
        .list();
```

Because the underlying database implements ternary logic, testing for null values requires some care. Remember that null = null doesn't evaluate to true in the database, but to null. All comparisons that use the null operator in fact evaluate to null. Both HQL and the Criteria API provide an SQL-style is null operator:

```
from User u where u.email is null
```

This query returns all users with no email address. The same semantic is available in the Criteria API:

```
session.createCriteria(User.class)
        .add( Expression.isNull("email") )
        .list();
```

We also need to be able to find users who *do* have an email address:

```
from User u where u.email is not null

session.createCriteria(User.class)
        .add( Expression.isNotNull("email") )
        .list();
```

Finally, the HQL where clause supports arithmetic expressions (but the Criteria API doesn't):

```
from Bid bid where ( bid.amount / 0.71 ) - 100.0 > 0.0
```

For string-based searches, you need to be able to perform case-insensitive matching and matches on fragments of strings in restriction expressions.

7.2.6 *String matching*

The `like` operator allows wildcard searches, where the wildcard symbols are `%` and `_`, just as in SQL:

```
from User u where u.firstname like "G%"
```

This expression restricts the result to users with a first name starting with a capital *G*. You can also negate the `like` operator, for example using a substring match expression:

```
from User u where u.firstname not like "%Foo B%"
```

For criteria queries, wildcard searches may use either the same wildcard symbols or specify a `MatchMode`. Hibernate provides the `MatchMode` as part of the `Criteria` query API; we use it for writing string match expressions without string manipulation. These two queries are equivalent:

```
session.createCriteria(User.class)
        .add( Expression.like("firstname", "G%") )
        .list();

session.createCriteria(User.class)
        .add( Expression.like("firstname", "G", MatchMode.START) )
        .list();
```

The allowed `MatchMode`s are `START`, `END`, `ANYWHERE`, and `EXACT`.

An extremely powerful feature of HQL is the ability to call arbitrary SQL functions in the `where` clause. If your database supports user-defined functions (most do), you can put this functionality to all sorts of uses, good or evil. For the moment, let's consider the usefulness of the standard ANSI SQL functions `upper()` and `lower()`. They can be used for case-insensitive searching:

```
from User u where lower(u.email) = 'foo@hibernate.org'
```

The `Criteria` API doesn't currently support SQL function calls. It does, however, provide a special facility for case-insensitive searching:

```
session.createCriteria(User.class)
        .add( Expression.eq("email", "foo@hibernate.org").ignoreCase() )
        .list();
```

Unfortunately, HQL doesn't provide a standard string-concatenation operator; instead, it supports whatever syntax your database provides. Most databases will allow the following:

```
from User user
    where ( user.firstname || ' ' || user.lastname ) like 'G% K%'
```

We'll return to some more exotic features of the HQL where clause later in this chapter. We only used single expressions for restrictions in this section; let's combine several with logical operators.

7.2.7 *Logical operators*

Logical operators (and parentheses for grouping) are used to combine expressions:

```
from User user
    where user.firstname like "G%" and user.lastname like "K%"

from User user
    where ( user.firstname like "G%" and user.lastname like "K%" )
    or user.email in ( "foo@hibernate.org", "bar@hibernate.org" )
```

If you add multiple `Criterion` instances to the one `Criteria` instance, they're applied conjunctively (that is, using and):

```
session.createCriteria(User.class)
        .add( Expression.like("firstname", "G%") )
        .add( Expression.like("lastname", "K%") )
```

If you need disjunction (or), you have two options. The first is to use `Expression.or()` together with `Expression.and()`:

```
Criteria crit = session.createCriteria(User.class)
                    .add(
                        Expression.or(
                            Expression.and(
                                Expression.like("firstname", "G%"),
                                Expression.like("lastname", "K%")
                            ),
                            Expression.in("email", emails)
                        )
                    );
```

The second option is to use `Expression.disjunction()` together with `Expression.conjunction()`:

```
Criteria crit = session.createCriteria(User.class)
                .add( Expression.disjunction()
                    .add( Expression.conjunction()
```

```
                         .add( Expression.like("firstname", "G%") )
                         .add( Expression.like("lastname", "K%") )
                     )
                 .add( Expression.in("email", emails) )
         );
```

We think both options are ugly, even after spending five minutes trying to format them for maximum readability. JDK 1.5 static imports would help improve readability considerably; but even so, unless you're constructing a query on the fly, the HQL string is much easier to understand. Complex criteria queries are useful only when they're created programmatically; for example, in the case of a complex search screen with several optional search criteria, we might have a `CriteriaBuilder` that translates user restrictions to `Criteria` instances.

7.2.8 *Ordering query results*

All query languages provide a mechanism for ordering query results. HQL provides an *order by* clause, similar to SQL.

This query returns all users, ordered by username:

```
from User u order by u.username
```

You specify ascending and descending order using `asc` or `desc`:

```
from User u order by u.username desc
```

Finally, you can order by multiple properties:

```
from User u order by u.lastname asc, u.firstname asc
```

The `Criteria` API provides a similar facility:

```
List results = session.createCriteria(User.class)
                 .addOrder( Order.asc("lastname") )
                 .addOrder( Order.asc("firstname") )
                 .list();
```

Thus far, we've only discussed the basic concepts of HQL and criteria queries. You've learned how to write a simple `from` clause and use aliases for classes. We've combined various restriction expressions with logical operators. However, we've focused on single persistent classes—that is, we've only referenced a single class in the `from` clause. An important query technique we haven't discussed yet is the *joining of associations* at runtime.

7.3 *Joining associations*

You use a *join* to combine data in two (or more) relations. For example, we might join the data in the ITEM and BID tables, as shown in figure 7.1. (Note that not all columns and possible rows are shown; hence the dotted lines.)

ITEM

ITEM_ID	NAME	INITIAL_PRICE
1	Foo	2.00
2	Bar	50.00
3	Baz	1.00

BID

BID_ID	ITEM_ID	AMOUNT
1	1	10.00
2	1	20.00
3	2	55.50

Figure 7.1
The ITEM and BID tables are obvious candidates for a join operation.

What most people think of when they hear the word *join* in the context of SQL databases is an *inner join*. An inner join is one of several types of joins, and it's the easiest to understand. Consider the SQL statement and result in figure 7.2. This SQL statement is an *ANSI-style join*.

If we join tables ITEM and BID with an inner join, using their common attributes (the ITEM_ID column), we get all items and their bids in a new result table. Note that the result of this operation contains only items that have bids. If we want all items, and null values instead of bid data when there is no corresponding bid, we use a *(left) outer join,* as shown in figure 7.3.

You can think of a table join as working as follows. First, you get a Cartesian product of the two tables by taking all possible combinations of ITEM rows with BID rows. Second, you filter these joined rows using a *join condition*. Note that the database has much more sophisticated algorithms to evaluate a join; it usually doesn't build a memory-consuming product and then filter all rows. The join condition is just a boolean expression that evaluates to true if the joined row is to be included in the result. In the case of the left outer join, each row in the (left) ITEM table that never

from ITEM I inner join BID B on I.ITEM_ID = B.ITEM_ID

ITEM_ID	NAME	INITIAL_PRICE	BID_ID	ITEM_ID	AMOUNT
1	Foo	2.00	1	1	10.00
1	Foo	2.00	2	1	20.00
2	Bar	50.00	3	2	55.50

Figure 7.2
The result table of an ANSI-style inner join of two tables

from ITEM I left outer join BID B on I.ITEM_ID = B.ITEM_ID

ITEM_ID	NAME	INITIAL_PRICE		BID_ID	ITEM_ID	AMOUNT	
1	Foo	2.00		1	1	10.00	
1	Foo	2.00		2	1	20.00	
2	Bar	50.00		3	2	55.50	
3	Baz	1.00		null	null	null	

Figure 7.3
The result of an ANSI-style left outer join of two tables

satisfies the join condition is also included in the result, with null values returned for all columns of BID. (A *right* outer join would retrieve all bids and null if a bid has no item—certainly not a sensible query in our situation.)

In SQL, the join condition is usually specified explicitly. (Unfortunately, it isn't possible to use the name of a foreign key constraint to specify how two tables are to be joined.) We specify the join condition in the on clause for an ANSI-style join or in the where clause for a so-called *theta-style join*, where I.ITEM_ID = B.ITEM_ID.

7.3.1 *Hibernate join options*

In Hibernate queries, you don't usually specify a join condition explicitly. Rather, you specify the name of a mapped Java class association. For example, the Item class has an association named bids with the Bid class. If we name this association in our query, Hibernate has enough information in the mapping document to then deduce the table join expression. This helps make queries less verbose and more readable.

HQL provides four ways of expressing (inner and outer) joins:

- An *ordinary* join in the from clause
- A *fetch* join in the from clause
- A *theta-style* join in the where clause
- An *implicit* association join

Later, we'll show you how to write a join between two classes that don't have an association defined (a theta-style join) and also how to write an implicit association join in the where or select (or group by, or order by, or having) clause. But often, a from clause join, either ordinary or fetch, is the clearest syntax—so we'll discuss these two options first. Remember that the semantics of HQL joins are close to SQL join operations but not necessarily the same.

Hibernate differentiates between the purposes for joining. Suppose we're querying `Items`. There are two possible reasons why we might be interested in joining the `Bids`.

We might want to limit the `Items` returned by the query on the basis of some criterion that should be applied to their `Bids`. For example, you might want all `Items` that have a bid of more than $100; hence this requires an *inner join.*

On the other hand, we may be primarily interested in the `Items` and not want the retrieved items and their `bids` loaded at the same time (the bids collection shouldn't be initialized). The `Items` are retrieved first, and Hibernate lazily loads all `Bids` with an additional select once we access the collection by calling, for example, `item.getBids().iterator()`.

Alternatively, we may want to execute an outer join to retrieve all the `Bids` for the queried `Items` in the same single select, something we called *eager fetching* earlier. Remember that we prefer to map all associations lazy by default, so an eager, outer-join fetch query is used to override the default fetching strategy at runtime.

Let's discuss this last case first.

7.3.2 *Fetching associations*

In HQL, you can specify that an association should be eagerly fetched by an outer join using the `fetch` keyword in the `from` clause:

```
from Item item
left join fetch item.bids
    where item.description like '%gc%'
```

This query returns all items with a description that contains the string gc, and all their bids, in a single select. When executed, it returns a list of `Item` instances, with their `bids` collections fully initialized. We call this a `from` clause *fetch join*. The purpose of a fetch join is performance optimization: We use this syntax only because we want eager initialization of the `bids` collections in a single SQL `select`.

We can do the same thing using the `Criteria` API:

```
session.createCriteria(Item.class)
        .setFetchMode("bids", FetchMode.EAGER)
        .add( Expression.like("description", "gc", MatchMode.ANYWHERE) )
        .list();
```

Both of these queries result in the following SQL:

```
select I.DESCRIPTION, I.CREATED, I.SUCCESSFUL_BID, B.BID_ID,
B.AMOUNT, B.ITEM_ID, B.CREATED
from ITEM I
left outer join BID B on I.ITEM_ID = B.ITEM_ID
where I.DESCRIPTION like '%gc%'
```

We can also prefetch many-to-one or one-to-one associations using the same syntax:

```
from Bid bid
left join fetch bid.item
left join fetch bid.bidder
    where bid.amount > 100

session.createCriteria(Bid.class)
        .setFetchMode("item", FetchMode.EAGER)
        .setFetchMode("bidder", FetchMode.EAGER)
        .add( Expression.gt("amount", new BigDecimal(100) ) )
        .list();
```

These queries execute the following SQL:

```
select I.DESCRIPTION, I.CREATED, I.SUCCESSFUL_BID,
B.BID_ID, B.AMOUNT, B.ITEM_ID, B.CREATED,
U.USERNAME, U.PASSWORD, U.FIRSTNAME, U.LASTNAME
from BID B
left outer join ITEM I on I.ITEM_ID = B.ITEM_ID
left outer join USER U on U.USER_ID = B.BIDDER_ID
where B.AMOUNT > 100
```

Note that the `left` keyword is optional in HQL, so we could rewrite the previous examples using `join fetch`. Although this looks straightforward to use, there are a couple of things to consider and remember:

- *HQL always ignores the mapping document eager fetch (outer join) setting.* If you've mapped some associations to be fetched by outer join (by setting `outer-join="true"` on the association mapping), any HQL query will ignore this preference. You must use an explicit fetch join if you want eager fetching in HQL. On the other hand, the criteria query will not ignore the mapping! If you specify `outer-join="true"` in the mapping file, the criteria query will fetch that association by outer join—just like `Session.get()` or `Session.load()` for retrieval by identifier. For a criteria query, you can explicitly disable outer join fetching by calling `setFetchMode("bids", FetchMode.LAZY)`. HQL is designed to be as flexible as possible: You can completely (re)define the fetching strategy that should be used at runtime.

- *Hibernate currently limits you to fetching just one collection eagerly.* This is a reasonable restriction, since fetching more than one collection in a single query would be a Cartesian product result. This restriction might be relaxed in a future version of Hibernate, but we encourage you to think about the size of the result set if more than one collection is fetched in an outer join. The amount of data that would have to be transported between database and application can easily grow into the megabyte range, and most of it would be thrown away immediately (Hibernate *flattens* the tabular result set to build the object graph). You may fetch as many one-to-one or many-to-one associations as you like.

- *If you fetch a collection, Hibernate doesn't return a distinct result list.* For example, an individual Item might appear several times in the result List, if you outer-join fetch the bids. You'll probably need to make the results distinct yourself using, for example: distinctResults = new HashSet(resultList);. A Set doesn't allow duplicate elements.

This is how Hibernate implements what we call *runtime association fetching strategies,* a powerful feature that is essential for achieving high performance in ORM. Let's continue with the other join operations.

7.3.3 *Using aliases with joins*

We've already discussed the role of the where clause in expressing restriction. Often, you'll need to apply restriction criteria to multiple associated classes (joined tables). If we want to do this using an HQL from clause join, we need to assign an alias to the joined class:

```
from Item item
join item.bids bid
    where item.description like '%gc%'
    and bid.amount > 100
```

This query assigns the alias item to the class Item and the alias bid to the joined Item's bids. We then use both aliases to express our restriction criteria in the where clause.

The resulting SQL is as follows:

```
select I.DESCRIPTION, I.CREATED, I.SUCCESSFUL_BID,
B.BID_ID, B.AMOUNT, B.ITEM_ID, B.CREATED
from ITEM I
inner join BID B on I.ITEM_ID = B.ITEM_ID
where I.DESCRIPTION like '%gc%'
and B.AMOUNT > 100
```

The query returns all combinations of associated Bids and Items. But unlike a fetch join, the bids collection of the Item isn't initialized by the query! So what do we mean by a *combination* here? We mean an ordered pair: (bid, item). In the query result, Hibernate represents an ordered pair as an array. Let's discuss a full code example with the result of such a query:

```
Query q = session.createQuery("from Item item join item.bids bid");
Iterator pairs = q.list().iterator();
```

```
while ( pairs.hasNext() ) {
        Object[] pair = (Object[]) pairs.next();
        Item item = (Item) pair[0];
        Bid bid = (Bid) pair[1];
}
```

Instead of a List of Items, this query returns a List of Object[] arrays. At index 0 is the Item, and at index 1 is the Bid. A particular Item may appear multiple times, once for each associated Bid.

This is all different from the case of a query with an eager fetch join. The query with the fetch join returned a List of Items, with initialized bids collections.

If we don't want the Bids in the query result, we can specify a select clause in HQL. This clause is optional (it isn't in SQL), so we only have to use it when we aren't satisfied with the result returned by default. We use the alias in a select clause to retrieve only the selected objects:

```
select item
from Item item
join item.bids bid
    where item.description like '%gc%'
    and bid.amount > 100
```

Now the generated SQL looks like this:

```
select I.DESCRIPTION, I.CREATED, I.SUCCESSFUL_BID,
from ITEM I
inner join BID B on I.ITEM_ID = B.ITEM_ID
where I.DESCRIPTION like '%gc%'
and B.AMOUNT > 100
```

The query result contains just Items, and because it's an *inner join*, only Items that have Bids:

```
Query q = session.createQuery("select i from Item i join i.bids b");
Iterator items = q.list().iterator();
while ( items.hasNext() ) {
        Item item = (Item) items.next();
}
```

As you can see, using aliases in HQL is the same for both direct classes and joined associations. We assign aliases in the from clause and use them in the where and in the optional select clause. The select clause in HQL is much more powerful; we discuss it in detail later in this chapter.

There are two ways to express a join in the Criteria API; hence there are two ways to use aliases for restriction. The first is the createCriteria() method of the Criteria interface. It means that you can nest calls to createCriteria():

```
Criteria itemCriteria = session.createCriteria(Item.class);
itemCriteria.add( Expression.like("description",
                                 "gc",
                                 MatchMode.ANYWHERE) );
Criteria bidCriteria = itemCriteria.createCriteria("bids");
bidCriteria.add( Expression.gt( "amount", new BigDecimal("100") ) );

List results = itemCriteria.list();
```

We'd usually write the query as follows (method chaining):

```
List results =
    session.createCriteria(Item.class)
     .add( Expression.like("description", "gc", MatchMode.ANYWHERE) )
     .createCriteria("bids")
      .add( Expression.gt("amount", new BigDecimal("100") ) )
     .list();
```

The creation of a `Criteria` for the `bids` of the `Item` results in an inner join between the tables of the two classes. Note that we may call `list()` on either `Criteria` instance without changing the query results.

The second way to express this query using the `Criteria` API is to assign an alias to the joined entity:

```
List results =
    session.createCriteria(Item.class)
            .createAlias("bids", "bid")
            .add( Expression.like("description", "%gc%") )
            .add( Expression.gt("bid.amount", new BigDeciml("100") ) )
            .list();
```

This approach doesn't use a second instance of `Criteria`. So, properties of the joined entity must be qualified by the alias assigned in `createAlias()`. Properties of the *root entity* (`Item`) may be referred to without the qualifying alias or by using the alias `"this"`. Thus the following is equivalent:

```
List results =
    session.createCriteria(Item.class)
            .createAlias("bids", "bid")
            .add( Expression.like("this.description", "%gc%") )
            .add( Expression.gt("bid.amount", new BigDecimal("100") ) )
            .list();
```

By default, a criteria query returns only the root entity—in this case, the `Items`—in the query result. Let's summarize with a full example:

```
Iterator items =
    session.createCriteria(Item.class)
            .createAlias("bids", "bid")
            .add( Expression.like("this.description", "%gc%") )
```

```
            .add( Expression.gt("bid.amount", new BigDecimal("100") ) )
            .list().iterator();
while ( items.hasNext() ) {
    Item item = (Item) items.next();
    // Do something
}
```

Keep in mind that the `bids` collection of each `Item` isn't initialized. A limitation of criteria queries is that you can't combine a `createAlias` with an eager fetch mode; for example, `setFetchMode("bids", FetchMode.EAGER)` isn't valid.

If we want to return both the matching `Items` and `Bids`, we must ask Hibernate to return each row of results as a `Map`:

```
Iterator itemBidMaps =
    session.createCriteria(Item.class)
            .createAlias("bids", "bid")
            .add( Expression.like("this.description", "%gc%") )
            .add( Expression.gt("bid.amount", new BigDecimal("100") ) )
            .returnMaps()
            .list().iterator();
while ( itemBidMaps.hasNext() ) {
    Map map = (Map) itemBidMaps.next();
    Item item = (Item) map.get("this");
    Bid bid = (Bid) map.get("bid");
    // Do something
}
```

This is a second difference between the default behaviors of HQL and criteria queries: by default, HQL queries return all queried entities if we don't select explicitly.

Sometimes you'd like a less verbose way to express a join. In Hibernate, you can use an *implicit association join*.

7.3.4 *Using implicit joins*

So far, we've used simple qualified property names like `bid.amount` and `item.description` in our HQL queries. HQL supports multipart property path expressions for two purposes:

- Querying components
- Expressing implicit association joins

The first use is straightforward:

```
from User u where u.address.city = 'Bangkok'
```

We express the parts of the mapped component `Address` with dot notation. This usage is also supported by the `Criteria` API:

```
session.createCriteria(User.class)
        .add( Expression.eq("address.city", "Bangkok") );
```

The second usage, implicit association joining, is available only in HQL. For example:

```
from Bid bid where bid.item.description like '%gc%'
```

This results in an implicit join on the many-to-one associations from `Bid` to `Item`. Implicit joins are always directed along many-to-one or one-to-one associations, never through a collection-valued association (you can't write `item.bids.amount`).

Multiple joins are possible in a single property path expression. If the association from `Item` to `Category` would be many-to-one (instead of the current many-to-many), we could write

```
from Bid bid where bid.item.category.name like 'Laptop%'
```

We frown on the use of this syntactic sugar for more complex queries. Joins are important, and especially when optimizing queries, you need to be able to see at a glance how many of them there are. Consider the following query (again, using a many-to-one from `Item` to `Category`):

```
from Bid bid
    where bid.item.category.name like 'Laptop%'
    and bid.item.successfulBid.amount > 100
```

How many joins are required to express this in SQL? Even if you get the answer right, we bet it takes you more than a few seconds. The answer is three; the generated SQL looks something like this:

```
select ...
from BID B
inner join ITEM I on B.ITEM_ID = I.ITEM_ID
inner join CATEGORY C on I.CATEGORY_ID = C.CATEGORY_ID
inner join BID SB on I.SUCCESSFUL_BID_ID = SB.BID_ID
where C.NAME like 'Laptop%'
and SB.AMOUNT > 100
```

It's more obvious if we express the same query like this:

```
from Bid bid
join bid.item item
    where item.category.name like 'Laptop%'
    and item.successfulBid.amount > 100
```

We can even be more verbose:

```
from Bid as bid
join bid.item as item
join item.category as cat
join item.successfulBid as winningBid
    where cat.name like 'Laptop%'
    and winningBid.amount > 100
```

Let's continue with `join` conditions using arbitrary attributes, expressed in *theta-style*.

7.3.5 *Theta-style joins*

A Cartesian product allows you to retrieve all possible combinations of instances of two or more classes. This query returns all ordered pairs of `User`s and `Category` objects:

```
from User, Category
```

Obviously, this generally isn't useful. There is one case where it's commonly used: *theta-style joins.*

In traditional SQL, a theta-style join is a Cartesian product, together with a join condition in the `where` clause, which is applied on the product to restrict the result.

In HQL, the theta-style syntax is useful when your join condition isn't a foreign key relationship mapped to a class association. For example, suppose we store the `User`'s name in log records instead of mapping an association from `LogRecord` to `User`. The classes don't "know" anything about each other, because they aren't associated. We can then find all the `User`s and their `LogRecord`s with the following theta-style join:

```
from User user, LogRecord log where user.username = log.username
```

The join condition here is the `username`, presented as an attribute in both classes. If both entities have the same `username`, they're joined (with an inner join) in the result. The query result consists of ordered pairs:

```
Iterator i = session.createQuery(
                        "from User user, LogRecord log " +
                        "where user.username = log.username"
                    )
                    .list().iterator();
while ( i.hasNext() ) {
    Object[] pair = (Object[]) i.next();
    User user = (User) pair[0];
    LogRecord log = (LogRecord) pair[1];
}
```

We can change the result by adding a `select` clause.

You probably won't need to use theta-style joins often. Note that the `Criteria` API doesn't provide any means for expressing Cartesian products or theta-style joins. It's also currently not possible in Hibernate to outer-join two tables that don't have a mapped association.

7.3.6 *Comparing identifiers*

It's extremely common to perform queries that compare primary key or foreign key values to either query parameters or other primary or foreign key values. If you think about this in more object-oriented terms, what you're doing is comparing object references. HQL supports the following:

```
from Item i, User u
    where i.seller = u and u.username = 'steve'
```

In this query, `i.seller` refers to the foreign key to the `USER` table in the `ITEM` table (on the `SELLER_ID` column), and `user` refers to the primary key of the `USER` table (on the `USER_ID` column). This query uses a theta-style join and is equivalent to the much preferred ANSI style:

```
from Item i join i.seller u
    where u.username = 'steve'
```

On the other hand, the following theta-style join *cannot* be re-expressed as a `from` clause join:

```
from Item i, Bid b
where i.seller = b.bidder
```

In this case, `i.seller` and `b.bidder` are both foreign keys of the `USER` table. Note that this is an important query in our application; we use it to identify people bidding for their own items.

We might also like to compare a foreign key value to a query parameter—for example, to find all `Comments` from a `User`:

```
User user = ...
Query q =
    session.createQuery("from Comment c where c.fromUser = :user");
q.setEntity("user", givenUser);
List result = q.list();
```

Alternatively, sometimes we'd prefer to express these kinds of queries in terms of identifier values rather than object references. You can refer to an identifier value by either the name of the identifier property (if there is one) or the special property name `id`. Every persistent entity class has this special HQL property, even if you don't implement an identifier property on the class (see chapter 3, section 3.4.2, "Database identity with Hibernate").

These queries are exactly equivalent to the previous queries:

```
from Item i, User u
    where i.seller.id = u.id and u.username = 'steve'
from Item i, Bid b
    where i.seller.id = b.bidder.id
```

However, we can now use the identifier value as a query parameter:

```
Long userId = ...
Query q =
    session.createQuery("from Comment c where c.fromUser.id = :id");
    q.setLong("id", userId);
List result = q.list();
```

You might have noticed that there is a world of difference between the following queries:

```
from Bid b where b.item.id = 1
```

```
from Bid b where b.item.description like '%gc'
```

The second query uses an implicit table join; the first has no joins at all.

We've now covered most of the features of Hibernate's query facilities that are commonly needed for retrieving objects for manipulation in business logic. In the next section, we'll change our focus and discuss features of HQL that are used mainly for analysis and reporting functionality.

7.4 *Writing report queries*

Reporting queries take advantage of the database's ability to perform efficient grouping and aggregation of data.

They're more relational in nature; they don't always return entities. For example, instead of retrieving Item entities that are transactional (and automatically dirty-checked), a report query might only retrieve the Item names and initial auction prices. If this is the only information we need (maybe even aggregated—the highest initial price in a category, and so on) for a report screen, we don't need transactional entities and can save the (albeit small) overhead of automatic dirty-checking and caching in the Session.

We won't talk about the Criteria API in this section, because it hasn't (yet) been adapted for reporting queries.

Let's consider the structure of an HQL query again.

The only required clause of an HQL query is the `from` clause. All other clauses are optional. The full structure of HQL is given by the following form:

```
[select ...] from ... [where ...]
    [group by ... [having ...]] [order by ...]
```

So far, we've discussed the `from`, `where`, and `order by` clauses. We used the `select` clause to declare which entities should be returned in a join query.

In reporting queries, you use the `select` clause for projection and the `group by` and `having` clauses for aggregation.

7.4.1 *Projection*

The `select` clause performs projection. It lets you specify which objects or properties of objects you need in the query result. For example, as you've already seen, the following query returns ordered pairs of `Item`s and `Bid`s:

```
from Item item join item.bids bid where bid.amount > 100
```

If we only need to use the `Item`s in our unit of work, we should use this query instead:

```
select item from Item item join item.bids bid where bid.amount > 100
```

Or, if we were just displaying a list screen to the user, it might be enough to retrieve only the properties we have to display:

```
select item.id, item.description, bid.amount
    from Item item join item.bids bid
    where bid.amount > 100
```

This query returns each row of results as an `Object[]` array of length 3. It's a report query; all objects in the result aren't Hibernate entities and aren't transactional. We use them in a read-only procedure. Let's execute it:

```
Iterator i = session.createQuery(
        "select item.id, item.description, bid.amount " +
        "from Item item join item.bids bid " +
        "where bid.amount > 100"
)
.list()
.iterator();

while ( i.hasNext() ) {
    Object[] row = (Object[]) i.next();

    Long id = (Long) row[0];
    String description = (String) row[1];
    BigDecimal amount = (BigDecimal) row[2];

    // ... show values in a report screen
}
```

Using dynamic instantiation

Since the previous example was verbose and not very object-oriented (working with a tabular data representation in arrays), we can define a class to represent each row of results and use the HQL select new construct:

```
select new ItemRow( item.id, item.description, bid.amount )
    from Item item join item.bids bid
    where bid.amount > 100
```

Assuming that the ItemRow class has an appropriate constructor (you have to write that class), this query returns newly instantiated (transient) instances of ItemRow, as you can see in the next example:

```
Iterator i = session.createQuery(
        "select new ItemRow( item.id, item.description, bid.amount ) " +
        "from Item item join item.bids bid " +
        "where bid.amount > 100"
)
.list()
.iterator();

while ( i.hasNext() ) {
    ItemRow row = (ItemRow) i.next();
    // Do something
}
```

The custom ItemRow class doesn't have to be a persistent class; it doesn't have to be mapped to the database or even be known to Hibernate. ItemRow is therefore only a data-transfer class, useful in report generation.

Getting distinct results

When you use a select clause, the elements of the result are no longer guaranteed to be unique. For example, Items descriptions aren't unique, so the following query might return the same description more than once:

```
select item.description from Item item
```

It's difficult to see how it could possibly be meaningful to have two identical rows in a query result, so if you think duplicates are likely, you should use the distinct keyword:

```
select distinct item.description from Item item
```

This eliminates duplicates from the returned list of Item descriptions.

Calling SQL functions

It's also possible (for some Hibernate SQL dialects) to call database-specific SQL functions from the select clause (remember, you can freely do it in the where clause). For example, the following query retrieves the current date and time from the database server (Oracle syntax), together with a property of Item:

```
select item.startDate, sysdate from Item item
```

The technique of database functions in the select clause is of course not limited to database-dependent functions, but to other, more generic (or standardized) SQL functions as well:

```
select item.startDate, item.endDate, upper(item.name)
    from Item item
```

This query returns an Object[] with the starting and ending date of an item auction, and the name of the item all in uppercase.

In particular, it's possible to call SQL *aggregate functions*.

7.4.2 Using aggregation

Hibernate recognizes the following aggregate functions: count(), min(), max(), sum(), and avg().

This query counts all the Items:

```
select count(*) from Item
```

The result is returned as an Integer:

```
Integer count =
    (Integer) session.createQuery("select count(*) from Item")
                     .uniqueResult();
```

Notice how we use *, which has the same semantics as in SQL.

The next variation of the query counts all Items that have a successfulBid:

```
select count(item.successfulBid) from Item item
```

This query calculates the total of all the successful Bids:

```
select sum(item.successfulBid.amount) from Item item
```

The query returns a BigDecimal. Notice the use of an implicit join in the select clause: We navigate the association (successfulBid) from Item to Bid by referencing it with a dot.

The next query returns the minimum and maximum bid amounts for a particular Item:

```
select min(bid.amount), max(bid.amount)
    from Bid bid where bid.item.id = 1
```

The result is an ordered pair of `BigDecimals` (two instances of `BigDecimal` in an `Object[]` array).

The special `count(distinct)` function ignores duplicates:

```
select count(distinct item.description) from Item item
```

When you call an aggregate function in the `select` clause without specifying any grouping in a `group by` clause, you collapse the result down to a single row containing your aggregated value(s). This means (in the absence of a `group by` clause) any `select` clause that contains an aggregate function must contain only aggregate functions.

So, for more advanced statistics and reporting, you'll need to be able to perform *grouping*.

7.4.3 *Grouping*

Just like in SQL, any property or alias that appears in HQL outside of an aggregate function in the `select` clause must also appear in the `group by` clause.

Consider the next query, which counts the number of users with each particular last name:

```
select u.lastname, count(u) from User u
    group by u.lastname
```

Now look at the generated SQL:

```
select U.LAST_NAME, count(U.USER_ID)
    from USER U
    group by U.LAST_NAME
```

In this example, the `u.lastname` isn't inside an aggregate function; we use it to group the result. We also don't need to specify the property we'd like to count in HQL. The generated SQL will automatically use the primary key if we use an alias that has been set in the `from` clause.

The next query finds the average bid amount for each item:

```
select bid.item.id, avg(bid.amount) from Bid bid
group by bid.item.id
```

This query returns ordered pairs of `Item` identifiers and average bid amount. Notice how we use the `id` special property to refer to the identifier of a persistent class no matter what the identifier's real property name is.

The next query counts the number of bids and calculates the average bid per unsold item:

```
select bid.item.id, count(bid), avg(bid.amount)
    from Bid bid
    where bid.item.successfulBid is null
    group by bid.item.id
```

This query uses an implicit association join. For an explicit ordinary join in the from clause (not a fetch join), we can re-express it as follows:

```
select bidItem.id, count(bid), avg(bid.amount)
    from Bid bid
        join bid.item bidItem
    where bidItem.successfulBid is null
    group by bidItem.id
```

To initialize the bids collection of the Items, we can use a fetch join and refer to the associations starting on the other side:

```
select item.id, count(bid), avg(bid.amount)
    from Item item
        fetch join item.bids bid
    where item.successfulBid is null
    group by item.id
```

Sometimes, you'll want to further restrict the result by selecting only particular values of a group.

7.4.4 Restricting groups with having

The where clause is used to perform the relational operation of restriction on rows. The having clause performs restriction on groups.

For example, the next query counts users with each last name that begins with *A*:

```
select user.lastname, count(user)
    from User user
    group by user.lastname
        having user.lastname like 'A%'
```

The same rules govern the select and having clauses: Only grouped properties may appear outside an aggregate function. The next query counts the number of bids per unsold item, returning results for only those items that have more than 10 bids:

```
select item.id, count(bid), avg(bid.amount)
    from Item item
        join item.bids bid
```

```
where item.successfulBid is null
group by item.id
    having count(bid) > 10
```

Most report queries use a `select` clause to choose a list of projected or aggregated properties. You've seen that when more than one property or alias is listed in the `select` clause, Hibernate returns the query results as tuples: Each row of the query result list is an instance of `Object[]`. Tuples are inconvenient and non-typesafe, so Hibernate provides the `select new` constructor as mentioned earlier. You can create new objects dynamically with this technique and also use it in combination with aggregation and grouping.

If we define a class called `ItemBidSummary` with a constructor that takes a `Long`, a `String`, and an `Integer`, we can use the following query:

```
select new ItemBidSummary( bid.item.id, count(bid), avg(bid.amount) )
    from Bid bid
    where bid.item.successfulBid is null
    group by bid.item.id
```

In the result of this query, each element is an instance of `ItemBidSummary`, which is a summary of an `Item`, the number of bids for that item, and the average bid amount. This approach is typesafe, and a data transfer class such as `ItemBidSummary` can easily be extended for special formatted printing of values in reports.

7.4.5 *Improving performance with report queries*

Report queries can have an impact on the performance of your application. Let's explore this issue in more depth.

The only time we've seen any significant overhead in Hibernate code compared to direct JDBC queries—and then only for unrealistically simple test cases—is in the special case of read-only queries against a local database. It's possible for a database to completely cache query results in memory and respond quickly, so benchmarks are generally useless if the dataset is small: Plain SQL and JDBC will always be the fastest option.

On the other hand, even with a small dataset, Hibernate must still do the work of adding the resulting objects of a query to the `Session` cache (perhaps also the second-level cache) and manage uniqueness, and so on. Report queries give you a way to avoid the overhead of managing the `Session` cache. The overhead of a Hibernate report query compared to direct SQL/JDBC isn't usually measurable, even in unrealistic extreme cases like loading one million objects from a local database without network latency.

Report queries using projection in HQL let you specify exactly which properties you wish to retrieve. For report queries, you aren't selecting entities, but only properties or aggregated values:

```
select user.lastname, count(user) from User user
    group by user.lastname
```

This query doesn't return a persistent entity, so Hibernate doesn't add a transactional object to the `Session` cache. This also means that no object must be watched for dirty state.

Reporting queries result in faster release of allocated memory, since objects aren't kept in the `Session` cache until the `Session` is closed—they may be garbage-collected as soon as they're dereferenced by the application, after executing the report.

These considerations are almost always extremely minor, so don't go out and rewrite all your read-only transactions to use report queries instead of transactional, cached, and monitored objects. Report queries are more verbose and (arguably) less object-oriented. They also make less efficient use of Hibernate's caches, which is much more important once you consider the overhead of remote communication with the database in production systems. You should wait until you find an actual case where you have a performance problem before using this optimization.

Let's get back to regular entity queries. There are still many Hibernate features waiting to be discovered.

7.5 Advanced query techniques

You'll use advanced query techniques less frequently with Hibernate, but you should know about them. In this section, we talk about programmatically building criteria with example objects, a topic we briefly introduced earlier.

Filtering collections is also a handy technique: You can use the database instead of filtering objects in memory. Subqueries and queries in native SQL will round out your knowledge of Hibernate query techniques.

7.5.1 Dynamic queries

It's common for queries to be built programmatically by combining several optional query criteria depending on user input. For example, a system administrator may wish to search for users by any combination of first name or last name, and to retrieve the result ordered by username. Using HQL, we could build the query using string manipulations:

```
public List findUsers(String firstname,
                      String lastname)
    throws HibernateException {

    StringBuffer queryString = new StringBuffer();
    boolean conditionFound = false;

    if (firstname != null) {
        queryString.append("lower(u.firstname) like :firstname ");
        conditionFound=true;
    }
    if (lastname != null) {
        if (conditionFound) queryString.append("and ");
        queryString.append("lower(u.lastname) like :lastname ");
        conditionFound=true;
    }

    String fromClause = conditionFound ?
                            "from User u where " :
                            "from User u ";

    queryString.insert(0, fromClause).append("order by u.username");

    Query query = getSession().createQuery( queryString.toString() );

    if (firstname != null)
        query.setString( "firstname",
                            '%' + firstname.toLowerCase() + '%' );
    if (lastname != null)
        query.setString( "lastname",
                            '%' + lastname.toLowerCase() + '%' );

    return query.list();
}
```

This code is tedious and noisy, so let's try a different approach. The `Criteria` API looks promising:

```
public List findUsers(String firstname,
                      String lastname)
    throws HibernateException {

    Criteria crit = getSession().createCriteria(User.class);

    if (firstname != null) {
        crit.add( Expression.ilike("firstname",
                                    firstname,
                                    MatchMode.ANYWHERE) );
    }
    if (lastname != null) {
        crit.add( Expression.ilike("lastname",
                                    lastname,
                                    MatchMode.ANYWHERE) );
    }
```

```
        crit.addOrder( Order.asc("username") );

        return crit.list();
    }
```

This code is much shorter. Note that the `ilike()` operator performs a case-insensitive match. There seems no doubt that this is a better approach. However, for search screens with many optional search criteria, there is an even better way.

First, observe that as we add new search criteria, the parameter list of `findUsers()` grows. It would be better to capture the searchable properties as an object. Since all the search properties belong to the `User` class, why not use an instance of `User`.

QBE uses this idea. You provide an instance of the queried class with some properties initialized, and the query returns all persistent instances with matching property values. Hibernate implements QBE as part of the `Criteria` query API:

```
public List findUsers(User u) throws HibernateException {

    Example exampleUser =
      Example.create(u).ignoreCase().enableLike(MatchMode.ANYWHERE);

    return getSession().createCriteria(User.class)
                      .add(exampleUser)
                      .list();
}
```

The call to `create()` returns a new instance of `Example` for the given instance of `User`. The `ignoreCase()` method puts the example query into a case-insensitive mode for all string-valued properties. The call to `enableLike()` specifies that the SQL `like` operator should be used for all string-valued properties, and specifies a `MatchMode`.

We've significantly simplified the code *again*. The nicest thing about Hibernate `Example` queries is that an `Example` is just an ordinary `Criterion`. So, you can freely mix and match QBE with QBC.

Let's see how this works by further restricting the search results to users with unsold `Items`. For this purpose, we add a `Criteria` to the example user, constraining the result using its `items` collection of `Items`:

```
public List findUsers(User u) throws HibernateException {

    Example exampleUser =
      Example.create(u).ignoreCase().enableLike(MatchMode.ANYWHERE);

    return getSession().createCriteria(User.class)
            .add( exampleUser )
                .createCriteria("items")
```

```
                        .add( Expression.isNull("successfulBid") )
                .list();
    }
```

Even better, we can combine `User` properties and `Item` properties in the same search:

```
public List findUsers(User u, Item i) throws HibernateException {

    Example exampleUser =
      Example.create(u).ignoreCase().enableLike(MatchMode.ANYWHERE);

    Example exampleItem =
      Example.create(i).ignoreCase().enableLike(MatchMode.ANYWHERE);

    return getSession().createCriteria(User.class)
            .add( exampleUser )
                .createCriteria("items")
                    .add( exampleItem )
            .list();
    }
```

At this point, we invite you to step back and consider how much code would be required to implement this search screen using handcoded SQL/JDBC. We won't reproduce it here; it would stretch for pages.

7.5.2 Collection filters

You'll commonly want to execute a query against all elements of a particular collection. For instance, we might have an `Item` and wish to retrieve all bids for that particular item, ordered by the time the bid was created. We already know one good way to write this query:

```
List results =
    session.createQuery("from Bid b where b.item = :item " +
                        "order by b.amount asc")
            .setEntity("item", item)
            .list();
```

This query works perfectly, since the association between bids and items is bidirectional and each `Bid` knows its `Item`. Imagine that this association was unidirectional: `Item` has a collection of `Bids`, but there is no inverse association from `Bid` to `Item`.

We could try the following query:

```
String query = "select bid from Item item join item.bids bid "
             + "where item = :item order by bid.amount asc";

List results = session.createQuery(query)
                        .setEntity("item", item)
                        .list();
```

This query is inefficient—it uses an unnecessary join. A better, more elegant solution is to use a *collection filter:* a special query that can be applied to a persistent collection (or array). It's commonly used to further restrict or order a result. We use it on an already loaded Item and its collection of bids:

```
List results = session.createFilter( item.getBids(),
                                      "order by this.amount asc" )
                 .list();
```

This filter is equivalent to the first query shown earlier and results in identical SQL. Collection filters have an implicit from clause and an implicit where condition. The alias this refers implicitly to elements of the collection of bids.

Hibernate collection filters are *not* executed in memory. The collection of bids may be uninitialized when the filter is called and, if so, will remain uninitialized. Furthermore, filters don't apply to transient collections or query results; they may only be applied to a persistent collection currently referenced by an object associated with the Hibernate session.

The only required clause of an HQL query is from. Since a collection filter has an implicit from clause, the following is a valid filter:

```
List results = session.createFilter( item.getBids(), "" ).list();
```

To the great surprise of everyone (including the designer of this feature), this trivial filter turns out to be useful! You can use it to paginate collection elements:

```
List results = session.createFilter( item.getBids(), "" )
                 .setFirstResult(50)
                 .setMaxResults(100)
                 .list();
```

Usually, however, we'd use an order by with paginated queries.

Even though you don't need a from clause in a collection filter, you can include one if you like. A collection filter doesn't even need to return elements of the collection being filtered. The next query returns any Category with the same name as a category in the given collection:

```
String filterString =
    "select other from Category other where this.name = other.name";

List results =
    session.createFilter( cat.getChildCategories(), filterString )
             .list();
```

The following query returns a collection of Users who have bid on the item:

```
List results =
    session.createFilter( item.getBids(),
                            "select this.bidder" )
            .list();
```

The next query returns all these users' bids (including those for other items):

```
List results = session.createFilter(
    item.getBids(),
    "select elements(this.bidder.bids)"
).list();
```

Note that the query uses the special HQL elements() function (explained later) to select all elements of a collection.

The most important reason for the existence of collection filters is to allow the application to retrieve some elements of a collection without initializing the entire collection. In the case of very large collections, this is important to achieve acceptable performance. The following query retrieves all bids made by a user in the past week:

```
List results =
    session.createFilter( user.getBids(),
                            "where this.created > :oneWeekAgo" )
            .setTimestamp("oneWeekAgo", oneWeekAgo)
            .list();
```

Again, this query does *not* initialize the bids collection of the User.

7.5.3 *Subqueries*

Subselects are an important and powerful feature of SQL. A subselect is a select query embedded in another query, usually in the select, from, or where clause.

HQL supports subqueries in the where clause. We can't think of many good uses for subqueries in the from clause, although select clause subqueries might be a nice future extension. (You might remember from chapter 3 that a *derived property* mapping is in fact a select clause subselect.) Note that some platforms supported by Hibernate don't implement subselects. In particular, only the latest versions of MySQL support subqueries. If you desire portability among many different databases, you shouldn't use this feature.

The result of a subquery might contain either a single row or multiple rows. Typically, subqueries that return single rows perform aggregation. The following subquery returns the total number of items sold by a user; the outer query returns all users who have sold more than 10 items:

```
from User u where 10 < (
    select count(i) from u.items i where i.successfulBid is not null
)
```

This is a *correlated subquery*—it refers to an alias (u) from the outer query. The next subquery is an *uncorrelated subquery:*

```
from Bid bid where bid.amount + 1 >= (
    select max(b.amount) from Bid b
)
```

The subquery in this example returns the maximum bid amount in the entire system; the outer query returns all bids whose amount is within one (dollar) of that amount.

Note that in both cases, the subquery is enclosed in parentheses. This is always required.

Uncorrelated subqueries are harmless; there is no reason not to use them when convenient, although they can always be rewritten as two queries (after all, they don't reference each other). You should think more carefully about the performance impact of correlated subqueries. On a mature database, the performance cost of a simple correlated subquery is similar to the cost of a join. However, it isn't necessarily possible to rewrite a correlated subquery using several separate queries.

If a subquery returns multiple rows, it's combined with *quantification.* ANSI SQL (and HQL) defines the following quantifiers:

- any
- all
- some (a synonym for any)
- in (a synonym for = any)

For example, the following query returns items where all bids are less than 100:

```
from Item item where 100 > all ( select b.amount from item.bids b )
```

The next query returns all items with bids greater than 100:

```
from Item item where 100 < any ( select b.amount from item.bids b )
```

This query returns items with a bid of exactly 100:

```
from Item item where 100 = some ( select b.amount from item.bids b )
```

So does this one:

```
from Item item where 100 in ( select b.amount from item.bids b )
```

HQL supports a shortcut syntax for subqueries that operate on elements or indices of a collection. The following query uses the special HQL `elements()` function:

```
List list = session.createQuery("from Category c " +
                           "where :item in elements(c.items)")
                .setEntity("item", item)
                .list();
```

The query returns all categories to which the item belongs and is equivalent to the following HQL, where the subquery is more explicit:

```
List results = session.createQuery("from Category c " +
                           "where :item in (from c.items)")
                .setEntity("item", item)
                .list();
```

Along with `elements()`, HQL provides `indices()`, `maxelement()`, `minelement()`, `maxindex()`, `minindex()`, and `size()`, each of which is equivalent to a certain correlated subquery against the passed collection. Refer to the Hibernate documentation for more information about these special functions; they're rarely used.

Subqueries are an advanced technique; you should question their frequent use, since queries with subqueries can often be rewritten using only joins and aggregation. However, they're powerful and useful from time to time.

By now, we hope you're convinced that Hibernate's query facilities are flexible, powerful, and easy to use. HQL provides almost all the functionality of ANSI standard SQL. Of course, on rare occasions you *do* need to resort to handcrafted SQL, especially when you wish to take advantage of database features that go beyond the functionality specified by the ANSI standard.

7.5.4 *Native SQL queries*

We can think of two good examples why you might use native SQL queries in Hibernate: HQL provides no mechanism for specifying SQL query hints, and it also doesn't support hierarchical queries (such as the Oracle CONNECT BY clause). We suppose that you'll stumble on other examples.

In these (relatively rare) cases, you're free to resort to using the JDBC API directly. However, doing so means writing the tedious code by hand to transform a JDBC ResultSet to an object graph. You can avoid all this work by using Hibernate's built-in support for native SQL queries.

You only need to learn one trick. An SQL query result may return the state of multiple entity instances in each row and even the state of multiple instances of the same entity. You need a way to distinguish between the different entities. Hibernate uses a naming scheme for the result column aliases to correctly map column values to the properties of particular instances. You wouldn't want the details of this naming scheme to be exposed to the user; instead, native SQL queries are specified with placeholders for the column aliases.

The following native SQL query shows what these placeholders—the names enclosed in braces—look like:

```
String sql = "select u.USER_ID as {uzer.id},"
        + " u.FIRSTNAME as {uzer.firstname},"
        + " u.LASTNAME as {uzer.lastname} from USERS u";
```

Each placeholder specifies an HQL-style property name. When we call this query in code, we must provide the entity class that is referred to by uzer in the placeholders. This tells Hibernate what type of entity is returned by the query:

```
List results =
    session.createSQLQuery(sql, "uzer", User.class).list();
```

If User is mapped to the USER table, it's verbose to respecify all the mappings from columns to properties in this way. Here's a shortcut:

```
List results =
    session.createSQLQuery("select {uzer.*} from USERS uzer",
                        "uzer", User.class)
            .list();
```

The {uzer.*} placeholder is replaced with a list of the mapped column names and correct column aliases for all properties of the User entity. The name used in the placeholder must be the same name that is used as the table alias in the SQL query (uzer in this example).

Note that the following variation works, but it isn't good style:

```
List results =
    session.createSQLQuery("select {users.*} from users",
                        "users",
                        User.class)
            .list();
```

In this case, there is no explicit table alias, so the implicit alias is the same as the table name users (note the lowercase).

A native SQL query may return tuples of entities (as usual, Hibernate represents a tuple as an instance of Object[]):

```
List tuples = session.createSQLQuery(
        "select {u.*}, {b.*} from USERS u inner join BID b" +
        " where u.USER_ID = b.BIDDER_ID",
```

```
    new String[] { "u", "b" },
    new Class[] {User.class, Bid.class} )
.list();
```

You may also have named SQL queries separate from application code in your Hibernate mapping files. We use the `<return>` element to specify the query return types:

```
<sql-query name="findUsersAndBids"><![CDATA[
    select {u.*}, {b.*} from USERS u inner join BID b
        where u.USER_ID = b.BIDDER_ID
    ]]>
    <return alias="u" class="User"/>
    <return alias="b" class="Bid"/>
</sql-query>
```

Since the native SQL is tightly coupled to the actual mapped tables and columns, we strongly recommend that you define all native SQL queries in the mapping document instead of embedding them in the Java code.

If, in some special cases, you need even more control over the SQL that is executed, or if you want to call a stored procedure using JDBC, Hibernate offers you a way to get a JDBC connection. A call to `session.connection()` returns the currently active JDBC `Connection` from the `Session`. It's not your responsibility to close this connection, just to execute whatever SQL statements you like and then continue using the `Session` (and finally, close the `Session`). The same is true for transactions; you must not commit or roll back this connection yourself (unless you completely manage the connection for Hibernate, without a connection pool or container datasource).

FAQ *How do I execute a stored procedure with Hibernate?* In Hibernate 2.x, there is no direct support for stored procedures. You have to get the JDBC connection and execute the SQL yourself. However, direct stored procedure support was implemented for the next major Hibernate version at the time of writing. You will soon be able to map CUD operations for entities to stored procedures and directly call any stored procedure using a Hibernate API.

When you're writing queries and testing them in your application, you may encounter one of the common performance issues with ORM. Fortunately, we know how to avoid (or, at least, limit) their impact. This process is called *optimizing object retrieval.* Let's walk through the most common issues.

7.6 *Optimizing object retrieval*

Performance-tuning your application should first include the most obvious settings, such as the best fetching strategies and use of proxies, as shown in chapter 4. (Note that we consider enabling the second-level cache to be the last optimization you usually make.)

The *fetch joins*, part of the *runtime fetching strategies*, as introduced in this chapter, deserve some extra attention. However, some design issues can't be resolved by tuning, but can only be avoided if possible.

7.6.1 *Solving the n+1 selects problem*

The biggest performance killer in applications that persist objects to SQL databases is the *n+1 selects problem*. When you tune the performance of a Hibernate application, this problem is the first thing you'll usually need to address.

It's normal (and recommended) to map almost all associations for lazy initialization. This means you generally set all collections to lazy="true" and even change some of the one-to-one and many-to-one associations to not use outer joins by default. This is the only way to avoid retrieving all objects in the database in every transaction. Unfortunately, this decision exposes you to the n+1 selects problem. It's easy to understand this problem by considering a simple query that retrieves all Items for a particular user:

```
Iterator items = session.createCriteria(Item.class)
    .add( Expression.eq("item.seller", user) )
    .list()
    .iterator();
```

This query returns a list of items, where each collection of bids is an uninitialized collection wrapper. Suppose that we now wish to find the maximum bid for each item. The following code would be one way to do this:

```
List maxAmounts = new ArrayList();
while (items.hasNext()) {
    Item item = (Item) items.next();
    BigDecimal maxAmount = new BigDecimal("0");
    for ( Iterator b = item.getBids().iterator(); b.hasNext(); ) {
        Bid bid = (Bid) b.next();
        if ( bid.getAmount().compareTo(maxAmount) == 1 )
            maxAmount = bid.getAmount();
    }
    maxAmounts.add( new MaxAmount( item.getId(), maxAmount ) );
}
```

But there is a huge problem with this solution (aside from the fact that this would be much better executed in the database using aggregation functions): Each time we access the collection of bids, Hibernate must fetch this lazy collection from the database for each item. If the initial query returns 20 items, the entire transaction requires 1 initial `select` that retrieves the items plus 20 additional `select`s to load the `bids` collections of each item. This might easily result in unacceptable latency in a system that accesses the database across a network. Usually you don't explicitly create such operations, because you should quickly see doing so is suboptimal. However, the n+1 selects problem is often hidden in more complex application logic, and you may not recognize it by looking at a single routine.

The first attempt to solve this problem might be to enable *batch fetching*. We change our mapping for the `bids` collection to look like this:

```
<set name="bids" lazy="true" inverse="true" batch-size="10">
```

With batch fetching enabled, Hibernate prefetches the next 10 collections when the first collection is accessed. This reduces the problem from n+1 selects to n/10 + 1 selects. For many applications, this may be sufficient to achieve acceptable latency. On the other hand, it also means that in some other transactions, collections are fetched unnecessarily. It isn't the best we can do in terms of reducing the number of round trips to the database.

A much, much better solution is to take advantage of HQL aggregation and perform the work of calculating the maximum bid on the database. Thus we avoid the problem:

```
String query = "select MaxAmount( item.id, max(bid.amount) )"
            + " from Item item join item.bids bid"
            + " where item.seller = :user group by item.id";

List maxAmounts = session.createQuery(query)
                        .setEntity("user", user)
                        .list();
```

Unfortunately, this isn't a complete solution to the generic issue. In general, we may need to do more complex processing on the bids than merely calculating the maximum amount. We'd prefer to do this processing in the Java application.

We can try enabling eager fetching at the level of the mapping document:

```
<set name="bids" inverse="true" outer-join="true">
```

The `outer-join` attribute is available for collections and other associations. It forces Hibernate to load the association eagerly, using an SQL `outer join`.

Note that, as previously mentioned, HQL queries ignore the `outer-join` attribute; but we might be using a criteria query.

This mapping avoids the problem as far as this transaction is concerned; we're now able to load all bids in the initial select. Unfortunately, any other transaction that retrieves items using `get()`, `load()`, or a criteria query will also retrieve all the bids at once. Retrieving unnecessary data imposes extra load on both the database server and the application server and may also reduce the concurrency of the system, creating too many unnecessary read locks at the database level.

Hence we consider eager fetching at the level of the mapping file to be almost always a bad approach. The `outer-join` attribute of collection mappings is arguably a misfeature of Hibernate (fortunately, it's disabled by default). Occasionally it makes sense to enable `outer-join` for a `<many-to-one>` or `<one-to-one>` association (the default is `auto`; see chapter 4, section 4.4.6.1, "Single point associations"), but we'd never do this in the case of a collection.

Our recommended solution for this problem is to take advantage of Hibernate's support for runtime (code-level) declarations of association fetching strategies. The example can be implemented like this:

```
List results = session.createCriteria(Item.class)
                        .add( Expression.eq("item.seller", user) )
                        .setFetchMode("bids", FetchMode.EAGER)
                        .list();

// Make results distinct
Iterator items = new HashSet(results).iterator();

List maxAmounts = new ArrayList();
for ( ; items.hasNext(); ) {
    Item item = (Item) items.next();
    BigDecimal maxAmount = new BigDecimal("0");
    for ( Iterator b = item.getBids().iterator(); b.hasNext(); ) {
        Bid bid = (Bid) b.next();
        if ( bid.getAmount().compareTo(maxAmount) == 1 )
            maxAmount = bid.getAmount();
    }
    maxAmounts.add( new MaxAmount( item.getId(), maxAmount ) );
}
```

We disabled batch fetching and eager fetching at the mapping level; the collection is lazy by default. Instead, we enable eager fetching for this query alone by calling `setFetchMode()`. As discussed earlier in this chapter, this is equivalent to a `fetch join` in the `from` clause of an HQL query.

The previous code example has one extra complication: The result list returned by the Hibernate criteria query isn't guaranteed to be distinct. In the case of a query that fetches a collection by outer join, it will contain duplicate items. It's the application's responsibility to make the results distinct if that is required. We implement this by adding the results to a `HashSet` and then iterating the set.

So, we have established a general solution to the n+1 selects problem. Rather than retrieving just the top-level objects in the initial query and then fetching needed associations as the application navigates the object graph, we follow a two-step process:

1. Fetch all needed data in the initial query by specifying exactly which associations will be accessed in the following unit of work.

2. Navigate the object graph, which will consist entirely of objects that have already been fetched from the database.

This is the only true solution to the mismatch between the object-oriented world, where data is accessed by navigation, and the relational world, where data is accessed by joining.

Finally, there is one further solution to the n+1 selects problem. For some classes or collections with a sufficiently small number of instances, it's possible to keep all instances in the second-level cache, avoiding the need for database access. Obviously, this solution is preferred where and when it's possible (it isn't possible in the case of the `bids` of an `Item`, because we wouldn't enable caching for this kind of data).

The n+1 selects problem may appear whenever we use the `list()` method of `Query` to retrieve the result. As we mentioned earlier, this issue can be hidden in more complex logic; we highly recommend the optimization strategies mentioned in chapter 4, section 4.4.7, "Tuning object retrieval" to find such scenarios. It's also possible to generate too many selects by using `find()`, the shortcut for queries on the `Session` API, or `load()` and `get()`.

There is a third query API method we haven't discussed yet. It's extremely important to understand when it's applicable, because it produces n+1 selects!

7.6.2 Using iterate() queries

The `iterate()` method of the `Session` and `Query` interfaces behaves differently than the `find()` and `list()` methods. It's provided specifically to let you take full advantage of the second-level cache.

Consider the following code:

```
Query categoryByName =
    session.createQuery("from Category c where c.name like :name");
categoryByName.setString("name", categoryNamePattern);
List categories = categoryByName.list();
```

This query results in execution of an SQL select, with all columns of the CATEGORY table included in the select clause:

```
select CATEGORY_ID, NAME, PARENT_ID from CATEGORY where NAME like ?
```

If we expect that categories are already cached in the session or second-level cache, then we only need the identifier value (the key to the cache). This will reduce the amount of data we have to fetch from the database. The following SQL would be slightly more efficient:

```
select CATEGORY_ID from CATEGORY where NAME like ?
```

We can use the iterate() method:

```
Query categoryByName =
    session.createQuery("from Category c where c.name like :name");
categoryByName.setString("name", categoryNamePattern);
Iterator categories = categoryByName.iterate();
```

The initial query only retrieves the category primary key values. We then iterate through the result, and Hibernate looks up each Category in the current session and in the second-level cache. If a cache miss occurs, Hibernate executes an additional select, retrieving the category by its primary key from the database.

In most cases, this is a minor optimization. It's usually much more important to minimize *row* reads than to minimize *column* reads. Still, if your object has large string fields, this technique may be useful to minimize data packets on the network and, therefore, latency.

Let's talk about another optimization, which also isn't applicable in every case. So far, we've only discussed caching the results of a lookup by identifier (including implicit lookups, such as loading a lazy association) in chapter 5. It's also possible to cache the results of Hibernate queries.

7.6.3 *Caching queries*

For applications that perform many queries and few inserts, deletes, or updates, caching queries can have an impact on performance. However, if the application performs many writes, the query cache won't be utilized efficiently. Hibernate expires a cached query result set when there is *any* insert, update, or delete of any row of a table that appears in the query.

Just as not all classes or collections should be cached, not all queries should be cached or will benefit from caching. For example, if a search screen has many different search criteria, then it's unlikely that the user will choose the same criterion twice. In this case, the cached query results won't be utilized, and we'd be better off not enabling caching for that query.

Note that the query cache does *not* cache the entities returned in the query result set, just the identifier values. Hibernate will, however, fully cache the value typed data returned by a projection query. For example, the projection query `"select u, b.created from User u, Bid b where b.bidder = u"` will result in caching of the identifiers of the users and the date object when they made their bids. It's the responsibility of the second-level cache (in conjunction with the session cache) to cache the actual state of entities. So, if the cached query you just saw is executed again, Hibernate will have the bid-creation dates in the query cache but perform a lookup in the session and second-level cache (or even execute SQL again) for each user that was in the result. This is similar to the lookup strategy of `iterate()`, as explained in the previous section.

The query cache must be enabled using a Hibernate property setting:

```
hibernate.cache.use_query_cache true
```

However, this setting alone isn't enough for Hibernate to cache query results. By default, Hibernate queries always ignore the cache. To enable query caching for a particular query (to allow its results to be added to the cache, and to allow it to draw its results *from* the cache), you use the `Query` interface:

```
Query categoryByName =
    session.createQuery("from Category c where c.name = :name");
categoryByName.setString("name", categoryName);
categoryByName.setCacheable(true);
```

Even this doesn't give you sufficient granularity, however. Different queries may require different query expiration policies. Hibernate allows you to specify a different named cache *region* for each query:

```
Query userByName =
    session.createQuery("from User u where u.username= :uname");
userByName.setString("uname", username);
userByName.setCacheable(true);
userByName.setCacheRegion("UserQueries");
```

You can now configure the cache expiration policies using the region name. When query caching is enabled, the cache regions are as follows:

- The default query cache region, `net.sf.hibernate.cache.QueryCache`

- Each named region

- The *timestamp cache*, `net.sf.hibernate.cache.UpdateTimestampsCache`, which is a special region that holds timestamps of the most recent updates to each table

Hibernate uses the timestamp cache to decide if a cached query result set is stale. Hibernate looks in the timestamp cache for the timestamp of the most recent insert, update, or delete made to the queried table. If it's later than the timestamp of the cached query results, then the cached results are discarded and a new query is issued. For best results, you should configure the timestamp cache so that the update timestamp for a table doesn't expire from the cache while queries against the table are still cached in one of the other regions. The easiest way is to turn off expiry for the timestamp cache.

Some final words about performance optimization: Remember that issues like the n+1 selects problem can slow your application to unacceptable performance. Try to avoid the problem by using the best fetching strategy. Verify that your object-retrieval technique is the best for your use case before you look into caching anything.

From our point of view, caching at the second level is an important feature, but it isn't the first option when optimizing performance. Errors in the design of queries or an unnecessarily complex part of your object model can't be improved with a "cache it all" approach. If an application only performs at an acceptable level with a *hot cache* (a full cache) after several hours or days of runtime, you should check it for serious design mistakes, unperformant queries, and n+1 selects problems.

7.7 *Summary*

We don't expect that you know everything about HQL and criteria after reading this chapter once. However, the chapter will be useful as a reference in your daily work with Hibernate, and we encourage you to come back and reread sections whenever you need to.

The code examples in this chapter show the three basic Hibernate query techniques: HQL, a query by criteria that includes a query by example mechanism, and direct execution of database-specific SQL queries.

We consider HQL the most powerful method. HQL queries are easy to understand, and they use persistent class and property names instead of table and column names. HQL is polymorphic: You can retrieve all objects with a given interface by querying for that interface. With HQL, you have the full power of arbitrary restrictions and projection of results, with logical operators and function calls just as in SQL, but always on the object level using class and property names. You can use named parameters to bind query arguments in a secure and typesafe way. Report-style queries are also supported, and this is an important area where other ORM solutions usually lack features.

Most of this is also true for criteria-based queries; but instead of using a query string, you use a typesafe API to construct the query. So-called *example objects* can be combined with criteria—for example, to retrieve "all items that look like the given example."

The most important part of object retrieval is the efficient loading of associated objects—that is, how you define the part of the object graph you'd like to load from the database in one operation. Hibernate provides lazy, eager, and batch fetching strategies, in mapping metadata and dynamically at runtime. You can use association joins and result iteration to prevent common problems such as the *n+1 selects problem*. Your goal is to minimize database roundtrips with many small queries, but at the same time, you also try to minimize the amount of data loaded in one query.

The best query and the ideal object-retrieval strategy depends on your use case, but you should be well prepared with the examples in this chapter and Hibernate's excellent runtime fetching strategies.

Writing Hibernate applications

Hibernate is intended to be used in just about any architectural scenario imaginable (as long as the application is written in Java). It might run inside a servlet engine—where you could use it with web application framework like Struts, Web-Work or Tapestry—or inside an EJB container, a Swing client, a lightweight container, or even a JMX server like JBoss.

Each of these environments requires infrastructure to integrate Hibernate with the way requests, transactions, and database resources are managed. The Hibernate core provides optional components for certain common integration scenarios, including integration with JTA, JNDI-bound datasources, JMX, JCA, and the transaction managers of all popular application servers. In addition, some frameworks like Spring and Keel ship with built-in Hibernate support, and plugin support is available for others including Tapestry, Apache Avalon, and PicoContainer. JBoss Application Server features special support for Hibernate archive deployment and integration of Hibernate as a JMX-managed component.

Even—perhaps *especially*—with all these options, it's often difficult to see exactly how Hibernate should be integrated into a particular Java-based architecture. Inevitably, you'll need to write infrastructural code to support your own application design. In this chapter, we'll describe some common Java architectures and show how Hibernate could be integrated into each scenario. However, we don't discuss integration with specific frameworks. We don't expect your application design to exactly match any of the scenarios we show, and we don't expect you to integrate Hibernate using exactly the code that we use. Rather, we'll demonstrate some common patterns and let you adapt them to your own tastes. For this reason, our examples are plain Java, using only the Java servlet and EJB APIs and no third-party frameworks.

In the first section of this chapter, we'll discuss application layering and show how it affects your persistence-related code. In the second part, we'll return to the interesting topic of application transactions (chapter 5) and show practical examples of the various ways application transactions can be implemented with Hibernate. In the third section, we'll discuss special types of data (especially legacy data) and show how you can use Hibernate with these data types. We'll also create a Hibernate persistence `Interceptor`, which is useful in many special cases.

8.1 Designing layered applications

We emphasized the importance of disciplined application layering in chapter 1. Layering helps you achieve separation of concerns, making code more readable by grouping code that does similar things. On the other hand, layering carries a price: Each extra layer increases the amount of code it takes to implement a simple piece of functionality—and more code makes the functionality itself more difficult to change.

We won't try to form any conclusions about the right number of layers to use (and certainly not about what those layers should be) since the "best" design varies from application to application and a complete discussion of application architecture is well outside the scope of this book. We merely observe that, in our opinion, overengineering has been endemic in the Java community, and overly ambitious multilayered architectures have significantly contributed to the cost of Java development and to the perceived complexity of J2EE. On the other hand, we do agree that a dedicated persistence layer is a sensible choice for most applications and that persistence-related code shouldn't be mixed with business logic or presentation.

In this section, we'll show you how to separate Hibernate-related code from your business and presentation layers, first in a servlet environment and then in an EJB environment. We need a simple use case from the CaveatEmptor application to demonstrate these ideas.

When a user places a bid on an item, CaveatEmptor must perform the following tasks, all in a single request:

1   Check that the amount entered by the user is greater than the maximum existing bid for the item.

2   Check that the auction hasn't yet ended.

3   Create a new bid for the item.

If either of the checks fails, the user should be informed of the reason for the failure; if both checks are successful, the user should be informed that the new bid has been made. These checks are our *business rules*. If a failure occurs while accessing the database, the user should be informed that the system is currently unavailable (an infrastructure concern).

Let's see how we can implement this in a servlet engine like Tomcat.

8.1.1   *Using Hibernate in a servlet engine*

First, we need a way for our application to obtain new Session instances. We'll write a simple *helper* (or utility) class to handle configuration and SessionFactory initialization (see chapter 2) and provide easy access to new Sessions. The full code for this class is shown in listing 8.1.

> **Listing 8.1   A simple Hibernate utility class**

```
public class HibernateUtil {

    private static final SessionFactory sessionFactory;   ❶

    static {   ❷
        try {
            Configuration cfg = new Configuration();
            sessionFactory = cfg.configure().buildSessionFactory();   ❸
        } catch (Throwable ex) {
            ex.printStackTrace(System.out);   ❹
            throw new ExceptionInInitializerError(ex);
        }
    }

    public static Session getSession() throws HibernateException {   ❺
        return sessionFactory.openSession();
    }
}
```

❶ The `SessionFactory` is bound to a `static` (and `final`) variable. All our threads can share this one constant, because `SessionFactory` is threadsafe.

❷ The `SessionFactory` is created in a *static initializer block*. This block is executed when a classloader loads the class.

❸ The process of building the `SessionFactory` from a `Configuration` is the same as always.

❹ We catch and wrap `Throwable` because we'd also like to catch `NoClassDefFound-Error` and other subclasses of `Error`, not just `Exception` and `RuntimeException`. Always log the exception; there are certain conditions when a static initializer exception might be swallowed. Of course, you should use your own logging mechanism rather than `System.out`.

❺ Our utility class has just one public method, a factory method for new `Sessions`. We could instead provide a `getSessionFactory()` method, but this version saves a line of code each time a `Session` is needed.

This (very trivial) implementation stores the `SessionFactory` in a static variable. You could even keep a reference to `SessionFactory` in the `ServletContext` or some other application-scope registry.

Note that this design is completely cluster-safe. The `SessionFactory` is essentially stateless (it keeps no state relative to running transactions), except for the second-level cache. It's the responsibility of the cache provider to maintain cache consistency across a cluster. So, you can safely have as many actual `SessionFactory` instances as you like (in practice, you want as *few* as possible, since the `SessionFactory` consumes significant resources and is expensive to initialize).

Now that we've solved the problem of where to put the `SessionFactory` (a FAQ), we continue with our use-case implementation. Most Java applications use some kind of *Model/View/Controller* (MVC) web application framework; even many of those that use plain servlets follow the MVC pattern by using JSPs or Velocity templates to implement the View, separating application control logic into a servlet or multiple servlets. Let's write such a controller servlet.

Writing a simple action servlet

With an MVC approach, we write the code that implements the "place bid" use case in an `execute()` method of an action named `PlaceBidAction` (see listing 8.2). We're assuming some kind of web framework, and we don't show how to read request parameters or how to forward to the next page. The code shown might even be the `doPost()` method of a plain servlet. (Note that we don't consider this first implementation to be a good one—we'll make substantial improvements later.)

Listing 8.2 Implementing a simple use case in one `execute()` method

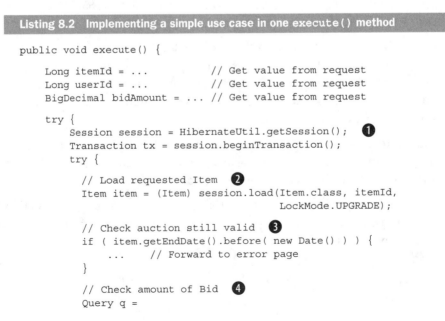

```
public void execute() {

    Long itemId = ...          // Get value from request
    Long userId = ...          // Get value from request
    BigDecimal bidAmount = ... // Get value from request

    try {
        Session session = HibernateUtil.getSession();    ❶
        Transaction tx = session.beginTransaction();
        try {

            // Load requested Item    ❷
            Item item = (Item) session.load(Item.class, itemId,
                                      LockMode.UPGRADE);

            // Check auction still valid    ❸
            if ( item.getEndDate().before( new Date() ) ) {
                ...    // Forward to error page
            }

            // Check amount of Bid    ❹
            Query q =
```

```
                session.createQuery("select max(b.amount)" +
                                    " from Bid b where b.item = :item");
            q.setEntity("item", item);
            BigDecimal maxBidAmount = (BigDecimal) q.uniqueResult();
            if (maxBidAmount.compareTo(bidAmount) > 0) {
                ...     // Forward to error page
            }

            // Add new Bid to Item     ❺
            User bidder = (User) session.load(User.class, userId);
            Bid newBid = new Bid(bidAmount, item, bidder);
            item.addBid(newBid);

            ...     // Place new Bid in scope for next page

            tx.commit();     ❻

            ...     // Forward to showSuccess.jsp page

        } catch (HibernateException ex) {     ❼
            if (tx != null) tx.rollback();
            throw ex;
        } finally {     ❽
            session.close();
        }
    } catch (HibernateException ex) {
        ... // Throw application specific exception
    }     ❾
}
```

❶ First, we get a new Session using our utility class and then start a database transaction.

❷ We load the Item from the database, using its identifier value, obtaining a pessimistic lock (this prevents two simultaneous bids for the same item).

❸ If the end date of the auction is earlier than the current date, we forward to an error page. Usually you'll want more sophisticated error handling for this exception, with a qualified error message.

❹ Using an HQL query, we check if there is a higher bid for the current item in the database. If there is, we forward to an error message.

❺ If all checks are successful, we place the new bid by adding it to the item. We don't have to save it manually; it will be saved using transitive persistence (cascading from the Item to Bid).

❻ Committing the database transaction flushes the current state of the Session to the database.

7 If any method in the inner `try-catch` block threw an exception, we have to roll back the transaction and rethrow the exception.

8 The `Session` must always be closed, freeing database resources.

9 The outer `try-catch` block is responsible for exceptions thrown by `Session.close()` and `Transaction.rollback()` and, of course, the rethrown inner exception.

The first thing wrong with this implementation is the clutter caused by all the session, transaction, and exception-handling code. Since this code is typically identical for all actions, we'd like to centralize it somewhere. One option is to place it in the `execute()` method of an abstract superclass of our actions.

We also have a problem with *lazy initialization* if we access the new bid on the `showSuccess.jsp` page: By the time we get to the JSP, the Hibernate session is already closed, so we can't access unfetched lazy associations. We encourage you to think about this issue; we made the experience that this might not be obvious for new Hibernate users.

A great solution to both problems is the *thread-local session* pattern.

The thread-local session

A thread-local session is a single session instance associated with a particular request. It lets you implement a *persistence context*, similar to the JTA notion of a transaction context. Any components called in the same request will share the same session and persistence context.

It's especially useful to include a JSP in the persistence context. The JSP pulls information from the domain model by navigating the object graph beginning at some persistent object in the session or request scope—for example, the newly created bid that was placed in the request scope by our action. However, the object graph might include uninitialized associations (proxies or collections) that must be traversed (and initialized) while rendering the view.

In our example, the JSP might list all items the current bidder has for sale by calling `newBid.getBidder().getItems().iterator()`. (This sounds a little contrived, but it's certainly possible.) Since the `items` association is lazy, it would be unfetched at this point.

But we already closed the Hibernate session at the end of the action's `execute()` method, so Hibernate will throw a `LazyInitializationException` when the association is accessed—the database connection is no longer available, and the object graph is detached, so Hibernate can't fetch the collection. It's possible to write our action to ensure that all needed associations are fully initialized before forwarding to the view (we discuss this later), but a more convenient approach is to leave the session open until the view is completely rendered.

FAQ   *Why can't Hibernate open a new connection (or session) if it has to lazy-load associations?* First, we think it's a better solution to fully initialize all required objects for a specific use case using eager fetching (this approach is less vulnerable to the n+1 selects problem). Furthermore, opening new database connections (and ad hoc database transactions!) implicitly and transparently to the developer exposes the application to transaction isolation issues. When do you close the session and end the ad hoc transaction—after each lazy association is loaded? We strongly prefer transactions to be clearly and explicitly demarcated by the application developer. If you want to enable lazy fetching for a detached instance, you can use lock() to attach it to a new session.

The thread-local session pattern allows you to have a single Hibernate session per request, spanning the view and potentially multiple action executes(). Java provides the ThreadLocal class for implementing thread scoped variables. The thread-local session pattern combines a ThreadLocal with an interceptor or servlet filter that closes the Session at the end of the request, after the view is rendered and just before the response is sent to the client.

First, we enhance the HibernateUtil helper. Instead of opening a new Session when getSession() is called, it returns a Session kept in a ThreadLocal variable, that is, it returns the Session associated with the current thread. The HibernateUtil class is also a good place to implement generic exception handling; hence we add some other static helper methods that wrap exceptions. The full code of our improved HibernateUtil is shown in listing 8.3.

Listing 8.3   An improved version of `HibernateUtil` using thread-local variables

```
public class HibernateUtil {

    private static final SessionFactory sessionFactory;

    private static final ThreadLocal threadSession =      ❶
                                        new ThreadLocal();
    private static final ThreadLocal threadTransaction =   ❷
                                        new ThreadLocal();
    static {
        // Initialize SessionFactory...
    }

    public static Session getSession() {    ❸
        Session s = (Session) threadSession.get();
        // Open a new Session, if this thread has none yet
```

```
        try {
            if (s == null) {
                s = sessionFactory.openSession();
                threadSession.set(s);
            }
        } catch (HibernateException ex) {
            throw new InfrastructureException(ex);
        }
        return s;
    }

    public static void closeSession() {   ❹
        try {
            Session s = (Session) threadSession.get();
            threadSession.set(null);
            if (s != null && s.isOpen())
                s.close();
        } catch (HibernateException ex) {
            throw new InfrastructureException(ex);
        }
    }

    public static void beginTransaction() {   ❺
        Transaction tx = (Transaction) threadTransaction.get();
        try {
            if (tx == null) {
                tx = getSession().beginTransaction();
                threadTransaction.set(tx);
            }
        } catch (HibernateException ex) {
            throw new InfrastructureException(ex);
        }
    }

    public static void commitTransaction() {   ❻
        Transaction tx = (Transaction) threadTransaction.get();
        try {
            if ( tx != null && !tx.wasCommitted()
                            && !tx.wasRolledBack() )
                tx.commit();
            threadTransaction.set(null);
        } catch (HibernateException ex) {
            rollbackTransaction();
            throw new InfrastructureException(ex);
        }
    }

    public static void rollbackTransaction() {   ❼
        Transaction tx = (Transaction) threadTransaction.get();
        try {
            threadTransaction.set(null);
            if ( tx != null && !tx.wasCommitted()
                            && !tx.wasRolledBack() ) {
```

```
                tx.rollback();
          }
      } catch (HibernateException ex) {
          throw new InfrastructureException(ex);
      } finally {
          closeSession();
      }
    }

  }
```

❶ The `Session` of the current thread is stored in this `ThreadLocal` variable.

❷ We use one database transaction for all operations, so we use another `ThreadLocal` for the `Transaction`. Both `Session` and `Transaction` are now associated with the thread, and many action executions in a thread can participate in the same database transaction.

❸ The `getSession()` method has been extended to use the thread-local variable; we also wrap the checked `HibernateException` in an unchecked `InfrastructureException` (part of CaveatEmptor).

❹ We also wrap the exceptions thrown by `Session.close()` in this static helper method.

❺ The code used to start a new database transaction is similar to the `getSession()` method.

❻ If committing the database transaction fails, we immediately roll back the transaction. We don't do anything if the transaction was already committed or rolled back.

❼ After rolling back the database transaction, the `Session` is closed.

This utility class is much more powerful than our first version: It provides thread-local sessions and database transactions, and it wraps all exceptions in a runtime exception defined by our application (or framework). This simplifies exception handling in application code significantly, and the thread-local pattern gives us the flexibility to share a single session among all actions and JSPs in a particular thread. The same is true for database transactions: You can either have a single database transactions for the whole thread or call `beginTransaction()` and `commitTransaction()` whenever you need to.

You can also see that calling `getSession()` for the first time in a particular thread opens a new `Session`. Let's now discuss the second part of the thread-local session design pattern: closing the `Session` after the view is rendered, instead of at the end of each `execute()` method.

We implement this second part using a servlet filter. Other implementations are possible, however; for example, the WebWork2 framework offers pluggable interceptors we could use. The job of the servlet filter is to close the `Session` before the response is sent to the client (and after all views are rendered and actions are executed). It's also responsible for committing any pending database transactions. See the `doFilter()` method of this servlet filter in listing 8.4.

Listing 8.4 The `doFilter()` method closes the Hibernate Session

```
public void doFilter(ServletRequest request,
                     ServletResponse response,
                     FilterChain chain)
        throws IOException, ServletException {

    try {

        chain.doFilter(request, response);
        HibernateUtil.commitTransaction();

    } finally {
        HibernateUtil.closeSession();
    }

}
```

We don't start a database transaction or open a session until an action requests one. Any subsequent actions, and finally the view, reuse the same session and transaction. After all actions (servlets) and the view are executed, we commit any pending database transaction. Finally, no matter what happens, we close the `Session` to free resources.

Now, we can simplify our action's `execute()` method to the following:

```
public void execute() {
    // Get values from request

    try {
        HibernateUtil.beginTransaction();
        Session session = HibernateUtil.getSession();

        // Load requested Item
        // Check auction still valid
        // Check amount of Bid
        // Add new Bid to Item
        // Place new Bid in scope for next page
        // Forward to showSuccess.jsp page
```

```
    } catch (HibernateException ex) {
        throw new InfrastructureException(ex);
    } catch (Exception ex) {
        // Throw application specific exception
    }

}
```

We've reduced the exception-handling code to a single try/catch block. We can safely rethrow checked exceptions such as HibernateException as runtime exceptions; we can use our application's (or framework's) exception hierarchy.

The thread-local session pattern isn't perfect, unfortunately. Changes made to objects in the Session are flushed to the database at unpredictable points, and we can only be certain that they have been executed successfully after the Transaction is committed. But our transaction commit occurs after the view has been rendered. The problem is the buffer size of the servlet engine: If the contents of the view exceed the buffer size, the buffer might get flushed and the contents sent to the client. The buffer may be flushed many times when the content is rendered, but the first flush also sends the HTTP status code. If the SQL statements executed at transaction commit time were to trigger a constraint violation in the database, the user might already have seen a successful output! We can't change the status code (for example, use a 500 Internal Server Error), because it's already been sent to the client (as 200 OK).

There are several ways to prevent this rare exception: You could adjust the buffer size of your servlet engine, or flush the Hibernate session before forwarding/redirecting to the view (add a flushSession() helper method to HibernateUtil). Some web frameworks don't immediately fill the response buffer with rendered content; they use their own OutputStream and flush it with the response only after the view has been completely rendered. So, we consider this a problem only with plain Java servlet programming.

Our action is already much more readable. Unfortunately, it still mixes together three distinctly different responsibilities: pageflow, access to the persistent store, and business logic. There is also a catch clause for the HibernateException that looks misplaced. Let's address the last responsibility first, since it's the most important.

Creating "smart" domain models

The idea behind the MVC pattern is that control logic (in our application, this is pageflow logic), view definitions, and business logic should be cleanly separated. Currently, our action contains some business logic—code that we might even be

able to reuse in the admittedly unlikely event that our application gained a new
user interface—and our domain model consists of "dumb" data-holding objects.
The persistent classes define state but no behavior.

We migrate the business logic into our domain model. Doing so adds a couple
of lines of code but also increases the potential for later reuse; it's also certainly
more object-oriented and therefore offers various ways to extend the business logic
(for example, using a strategy pattern for different bid strategies). First, we add the
new method placeBid() to the Item class:

```
public Bid placeBid(User bidder, BigDecimal bidAmount)
    throws BusinessException {

    // Auction still valid
    if ( this.getEndDate().before( new Date() ) ) {
        throw new BusinessException("Auction already ended.");
    }

    // Create new Bid
    Bid newBid = new Bid(bidAmount, this, bidder);

    // Place bid for this Item
    this.addBid(newBid);
    return newBid;
}
```

This code enforces business rules that constrain the state of our business objects
but don't execute data-access code. The motivation is to encapsulate business
logic in classes of the domain model without any dependency on persistent data
access. You might have discovered that this method of Item doesn't implement the
check for the highest bid. Keep in mind that these classes should know nothing
about persistence because we might need them outside the persistence context
(for example, in the presentation tier). We could even implement "Check the
highest bid amount" in this placeBid() method by iterating the collection of bids
for the item and finding the highest amount. This isn't as performant as an HQL
query, so we prefer to implement the check elsewhere later. Now, we simplify our
action to the following:

```
public void execute() {

    // Get values from request

    try {
        HibernateUtil.beginTransaction();
        Session session = HibernateUtil.getSession();

        // Load requested Item
        Item item = (Item) session.load(Item.class, itemId);
```

```
            // Check amount of Bid with a query
            Query q =
                session.createQuery("select max(b.amount)" +
                                " from Bid b where b.item = :item");
            q.setEntity("item", item);
            BigDecimal maxBidAmount = (BigDecimal) q.uniqueResult();
            if (maxBidAmount.compareTo(bidAmount) > 0) {
                throw new BusinessException("Bid amount too low.");
            }

            // Place Bid
            User bidder = (User) session.load(User.class, userId);
            Bid newBid = item.placeBid(bidder, bidAmount);

            // Place new Bid in scope for next page
            // Forward to showSuccess.jsp page

    } catch (HibernateException ex) {
        throw new InfrastructureException(e1);

    } catch (BusinessException ex) {
        // Execute exception specific code

    } catch (Exception ex) {
        // Throw application specific exception
    }

}
```

The business logic for placing a bid is now (almost completely) encapsulated in the placeBid() method and control logic in the action. We can even design a different pageflow by catching and forwarding specific exceptions. But the MVC pattern doesn't say much about where P for Persistence should go. We're sure the Hibernate code doesn't belong in the action, however: Persistence code should be isolated in the persistence layer. Let's encapsulate that code with a DAO and create a façade for persistence operations.

Data access objects

Mixing data access code with control logic violates our emphasis on separation of concerns. For all but the simplest applications, it makes sense to hide Hibernate API calls behind a façade with higher level business semantics. There is more than one way to design this façade—some small applications might use a single PersistenceManager object; some might use some kind of command-oriented design—but we prefer the DAO pattern.

The DAO design pattern originated in Sun's Java BluePrints. It's even used in the infamous Java Petstore demo application. A DAO defines an interface to persistence operations (CRUD and finder methods) relating to a particular persistent entity; it advises you to group code that relates to persistence of that entity.

Let's create an `ItemDAO` class, which will eventually implement all persistence code related to `Items`. For now, it contains only the `getItemById()` method, along with `getMaximumBidAmount()`. The full code of the DAO implementation is shown in listing 8.5.

Listing 8.5 A simple DAO abstracting item-related persistence operations

```
public class ItemDAO {

    public ItemDAO() {
        HibernateUtil.beginTransaction();
    }

    public Item getItemById(Long itemId) {
        Session session = HibernateUtil.getSession();
        Item item = null;
        try {

            item = (Item) session.load(Item.class, itemId);

        } catch (HibernateException ex) {
            throw new InfrastructureException(ex);
        }
        return item;
    }

    public BigDecimal getMaxBidAmount(Long itemId) {
        Session session = HibernateUtil.getSession();
        BigDecimal maxBidAmount = null;
        try {

            String query = "select max(b.amount)" +
                            " from Bid b where b.item = :item";
            Query q = session.createQuery(query);
            q.setLong("itemId", itemId.longValue());
            maxBidAmount = (BigDecimal) q.uniqueResult();

        } catch (HibernateException ex) {
            throw new InfrastructureException(ex);
        }
        return maxBidAmount;
    }
}
```

Whenever a new `ItemDAO` is created, we start a new database transaction or join the current database transaction of the running thread. Whether `getMaximumBid-Amount()` belongs on `ItemDAO` or a `BidDAO` is perhaps a matter of taste; but since the argument is an `Item` identifier, it seems to naturally belong here. By letting the DAO wrap all HibernateExceptions in our application's InfrastructureException, we've finally managed to move all Hibernate exception handling out of the action.

We also need a UserDAO, which, for now, contains just a getUserById() method:

```
public class UserDAO {

    public UserDAO() {
        HibernateUtil.beginTransaction();
    }

    public User getUserById(Long userId) {
        Session session = HibernateUtil.getSession();
        User user = null;
        try {
            user = (User) session.load(User.class, userId);
        } catch (HibernateException ex) {
            throw new InfrastructureException(ex);
        }
        return user;
    }

}
```

You can begin to see a new advantage of the thread-local session pattern. All our DAOs can share the same Hibernate session (and even database transaction) without the need for you to pass the session explicitly as a parameter to the DAO instance. This is a powerful advantage that becomes more important as your application grows and layering becomes more complex.

Armed with our new DAO classes, we can further simplify our action code to the following:

```
public void execute() {

    // Get values from request

    try {
        ItemDAO itemDAO = new ItemDAO();
        UserDAO userDAO = new UserDAO();

        if (itemDAO.getMaxBidAmount(itemId).compareTo(bidAmount) > 0)
            throw new BusinessException("Bid amount too low.");

        Item item = itemDAO.getItemById(itemId);
        Bid newBid =
            item.placeBid(userDAO.getUserById(userId), bidAmount);

        // Place new Bid in scope for next page
        // Forward to showSuccess.jsp page
    } catch (BusinessException ex) {
        // Forward to error page
```

```
    } catch (Exception ex) {
        // Throw application specific exception
    }
}
```

Notice how much more self-documenting this code is than our first implementation. Someone who knows nothing about Hibernate can still understand immediately what this method does, without the need for code comments.

We're now almost satisfied with our implementation of this use case. Our methods are all short, readable, and somewhat reusable. Messy exception- and transaction-related code is completely externalized to infrastructure. However, there is still a mix of concerns. One piece of our business logic is still visible in the action implementation: the check against the current maximum bid. Code that throws a BusinessException should be in the domain model.

An important question arises: If we moved this routine into the placeBid() method of Item, the domain model implementation will have a dependency on the persistence API, the DAOs. This should be avoided, because it would complicate unit testing of the domain objects and business logic (the "persistence" concern leaked into the domain model implementation). So, do we have no other choice but to keep this piece of business code with our control logic?

The solution for this problem is some slight refactoring of the placeBid() method, two new methods on the ItemDAO class, and some changes to our control code, summarized in the following code snippet:

```
BigDecimal currentMaxAmount = itemDAO.getMaxBidAmount(itemId);
BigDecimal currentMinAmount = itemDAO.getMinBidAmount(itemId);
Item item = itemDAO.getItemById(itemId);
User user = userDAO.getUserById(userId)
newBid = item.placeBid(user, newAmount,
                       currentMaxAmount, currentMinAmount);
```

We changed several things. First, we moved the business logic and exception to the placeBid() method. We call this method with new arguments: the current maximum and minimum bid amounts. We retrieve the two values using new methods of the ItemDAO. Now, all that's left in our action servlet are calls to the persistence layer and calls that start the execution of some business logic. Our business logic is encapsulated in the domain model and fully reusable; there is no dependency on the persistence layer's DAO interface. You will likely face challenges like this is your own application, so be prepared to re-think and refactor your code for clean layering.

Let's get back to our discussion of the DAO pattern. Actually, a DAO is barely a pattern at all—there are many ways to implement this basic idea. Some developers go so far as to combine their DAO framework with an abstract factory pattern, allowing runtime switching of the persistence mechanism. This approach is usually motivated by the need to remain independent of vendor-specific SQL. Since Hibernate already does a good (although not a complete) job of abstracting our Java code away from the vendor-specific SQL dialect, we prefer to keep things simple for now.

The next step is to see how we can take this code and adapt it to run in an EJB container. Obviously, we'd like to change as little as possible. We've been arguing all along that one advantage of POJOs and transparent persistence is portability between different runtime environments. If we now have to rewrite all the code for placing a bid, we're going to look a bit silly.

8.1.2 *Using Hibernate in an EJB container*

From our point of view, the most important difference between a servlet-based application and an application where business logic and data access executes in the EJB container is the possibility of physical separation of tiers. If the EJB container runs in a different process than the servlet engine, it's absolutely essential to minimize requests from the servlet tier to the EJB tier. Latency is added by every interprocess request, increasing the application response time and reducing concurrency due to the need for either more database transactions or longer transactions.

Hence it's essential that all data access related to a single user request occur within a single request to the EJB tier. This means you can't use the previous lazy approach, where the view was allowed to pull data from the domain model objects as needed. Instead, the business (EJB) tier must accept responsibility for fetching all data that will be needed subsequently for rendering the view.

In existing systems that use entity beans, you can already see this idea. The *session façade* pattern allows these systems to group all activity related to a particular user request into a single request to the EJB tier. The ubiquitous *data-transfer object* (DTO) pattern provides a way of packaging together the data that the view will need. A DTO is a class that holds the state of a particular entity; you can think of a DTO as a JavaBean or POJO without any business methods. DTOs are required in an entity bean environment, since entity beans aren't serializable and can't be transported across tiers. In our case, we can easily make our POJOs serializable, so we naturally find ourselves questioning the need for DTOs.

Rethinking data transfer objects

The notion that, in an EJB-based application, the web tier shouldn't communicate directly with the domain model, is deeply embedded in J2EE practices and thinking. We doubt that this idea will vanish overnight, and there are certain reasonable arguments in favor of this notion. However, you shouldn't mistake these arguments for the real reason why DTOs became so universally accepted.

The DTO pattern originated when the J2EE community observed that the use of fine-grained remote access to entity beans was slow and unscalable. In addition, the entity beans themselves weren't serializable, so some other type of object was needed to package and carry the state of the business objects between tiers.

There are now twin justifications for the use of DTOs: first, DTOs implement *externalization* of data between tiers; second, DTOs enforce *separation* of the web tier from the business logic tier. Only the second justification applies to us, and the benefit of this separation is questionable when weighed against its cost. We won't tell you to never use DTOs (in other places, we're sometimes less reticent). Instead, we'll list some arguments for and against use of the DTO pattern in an application that uses Hibernate and ask you to carefully weigh these arguments in the context of your own application.

It's true that the DTO removes the direct dependency of the view on the domain model. If your project partitions the roles of Java developer and web page designer, this might be of some value. In particular, the DTO lets you flatten domain model associations, transforming the data into a format that is perhaps more convenient for the view. However, in our experience, it's normal for all layers of the application to be highly coupled to the domain model, with or without the use of DTOs. We don't see anything wrong with that, and we suggest that it might be possible to embrace the fact.

The first clue that something is wrong with DTOs is that, contrary to their title, they aren't objects at all. DTOs define state without behavior. This is immediately suspect in the context of object-oriented development. Even worse, the state defined by the DTO is often identical to the state defined in the business objects of the domain model—the supposed separation achieved by the DTO pattern could also be viewed as mere *duplication*.

The DTO pattern exhibits two of the code smells described in Fowler [1999]: the *shotgun change* smell, where a small change to some system requirement requires changes to multiple classes; and the *parallel class hierarchies* smell, where two different class hierarchies contain similar classes in a one-to-one correspondence. The parallel class hierarchy is evident in this case—systems that use the DTO pattern have `Item` and `ItemDTO`, `User` and `UserDTO`, and so on. The shotgun change smell manifests itself when we add a new property to `Item`. We must change not only the view and the `Item` class, but also the `ItemDTO` and the code that assembles the `Item-DTO` instance from the properties of an `Item` (this last piece of code is especially tedious and fragile).

Of course, DTOs aren't all bad. The code we just referred to as "tedious and fragile"—the *assembler*—does have some value even in the context of Hibernate. DTO assembly provides you with a convenient point at which to ensure that all data the view will need is fully fetched before returning control to the web tier. If you find yourself wrestling with Hibernate `LazyInitializationExceptions` in the web tier, one possible solution is to try the DTO pattern, which naturally imposes extra discipline by requiring that all needed data is copied explicitly from the business objects (we don't find that we need this discipline, but your experience may vary).

Finally, DTOs may have a place in data transfer between loosely coupled applications (our discussion has focused on their use in data transfer between tiers of the *same* application). However, JMS or SOAP seems to be better adapted to this problem.

We won't use DTOs in the CaveatEmptor application. Instead, the EJB tier session façade will return domain model business objects to the web tier.

The session façade pattern

The *session façade* pattern is used in most J2EE applications today and is well known to most Java developers [Marinescu 2002]. A session façade is an EJB session bean that acts as the external interface to some business-oriented software component. The use of a session bean lets you take advantage of EJB declarative transactions and security, and provides services that are sufficiently coarse-grained that you avoid the latency of many fine-grained interprocess calls. We won't spend much time discussing this pattern, since it's well understood and noncontroversial. Instead, we'll demonstrate how our previous action example can be rewritten using a session façade.

We make two major changes to our code from the previous section. First, we change the `HibernateUtil` class so that the Hibernate `SessionFactory` is kept in the JNDI registry rather than in a static variable. There's no especially compelling reason for this, apart from consistency with how other similar objects (such as the JTA `UserTransaction`) are handled in an EJB environment. We have to change the static initializer of the `HibernateUtil` class and remove the static `sessionFactory` variable:

```
static {
    try {
        new Configuration().configure().buildSessionFactory();
        // SessionFactory is now in JNDI, see hibernate.cfg.xml
    } catch (Throwable ex) {
        ex.printStackTrace(System.out);
        throw new ExceptionInInitializerError(ex);
    }
}

public static SessionFactory getSessionFactory() {
    SessionFactory sessions = null;
    try {
        Context ctx = new InitialContext();
        String jndiName = "java:hibernate/HibernateFactory";
        sessions = (SessionFactory)ctx.lookup(jndiName);
    } catch (NamingException ex) {
        throw new InfrastructureException(ex);
    }
    return sessions;
}
```

Note that we have to use the getSessionFactory() helper method now whenever we need the SessionFactory—for example, in the getSession() routine. We also have to configure Hibernate to place the SessionFactory in JNDI after the call to buildSessionFactory(), as described in chapter 2, section 2.4.2, "JNDI-bound SessionFactory."

In the next step, we move some of the code from the servlet action into the bidForItem() method of a new CaveatEmptorFacade session bean. This change highlights a limitation of the EJB specification. In our servlet-only implementation, we were able to perform all exception and transaction handling in a servlet filter and our utility class. A servlet filter is the servlet specification's implementation of the *interceptor* pattern. Unbelievably, the EJB specification provides no standard way to implement interceptors for EJB method calls. Certain containers, such as JBoss and WebLogic, provide vendor-specific interception APIs, and we encourage you to use these facilities if portability isn't an immediate goal. In our case, we need to demonstrate code that will work with all vendors' products, so we need to move the tedious exception and transaction handling code into the bidForItem() method. (In the next section, we'll use the EJB command pattern to pull it back out again!)

The remote interface of our session façade is simple enough:

```
public interface CaveatEmptorFacade extends javax.ejb.EJBObject {
    public Bid bidForItem(Long userId,
                          Long itemId,
                          BigDecimal bidAmount)
        throws RemoteException;
}
```

The bean implementation class is as follows:

```
public class CaveatEmptorFacadeBean
        implements javax.ejb.SessionBean {
    public void setSessionContext(SessionContext sessionContext)
                throws EJBException, RemoteException {}
    public void ejbRemove()
                throws EJBException, RemoteException {}
    public void ejbActivate()
                throws EJBException, RemoteException {}
    public void ejbPassivate()
                throws EJBException, RemoteException {}

    public Bid bidForItem(Long userId,
                        Long itemId, BigDecimal bidAmount)
        throws RemoteException {

    Bid newBid = null;
    try {
        ItemDAO itemDAO = new ItemDAO();
        UserDAO userDAO = new UserDAO();

        BigDecimal currentMaxAmount =
                        itemDAO.getMaxBidAmount(itemId);
        BigDecimal currentMinAmount =
                        itemDAO.getMinBidAmount(itemId);
        Item item = itemDAO.getItemById(itemId);
        User user = userDAO.getUserById(userId)

        newBid = item.placeBid(user, newAmount,
                    currentMaxAmount, currentMinAmount);

        HibernateUtil.commitTransaction();

    } finally {
        HibernateUtil.closeSession();
    }

    return newBid;
}
```

Note that the call to `HibernateUtil.commitTransaction()` might not actually commit the database transaction: Hibernate transparently handles the fact that it's running in an EJB container with JTA, so the database transaction might remain in effect until the container commits it. However, a Hibernate `Session` flush occurs at this point.

The failure of one of our business rules is indicated by throwing a `BusinessException` back to the client of this session bean. A failure of an infrastructure part of the application will throw an `InfrastructureException`; both will be wrapped in an `EJBException`, which in turn will be sent to the client wrapped in a `RemoteException` (all of this is handled by the EJB container). It will be the job of the action (on the web tier) to interpret these wrapped exceptions and display a meaningful message to the user. The action code therefore becomes

```
public void execute() {

    // Get values from request
    try {
        Context ctx = new InitialContext();
        String jndiName = "java:comp/ejb/CaveatEmptorFacade";
        CaveatEmptorFacade ejbFacade =
                        (CaveatEmptorFacade) ctx.lookup(jndiName);

        Bid newBid = ejbFacade.bidForItem(userId, itemId, bidAmount);

        // Place new Bid in scope for next page

        // Forward to success page
    } catch (RemoteException ex) {

        // Get the EJBException that contains our runtime
        // Infrastructure and Business exceptions.
    }
}
```

We will now abandon the session façade pattern and use a design based on the command pattern, an approach that has proven to be flexible and, in some situations, better than a session façade.

The EJB command pattern

The *EJB command pattern* replaces the methods of a session façade—such as bid-ForItem() in our example—with command classes. We have a BidForItemCommand. The execute() method of this command is called by a stateless session bean known as the *command handler*. The command handler lets you take advantage of container transactions and security and implements generic exception handling (it could even provide a full interceptor framework). The command itself encapsulates a unit of application logic, input parameters, and output parameters. It's instantiated by the client action, dispatched to the command handler, executed in the context of the EJB tier, and finally returned to the client with the result of the operation.

The command pattern lets you reduce code by handling some concerns generically and also by reducing the amount of noise involved in EJB development. The commands are simple POJOs and are easy to write and reuse; they may even be reused outside of the EJB container (just like the POJO domain model). The only requirement is that commands implement the following interface:

```
public interface Command extends Serializable {
    public void execute() throws CommandException;
}
```

Notice that commands must be serializable so they can be passed between tiers. This interface defines a contract between the command and the command handler. The remote interface of the command handler is simple:

```
public interface CommandHandler extends javax.ejb.EJBObject {
    public Command executeCommand(Command command)
        throws RemoteException, CommandException;
}
```

First, we implement a generic command handler with an EJB stateless session bean:

```
public class CommandHandlerBean
    implements javax.ejb.SessionBean {

    public void setSessionContext(SessionContext sessionContext)
                throws EJBException, RemoteException {}
    public void ejbRemove()
                throws EJBException, RemoteException {}
    public void ejbActivate()
                throws EJBException, RemoteException {}
    public void ejbPassivate()
                throws EJBException, RemoteException {}

    public Command executeCommand(Command command)
        throws RemoteException, CommandException {

        try {
            command.execute();
        } catch (CommandException ex) {
            HibernateUtil.rollbackTransaction();
            throw ex;
        }
        return command;
    }

}
```

You can see that this code is generic (we don't even have to implement the session bean methods): This handler catches any exception thrown by the command and sets the current running container transaction to rollback state (remember that Hibernate handles JTA transparently). If no exception occurs, the execute() method returns the command, possibly with output parameters for the rendering of the view. Note that we could even let the container roll back the transaction, by not catching our application exception (CommandException). The client servlet action implementation calling this handler is very similar to our previous version:

```
public void execute() {

    // Get values from request

    BidForItemCommand bidForItem =
                new BidForItemCommand(userId, itemId, bidAmount);

    try {
        Context ctx = new InitialContext();
        String jndiName = "java:comp/ejb/CaveatEmptorCommandHandler";
        CommandHandler handler =
                        (CommandHandler) ctx.lookup(jndiName);
        bidForItem =
            (BidForItemCommand) handler.executeCommand(bidForItem);

        // Place new Bid in scope for next page
        // bidForItem.getNewBid();

        // Forward to showSuccess.jsp page
    } catch (CommandException ex) {
        // Unwrap and forward to error page
        // ex.getCause();
    } catch (Exception ex) {
        // Throw application specific exception
    }

}
```

First we create a new `BidForItemCommand` and set the input values we got earlier
from the HTTP request. Then, after looking up the handler session bean, we execute the command. We can access the newly created `Bid` as one of the output
parameters of the command by calling the command's `getNewBid()` accessor
method. A command is just a simple JavaBean with an additional `execute()`
method called by the handler:

```
public class BidForItemCommand
    implements Command {

    private Long userId;
    private Long itemId;
    private BigDecimal bidAmount;

    private Bid newBid;

    public BidForItemCommand(Long userId,
                            Long itemId,
                            BigDecimal bidAmount) {
        this.userId = userId;
        this.itemId = itemId;
        this.bidAmount = bidAmount;
    }

    public Bid getNewBid() {
        return newBid;
```

```
    }

    public void execute() throws CommandException {

      try {
        ItemDAO itemDAO = new ItemDAO();
        UserDAO userDAO = new UserDAO();

        BigDecimal currentMaxAmount =
                          itemDAO.getMaxBidAmount(itemId);
        BigDecimal currentMinAmount =
                          itemDAO.getMinBidAmount(itemId);
        Item item = itemDAO.getItemById(itemId);
        User user = userDAO.getUserById(userId)

        newBid = item.placeBid(user, newAmount,
                    currentMaxAmount, currentMinAmount);

        HibernateUtil.commitTransaction();

      } catch (InfrastructureException ex) {
        // Rethrow as a checked exception
        throw new CommandException(ex);

      } catch (BusinessException ex) {
        // Rethrow as a checked exception
        throw new CommandException(ex);

      } finally {
        HibernateUtil.closeSession();
      }

    }

  }
```

The first few lines aren't very interesting; we use the standard JavaBean attributes and accessor method syntax to declare the input and output parameters of this command. The `execute()` method should look familiar, because it encapsulates the control logic and exception handling we previously had in our session bean. You can easily extend this `execute()` method—for example, by querying/initializing some part of the object graph you need or by adding output parameters that are required to render a view.

NOTE *Hibernate libraries on the client*—Since the `BidForItemCommand` needs our DAOs, we have to include all persistence libraries on the servlet classpath (even if the command is executed only on the business tier). This is a serious drawback of the command pattern. One solution for this problem is to treat commands only as an input and output transport mechanism and keep business logic on the server in stateless session beans. However, this is close to the DTO (anti-) pattern, so you have to decide what's appropriate in your situation.

Since we have just one command, the command pattern seems like more work than the session façade pattern. However, as the system grows, adding new commands is simplified because cross-cutting concerns like exception handling can be implemented in the command handler. Commands are easy to implement and extremely reusable (it's easy to compose and extend commands using delegation or inheritance). But the command pattern has other nice features. The session bean need not be the only command handler! It's easy to implement a JMS-based command handler that executes commands asynchronously. You can even store a command in the database for scheduled execution. Commands can be used outside the EJB environment—in a batch process or JUnit test case, for example. In practice, this architecture works nicely.

We've come to the end of our discussion of layering. There are many variations on, and permutations of, the ideas we've shown here. We haven't talked about the use of Hibernate in lightweight containers such as the Spring Framework or PicoContainer because, although the code looks different, the basic concepts remain similar.

Our "bid for an item" use case was simple in one important respect: The application transaction spanned just one user request and so could be implemented using exactly one database transaction. Real application transactions might span multiple user requests and require that the application (and database) hold state relating to the application transaction while waiting for user response. In the next section, we'll show you how application transactions may be implemented in layered architectures such as the ones we just described.

8.2 Implementing application transactions

We discussed the notion of an *application transaction* in chapter 5, section 5.2, "Working with application transactions." We also discussed how Hibernate helps detect conflicts between concurrent application transactions using managed versioning. We didn't discuss how application transactions are used in Hibernate applications, so we now return to this essential subject.

There are three ways to implement application transactions in an application that uses Hibernate: using a *long session*, using *detached objects*, and doing it the *hard way*. We'll start with the hard way, since if you've been using EJB entity beans, the hard way is what you're already familiar with. First, we need a use case to illustrate these ideas.

8.2.1 Approving a new auction

Our auction has an approval cycle. A new item is created in the *Draft* state. The user who created the auction may place the item in *Pending* state when the user is satisfied with the item details. System administrators may then approve the auction, placing the item in the *Active* state and beginning the auction. At any time before the auction is approved, the user or any administrator may edit the item details. Once the auction is approved, no user or administrator may edit the item. It's essential that the approving administrator sees the most recent revision of the item details before approving the auction and that an auction can't be approved twice. Figure 8.1 shows the item approval cycle.

The application transaction is auction approval, which spans two user requests. First, the administrator selects a pending item to view its details; second, the administrator approves the auction, moving the item to the Active state. The second request must perform a version check to verify that the item hasn't been updated or approved since it was retrieved for display.

The business logic for approving an auction should, as usual, be implemented by the domain model. In this case, we add an approve() method to the Item class:

```
public void approve(User byUser) throws BusinessException {

    if ( !byUser.isAdmin() )
        throw new PermissionException("Not an administrator.");

    if ( !state.equals(ItemState.PENDING) )
        throw new IllegalStateException("Item not pending.");

    state = ItemState.ACTIVE;
    approvedBy = byUser;
    approvalDatetime = new Date();
}
```

But it's the code that calls this method that we're interested in.

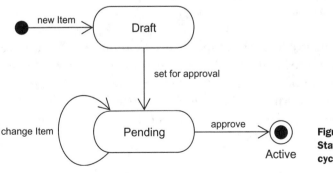

Figure 8.1
State chart of the item approval cycle in CaveatEmptor

FAQ   *Are application transactions really transactions?* Most books define *transaction* in terms of the ACID properties: *atomicity, consistency, isolation,* and *durability.* Is an application transaction really a transaction by that definition? Consistency and durability don't seem to be a problem, but what about atomicity and isolation? Our example is both atomic and isolated, since all update operations occur in the last request/response cycle (that is, the last database transaction). However, our definition of an application transaction permits update operations to occur in any request/response cycle. If an application transaction performs an update operation in any but the final database transaction, it isn't atomic and may not even be isolated. Nevertheless, we feel that the term *transaction* is still appropriate, since systems with this kind of application transaction usually have functionality or a business process that allows the user to compensate for this lack of atomicity (allowing the user to roll back steps of the application transaction manually, for example).

Now that we have our use case, let's look at the different ways we can implement it. We'll start with an approach we don't recommend.

8.2.2 Doing it the hard way

The hard way to implement application transactions is to discard all persistent instances between each request. The justification for this approach is that, since the database transaction is ended, the persistent instances are no longer guaranteed to be in a state that is consistent with the database. The longer the administrator spends deciding whether to approve the auction, the greater the risk that some other user has edited the auction details and that the Item instance now holds stale data.

Suppose our first request executed the following code to retrieve the auction details:

```
public Item viewItem(Long itemId) {
    return ItemDAO.getItemById(itemId);
}
```

This line of thinking would advise us to discard the returned Item after rendering the view, storing only the identifier value for use in the next request. It seems superficially reasonable that we should retrieve the Item instance again at the start of the second request. (This is what would be done in a system that uses entity beans for persistence.) We could then be certain that the Item held nonstale data for the duration of the second database transaction.

There is one problem with this notion: The administrator already used the possibly stale data to arrive at the decision to approve! Reloading the Item in the second request is useless, since the reloaded state *will not be used for anything*—at least, it can't be used in deciding whether the auction should be approved, which is the important thing.

In order to ensure that the details that were viewed and approved by the administrator are still the current details during the second database transaction, we must perform an explicit *manual version check*. The following code demonstrates how this could be implemented in a controller servlet:

```
public void approveAuction(Long itemId,
                           int itemVersion,
                           Long adminId)
      throws BusinessException {

    Item item = new ItemDAO().getItemById(itemId);

    if ( !( itemVersion==item.getVersion() ) )
        throw new StaleItemException();

    User admin = new UserDAO().getUserById(adminId);
    item.approve(admin);
}
```

In this case, the manual version check isn't especially difficult to implement.

Are we justified in calling this approach *hard?* In more complex cases involving relationships, it's tedious to perform all the checks manually for all objects that are to be updated. These manual version checks should be considered noise—they implement a purely systemic concern not expressed in the business problem.

More important, the previous code snippet contains other unnecessary noise. We already retrieved the Item and User in previous requests. Is it necessary to reload them in each request? It should be possible to simplify our control code to the following:

```
public approveAuction(Item item, User admin)
      throws BusinessException {
    item.approve(admin);
}
```

Doing so not only saves three lines of code, but is also arguably more object oriented—our system is working mainly with domain model instances instead of passing around identifier values. Furthermore, this code would be quicker, since it saves two SQL SELECT queries that uselessly reload data. How can we achieve this simplification using Hibernate?

8.2.3 *Using detached persistent objects*

Suppose we kept the `Item` as a detached instance, storing it in the user's HTTP session, for example. We could reuse it in the second database transaction by reassociating it with the new Hibernate session using either `lock()` or `update()`. Let's see what these two options look like.

In the case of `lock()`, we adjust the `approveAuction()` method to look like this:

```
public void approveAuction(Item item, User admin)
        throws BusinessException {
    try {

        HibernateUtil.getSession().lock(item, LockMode.NONE);

    } catch (HibernateException ex) {
        throw new InfrastructureException(ex);
    }

    item.approve(admin);

}
```

The call to `Session.lock()` reassociates the item with the new Hibernate session and ensures that any subsequent change to the state of the item is propagated to the database when the session is flushed (for a discussion of the different Lock-Modes, see chapter 5, section 5.1.7, "Using pessimistic locking"). Since `Item` is versioned (if we map a `<version>` property), Hibernate will check the version number when synchronizing with the database, using the mechanism described in chapter 5, section 5.2.1, "Using managed versioning." You therefore don't have to use a pessimistic lock, as long as it would be allowed for concurrent transactions to read the item in question while the approval routine runs.

Of course, it would be better to hide Hibernate code in a new DAO method, so we add a new `lock()` method to the `ItemDAO`. This allows us to simplify the `approveAuction()` method to

```
public approveAuction(Item item, User admin)
        throws BusinessException {
    new ItemDAO().lock(item,false);    // Don't be pessimistic
    item.approve(admin);
}
```

Alternatively, we could use `update()`. For our example, the only real difference is that `update()` may be called after the state of the item has been modified, which would be the case if the administrator made changes before approving the auction:

```
public approveAuction(Item item, User admin)
        throws BusinessException {
    item.approve(admin);
    new ItemDAO().saveOrUpdate(item);
}
```

The new `saveOrUpdate()` method of `ItemDAO` calls `HibernateUtil.getSession().saveOrUpdate(item)`. Again, Hibernate will perform a version check when updating the item.

Is this implementation, using detached objects really any simpler than the hard way? We still need an explicit call to the `ItemDAO`, so the point is arguable. In a more complex example involving associations, we'd see more benefit, since the call to `lock()` or `update()` might cascade to associated instances. And let's not forget that this implementation is more efficient, avoiding the unnecessary SELECTs.

But we're still not satisfied. Is there a way to avoid the need for explicit reassociation with a new session? One way would be to use the same Hibernate session for both database transactions, a pattern we described in chapter 5 as *session-per-application-transaction*.

8.2.4 *Using a long session*

A *long session* is a Hibernate session that spans a whole application transaction, allowing reuse of persistent instances across multiple database transactions. This approach avoids the need to reassociate detached instances created or retrieved in previous database transactions.

A session contains two important kinds of state: It holds a cache of persistent instances and a JDBC `Connection`. We've already stressed the importance of not holding database resources open across multiple requests. Therefore, the session needs to release its connection between requests, if you intend to keep it open for more than one request.

The `disconnect()` method releases the session's JDBC connection without closing the session; the `reconnect()` method acquires a new connection for the same session. These methods let you have a session that spans multiple requests (a long session) without tying up expensive resources.

Currently, we're storing the session only in a `ThreadLocal`. Since each request is processed in a different thread, and since the session is now to be reused in multiple requests, we need a different solution. In a servlet-only environment, the perfect place to keep a reference to the Hibernate session between requests is in an `HttpSession` attribute.

It's simple to change the Hibernate servlet filter we wrote earlier to disconnect the Session between requests instead of completely closing it. This filter is also the best place to handle reconnection of the Session. The new doFilter() method is shown in listing 8.6. (Note that our example uses a servlet filter, but the same ideas are applicable to any other kind of interceptor.)

Listing 8.6   The doFilter() method for long sessions

```
public void doFilter(ServletRequest request,
                     ServletResponse response,
                     FilterChain chain)
        throws IOException, ServletException {

    // Try to get a Hibernate Session from the HttpSession
    HttpSession userSession =
            ((HttpServletRequest) request).getSession();
    Session hibernateSession =
            (Session) userSession.getAttribute("HibernateSession");

    // and reconnect it to the current thread
    if (hibernateSession != null)
        HibernateUtil.reconnect(hibernateSession);

    try {
        chain.doFilter(request, response);

        // Commit any pending database transaction.
        HibernateUtil.commitTransaction();

    } finally {

        // Disconnect the Session
        hibernateSession = HibernateUtil.disconnectSession();

        // and store it in the user's HttpSession
        userSession.setAttribute("HibernateSession", hibernateSession);
    }
}
```

Instead of closeSession(), we call disconnectSession() in the finally block. Before running the filter chain, we check whether the user session contains an existing Hibernate Session and, if found, reconnect() it and associate it with the current thread. The *disconnect* and *reconnect* operations detach the Hibernate session from the old and attach it to a new JDBC Connection.

Unfortunately, this implementation *never* closes the Hibernate session. Our Hibernate session has the same lifespan as the user session. So, all subsequent application transactions will reuse the same Hibernate session. This session holds a cache of persistent instances that grows increasingly stale over time; this is unacceptable.

At the beginning of each new application transaction, we *do* need to ensure that we have a completely clean Hibernate session. We need a new method to demarcate the beginning of an application transaction. This method must close the existing session and open a new one. Together with the disconnect() and reconnect() methods, we add the newApplicationTx() method to the HibernateUtil class:

```
public static void reconnect(Session session)
    throws InfrastructureException {
    try {
        session.reconnect();
        threadSession.set(session);
    } catch (HibernateException ex) {
        throw new InfrastructureException(ex);
    }
}

public static Session disconnectSession()
    throws InfrastructureException {

    Session session = getSession();
    try {
        threadSession.set(null);
        if (session.isConnected() && session.isOpen())
            session.disconnect();
    } catch (HibernateException ex) {
        throw new InfrastructureException(ex);
    }
    return session;
}

public static void newApplicationTx() {
    closeSession();
}
```

We must call the newApplicationTx() method at the beginning of the application transaction, just before the item for approval is shown to the administrator (before viewItem(itemId) in a controller servlet is called):

```
HibernateUtil.newApplicationTx();
viewItem(itemId);
```

Our viewItem() method would remain, as ever:

```
public Item viewItem(Long itemId) {
    return ItemDAO.getItemById(itemId);
}
```

And, as promised, the approveAuction() method now finally simplifies as follows:

```
public approveAuction(Item item, User admin)
        throws BusinessException {
    item.approve(admin);
}
```

More complex application transactions sometimes make changes to the domain model in several sequential requests. Since the session is flushed by our interceptor at the end of each request, the application transaction would be nonatomic if data was written in a request in the middle. In applications that require recovery of incomplete application transactions in the case of a system failure, this is correct. However, other applications require atomicity, and hence changes should be flushed to the database only on the final request. This is easy to implement using detached objects but not as natural with the long session approach.

The solution is to set the Hibernate session to FlushMode.NEVER and explicitly flush it at the end of the application transaction. All changes are held in memory (actually, in the users HttpSession) until the explicit flush. Note that queries won't be aware of these unflushed changes and might return stale data.

There's one final complication relating to the long session approach. A Hibernate Session isn't threadsafe, and the servlet engine allows multiple requests from the same user to be processed concurrently. So, it's possible that two concurrent requests could obtain the same Hibernate Session from the HttpSession if, for example, the user clicked a submit button twice. This would result in unpredictable behavior. This problem also affects the previous approach, where we used detached objects, since detached objects also aren't threadsafe. Indeed, this problem affects any web application that keeps mutable state in the HttpSession.

Since this is a generic problem that affects almost all web applications, we'll leave it to you to find an appropriate solution. A good solution for some applications might be to reject any new request if a request is already being processed for the same user. You could easily implement this approach in a servlet filter. Other applications might need to serialize requests from the same user (which can be achieved by synchronizing on the HttpSession object in a servlet filter).

Still other applications (multiwindow applications, for example) may need to support multiple concurrent application transactions. In this case, the application might allocate more than one long session to each user, with some mapping between the window that was the source of a request and the long session that services the associated application transaction.

This worked nicely for our servlet-only architecture. But what about EJB applications? If the Hibernate Session is accessed only from the EJB tier, storing it in the user session in the web tier isn't an option. More generally, *when* are each of the three application transaction approaches we've discussed relevant?

8.2.5 *Choosing an approach to application transactions*

You can probably guess from the fact that we called something the hard way that we don't think it's a good technique. We wouldn't use this approach in our own applications. However, if your architecture specifies that the web tier should never access the domain model directly (and so the domain model is completely hidden from the presentation layer behind an intermediate DTO abstraction layer), and if you're unable to keep state associated with the user in the EJB tier (you're using only stateless session beans), then you have essentially no other choice. It's possible to build Hibernate applications this way, and Hibernate was designed to support this approach. At least this approach frees you from having to consider the difference between persistent and detached instances, and it eliminates the possibility of LazyInitializationExceptions thrown by detached objects.

Currently, most Hibernate applications choose the detached objects approach, with a new session per database transaction. In particular, this is the method of choice for an application where business logic and data access execute in the EJB tier but where the domain model is also used in the web tier, avoiding the need for tedious DTOs. This approach is even being used successfully in servlet-only applications. We're inclined to think that it isn't the best approach for servlet-only applications, however.

Instead, we'd use the long session approach in the case of a servlet-only application. So far, we've found this approach difficult to explain, and it isn't well understood in the Hibernate community. We suppose this is because the notion of an application transaction isn't well understood in the Java community, and most developers aren't used to thinking about problems in terms of application transactions. We hope this situation changes soon, because this idea is useful even if you don't use the long session approach.

If you want to use long sessions in an EJB application, you need to find a way to associate a Hibernate session with a particular user without leaving the EJB tier. But should you be keeping state associated with users in the EJB tier at all? This kind of practice is usually frowned on.

As far as we can see, there is no *a priori* reason why it should be less efficient to keep state associated with a user session in the business tier than in the web tier. On the contrary, it looks as if it would be much *more* efficient to keep state associated with the application transaction right there in the middle tier where it belongs, rather than serializing it to and from the database and/or web tier in each request. The EJB specification provides stateful session beans for precisely this purpose. A stateful bean could store a Hibernate session in an instance variable, disconnecting the session between requests. However, many application servers are known to implement inefficient stateful session bean support. You have to evaluate your vendor and product before using this approach.

Our discussion about basic application design is now finished. Let's turn to more exotic problems that usually occur when you have to handle legacy or other special kinds of data.

8.3 *Handling special kinds of data*

Some data requires special treatment in addition to the general principles we've discussed in the rest of the book. In this section, we'll describe important kinds of data that introduce extra complexity into your Hibernate code.

The first and most important problem is *legacy* data. Relatively few projects have the luxury of working completely from scratch with a brand-new database; most applications share data with existing legacy applications. In this case, it's difficult to change the database schemas, and your new application may be forced to work with a data model that is less than optimal from your point of view. It's even possible to find yourself tied to a legacy database with such a crazy design that use of Hibernate is impossible (this is exceedingly rare, however).

A second interesting case is data that is *auditable*. Any change to auditable data requires that the change be recorded in the database along with the date and time when the change was made and the name of the user who made the change. Hibernate has special facilities for implementing audit logs (and other similar aspects that require a persistence event mechanism).

Let's first look at legacy data mappings and some of the resulting application design issues.

8.3.1 *Legacy schemas and composite keys*

When your application inherits an existing legacy database schema, you want to make as few changes to the existing schema as possible. Every change you make could break other existing applications that access the database and require expensive migration of existing data. In general, it isn't possible to build a new application and make *no* changes to the existing data model—a new application usually means additional business requirements that naturally require evolution of the database schema.

We'll therefore consider two types of problems: problems that relate to changing business requirements (which generally can't be solved without schema changes) and problems that relate only to how you wish to represent the same business problem in your new application (which can usually—but not always—be solved without database schema changes). You can usually spot the first kind of problem by looking at the *logical* data model. The second type more often relates to the implementation of the logical data model as a physical database schema.

If you accept this observation, you'll see that the kinds of problems that require schema changes are those that call for addition of new entities, refactoring of existing entities, addition of new attributes to existing entities, and modification of the associations between entities. The problems that can be solved *without* schema changes usually involve inconvenient column definitions for a particular entity.

Let's now concentrate on the second kind of problems. These inconvenient column definitions most commonly fall into two categories:

- Use of natural (especially composite) keys
- Inconvenient column types

We've mentioned that we think natural primary keys are a bad idea. Natural keys often make it difficult to refactor the data model when business requirements change. They may even, in extreme cases, impact performance. Unfortunately, many legacy schemas use (natural) composite keys heavily, and, for the very reason that we discourage the use of composite keys, it may be difficult to change the legacy schema to use surrogate keys. Therefore, Hibernate supports the use of natural keys. If the natural key is a composite key, support is via the <composite-id> mapping.

The second category of problems can usually be solved using a custom Hibernate mapping type (a UserType or CompositeUserType), as described in chapter 6.

Let's look at some examples that illustrate the solutions for both problems. We'll start with natural key mappings.

Mapping a table with a natural key

Our USER table has a synthetic primary key, USER_ID, and a unique key constraint on USERNAME. Here's a portion of our Hibernate mapping:

```
<class name="User" table="USER">
    <id name="id" column="USER_ID" unsaved-value="null">
        <generator class="native"/>
    </id>

    <version name="version"
             column="VERSION"/>

    <property name="username"
             column="USERNAME"
```

```
                            unique="true"
                            not-null="true"/>
        . . .
    </class>
```

Notice that a synthetic identifier mapping may specify an `unsaved-value`, allowing Hibernate to determine whether an instance is a detached instance or a new transient instance. Hence, the following code snippet may be used to create a new persistent user:

```
User user = new User();
user.setUsername("john");
user.setFirstname("John");
user.setLastname("Doe");
session.saveOrUpdate(user); // Generates id value by side-effect
System.out.println( session.getIdentifier(user) ); // Prints  1
session.flush();
```

If you encountered a USER table in a legacy schema, USERNAME would probably be the primary key. In this case, we would have no synthetic identifier; instead, we'd use the `assigned` identifier generator strategy to indicate to Hibernate that the identifier is a natural key assigned by the application before the object is saved:

```
<class name="User" table="USER">
    <id name="username" column="USERNAME">
        <generator class="assigned"/>
    </id>

    <version name="version"
             column="VERSION"
             unsaved-value="negative"/>
    . . .
</class>
```

We removed the `unsaved-value` attribute from the `<id>` mapping. An assigned identifier can't be used to determine whether an instance is detached or transient—since it's assigned by the application, it's never null. Instead, we specify an `unsaved-value` mapping for the `<version>` property. Doing so achieves the same effect by essentially the same mechanism. The code to save a new User isn't changed:

```
User user = new User();
user.setUsername("john"); // Assign a primary key value
user.setFirstname("John");
user.setLastname("Doe");
session.saveOrUpdate(user); // Will save, since version is -1
System.out.println( session.getIdentifier(user) ); // Prints "john"
session.flush();
```

However, we will have to change the declaration of the version property in the `User` class to assign a negative value (`private int version = -1`).

If a class with a natural key does *not* declare a version or timestamp property, it's more difficult to get `saveOrUpdate()` and cascades to work correctly. You might use a custom Hibernate `Interceptor` as discussed later in this chapter. (On the other hand, if you're happy to use explicit `save()` and explicit `update()` instead of `saveOrUpdate()` and cascades, Hibernate doesn't need to be able to distinguish between transient and detached instances; so, you can safely ignore this advice.)

Composite natural keys extend the same ideas.

Mapping a table with a composite key

As far as Hibernate is concerned, a composite key may be handled as an assigned identifier of value type (the Hibernate type is a component). Suppose the primary key of our user table consisted of a `USERNAME` and an `ORGANIZATION_ID`. We could add a property named `organizationId` to the `User` class and use the following mapping:

```
<class name="User" table="USER">

    <composite-id>
        <key-property name="username"
                      column="USERNAME"/>

        <key-property name="organizationId"
                      column="ORGANIZATION_ID"/>
    </composite-id>

    <version name="version"
             column="VERSION"
             unsaved-value="0"/>
    ...
</class>
```

The code to save a new `User` would look like this:

```
User user = new User();

// Assign a primary key value
user.setUsername("john");
user.setOrganizationId(42);

// Set property values
user.setFirstname("John");
user.setLastname("Doe");
session.saveOrUpdate(user); // will save, since version is 0
session.flush();
```

But what object could we use as the identifier when we called `load()` or `get()`? It's possible to use an instance of the `User`; for example:

```
User user = new User();

// Assign a primary key value
user.setUsername("john");
user.setOrganizationId(42);

// Load the persistent state into user
session.load(User.class, user);
```

In this code snippet, User acts as its own identifier class. Note that we now have to implement Serializable and equals()/hashCode() for this class. It's much more elegant to define a separate *composite identifier class* that declares just the key properties. We call this class UserId:

```
public class UserId extends Serializable {
    private String username;
    private String organizationId;

    public UserId(String username, String organizationId) {
        this.username = username;
        this.organizationId = organizationId;
    }

    // Getters...

    public boolean equals(Object o) {
        if (this == o) return true;
        if (o = null) return false;
        if (!(o instanceof UserId)) return false;
        final UserId userId = (UserId) o;
        if (!organizationId.equals(userId.getOrganizationId()))
            return false;
        if (!username.equals(userId.getUsername()))
            return false;
        return true;

    }
    public int hashCode() {
        return username.hashCode();
    )
}
```

It's critical that we implement equals() and hashCode() correctly, since Hibernate uses these methods to do cache lookups. Composite key classes are also expected to implement Serializable.

Now, we'd remove the userName and organizationId properties from User and add a userId property. We'd use the following mapping:

```
<class name="User" table="USER">

    <composite-id name="userId" class="UserId">
        <key-property name="userName"
                      column="USERNAME"/>

        <key-property name="organizationId"
                      column="ORGANIZATION_ID"/>
    </composite-id>

    <version name="version"
             column="VERSION"
             unsaved-value="0"/>
    ...
</class>
```

We could save a new instance using this code:

```
UserId id = new UserId("john", 42);

User user = new User();

// Assign a primary key value
user.setUserId(id);

// Set property values
user.setFirstname("John");
user.setLastname("Doe");

session.saveOrUpdate(user); // will save, since version is 0
session.flush();
```

The following code shows how to load an instance:

```
UserId id = new UserId("john", 42);

User user = (User) session.load(User.class, id);
```

Now, suppose the ORGANIZATION_ID was a foreign key to the ORGANIZATION table, and that we wished to represent this association in our Java model. Our recommended way to do this is to use a <many-to-one> association mapped with insert="false" update="false", as follows:

```
<class name="User" table="USER">

    <composite-id name="userId" class="UserId">
        <key-property name="userName"
                      column="USERNAME"/>

        <key-property name="organizationId"
                      column="ORGANIZATION_ID"/>
    </composite-id>
```

```
<version name="version"
        column="VERSION"
        unsaved-value="0"/>

<many-to-one name="organization"
        class="Organization"
        column="ORGANIZATION_ID"
        insert="false" update="false"/>
...
</class>
```

This use of insert="false" update="false" tells Hibernate to ignore that property when updating or inserting a User, but we may of course read it with john.getOrganization().

An alternative approach is to use a <key-many-to-one>:

```
<class name="User" table="USER">

    <composite-id name="userId" class="UserId">
        <key-property name="userName"
                    column="USERNAME"/>

        <key-many-to-one name="organization"
                    class="Organization"
                    column="ORGANIZATION_ID"/>
    </composite-id>

    <version name="version"
            column="VERSION"
            unsaved-value="0"/>
    ...
</class>
```

However, it's usually inconvenient to have an association in a composite identifier class, so this approach isn't recommended except in special circumstances.

Since USER has a composite primary key, any referencing foreign key is also composite. For example, the association from Item to User (the seller) is now mapped to a composite foreign key. To our relief, Hibernate can hide this detail from the Java code. We can use the following association mapping for Item:

```
<many-to-one name="seller" class="User">
    <column name="USERNAME"/>
    <column name="ORGANIZATION_ID"/>
</many-to-one>
```

Any collection owned by the User class will also have a composite foreign key—for example, the inverse association, items, sold by this user:

```
<set name="items" lazy="true" inverse="true">
    <key>
        <column name="USERNAME"/>
```

```
        <column name="ORGANIZATION_ID"/>
    </key>
    <one-to-many class="Item"/>
</set>
```

Note that the order in which columns are listed is significant and should match the order in which they appear inside the <composite-id> element.

Let's turn to our second legacy schema problem, inconvenient columns.

Using a custom type to map legacy columns

The phrase *inconvenient column type* covers a broad range of problems: for example, use of the CHAR (instead of VARCHAR) column type, use of a VARCHAR column to represent numeric data, and use of a special value instead of an SQL NULL. It's straightforward to implement a UserType to handle legacy CHAR values (by trimming the String returned by the JDBC driver), to perform type conversions between numeric and string data types, or to convert special values to a Java null. We won't show code for any of these common problems; we'll leave that to you—they're all easy if you study chapter 6, section 6.1.3, "Creating custom mapping types" carefully.

We'll look at a slightly more interesting problem. So far, our User class has two properties to represent a user's names: firstname and lastname. As soon as we add an initial, our User class will become messy. Thanks to Hibernate's component support, we can easily improve our model with a single name property of a new Name Java type (which encapsulates the details).

Also suppose that there is a single NAME column in the database. We need to map the concatenation of three different properties of Name to one column. The following UserType demonstrates how this can be accomplished (we make the simplifying assumption that the initial is never null):

```
public class NameUserType implements UserType {

    private static final int[] TYPES = { Types.VARCHAR };
    public int[] sqlTypes() { return TYPES; }
    public Class returnedClass() { return Name.class; }

    public boolean isMutable() {
        return true;
    }

    public Object deepCopy(Object value) throws HibernateException {
        Name name = (Name) value;
        return new Name(name.getFirstname(),
                        name.getInitial(),
                        name.getLastname());
    }
```

```
public boolean equals(Object x, Object y)
        throws HibernateException {
    // use equals() implementation on Name class
    return x==null ? y==null : x.equals(y);
}

public Object nullSafeGet(ResultSet resultSet,
                          String[] names,
                          Object owner)
    throws HibernateException, SQLException {

    String dbName =
        (String) Hibernate.STRING.nullSafeGet(resultSet, names);

    if (dbName==null) return null;

    StringTokenizer tokens = new StringTokenizer(dbName);
    Name realName =
        new Name( tokens.nextToken(),
                  String.valueOf(tokens.nextToken().charAt(0)),
                  tokens.nextToken() );
    return realName;
}

public void nullSafeSet(PreparedStatement statement,
                        Object value,
                        int index)
    throws HibernateException, SQLException {

    Name name = (Name) value;

    String nameString = (name==null) ?
        null :
        name.getFirstname()
        + ' ' + name.getInitial()
        + ' ' + name.getLastname();
    Hibernate.STRING.nullSafeSet(statement, nameString, index);
}

}
```

Notice that this UserType delegates to one of the Hibernate built-in types for some functionality. This is a common pattern, but it isn't a requirement.

We hope you can now see how many different kinds of problems having to do with inconvenient column definitions can be solved by clever user of Hibernate custom types. Remember that every time Hibernate reads data from a JDBC ResultSet or writes data to a JDBC PreparedStatement, it goes via a Type. In almost every case, that Type could be a custom type. (This includes associations—a Hibernate ManyToOneType, for example, delegates to the identifier type of the associated class, which might be a custom type.)

One further problem often arises in the context of working with legacy data: integrating database triggers.

Working with triggers

There are some reasonable motivations for using triggers even in a brand-new database, so legacy data isn't the only context in which problems arise. Triggers and ORM are often a problematic combination. It's difficult to synchronize the effect of a trigger with the in-memory representation of the data.

Suppose the ITEM table has a CREATED column mapped to a CREATED property of type Date, which is initialized by an insert trigger. The following mapping is appropriate:

```
<property name="created"
          type="timestamp"
          column="CREATED"
          insert="false"
          update="false"/>
```

Notice that we map this property insert="false" update="false" to indicate that it isn't to be included in SQL INSERTs or UPDATEs.

After saving a new Item, Hibernate won't be aware of the value assigned to this column by the trigger, since it occurs after the INSERT or the item row. If we need to use the value in our application, we have to tell Hibernate explicitly to reload the object with a new SQL SELECT. For example:

```
Item item = new Item();
...
HibernateUtil.beginTransaction();
Session session = HibernateUtil.getSession();

session.save(item);
session.flush(); // Force the INSERT to occur
session.refresh(item); // Reload the object with a SELECT

System.out.println( item.getCreated() );

HibernateUtil.commitTransaction();
HibernateUtil.closeSession();
```

Most problems involving triggers may be solved this way, using an explicit flush() to force immediate execution of the trigger, perhaps followed by a call to refresh() to retrieve the result of the trigger.

You should be aware of one special problem when you're using detached objects with a database with triggers. Since no snapshot is available when a detached object is reassociated with a session using update() or saveOrUpdate(), Hibernate may execute unnecessary SQL UPDATE statements to ensure that the database state is completely synchronized with the session state. This may cause an UPDATE trigger to fire inconveniently. You can avoid this behavior by enabling select-before-update in the mapping for the class that is persisted to the table with the trigger. If the ITEM table has an update trigger, we can use the following mapping:

```
<class name="Item"
    table="ITEM"
    select-before-update="true">
    ...
</class>
```

This setting forces Hibernate to retrieve a snapshot of the current database state using an SQL SELECT, enabling the subsequent UPDATE to be avoided if the state of the in-memory Item is the same.

Let's summarize our discussion of legacy data models: Hibernate offers several strategies to deal with (natural) composite keys and inconvenient columns. However, our recommendation is that you carefully examine whether a schema change is possible. In our experience, many developers immediately dismiss database schema changes as too complex and time-consuming, and they look for a Hibernate solution. Sometimes this opinion isn't justified, and we urge you to consider schema evolution as a natural part of your data's lifecycle. If making table changes and exporting/importing data solves the problem, one day of work might save many days in the long run—when many workarounds and special cases become a burden.

We'll now look more closely at audit logging and tracking object state changes in the database.

8.3.2 Audit logging

An *audit log* is a database table that contains information about changes made to other data, specifically about the *event* that results in the change. For example, we might record information about creation and update events for auction Items. The information that's recorded usually includes the user, the date and time of the event, what type of event occurred, and the item that was changed.

Audit logs are often handled using database triggers, and we think this is an excellent approach. However, it's sometimes better for the application to take responsibility, especially if portability between different databases is required.

You need to perform several steps to implement audit logging:

1 Mark the persistent classes for which you want to enable logging.

2 Define the information that should be logged: user, date, time, type of modification, and so on.

3 Tie it all together with a Hibernate `Interceptor` that automatically creates the audit trail for you.

Creating the marker interface

We first create a marker interface, `Auditable`. We use this interface to mark all persistent classes that should be automatically audited:

```
package org.hibernate.auction.model;

public interface Auditable {
    public Long getId();
}
```

This interface requires that a persistent entity class expose its identifier with a getter method; we need this property to log the audit trail. Enabling audit logging for a particular persistent class is then trivial; we just add it to the class declaration. Here's an example, for `Item`:

```
public class Item implements Serializable, Auditable {
    ...
}
```

Creating and mapping the log record

Now we create a new persistent class, `AuditLogRecord`. This class represents the information we want to log in the audit database table:

```
public class AuditLogRecord {

    public String message;
    public Long entityId;
    public Class entityClass;
    public Long userId;
    public Date created;

    AuditLogRecord() {}

    public AuditLogRecord(String message,
                          Long entityId,
                          Class entityClass,
                          Long userId) {
        this.message = message;
        this.entityId = entityId;
        this.entityClass = entityClass;
        this.userId = userId;
        this.created = new Date();
    }
}
```

You shouldn't consider this class part of your domain model. Hence you don't need to be as cautious about exposing public attributes. The `AuditLogRecord` is part of your persistence layer and possibly shares the same package with other persistence-related classes, such as `HibernateUtil` or your custom mapping types.

Next, we map this class to the `AUDIT_LOG` database table:

```
<hibernate-mapping>

<class name="org.hibernate.auction.persistence.audit.AuditLogRecord"
       table="AUDIT_LOG"
       mutable="false">

    <id type="long" column="AUDIT_LOG_ID">
       <generator class="native"/>
    </id>

    <property    name="message" column="MESSAGE"
                 not-null="true" access="field"/>

    <property    name="entityId" column="ENTITY_ID"
                 not-null="true" access="field"/>

    <property    name="entityClass" column="ENTITY_CLASS"
                 not-null="true" access="field"/>

    <property    name="userId" column="USER_ID"
                 not-null="true" access="field"/>

    <property    name="created" column="CREATED"
                 type="java.util.Date" not-null="true"
                 access="field"/>

</class>

</hibernate-mapping>
```

We marked the class `mutable="false"`, since `AuditLogRecords` are immutable, Hibernate will now no longer update the record, even if you try to. Note that we don't declare an identifier property in the class; Hibernate will therefore manage the surrogate key of an `AuditLogRecord` internally.

The audit logging concern is somewhat orthogonal to the business logic that causes the loggable event. It's possible to mix logic for audit logging with the business logic, but in many applications it's preferable that audit logging be handled in a central piece of code, transparently to the business logic. We wouldn't manually create a new `AuditLogRecord` and save it whenever an `Item` is modified.

Hibernate offers an extension point, so you can plug in an audit-log routine (or any other similar event listener). This extension is known as a Hibernate `Interceptor`.

Writing an interceptor

We'd prefer that a logEvent() method be called automatically when we call save(). The best way to do this with Hibernate is to implement the Interceptor interface. Here's an example:

```
public class AuditLogInterceptor implements Interceptor {

    private Session session;
    private Long userId;

    private Set inserts = new HashSet();
    private Set updates = new HashSet();

    public void setSession(Session session) {
        this.session=session;
    }
    public void setUserId(Long userId) {
        this.userId=userId;
    }
    public boolean onSave(Object entity,
                          Serializable id,
                          Object[] state,
                          String[] propertyNames,
                          Type[] types)
            throws CallbackException {

        if (entity instanceof Auditable)
            inserts.add(entity);

        return false;
    }

    public boolean onFlushDirty(Object entity,
                                Serializable id,
                                Object[] currentState,
                                Object[] previousState,
                                String[] propertyNames,
                                Type[] types)
            throws CallbackException {

        if (entity instanceof Auditable)
            updates.add(entity);

        return false;
    }

    public void postFlush(Iterator iterator)
            throws CallbackException {
        try {
```

```
        for (Iterator it = inserts.iterator(); it.hasNext();) {
            Auditable entity = (Auditable) it.next();
            AuditLog.logEvent("create",
                                entity,
                                userId,
                                session.connection());
        }
        for (Iterator it = updates.iterator(); it.hasNext();) {
            Auditable entity = (Auditable) it.next();
            AuditLog.logEvent("update",
                                entity,
                                userId,
                                session.connection());
        }
    } catch (HibernateException ex) {
        throw new CallbackException(ex);
    } finally {
        inserts.clear();
        updates.clear();
    }
}
...
}
```

The Hibernate `Interceptor` API has many more methods than are shown in this example. We assume you'll implement them with default semantics (that is, you'll usually return `false` or `null`, following the API documentation).

This particular interceptor has two interesting aspects. First, the `session` and `userId` are attributes this interceptor needs to do its work, so a client using this interceptor will have to set both properties when enabling the interceptor. The other interesting aspect is the audit log routine in `onSave()` and `onFlushDirty()`, where we add new and updated entities to collections. The `onSave()` interceptor method is called whenever Hibernate saves an entity; the `onFlushDirty()` method is called whenever Hibernate detects a dirty object. The audit logging is done in the `postFlush()` method, which Hibernate calls after executing the synchronization SQL. We use the static call `AuditLog.logEvent()` (a class and method we discuss next) to log the event. Note that we can't log events in `onSave()`, because the identifier value of a new entity might not be known at this point. Hibernate is guaranteed to have set all entity identifiers after flushing, so `postFlush()` is a good place to perform audit logging.

Also note how we use the `session`: We pass the JDBC connection of a given `Session` to the static call to `AuditLog.logEvent()`. There is a good reason for doing this, as we'll discuss in more detail. Let's first tie it all together and see how you enable the new interceptor.

Enabling the interceptor

You need to assign the `Interceptor` to a Hibernate `Session` when you first open the session:

```
AuditLogInterceptor interceptor = new AuditLogInterceptor();

Session session =
    HibernateUtil.getSessionFactory().openSession(interceptor);
Transaction tx = session.beginTransaction();

interceptor.setSession(session);
interceptor.setUserId( currentUser.getId() );

session.save(newItem); // Triggers onSave() of the Interceptor

tx.commit();            // Triggers postFlush() of the Interceptor
session.close();
```

Note that we no longer use `HibernateUtil.getSession()`, and so on, in this example. If we get a `Session` from `HibernateUtil`, it won't have the interceptor enabled. Therefore, we get the `SessionFactory` and manage the `Session` ourselves, as we did before we had `HibernateUtil`. However, it's straightforward to enhance the `HibernateUtil` class with interceptor handling. We leave this as an exercise for you: Try adding a `HibernateUtil.registerInterceptor()` method that holds the currently active `Interceptor` in a thread-local variable.

Let's get back to that interesting `Session`-handling code inside the interceptor and find out why we passed the `connection()` of the current `Session` to `AuditLog.logEvent()`.

Using a temporary Session

It should be clear why we require a `Session` inside the `AuditLogInterceptor`. The interceptor has to create and persist `AuditLogRecord` objects, so a first attempt for the `onSave()` method could have been the following routine:

```
if (entity instanceof Auditable) {
    try {

        AuditLogRecord logRecord = new AuditLogRecord( ... );
        // ... set the log information

        session.save(logRecord);
    } catch (HibernateException ex) {
        throw new CallbackException(ex);
    }
}
```

This seems straightforward: create a new `AuditLogRecord` instance and save it, using the current `Session`. However, it doesn't work.

It's illegal to invoke the original Hibernate `Session` from an `Interceptor` call-back. The session is in a fragile state during interceptor calls. A nice trick that avoids this issue is to open a new `Session` for the sole purpose of saving a single `AuditLogRecord` object. To keep this as fast as possible, you reuse the JDBC connection from the original `Session`.

This *temporary session* handling is encapsulated in the `AuditLog` helper class:

```
public class AuditLog {

    public static void logEvent(
        String message,
        Auditable entity,
        Long userId,
        Connection connection)
        throws CallbackException {

        Session tempSession =
          HibernateUtil.getSessionFactory().openSession(connection);

        try {
            AuditLogRecord record =
                new AuditLogRecord(message,
                                   entity.getId(),
                                   entity.getClass(),
                                   userId );

            tempSession.save(record);
            tempSession.flush();
        } catch (Exception ex) {
            throw new CallbackException(ex);

        } finally {
            try {
                tempSession.close();
            } catch (HibernateException ex) {
                throw new CallbackException(ex);
            }
        }
    }
}
```

Note that this method never commits or starts any database transactions; all it does is execute additional INSERT statements on an existing JDBC connection and inside the current database transaction. Using a temporary `Session` for some operations on the same JDBC connection and transaction is a nice trick you may also find useful in other scenarios.

We encourage you to experiment and try different interceptor design patterns. For example, you could redesign the auditing mechanism to log any entity, not only `Auditable`. The Hibernate website also has examples using nested interceptors or logging a complete history (including updated property and collection information) for an entity.

8.4 Summary

This chapter focused on application design and special cases you may encounter in your daily work writing Hibernate applications. We first talked about application design in a simple servlet-based scenario. The HibernateUtil helper class is essential to our layered application design, cleanly separating SessionFactory, Session, and Hibernate exception handling from other concerns of our application. We then showed the advantages of "smart" domain models by implementing business logic in the CaveatEmptor Item class.

We used the DAO pattern to create a façade for the persistence layer, hiding Hibernate internals from control, presentation, and business logic. We then evolved our servlet-based example to a three-tiered EJB architecture with the *session facade* and *EJB command* patterns. Thanks to Hibernate's detached object support, we can avoid the DTO pattern and eliminate a great deal of tedious code.

Detached Hibernate objects are also useful when you're implementing long-running application transactions. We used a servlet filter as an interceptor to implement application transactions with a long-running Hibernate Session.

In the second part of the chapter, we examined more exotic scenarios involving legacy data schemas. You learned how to map (natural) composite keys and how to handle them in application code. We also saw how to deal with triggers and use Hibernate custom types when mapping legacy data.

Finally, we implemented audit logging for persistent entities with a Hibernate Interceptor. Our custom interceptor uses a temporary Session trick to track modification events in an audit history table.

Using the toolset 9

Good ORM software comes bundled with a set of tools, and so does Hibernate. In this chapter, we'll discuss the Hibernate toolset. These tools can automatically generate mapping metadata, SQL database schemas, and even Java POJO source code. However, you have to use the right tool for your specific *development process*.

9.1 Development processes

In some projects, the development of a domain model is driven by developers analyzing the business domain in object-oriented terms. In others, it's heavily influenced by an existing relational data model: either a legacy database or a brand-new schema designed by a professional data modeler.

Since different projects start from different points, we need to consider different development scenarios and the different tools that may be used in each case. An overview of the tools and the artifacts they use as source and output is shown in figure 9.1. You may want to refer to this diagram while reading this chapter.

> **NOTE**   Note that *AndroMDA*, a tool that generates POJO source code from UML diagram files, isn't strictly considered part of the common Hibernate toolset; hence we don't discuss it in this chapter. See the community area on the Hibernate website for more information about the Hibernate modules in AndroMDA.

Before we begin looking closely at any of the particular tools you can use with Hibernate, we'll briefly survey the main scenarios and mention the tools that are most appropriate to each.

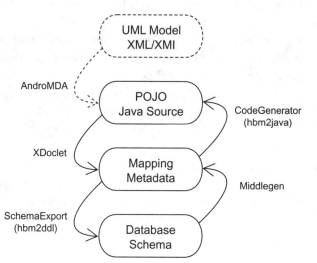

Figure 9.1
Input and output of the tools
used for Hibernate development

9.1.1 *Top down*

In *top-down development*, you start with an existing Java domain model (ideally implemented with POJOs/JavaBeans) and complete freedom with respect to the database schema. You must create a mapping document—either manually using a text editor (recommended is an IDE with XML auto-completion) or automatically using XDoclet—and then let Hibernate's `hbm2ddl` tool generate the database schema. In the absence of an existing data model, this is the most comfortable development style for most Java developers. You can even use the Hibernate tools to automatically refresh the database schema on every application restart in development.

9.1.2 *Bottom up*

Conversely, *bottom-up development* begins with an existing database schema and data model. In this case, the easiest way to proceed is to use Middlegen to generate Hibernate mapping documents and then run the `hbm2java` tool and generate skeletal POJO persistent classes. You'll usually have to enhance and modify the generated Hibernate mapping by hand, because not all class association details and Java-specific meta-information can be automatically generated from an SQL schema.

9.1.3 *Middle out (metadata oriented)*

Neither Java classes (without XDoclet annotations) nor DDL schemas contain enough information to be able to completely deduce an ORM. Hence, if you wish to *generate* the Hibernate mapping document instead of writing it by hand, you'll need extra input from the user. In the case of XDoclet, this information is provided by XDoclet attributes embedded in the source code. In the case of Middlegen, it's provided via the Middlegen GUI.

On the other hand, the mapping document does provide sufficient information to completely deduce the DDL schema and to generate working JavaBeans. Furthermore, the mapping document isn't too verbose. So, you may prefer *middle-out development*, where you begin with a handwritten Hibernate mapping document and generate the DDL using `hbm2ddl` and Java classes using `hbm2java`.

9.1.4 *Meet in the middle*

The most difficult scenario combines existing Java classes and an existing relational schema. In this case, there is little that the Hibernate toolset can do to help. It isn't possible to map arbitrary Java domain models to a given schema, so this scenario usually requires at least some refactoring of the Java classes, database schema, or both. The mapping document must almost certainly be written by hand (although it might be possible to use XDoclet). This is an incredibly painful scenario that is, fortunately, exceedingly rare.

9.1.5 Roundtripping

The notion of *roundtripping* is that any one of the three kinds of artifacts (Java classes, mapping documents, database schema) should be sufficient to reproduce the other two. Each tool should be completely reversible. You've already seen that this isn't the case. At the very least, you must add XDoclet annotations to the Java classes. Worse, it's never possible to fully reproduce the Java domain model or ORM from only the database schema.

Nevertheless, the Hibernate team is attempting to achieve a slightly less ambitious goal for the Hibernate toolset. Suppose you start with an existing database schema. Then the following steps should reproduce this schema exactly, with minimal user intervention:

1 Use Middlegen to create a mapping document

2 Use hbm2java to generate annotated Java classes

3 Use XDoclet to regenerate the mapping document

4 Use hbm2ddl to generate the DDL

At the time of this writing, there is still work to be done before this approach works perfectly, because it involves many different tools and metamodel conversions.

We'll now look more closely at each of the tools we've mentioned, starting with hbm2ddl. This tool is used to automatically generate SQL DDL from Hibernate mapping metadata. We assume that you've already created some POJO persistent classes and the relevant Hibernate mappings and are now looking for a way to simplify the creation of the schema in the database.

9.2 Automatic schema generation

Schemas for SQL-based database management systems are written in the SQL DDL. This includes well-known statements such as CREATE and ALTER.

The tool used for the generation process is called hbm2ddl. Its class is net.sf.hibernate.tool.hbm2ddl.SchemaExport; hence it's also sometimes called SchemaExport.

NOTE   *The Hibernate extensions package*—You may have noticed that `hbm2ddl` resides inside the main Hibernate distribution and isn't packaged with the other tools in `HibernateExtensions`. The Hibernate team decided that `hbm2ddl` is much closer to the core functionality of Hibernate than any of the other tools and should be bundled with Hibernate itself. In addition, you can run `hbm2ddl` from an application to automatically generate a database schema at runtime. This ability is especially useful if you'd like to initialize the database every time the application in development restarts.

In Hibernate, the prerequisite for automatically generating SQL DDL is always a Hibernate mapping metadata definition in XML. We assume that you've designed and implemented your POJO classes and written mapping metadata, but you probably haven't paid much attention to database-specific details (like table and column names).

Some special elements and attributes can be used in the mapping files; most of them are relevant only for a customized schema. Hibernate tries to use sensible defaults if you don't specify your own names and strategies; however, be warned that a professional DBA might not accept this default schema without manual changes. Nevertheless, the defaults may be satisfactory for a development or prototype environment.

9.2.1 *Preparing the mapping metadata*

In this example, we've marked up the mapping for the `Item` class with `hbm2ddl`-specific attributes and elements. These optional definitions integrate seamlessly with the other mapping elements, as you can see in listing 9.1.

Listing 9.1   Additional elements in the `Item` mapping for `SchemaExport`

```
<class name="Item" table="ITEM">

<id name="id" type="string">
    <column name="ITEM_ID" sql-type="char(32)"/>    ❶
    <generator class="uuid.hex"/>
</id>

<property name="name" type="string">
    <column name="NAME"
            not-null="true"
            length="255"
            index="IDX_ITEMNAME"/>    ❷
</property>

<property name="description"
          type="string"
```

```
            column="DESCRIPTION"
            length="4000"/>   ❸

<property name="initialPrice"
        type="customtype.MonetaryAmount">
    <column name="INITIAL_PRICE" check="INITIAL_PRICE > 0"/>   ❹
    <column name="INITIAL_PRICE_CURRENCY"/>
</property>

<set name="categories" table="CATEGORY_ITEM" cascade="none">
    <key
        <column="ITEM_ID" sql-type="char(32)"/>   ❺
    </key>
    <many-to-many class="Category">
        <column name="CATEGORY_ID" sql-type="char(32)/>
    </many-to-many>
</set>

...

</class>
```

❶ hbm2ddl automatically generates a VARCHAR typed column if a property (even the identifier property) is of mapping type string. We know the identifier generator uuid.hex always generates strings that are 32 characters long; so, we use a CHAR SQL type and also set its size fixed at 32 characters. The nested <column> element is required for this declaration because there is no attribute to specify the SQL datatype on the <id> element.

❷ The column, not-null, and length attributes are also available on the <property> element, but we want to create an additional index in the database, hence we again use a nested <column> element. This index will speed our searches for items by name. If we reuse the same index name on other property mappings, we can create an index that includes multiple database columns. The value of this attribute is also used to name the index in the database catalog.

❸ For the description field, we chose the lazy approach, using the attributes on the <property> element instead of a <column> element. The DESCRIPTION column will be generated as VARCHAR(4000).

❹ The custom user-defined type MonetaryAmount requires two database columns to work with. We have to use the <column> element. The check attribute triggers the creation of a *check constraint*; the value in that column must match the given arbitrary SQL expression. Note that there is also a check attribute for the <class> element, which is useful for multicolumn check constraints.

⑤ A <column> element can also be used to declare the foreign key fields in an association mapping. Otherwise, the columns of our association table CATEGORY_ITEM would be VARCHAR(32) instead of the more appropriate CHAR(32) type.

We've grouped all attributes relevant for schema generation in table 9.1; some of them weren't included in the previous Item mapping example.

Table 9.1   XML mapping attributes for hbm2ddl

Attribute	Value	Description
column	string	Usable in most mapping elements; declares the name of the SQL column. hbm2ddl (and Hibernate's core) defaults to the name of the Java property) if the column attribute is omitted and no nested <column> element is present. This behavior may be changed by implementing a custom NamingStrategy; see the section "Naming conventions" in chapter 3.
not-null	true/false	Forces the generation of a NOT NULL column constraint. Available as an attribute on most mapping elements and also on the dedicated <column> element.
unique	true/false	Forces the generation of a single-column UNIQUE constraint. Available for various mapping elements.
length	integer	Can be used to define a "length" of a datatype. For example, length="4000" for a string mapped property generates a VARCHAR(4000) column. This attribute is also used to define the precision of decimal types.
index	string	Defines the name of a database index that can be shared by multiple elements. An index on a single column is also possible. Only available with the <column> element.
unique-key	string	Enables unique constraints involving multiple database columns. All elements using this attribute must share the same constraint name to be part of a single constraint definition. This is a <column> element-only attribute.
sql-type	string	Overrides hbm2ddl's automatic detection of the SQL datatype; useful for database specific data types. Be aware that this effectively prevents database independence: hbm2ddl will automatically generate a VARCHAR or VARCHAR2 (for Oracle), but it will always use a declared SQL-type instead, if present. This attribute can only be used with the dedicated <column> element.
foreign-key	string	Names a foreign-key constraint, available for <many-to-one>, <one-to-one>, <key>, and <many-to-many> mapping elements. Note that inverse="true" sides of an association mapping won't be considered for foreign key naming, only the non-inverse side. If no names are provided, Hibernate generates unique random names.

After you've reviewed (probably together with a DBA) your mapping files and added schema-related attributes, you can create the schema.

9.2.2 *Creating the schema*

The `hbm2ddl` tool can be called from the command line:

```
java -cp classpath net.sf.hibernate.tool.hbm2ddl.SchemaExport
  options mapping_files
```

You have to make sure that Hibernate and its third-party libraries are in the classpath, along with your compiled persistent classes.

Table 9.2 shows the options for `hbm2ddl`.

Table 9.2   Command-line `hbm2ddl` configuration options

Option	Description
–quiet	Don't output the script to *stdout*.
–drop	Only drop the tables and clean the database.
–text	Don't export the DDL directly to the database, but only to *stdout*.
–output=*filename*	Output the DDL script to the given file.
–config=*filename*	Read the database configuration from a Hibernate XML configuration file.
–properties=*filename*	Read database properties from a Hibernate properties file.
–format	Format the generated SQL nicely in the script instead of using one row for each statement.
–delimiter=x;	Set an end-of-line delimiter for the script (usually a semicolon). The default is to not output an end-of-line delimiter. This delimiter is used only in textual output; it isn't relevant if the DDL is executed immediately.

As you can see from these options, the DDL can be directly executed. Doing so requires database connection settings in a properties file (or XML-based configuration). The DDL generated by `hbm2ddl` will always drop all tables and regenerate them; this is especially useful in development. Remember that a Hibernate database dialect is required in the configuration, because SQL DDL is highly vendor-specific.

One of the reasons `hbm2ddl` is distributed with the core Hibernate package is its ability to be started from inside an application, as shown here:

```
Configuration cfg = new Configuration();
SchemaExport schemaExport = new SchemaExport(cfg);
schemaExport.create(false, true);
```

A new `SchemaExport` object is created from a `Configuration`. If you use a hibernate.cfg.xml, the database connection settings and the dialect will be available in the `Configuration` and passed to the `SchemaExport` constructor. The create(false, true) call triggers the DDL creation process without any SQL printed to stdout (false) but with DDL immediately executed in the database (true). See the `SchemaExport` API for more information; all command-line options are also available directly in Java and can be set on the `SchemaExport` object.

The `hbm2ddl` tool can also be globally controlled by Hibernate configuration properties—for example, in the `hibernate.properties`:

```
hibernate.hbm2ddl.auto create-drop
```

Setting `hibernate.hbm2ddl.auto` to `create-drop` enforces a drop and a create of the database schema if buildSessionFactory() is called (usually, when a Hibernate application starts). Once you close() the `SessionFactory`, the schema is dropped again. Setting this parameter to `create` only drops and creates the schema when the `SessionFactory` is created. There is also an `update` setting for automatic updates of schema for schema evolution. The `SchemaUpdate` tool is used for that purpose, as discussed in the next section.

You may not be satisfied with these three options. Running `hbm2ddl` from the command line feels awkward, and using it inside your application isn't helpful in all development scenarios. If you, like most Java developers, use Ant to built projects, you can use an Ant task for automatic schema generation:

```
<target name="schemaexport">
    <taskdef name="schemaexport"
            classname="net.sf.hibernate.tool.hbm2ddl.SchemaExportTask"
            classpathref="class.path"/>

    <schemaexport
        config="${basedir}/etc/hibernate_export.cfg.xml"
        quiet="no"
        text="no" drop="no"
        delimiter=";"
        output="schema-export.sql">
        <fileset dir="src">
            <include name="**/*.hbm.xml"/>
        </fileset>
    </schemaexport>
</target>
```

This example uses an Ant task definition, and the task may be called with different options. In this case, the DDL is exported to a file (schema-export.sql) with a semicolon as a line delimiter. We also enable the DDL generation for all mapping files found in the src directory and export it directly to the database (text="no"). The database connection settings (and the dialect) are read from the hibernate_ export.cfg.xml found in the etc/ subdirectory.

9.2.3 *Updating the schema*

Once you've deployed an application, it becomes difficult to alter the database schema. This can even be the case in development, if your scenario requires test data that has to be redeployed after every schema change. With hbm2ddl, your only choice is to drop the existing structure and create it again, possibly followed by a time-consuming test data import.

Hibernate comes bundled with a tool for schema evolution, SchemaUpdate, which is used to update an existing SQL database schema; it drops obsolete tables, columns, and constraints. It uses the JDBC metadata and creates new tables and constraints by comparing the old schema with the updated mapping information. Note that SchemaUpdate depends on the quality of the metadata provided by the JDBC drivers, so it may not work as expected with some databases and drivers. (We actually think that SchemaUpdate is not very usable in practice at the time of writing.)

You can run SchemaUpdate from inside an application, as shown here:

```
Configuration cfg = new Configuration();
SchemaUpdate schemaUpdate = new SchemaUpdate(cfg);
schemaUpdate.execute(false, true);
```

A SchemaUpdate object is created from an existing Configuration. It requires the same settings (database connection and dialect) as hbm2ddl. This example only updates the database, without any DDL statements printed to stdout (as specified by false).

Of course, you can also use SchemaUpdate in an Ant build script:

```
<target name="schemaupdate">
    <taskdef name="schemaupdate"
            classname="net.sf.hibernate.tool.hbm2ddl.SchemaUpdateTask"
            classpathref="class.path"/>

    <schemaupdate
        properties="hibernate.properties"
        quiet="no">
        <fileset dir="src">
            <include name="**/*.hbm.xml"/>
        </fileset>
    </schemaupdate>
</target>
```

This task updates the database schema for all mapping files found in the src directory and also prints the DDL to stdout. Database connection settings are read from the hibernate.properties file found in the classpath.

The hbm2ddl tool is popular; most Hibernate projects use it in a top-down development process. It uses the Hibernate mapping metadata to generate a database schema that should conform with the expectations of any DBA. However, it isn't the only Hibernate tool that utilizes mapping metadata. In a bottom-up or middle-out development process, you can also generate Java source for persistent classes.

9.3 *Generating POJO code*

Hibernate's tool for automatic generation of persistent classes is called hbm2java; its main class is net.sf.hibernate.tool.hbm2java.CodeGenerator. This tool is also known as CodeGenerator, and it's available in the optional HibernateExtensions distribution.

You should use hbm2java for

- POJO source generation from Hibernate mapping files, using a middle-out development approach
- POJO source generation from mapping files that have also been automatically generated by Middlegen from an existing (legacy) database schema

hbm2java is highly customizable; you use extra metadata in the mapping files as with hbm2ddl. The Hibernate toolset documentation explains the basic usage of the tool and includes an overview of all possible configuration parameters. Instead of repeating them here, we'll discuss a practical example.

9.3.1 *Adding meta-attributes*

Let's assume that we have an existing Hibernate mapping file for the User class, and we'd like to generate the source for the class using the POJO conventions. As discussed in chapter 3, a POJO implements Serializable and has a no-arguments constructor, getters and setters for all properties, and an encapsulated implementation.

We generally use Hibernate's defaults in the mapping metadata and try to write as little metadata as possible. Some of the Hibernate defaults are generated using reflection on existing persistent classes. Of course, you can't rely on this auto-detection mechanism when you're using hbm2java, because there are no classes to reflect on.

Therefore, our first step is to improve the mapping metadata, so hbm2java will be able to run without errors. For example, if we've mapped the username of the User as

```
<property name="username"/>
```

we now explicitly include the type of the property, using either Hibernate mapping types or Java class names:

```
<property name="username" type="string"/>
```

After completing our mapping with type information, we continue with settings for the code-generation process.

By default, hbm2java produces a simple POJO persistent class. The class implements the Serializable marker interface, it has the required constructor and accessor methods, and it implements the recommended toString() and equals()/hashCode() methods with default semantics. All attributes of the class have private visibility, as expected. We can change that behavior with the <meta> element and attributes in our mapping files.

One of the first improvements we make is a more restrictive visibility scope for the User's properties. By default, all accessor methods are generated with public visibility. If our User objects were immutable, we wouldn't expose the setter methods on the public interface—only the getter methods. Instead of enhancing the mapping of each property with a <meta> element, we can declare a meta-attribute at the class level, thus applying the setting to all properties in that class:

```
<class name="User"
          table="USER">

    <meta attribute="scope-set">private</meta>

          . . .

</class>
```

The scope-set attribute defines the visibility of property setter methods. hbm2java also accepts meta-attributes on the next higher level, in the hbm2java configuration file discussed later in this section. This global meta-attribute affects source generation for all classes. We can also add fine-grained meta-attributes to single property, collection, or component mappings, as you'll see next.

One (albeit small) improvement is the inclusion of the User's username in the output of the generated toString() method. By default, toString() only shows the identifier value of an object. The username will be a good visual control element in our application's log output. So, we change the mapping of User to include it in the generated code:

```
<property name="username"
          type="string">
   <meta attribute="use-in-tostring">true</meta>
</property>
```

The generated code of the toString() method in User.java looks like this:

```
public String toString() {
    return new ToStringBuilder(this)
            .append("id", getId())
            .append("username", getUsername())
            .toString();
}
```

Note that hbm2java uses utility classes, in this case the ToStringBuilder of the commons-lang open source project. You have to include these utility libraries in your project if you want to compile the generated code without manual modification.

As we mentioned earlier, meta-attributes can be inherited—that is, if we declare a use-in-tostring at the level of a <class> element, all properties of that class are included in the toString() method. This inheritance mechanism works for all hbm2java meta-attributes, but we can turn it off selectively:

```
<meta attribute="scope-class" inherit="false">public abstract</meta>
```

Setting inherit to false in the scope-class meta-attribute creates the current class as public abstract, but not its subclasses.

At the time of this writing, hbm2java supports 21 meta-attributes for fine-tuning code generation. Most are related to visibility, interface implementation, class extension, and predefined Javadoc comments. Two of the meta-attributes are more interesting, because they control the automatic generation of *finder methods*.

9.3.2 *Generating finders*

A *finder* is a static method that may be called by application code to retrieve objects from the database. It's part of a *finder class*; the interface of that class can be regarded as a part of the public visible API of the persistence layer.

A full persistence layer would require all kinds of interfaces to manage objects: for example, a full DAO API, as described in chapter 8. You can use the automatically generated finders as the skeleton for that implementation.

hbm2java generates finder methods for single properties. We add a finder meta-attribute to our mapping declaration:

```
<property name="username"
        type="string">
    <meta attribute="use-in-tostring">true</meta>
    <meta attribute="finder-method">findByUsername</meta>
</property>
```

The `finder` attribute declares the name for the finder method, `findByUsername` in this case. The generated static method therefore is

```
public static List findByUsername(Session session, String username)
        throws SQLException, HibernateException {

    List finds = session.find("from User as user where user.username=?",
                            username, Hibernate.STRING);
    return finds;
}
```

This method accepts a `username` as an argument and returns a `List` of all `User`s with that name. The class of this method is called `UserFinder`:

```
public class UserFinder implements Serializable {

    public static List findAll(Session session)
        throws SQLException, HibernateException {

        List finds = session.find("from User ");
        return finds;
    }

}
```

Note that a generated finder class has at least one method, `findAll()`, which returns all objects of that class.

Also note how the finder methods use the Hibernate `Session`: It must be passed as an argument to each method call. This can be inconvenient, especially if an application uses a `ThreadLocal` mechanism for `Session` handling, as discussed in chapter 8.

We can set a static helper method that we'd like to use instead of the `Session` argument by adding the `session-method` meta-attribute to the class mapping:

```
<class name="User"
        table="USER">

        <meta attribute="session-method">
            HibernateUtil.getSession();
        </meta>
        ...

</class>
```

The generated finder method then uses a call to this helper method to obtain a `Session`:

```
public static List findAll()
    throws SQLException, HibernateException {

    Session session = HibernateUtil.getSession();
    List finds = session.find("from User");
    return finds;
}
```

We recommend this approach instead of the clumsy additional parameter for each finder method. See chapter 8 for more information on the thread-local session and the HibernateUtil class.

Finally, you can control the generation of basic POJO persistent classes and finder classes with the hbm2java configuration file.

9.3.3 *Configuring hbm2java*

Without a configuration file, hbm2java uses only the meta-attributes in the mapping metadata and its BasicRenderer for source generation. This renderer produces POJO persistent classes but not finder classes. We have to add the FinderRenderer to the configuration:

```
<codegen>

    <meta attribute="implements">
        org.hibernate.auction.model.Auditable
    </meta>

    <generate
        renderer="net.sf.hibernate.tool.hbm2java.BasicRenderer"/>

    <generate
        renderer="net.sf.hibernate.tool.hbm2java.FinderRenderer"
        package="org.hibernate.auction.finder"
        suffix="Finder"/>

</codegen>
```

We also added a global meta-attribute to this configuration; it's effective for all classes in all mapping declarations. We set the BasicRenderer for POJO persistent classes. The FinderRenderer can be customized with two settings: the package and the suffix for the generated classes. The full name of the finder class for User therefore is org.hibernate.auction.finder.UserFinder.java.

One of the newer features of hbm2java is a renderer that uses the Velocity template engine. BasicRenderer and FinderRenderer use hard-coded templates for the code generation, whereas VelocityRenderer can be fully customized with user-defined templates. It replaces the other two renderers in the hbm2java configuration file:

```
<codegen>
    <generate
        renderer="net.sf.hibernate.tool.hbm2java.VelocityRenderer">
        <param name="template">pojo.vm</param>
    </generate>
</codegen>
```

This renderer uses the `template` parameter as the name of the template used for code generation. This template is written in Velocity's language and must be available on the classpath on execution. `hbm2java` comes bundled with a default `pojo.vm` template file, which you might use as a skeleton for your own application-specific templates. Note that Velocity-based code generation is still in its early stages, and the default template isn't as sophisticated as the `BasicRenderer`. We also consider implementing your own render class as a more powerful approach, because Velocity unfortunately isn't very flexible for code generation. So, if you don't have time to learn Velocity, you should be able to produce a custom method quickly by using the `BasicRenderer` and `FinderRenderer` source code as a template.

You can start `hbm2java` either on the command line or with the `hbm2java` Ant task in the regular build process.

9.3.4 *Running hbm2java*

You can easily start `hbm2java` from the command line:

```
java -cp classpath net.sf.hibernate.tool.hbm2java.CodeGenerator
    options mapping_files
```

`hbm2java` supports two options: `output` sets the directory for generated code, and `config` can be used to set a configuration file. Each mapping file that should be included in the source generation process must be named explicitly.

An Ant task might be more appropriate in most projects. Here's an example:

```
<target name="codegen">

    <taskdef name="hbm2java"
            classname="net.sf.hibernate.tool.hbm2java.Hbm2JavaTask"
            classpathref="class.path"/>

    <hbm2java config="codegen.cfg.xml"
            output="generated/src/">

        <fileset dir="mappings/">
            <include name="**/*.hbm.xml"/>
        </fileset>

    </hbm2java>

</target>
```

This target produces Java source files in the `generated_src` directory. `hbm2java` uses the `codegen.cfg.xml` file from the current directory as its configuration and reads all Hibernate mapping files from the `mappings` directory (and its subdirectories).

Remember to provide a classpath reference to this task that includes not only the `hibernate-tools.jar` of the `HibernateExtensions` distribution but also the Hibernate core JAR and all required third-party libraries for Hibernate (and Velocity, if required).

The `hbm2java` tool can significantly improve your application development process, especially if you have a large number of existing database tables and also automatically generate Hibernate mapping metadata from that schema. Generating the mapping metadata from a schema is the job of Middlegen.

9.4   *Existing schemas and Middlegen*

Many developers use Hibernate in projects with legacy databases and existing schemas. In those cases, you usually can't modify the schema for easier integration with Hibernate. SQL databases traditionally have problems with schema evolution; some products even have problems renaming a table column.

If your only choice is to work with an existing schema, you may as well try to automatically generate Hibernate mapping metadata from that schema. Doing so is especially useful if the schema contains many tables (say, more than 50) and the application working with that data has to be up and running as early as possible (which is also usually the case). You can use Middlegen to generate a mapping skeleton from database metadata and then refine the mappings by hand.

Middlegen isn't limited to Hibernate metadata; it can also generate EJB entity bean code or Struts actions and JSP code through its plugins architecture. However, we'll focus on the Hibernate plugin in this section. Middlegen also offers a nice GUI, so you can rearrange the tables and customize the metadata generation process graphically.

9.4.1   *Starting Middlegen*

The preferred way to start Middlegen is with Ant, using the bundled `middlegen.MiddlegenTask`. As always, you declare it in the `build.xml` after you copy the Middlegen core and Hibernate plugin JAR libraries to the classpath (Don't forget your JDBC driver!):

```
<taskdef name="middlegen"
    classname="middlegen.MiddlegenTask"
    classpathref="class.path"/>
```

You can now use this `middlegen` task in whatever target you like and start the Middlegen GUI:

```
<middlegen appname="CaveatEmptor"
           prefsdir="${basedir}" gui="true"
           databaseurl="jdbc:oracle:thin:@localhost:1521:orac"
           driver="oracle.jdbc.driver.OracleDriver"
           username="test"
           password="test"
           schema="auction">
    <hibernate destination="generated/src"
               package="org.hibernate.auction.model"/>
</middlegen>
```

The previous example shows the minimum configuration options for Middlegen with the Hibernate plugin. You have to specify the database connection settings, such as JDBC driver, database URL, and login. The schema name is also important; otherwise, Middlegen will use all tables the user has access to, not only the tables owned by the user/schema.

Middlegen saves the user's preferences (settings such as the position of the tables in the graphical interface and customization options); it uses the base directory of your project as the save path. The name of the preferences file is the same as the application name: in this case, `CaveatEmptor-prefs.properties`.

Finally, you configure the Hibernate plugin. You have to set the target directory for the generated mapping files. In this example, we use the same directory that we might later use for the generated POJO source files (with `hbm2java`), so XML mapping files and persistent classes are in the same path. The package setting is used for all classes in the mapping metadata.

Executing this target with Ant starts Middlegen. After automatically connecting to the local Oracle database, Middlegen reads the schema metadata and shows a graphical interface. This interface has a view of the database tables in the top half and a dialog with various options at the bottom. Figure 9.2 shows the table view.

If you start Middlegen for the first time (without an existing configuration), the tables and relationships in the overview may look chaotic. Some manual work is required to get a good overview; luckily this must be done only once, because Middlegen saves the layout in the preferences. You can click and drag tables in the view and also select relationships for further customization (see the highlighted relationship between CATEGORY and CATEGORY_ITEM). After some work, we get a view of the CaveatEmptor database as shown in the figure; notice that the canvas extends to the right side with all other tables and relationships that have been found in our schema.

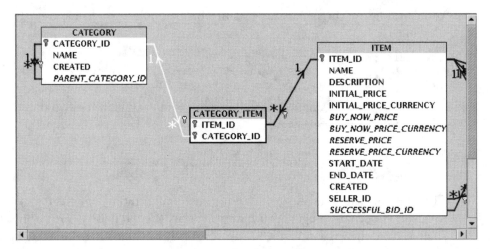

Figure 9.2 Middlegen showing the tables of the CaveatEmptor database

The first thing we want to customize is the association table between the CATEGORY and ITEM tables. In our application, the CATEGORY_ITEM table should be used to implement the many-to-many association between the Category and Item classes. However, it will be generated as a separate entity (a CategoryItem persistent class) if we don't change the Middlegen defaults.

Most Middlegen options can be modified graphically; but this change must be made before startup, in Middlegen's Ant configuration.

9.4.2 *Restricting tables and relationships*

Association tables that are part of a many-to-many relationship must be declared in the Middlegen Ant task as a jointable:

```
<hibernate destination="generated/src/"
        package="org.hibernate.auction.model"/>

<many2many>
    <tablea name="CATEGORY"/>
    <jointable name="CATEGORY_ITEM" generate="false"/>
    <tableb name="ITEM"/>
</many2many>
```

The <many2many> element indicates a many-to-many association. Middlegen now generates only a single association in the mapping files instead of an additional entity and two one-to-many associations. By declaring generate="false" for the association table, we tell Middlegen to analyze the table (for association generation) but not generate any dedicated class for it.

We now get a different graphical view of the tables; see figure 9.3.

The relationship between CATEGORY and ITEM is now correct, and the lines and arrows (and all other tables) on the right side of our canvas are gone (which you might not have expected).

With the new many2many option set in the Ant task, Middlegen now only considers the named tables, not all tables. Because we only named the two tables (and the association table), Middlegen ignores all others. We can use the <table> element in the Ant task to declare additional tables manually:

```
<hibernate>
    ...
    <many2many>
       ...
    <table name="BID"/>
```

Middlegen now also reads (and generates code for) the BID table (and the relationships between ITEM and BID). The table element is independent of the many2many; you can use it alone to specify the subset of tables in a schema for which mapping metadata should be generated.

The table element has attributes for further customization, such as a setting for singular and plural names (useful for automatic property naming in associations—for example, Item.getCategorys() versus Item.getCategories()). The few other options are rarely used; you can find a description in the Middlegen documentation.

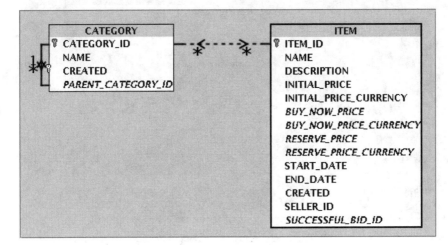

Figure 9.3 A many-to-many relationship between CATEGORY and ITEM

Some other interesting (Hibernate-specific) Ant task options exist, but first we'll discuss the graphical customization with the Middlegen GUI. After all, we now have all our tables and relationships loaded by Middlegen.

9.4.3 *Customizing the metadata generation*

In the table overview, you can select tables, association lines, and individual columns by clicking on them. You can change the multiplicity and the navigation option of a relationship by clicking on the ends of the associations (on the arrows) while holding down the Ctrl or Shift key. The multiplicity controls the generation of a collection-valued or single-entity-valued property for this association; it switches between one-to-one and one-to-many (and many-to-one) association generation.

Furthermore, you can select tables, single fields, or all fields of a table, and then modify the Hibernate mapping generation with the Middlegen controls. In figure 9.4, we've selected the ITEM table.

Middlegen has some defaults, such as the name (Item) for the generated class mapping. The other options reflect the Hibernate mapping elements and attributes; you can change the key assignment strategy, visibility, and interfaces of

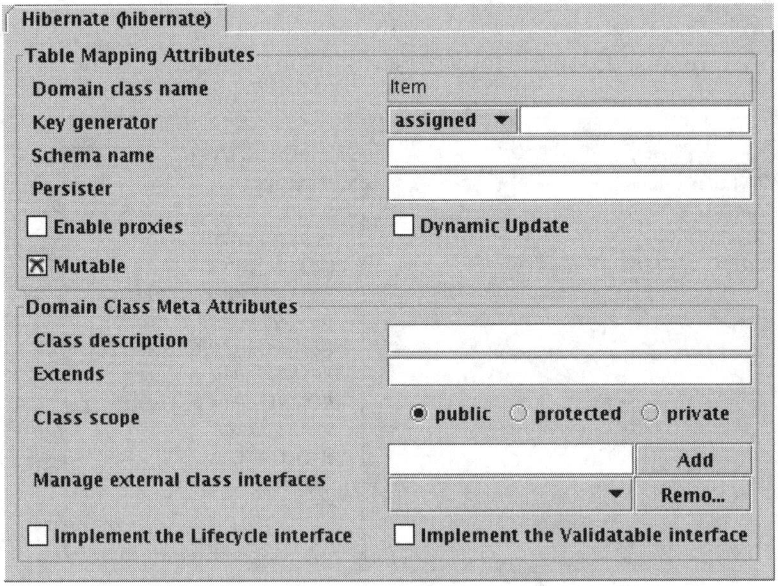

Figure 9.4 Mapping generation options in Middlegen for the ITEM table

the persistent class. All options for a single table are related to the `<class>` Hibernate mapping element.

You can customize a single property by selecting a column in the overview (see figure 9.5).

In this example, the INITIAL_PRICE column of the ITEM table is selected, its default Java type is shown as BigDecimal. Middlegen automatically suggests this type by reading the (possibly vendor-specific) SQL type in the schema metadata (such as NUMBER(10,2) in Oracle).

The default mechanism used for type detection isn't perfect, however. Consider the RANKING column in the USER table. The SQL data type in Oracle for this column is NUMBER(10,0). Middlegen will by default generate the following Hibernate mapping XML:

```
<property
    name="ranking"
    type="long"
    column="RANKING"
    not-null="false"
    length="10"/>
```

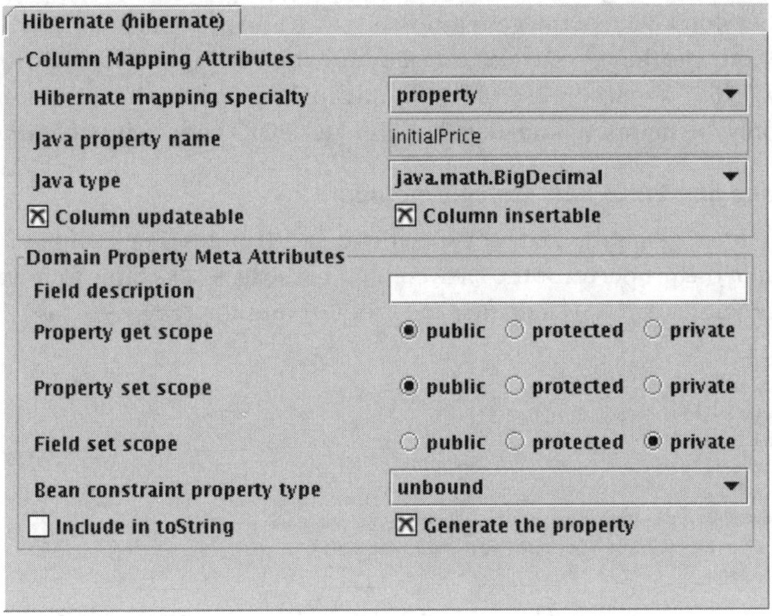

Figure 9.5 Mapping generation options for the INITIAL_PRICE column

This looks fine, but what if our Java class shouldn't have a primitive, but rather a `java.lang.Long` as the property type? If you look at the RANKING column again, you can see that we have to change the type to `java.lang.Long`: the primitive `long` can't be `null`, but the field in the database can be.

Selecting each column in the table overview and changing its property type manually isn't the best way to solve this problem. Hibernate's plugin for Middlegen comes bundled with a custom type-mapper that helps; it has to be turned on in the Middlegen Ant task:

```
<hibernate destination="${gensrc.home}"
           package="org.hibernate.auction.model"
           javaTypeMapper=
⇒"middlegen.plugins.hibernate.HibernateJavaTypeMapper"/>
```

This mapper automatically detects nullable columns and changes the default mapping (or Java) type to a nonprimitive type. You can also supply your own type mapping strategy and use the `HibernateJavaTypeMapper` as a starting point. The source code is, as always, freely available.

Let's go back to the customization dialog in Middlegen. The Domain Property Meta Attributes dialog isn't directly relevant for the Hibernate mapping XML—that is, they don't control the generation of a POJO mapping element. As the name implies, you use these controls to customize the additional meta-attributes for `hbm2java`. This is especially useful for roundtrip development if you want to generate not only the mapping metadata but also Java POJO code using that metadata.

9.4.4 *Generating hbm2java and XDoclet metadata*

Middlegen can generate `hbm2java`-specific meta-attributes. For example, if we set the scope of the property for the NAME column in the CATEGORY table to private, Middlegen generates this XML for the `name` property and the `Category` class:

```
<property
    name="name"
    type="java.lang.String"
    column="NAME"
    not-null="true"
    length="255">
    <meta attribute="scope-get">private</meta>
    <meta attribute="scope-set">private</meta>
</property>
```

The `<meta>`-element is used by the POJO `hbm2java` as discussed earlier in this chapter. The generated POJO class `Category` will have private accessor methods for the `name` property.

This isn't the last stage; you can go one step further and include XDoclet tags in the generate POJO source. That means you can generate Hibernate mapping metadata from a database schema, generate POJO source from the metadata, and then run XDoclet on that source to generate mapping metadata again. This is especially useful if Middlegen is only used for an initial import of the schema and you'd like to continue from that with customization of POJO source and/or metadata only. The trick is again the meta-attribute for `hbm2java`; you can use the *description* meta-attributes to place XDoclet tags in the generated Javadoc of your source files.

First, we have to turn on the XDoclet option in Middlegen's Ant target:

```
<hibernate destination="generated_src/"
           package="org.hibernate.auction.model"
           genXDocletTags="true"/>
```

Consider the `NAME` column of `CATEGORY` again. Middlegen now generates the following Hibernate mapping XML:

```
<property
    name="name"
    ...

>

        <meta attribute="field-description">
          @hibernate.property
          column="NAME"
          length="255"
          not-null="true"
      </meta>
  </property>
```

Running `hbm2java` with this XML generates POJO Java source with XDoclet tags in comments:

```
/**
 * @hibernate.property
 * column="NAME"
 * length="255"
 * not-null="true"
 */
public String getName() { return name; }
```

After generating the Hibernate mapping metadata skeleton with Middlegen and POJO source code with `hbm2java`, you can switch to top-down development to further customize your persistent classes and mappings.

9.5 *XDoclet*

With a top-down development process, you start your implementation by writing persistent Java classes (or generating them automatically with AndroMDA or `hbm2java`). In this scenario, *attribute-oriented programming* for automatic metadata generation is the preferred approach. As we discussed in chapter 3, Java has no language constructs for metadata (JSR-175 and JDK 1.5 will solve that, however). You use Javadoc tags (such as `@attribute`) to specify class-, field-, or method-level metadata attributes in your source code.

XDoclet is the tool that reads these meta-attributes and generates Hibernate mapping files. XDoclet isn't limited to Hibernate; it can generate all kinds of XML-based descriptor files, such as EJB or web service deployment descriptors. In this section, we use XDoclet version 1.2; it can generate either the old Hibernate 1.x mapping files or metadata for Hibernate 2.x.

We already discussed the advantages and disadvantages of XDoclet (and the future of attribute-oriented programming) in chapter 3, section 3.3.3, "Attribute-oriented programming." In this section, we'll look more closely at XDoclet and use it to generate the mapping metadata for several CaveatEmptor persistent classes. The first class is the `User`.

9.5.1 *Setting value type attributes*

The `User` class is an entity with an identifier property, various other value-typed properties (and a component, `Address`), and associations to other entities. First, we declare the mapping for the `User`:

```
/**
 * @hibernate.class
 * table="USERS"
 */
public class User implements Serializable {
...
```

The XDoclet tags for Hibernate always have the syntax `@hibernate.`*`tagname`* *`(optional) attributes`*. The tagname is related to the element in XML mapping declarations; in the previous example, a `hibernate.class` tag refers to a `<class>` mapping element. The attribute `table` is set to `USERS`.

An excerpt of the generated mapping file from this tag looks like this:

```
<hibernate-mapping>
    <class
        name="User"
        table="USERS">
...
```

Note that we've reformatted all generated example mappings in this section for better readability; we've also removed attributes if they've been set to default values by XDoclet. Your result might look different, but it has the same semantics.

Users are entities, so we need an identifier property. In the persistent class source, all properties (value typed or entity association attributes) are marked with XDoclet tags on the getter method. For the `id` property, we add a Javadoc comment to `getId()`:

```
/**
 * @hibernate.id
 * column="USER_ID"
 * unsaved-value="null"
 * generator-class="native"
 */
public Long getId() {
    return id;
}
```

The attributes of the `hibernate.id` tag are the same as the attributes for the `<id>` element. We continue with a simple property, the `username`:

```
/**
 * @hibernate.property
 * column="USERNAME"
 * length="16"
 * not-null="true"
 * unique="true"
 * update="false"
 */
public String getUsername() {
    return username;
}
```

A `hibernate.property` tag has all the attributes of a `<property>` element. You may have noticed the pattern by now. Also remember that you can rely on the Hibernate defaults: If you added the `@hibernate.property` tag to the getter *without* any attributes, your mapping would be `<property name="username"/>`; you'd then use default values for all other possible attributes. This technique allows rapid prototyping of your domain model with XDoclet.

We have one more value-typed property in `User`, the `Address` component:

```
/**
 * @hibernate.component
 */
public Address getAddress() {
    return address;
}
```

This time, the Hibernate defaults are used for the `hibernate.component` declaration. In addition to this declaration of a component mapping, the individual properties of `Address` must also be mapped: In the `Address` source code, we add `hibernate.property` tags to the `getStreet()`, `getZipcode`, and `getCity()` getter methods. We don't mark up the `Address` class itself—it isn't an entity (only a component of `User` and possibly others), and it doesn't even have an identifier property. Only the getter methods of the component properties have to be tagged.

Let's complete the mapping declaration for `User` with tags for entity association mapping.

9.5.2 *Mapping entity associations*

Mapping entity associations with XDoclet is basically the same as for value-typed properties; XDoclet tags are added to the getter methods for all association related properties. For example, the association from `User` to `Item` looks like this:

```
/**
 * @hibernate.set
 * inverse="true"
 * lazy="true"
 * cascade="save-update"
 * @hibernate.collection-key
 * column="SELLER_ID"
 * @hibernate.collection-one-to-many
 * class="Item"
 */
public Set getItems() {
    return items;
}
```

The first thing that's different from a simple value-typed property is the number of tags we need for the mapping. We're mapping the "many" end of a bidirectional one-to-many association; hence the use of a collection type. The attributes for the `hibernate.set` are the same as always: `inverse` for the bidirectional aspect and, of course, lazy loading. The other two tags are also related to well-known Hibernate XML elements, `<key>` and `<one-to-many>`. Notice that we name the foreign key column in the Item's table `SELLER_ID` (`USER_ID` would be more obvious, but less expressive) and that we have to explicitly name the class of entities referenced by the `Set`.

We also have to map the other end of this association. In the `Item` class, we map the `seller`:

```
/**
 * @hibernate.many-to-one
 * column="SELLER_ID"
```

```
 * cascade="none"
 * not-null="true"
 */
public User getSeller() {
    return seller;
}
```

For the "one" side of the association, we may omit the class of the referenced entity; it's implicit from the property's type. We now have both ends of the association mapped and can continue generating the XML files—that is, run XDoclet.

9.5.3 *Running XDoclet*

Generating mapping files with XDoclet is easy, because it's available as an Ant task. As always, we first have to declare the new task in the Ant build.xml:

```
<taskdef name="hibernatedoclet"
         classname="xdoclet.modules.hibernate.HibernateDocletTask"
         classpathref="class.path"/>
```

The classpath for this task should include xdoclet-X.X.X.jar, xdoclet-hibernate-module-X.X.X.jar, xdoclet-xdoclet-module-X.X.X.jar, and xjavadoc-X.X.X.jar. These libraries are all in the XDoclet main distribution, as are several required third-party libraries, such as commons-lang.jar, commons-collections.jar, and commons-logging.jar. The Hibernate library (and its third-party libraries) aren't required by the XDoclet process.

The next step is to include the task we defined in the target we'll call. We use a new target called xdoclet, as shown here:

```
<target name="xdoclet">
    <hibernatedoclet
                destdir="mappings/"
                excludedtags="@version,@author,@todo"
                force="true"
                mergedir="merge/">

        <fileset dir="src">
            <include name="**/org/hibernate/auction/*.java"/>
        </fileset>

        <hibernate version="2.0"/>

    </hibernatedoclet>
</target>
```

First, the destdir attribute defines the target directory for the generated mapping files. We exclude the standard Javadoc tags from the generation process, and force a processing of Java source files each time XDoclet runs (otherwise, only mappings for updated source files would be generated). The `mergedir` can be used to automatically include user-defined mappings in the generated files.

Next, all Java source files in the directory `src` and subdirectory (package) `org.hibernate.auction` are checked for XDoclet tags. Finally, we switch the XDoclet Hibernate module to Hibernate2, otherwise XDoclet generates Hibernate 1.x mapping descriptors.

XDoclet for Hibernate metadata generation has an impact on the development environment and how a team of developers works together. You should be aware of the consequences.

The `mergedir` setting of the Ant task helps if you have to implement exceptional cases specific to your development environment and process. If you place a file named `hibernate-properties-class.xml` in the `mergedir`, its contents will be added to the mapping file of the `class`. This allows you to use additional mappings, separated from the XDoclet-tagged Java source.

One final word about XDoclet: You may be tempted to use it in all situations, even if it isn't appropriate. XDoclet with Hibernate is best suited for clean-room top-down development, but it may not be the best tool if you have to work with an existing database schema. It's especially difficult—and even impossible in some cases—to map composite key structures and certain ternary associations with XDoclet tags. However, most class, property, and association mappings can be declared easily.

9.6 Summary

Sometimes the development process is fixed: With legacy databases, you can only start from an existing schema, and you'll usually want to automatically generate POJO classes that represent your data model. You use `hbm2java` to generate Java source code from Hibernate mapping metadata. This metadata can also be automatically generated from an existing database schema with Middlegen, thus completing the bottom-up development process.

If you're working from the top down, you start with POJO persistent classes. Instead of manually creating the mapping metadata and the database schema for these classes, you mark up your source with custom Javadoc tags and generate Hibernate mapping files with XDoclet. The Hibernate tool `hbm2ddl` creates SQL files with DDL from Hibernate mapping metadata, completing the top-down development process.

If you use the Hibernate toolset (and open source projects such as AndroMDA, Middlegen, and XDoclet), you always have to be aware of conceptual limitations:

A fully automated, perfect generation of either POJO classes or mapping metadata, no matter from what source, isn't possible. You always have to customize the generation process or modify the end result manually.

This isn't a limitation of the tools, which we consider quite capable, but a restriction that stems from the fact that not every detail can be extracted from each source. One exception is the top-down approach (hence its popularity): With POJO classes and mapping metadata in place, you can generate an SQL DDL script with `hbm2ddl`. In our experience, this script is (almost) as good as any hand-coded schema declaration.

It's a good idea to start learning Hibernate without any of the tools. The goal of the tools is to relieve you from having to perform the repetitive tasks that will occur when you work with Hibernate in a project. This is different from a graphical mapping workbench or other such gimmick, which may help at first but slow you down later. Take the time to learn the basics, and then double your speed with the tools.

SQL fundamentals

A table, with its rows and columns, is a familiar sight to anyone who has worked with an SQL database. Sometimes you'll see tables referred to as relations, rows as tuples, and columns as attributes. This is the language of the relational data model, the mathematical model that SQL databases (imperfectly) implement.

The relational model allows you to define data structures and constraints that guarantee the integrity of your data (for example, by disallowing values that don't accord with your business rules). The relational model also defines the relational operations of restriction, projection, Cartesian product, and relational join [Codd 1970]. These operations let you do useful things with your data, such as summarizing or navigating it.

Each of the operations produces a new table from a given table or combination of tables. SQL is a language for expressing these operations in your application (therefore called a data language) and for defining the base tables on which the operations are performed.

You write SQL DDL statements to create and manage the tables. We say that DDL defines the database schema. Statements such as CREATE TABLE, ALTER TABLE, and CREATE SEQUENCE belong to DDL.

You write SQL DML statements to work with your data at runtime. Let's describe these DML operations in the context of tables from the CaveatEmptor application.

In CaveatEmptor, we naturally have entities like *item, user,* and *bid.* We assume that the SQL database schema for this application includes an ITEM table and a BID table, as shown in figure A.1. The datatypes, tables, and constraints for this schema have been created with SQL DDL (CREATE and ALTER operations).

Insertion is the operation of creating a new table from an old table by adding a row. SQL databases perform this operation in place, so the new row is added to the existing table:

```
insert into ITEM values (4, 'Fum', 45.0)
An SQL update modifies an existing row:

update ITEM set INITIAL_PRICE = 47.0 where ITEM_ID = 4
```

ITEM

ITEM_ID	NAME	INITIAL_PRICE
1	Foo	2.00
2	Bar	50.00
3	Baz	1.00

BID

BID_ID	ITEM_ID	AMOUNT
1	1	10.00
2	1	20.00
3	2	55.50

Figure A.1
**The ITEM and BID tables
of an auction application**

A *deletion* removes a row:

```
delete from ITEM where ITEM_ID = 4
```

The real power of SQL lies in querying data. A single query might perform many relational operations on several tables. Let's look at the basic operations.

First, *restriction* is the operation of choosing rows of a table that match a particular criterion. In SQL, this criterion is the expression that occurs in the where clause:

```
select * from ITEM where NAME like 'F%'
```

Projection is the operation of choosing columns of a table and eliminating duplicate rows from the result. In SQL, the columns to be included are listed in the select clause. You can eliminate duplicate rows by specifying the distinct keyword:

```
select distinct NAME from ITEM
```

A *Cartesian product* (also called a *cross join*) produces a new table consisting of all possible combinations of rows of two existing tables. In SQL, you express a Cartesian product by listing tables in the from clause:

```
select * from ITEM i, BID b
```

A relational *join* produces a new table by combining the rows of two tables. For each pair of rows for which a *join condition* is true, the new table contains a row with all field values from both joined rows. In ANSI SQL, the join clause specifies a table join; the join condition follows the on keyword. For example, to retrieve all items that have bids, you join the ITEM and the BID table on their common ITEM_ID attribute:

```
select * from ITEM i inner join BID b on i.ITEM_ID = b.ITEM_ID
```

A join is equivalent to a Cartesian product followed by a restriction. So, joins are often instead expressed in theta style, with a product in the from clause and the join condition in the where clause. This SQL theta-style join is equivalent to the previous ANSI-style join:

```
select * from ITEM i, BID b where i.ITEM_ID = b.ITEM_ID
```

Along with these basic operations, relational databases define operations for aggregating rows (GROUP BY) and ordering rows (ORDER BY):

```
select b.ITEM_ID, max(b.AMOUNT)
from BID b
group by b.ITEM_ID
having max(b.AMOUNT) > 15
order by b.ITEM_ID asc
```

SQL was called a *structured* query language in reference to a feature called *subselects*. Since each relational operation produces a new table from an existing table or tables, an SQL query might operate on the result table of a previous query. SQL lets you express this using a single query, by nesting the first query inside the second:

```
select *
from (
    select b.ITEM_ID as ITEM, max(b.AMOUNT) as AMOUNT
    from BID b
    group by b.ITEM_ID
)
where AMOUNT > 15
order by ITEM asc
```

The result of this query is equivalent to the previous one.

A subselect may appear anywhere in an SQL statement; the case of a subselect in the where clause is the most interesting:

```
select * from BID b where b.AMOUNT >= (select max(c.AMOUNT) from BID c)
```

This query returns the largest bid in the database. where clause subselects are often combined with *quantification*. The following query is equivalent:

```
select * from BID b where b.AMOUNT >= all(select c.AMOUNT from BID c)
```

An SQL restriction criterion is expressed in a sophisticated expression language that supports mathematical expressions, function calls, string matching, and even more sophisticated features such as full text searches:

```
select * from ITEM i
    where lower(i.NAME) like '%gc%'
          or lower(i.NAME) like '%excellent%'
```

*B*ORM
implementation
strategies

In this appendix, we'll provide some insight into Hibernate internals; we'll show you how Hibernate detects object state changes and what techniques other solutions use. An ORM user generally shouldn't care about this detail, but the reality is sometimes different; hence it may have some impact on your development process.

At runtime, the ORM implementation interacts with instances of persistent classes to populate property values and detect state changes made by the application (dirty checking). The ORM implementation must also detect access to lazy associations. Traditionally, there were a number of different ways of implementing this interaction, many of which intruded on the implementation of the domain model. Inheritance from generated source code, source code processing, compiled bytecode processing, and runtime reflection have all been used. The strategy (or the mix of strategies) chosen determines how transparent a tool can be.

Before we compare these different techniques, we should mention that there are two basic approaches to dirty checking and two views on exactly what gets persisted.

B.1 Properties or fields?

In object-oriented development, it's good practice to access the attributes of a class via accessor methods. This allows a class to have an internal representation of its own state that's different than the representation visible to its clients. In particular, it allows a class like `Calendar` to have one internal representation and several external views; it even lets a class like `ComplexNumber` use several alternate internal representations while exposing a consistent view to clients. In addition, property accessors allow the class to perform validation of new values when properties are modified, or access authorization checks.

There is some disagreement over whether an ORM solution should work with these externally visible property values, interacting with the class via its accessors or directly with the internal instance variables. The Hibernate team considers it a very good practice to decouple the persistent representation of a JavaBean from the bean's internal data structure. In particular, persistence of property values allows the property implementation to be overridden in a subclass. So, by default, Hibernate persists property values. Hibernate will access instance variables directly only if you specify `access="field"` in the property mapping. We discourage this usage.

Of course, not all class attributes are meant to be `public` and visible to all clients. Hibernate lets you declare accessors for persistent properties as `protected`, `private`, or package visible.

Regardless of the way persistent attributes are accessed, there are two possible ways to implement the detection of modified object state for dirty checking: interception and inspection.

B.2   Dirty-checking strategies

The first approach, *interception*, has the ORM implementation interpose itself between the application and the persistent object's fields (or properties), intercepting the assignment of new values to the fields. The second approach, *inspection*, compares an object's property values at the end of a transaction to a saved snapshot of the state of the object when it was loaded from the database. Some people have argued that interception might be expected to perform better than inspection, but we have seen no evidence of this—our own tests show that the difference is negligible, at most (at least, compared to other costs such as database access).

For dirty checking, Hibernate chooses the second approach, since it can be implemented without the need for intervention at buildtime or class-loading time. Unfortunately, the Java runtime environment doesn't provide hooks to allow generic code to intercept method calls or instance variable access. (Other interpreted languages do provide such functionality, so it's curious that Java doesn't.) In Java, interception requires processing of the source code or bytecode at buildtime, or of the bytecode at class-loading time.

To avoid this requirement, Hibernate performs inspection of all persistent objects associated with a session when the session is flushed. Hibernate (like any ORM solution) *does* use interception to implement lazy association fetching.

We'll now briefly consider how various ORM solutions implement interception and/or inspection. This isn't an exhaustive list of all possible approaches, but it does cover the most popular possibilities, past and present.

B.2.1   Inheritance from generated code

This is the most intrusive approach. At development time, an abstract superclass is generated from mapping metadata. You implement behavior and transient state on a subclass. This approach works reasonably well in languages with support for multiple inheritance, but it's inappropriate for Java's single inheritance model. It's certainly contrary to the notion of transparent persistence for POJOs. This should be considered an old-fashioned approach; modern ORM implementations all use some other means.

B.2.2 Source-code processing

You can use buildtime source processing to implement interception. Usually, an intermediate Java file is generated before compilation. (Theoretically, the processor could process the source in place by modifying the original file, but this approach would be much less transparent to the developer.)

This strategy has two problems. First, line numbers reported in stack traces and by the debugger won't correctly reflect the original source code—they will be line numbers of the intermediate enhanced code. On the other hand, the processed source *is* available for you to debug if necessary, which might be an advantage of this approach. Second, running the source processor might be a hassle at development time. This concern doesn't apply if you're using an Ant build during development—but it may be less convenient if you use an IDE with incremental compilation.

B.2.3 Bytecode processing

Source-code processing is often clumsy in practice. A currently popular approach is to process the compiled bytecode. Bytecode processing is usually implemented as a post-compile step in the build process. It can also be done at class-loading time in environments where the persistence mechanism can gain control of the classloader.

Bytecode processing is transparent at the code level and may be convenient if your IDE is closely integrated with the enhancer. We prefer that an ORM implementation do all its work at runtime rather than buildtime, since this is the simplest way to short-circuit any possible problems with toolset integration—but we'll leave you to make up your own mind. Of the buildtime techniques available, bytecode processing is our preference.

B.2.4 Reflection

Runtime reflection has an image problem in the Java community: Reflective systems are perceived to be slow. This is partly untrue—reflection is much faster in modern JVMs than in JDK 1.2—and partly irrelevant to our class of problems. Even if reflection was really as slow as some people assume, the overhead is insignificant compared to the cost of disk access and interprocess (even network) communication that dominates data access. There really is no good reason to avoid the use of reflection in a persistence layer.

On the other hand, there is one excellent reason to choose reflection over other techniques such as code generation: Reflection doesn't intrude on the build cycle or on the performance of system initialization. This has a definite positive effect on *developer* performance.

Early versions of Hibernate used reflection exclusively for interaction with the domain objects. This solution was popular with users and was shown to cause only a slight performance overhead. However, JDK reflection was found insufficient when it came to the problem of lazy fetching.

To implement lazy fetching of associations, Hibernate uses *proxies*. A proxy is an object that implements the public interface of a business object and intercepts all messages sent to that object by its clients. In the case of Hibernate, interception is used to load the proxied object's state from the database the first time it's used.

For proxying many-valued associations, Hibernate uses implementations of the collection interfaces defined in `java.util`. For single-point associations (an object reference to a user-defined class), more sophisticated machinery is required.

Java provides `java.lang.reflect.Proxy` for JDK 1.3 and above. An instance of `Proxy` may be instantiated at runtime, implementing a given list of interfaces. This solution is great if your persistent objects are accessed by clients only via an interface, but what if the persistent class doesn't implement an interface at all? You don't want to force the unwieldy EJB-style local interfaces on your POJOs. They're supposed to be plain, remember!

So, if Java reflection can't solve all your problems, what option remains?

B.2.5 *Runtime bytecode generation*

Fortunately, exactly when the Hibernate team needed it, another open source project came along and neatly solved this problem. The *CGLIB* project describes itself as a "code generation library," but we prefer to think of it as an alternative reflection package for Java—a replacement for `java.lang.reflect`.

CGLIB uses runtime bytecode generation to implement some of the same features provided by the Java reflection API, only more efficiently. Most important, CGLIB can create proxies that inherit a class, as well as implement interfaces! This allows Hibernate to implement lazy association fetching almost completely transparently. At runtime, clients may hold a reference to a proxy that is a generated subclass of the associated persistent class. When the client invokes a method of the proxy, Hibernate intercepts that method call and loads the state of the proxied object from the database.

For classes with all nonprivate property accessor methods, CGLIB also can be used to bypass reflection and get/set property values with normal Java method invocation (in generated bytecode). Hibernate uses this feature whenever possible.

Some Hibernate users found that the bytecode generation step, which occurs at system-initialization time, was slow in earlier versions of Hibernate. The current release of Hibernate integrates CGLIB 2.0, which vastly improves the performance of bytecode generation and helps reduce the startup time of the Hibernate application.

CGLIB is an amazingly useful library. If you have generic programming problems, we encourage you to see if CGLIB can help.

B.2.6 "Generic" objects

Some persistence layers, which we hesitate to consider ORM implementations, persist objects consisting of a dynamic set of properties—collections of name/value pairs. (Some even encourage you to extend the dynamic class with application classes that add typesafe property access.) We won't pay much attention to this kind of approach since we're most interested in persistence for POJOs. However, this approach fills its own important niche: metadata-driven applications. Typesafe domain models aren't appropriate for applications where the business model is defined in metadata.

A great example of this approach is the OFBiz entity engine. But Hibernate 3 (which is in an early stage of development at the time of this writing) supports this kind of application by allowing domain models to be represented as a graph of Maps containing property name/value pairs.

Back in the real world

Hibernate, as an open source project, has a different relationship with its users than a traditional software company that sells software licenses to its customers. The users take responsibility for the project, but even more interesting (and sometimes entertaining) is the fact that all free support is made public. This gives us the opportunity to discuss real-world problems—questions asked by actual users. As we all know, you can't avoid all problems by reading good books and documentation before you begin a project. All of us have struggled with unsolvable problems; often, asking for help in a user forum is the best option.

The same is true for the Hibernate users, so we'd like to show you some of the questions asked and discuss possible answers. There is often a big difference between book theory and the daily reality as a software developer. So, we'll keep things in perspective and show you that you aren't alone in a "Dilbert" world. Read on.

C.1 *The strange copy*

> *Due to some strange requirements from our Oracle DBAs, I cannot access our databases "live"; I must copy the data from Oracle to a local MySQL database (yes, it's very lame but totally out of my control). I have written a utility to do this (not using Hibernate, just straight JDBC as it's "legacy"). The problem that I run into is that I run this via cron, outside of the web app and again not using Hibernate, and when it is done running, the web app cannot access the database for a while (until a cache timeout?).*

There are two problems here. The first is the DBA and the requirement to copy to a local MySQL database. This is a strange requirement, and we can't imagine why it exists. Remember that many commercial databases have free developer licenses—if you can't switch databases, use Hibernate for the data import and export. Hibernate has an experimental XMLDatabinder feature, which can serialize a graph of persistent objects to an XML file. The ReverseXMLDatabinder is then used to restore the saved file, saving the objects to a database. This works cross-platform with all Hibernate supported databases. Search the Hibernate website and forum for tips on XML databinding.

Your real problem looks like MySQL is locking (and not releasing) the tables for the import, a question that's best answered by the MySQL community or company.

C.2 *The more the better*

> *We've got a table with 700 columns. This table is in 3rd normal form, as far as I can tell. We could break chunks of cols off to separate tables, but they would have 1:1 relationships with "mother" :-). Would this be preferable to 1 table with 700 cols?*

First, database performance depends on many factors, not necessarily the number of columns in a table. We're much more interested in reducing row reads, not column reads; if you have to worry about "too many columns," try to use projection queries. However, large tables may have an impact on caching on the database side, because you get fewer rows into the block buffer cache if each row has 700 columns. This makes it even more important to tune your database properly, especially indexed access.

The second problem is the amount of data the JDBC driver has to deal with: Every time you load or save an object, huge SQL statements (in the range of several kilobytes of text) have to be sent. Also think about the mapping of a query result to persistent Hibernate objects: The JDBC driver may create a large number of objects behind the scenes when Hibernate extracts the data from the result set. This is usually a very fast operation and negligible compared to the other costs in a typical data-access scenario. It's a factor if you have an enormous number of columns, but at least it scales linearly.

Do some performance tests with straight JDBC and SQL and see how long they take. Also consider how often the query will run in your application, so you don't spend too much time optimizing unnecessarily.

C.3 *We don't need primary keys*

> *I have a simple question. If I have a table which has no key definition, and if I try to map this, what happens? I mean, can Hibernate handle tables without key definitions? Actually, I already tried such a thing, because I have some tables to map which have no keys, and I am not allowed to change. I could save new instances, but in querying there were problems.*

Relational products that don't enforce a primary key attribute definition for a relation are broken (that is, they allow bags of tuples, not sets). A relational value is a set of tuples, hence no duplicate rows are allowed. Unfortunately, many SQL databases are broken that way; they allow duplicate rows and, in general, make primary keys optional.

You need a primary key for a table to work with Hibernate; otherwise there is no way to distinguish rows. This is true not only for Hibernate but for every other system (and user) of your database. We recommend that you clean up the database. As a last resort, you can use a composite key mapping in Hibernate and include all columns as a composite key.

C.4 Time isn't linear

I realized that after daylight savings took effect, every call to update an entry into my database created before daylight savings took effect would result in a StaleObjectStateException.

If your timestamp datatype doesn't include a daylight saving time attribute, you'll run into problems with Hibernate's automatic versioning.

There aren't many reasons to use a timestamp instead of a simple version number. One might be the additional information that can be used for reporting or ad-hoc queries with a "last updated" timestamp. The version is a meaningless internal number, and meta-information such as *time of creation, last updated,* and *updated by* have to be added in additional columns. With a requirement like this, consider a full audit log implementation (see section 8.3.2, "Audit logging").

A version property is less problematic for automatic versioning; hence we recommend it.

C.5 Dynamically unsafe

I'm just starting with Hibernate, and the concept of using Dynabeans appeals to me. I'm seriously considering it. I came from an environment that took the opposite approach of Hibernate: Everything used a database object; it contained a set of table objects, which contained Record objects, which contained Field Objects. This basically meant we didn't need getters or setters on the back end. I practically resent their presence to be honest! I'm trying to find some way to do that with Hibernate. Any chance?

Hibernate supports Maps as dynamic components. Keep in mind that this is no longer a data model that ensures data integrity, which should be the primary goal of any database. Such a data model of unprotected values is only good enough for quick prototyping. However, prototypes often aren't thrown away but are used as a foundation for the real implementation in a project. If this setup isn't changed to a normalized relational data model, serious problems may appear in the future, including unpredictable behavior, lost data, and expensive maintenance. However, it might be acceptable to use this dynamic approach in some use cases (usually exceptional ones), in addition to a solid data model.

Keep in mind that data (and a database) usually lives much longer than any application. With a dynamic map model, the semantics of the data structure and the (often very crude) handcoded data-integrity rules will be lost when an application is no longer useful. Costly and time-consuming data migration is often the result. If the time to market is really a problem and an argument for unsafe data, use Hibernate instead and save time from the start without losing any power.

C.6 *To synchronize or not?*

> *I've been using Hibernate for a while, and I really like it. But I find that there is a major, major issue. Synchronization. We lose data! We have a web based application where different people can simultaneously add or update data—we have to synchronize!*

Don't lock or in any other way serialize access to objects in the application. You don't have to do anything to ensure that concurrent modification doesn't destroy your data; that is the job of Hibernate and the underlying database.

This question is sometimes asked as follows: "How does Hibernate ensure that an object modified in Session A is synchronized with the same loaded object in Session B?" It isn't the same object. Both objects may have the same database identity, but because they're loaded in different Sessions, they're two distinct instances in the JVM. This is called *transaction-scoped identity*, and there is no need to synchronize two objects that have only the database identity in common. In other words, all operations in concurrently running transactions are isolated from each other. So how do you solve this concurrent access to the same resource?

Hibernate uses existing mechanisms present in any database-management system to resolve the conflict. The Hibernate Session inherits the transaction semantics and transaction isolation level of the standard JDBC connection it's started with. This means you'll experience the typical problems of not having fully isolated access to a shared resource (dirty reads, nonrepeatable reads, phantom reads), depending on the transaction isolation level of your database connection and transaction. Conflicting updates, however, are resolved with an optimistic approach at commit time (using a version check). With Hibernate's automatic versioning, you can ensure that an object loaded and modified in Session A can't overwrite the changes made to an object in Session B if the database transaction of Session B (manipulating the "same" object) was committed earlier than Session A's. In rare cases, and when handling critical data, you may use a pessimistic approach. By setting a pessimistic exclusive lock (using a LockMode) in the database, you prevent Session B from loading the "same" object; it must wait (or immediately fail) until Session A releases the lock.

The question sometimes also refers to an automatic update of a loaded object if it has been modified while it's loaded. For example, if Session B displays an object to the user and Session A modifies that object, the display in Session B must be updated.

Hibernate has no automatic push mechanism; therefore, the application has to poll the database for updates. This is consistent with the transaction semantics of Hibernate and the database. You may in rare cases implement a Hibernate Interceptor and trigger a refresh() call in all other units of work if an object has been modified, but doing so will always require synchronized access that might become a bottleneck for scalability.

C.7 *Really fat client*

Our application will use JWS technology. We will use Hibernate and a J2EE architecture, and we would like to keep all Hibernate stuff on the server side. We noticed that if we use a proxy, we miss some Hibernate classes while de-serializing the object on the client side. Do we have to put all of Hibernate and related libraries on the client? They are quite big.

You only need the following libraries (about 1 MB) on the client to successfully deserialize a detached object graph: hibernate2.jar, odmg.jar, commons-logging.jar, and cglib2.jar. (It might also be possible to package a minimalistic hibernate-client.jar.)

Keep in mind that the leaf nodes of the graph are uninitialized collections or associations to proxies. Accessing the graph past these nodes on the client will give you an exception. The solution for this problem is to fully initialize all required objects before sending them to the client. We don't recommend (and Hibernate doesn't implement) any automatic lazy loading triggered by client code. Data access, graph closures, and transaction semantics should be well known in any application and not be ad hoc.

Use the good old data transfer object pattern if client code size is the most important issue. You'll lose the main advantage of detached POJOs with Hibernate: automatic reattachment to a new transaction with an optimistic concurrency check.

C.8 *Resuming Hibernate*

> *I start my PC, after completion of my work, I Hibernate it. After some time when I resume my PC, it will run within no time. The problem is that when I resume my PC if electricity is fluctuated, and the PC is suddenly off without Hibernating, is it possible in Windows XP that I restore my PC?*

Frankly, we don't know. However, we take great care not to make Hibernate appear to be a silver bullet. It isn't a solution that will make all your database (or Windows XP) problems go away magically.

Writing database applications is one of the more challenging tasks in software development. Hibernate's job is to *reduce* the amount of code you have to write for the most common 90 percent of use cases (common CRUD and reporting). The next 5 percent are more difficult; queries become complex, transaction semantics are unclear at first, and performance bottlenecks are hidden. You can solve these problems with Hibernate elegantly and keep your application portable, but you'll also need some experience to get it right.

Hibernate's learning curve is high at first. In our experience, a developer needs at least two to four weeks to learn the basics. Don't jump on Hibernate one week before your project deadline—it won't save you. Be prepared to invest more time than you would need for another web application framework or simple utility.

Finally, use SQL, JDBC, and stored procedures for the 5 percent of use cases you can't implement with Hibernate, such as mass data manipulation or complex reporting queries with vendor-specific SQL functions.

Use the right tool for the right job. (And try reinstalling Windows XP.)

references

[Ambler 2002] Ambler, Scott. 2002. Mapping Objects to Relational Databases. AmbySoft Inc. white paper. www.ambysoft.com/mappingObjects.html.

[Codd 1970] Codd, E. F. 1970. A Relational Model of Data for Large Shared Data Banks. *Communications of the ACM* 13, no. 6 (June): 377–387. http://doi.acm.org/10.1145/362384.362685.

[Date 2004] Date, C. J. 2004. *An Introduction to Database Systems*, 8th ed. Boston: Pearson/Addison Wesley.

[Evans 2004] Evans, Eric. 2004. *Domain-Driven Design*. Boston: Addison-Wesley.

[Fowler 1999] Fowler, Martin. 1999. *Refactoring: Improving the Design of Existing Code*. Reading, MA: Addison-Wesley.

[Fowler 2003] ———. 2003. *Patterns of Enterprise Application Architecture*. Boston: Addison-Wesley.

[Fussel 1997] Fussel, Mark L. 1997. Foundations of Object Relational Mapping. ChiMu Corporation. www.chimu.com/publications/objectRelational/.

[Gamma et al 1995] Gamma, Erich, Richard Helm, Ralph Johnson, and John Vlissides. 1995. *Design Patterns: Elements of Reusable Object-Oriented Software*. Reading, MA: Addison-Wesley.

[Marinescu 2002] Marinescu, Floyd. 2002. EJB *Design Patterns: Advanced Patterns, Processes, and Idioms*. New York: John Wiley.

[Tow 2003] Tow, Dan. 2003. *SQL Tuning*. Sebastopol, CA: O'Reilly.

[Walls and Richards 2004] Walls, Craig and Norman Richards. 2004. *XDoclet in Action*. Greenwich, CT: Manning.

index